My Glorious Master

My Glorious Master

Remembrances of Śrīla Prabhupāda's Mercy on a Fallen Soul

BHŪRIJANA DĀSA

VIHE PUBLICATIONS

Published by VIHE Publications.

Cover design by Raghu Consbruck.
www.raghudesigns.com

ISBN-13: 978-0-9925219-4-3

For furher information on VIHE Publications,
visit our website at www.vihepublications.com

Printed in India by Replika Press Pvt. Ltd.

sei bhakta dhanya, ye nā chāḍe prabhura caraṇa
sei prabhu dhanya, ye nā chāḍe nija-jana
durdaive sevaka yadi yāya anya sthāne
sei ṭhākura dhanya tāre cule dhari' āne

Glorious is that devotee who does not give up the shelter of his Lord, and glorious is that Lord who does not abandon His servant. If by chance a servant falls down and goes somewhere else, glorious is that master who captures him and brings him back by the hair.

– *Caitanya-caritāmṛta, Antya* 4.46–47

I offer thousands of prostrated obeisances to my spiritual master, His Divine Grace A.C. Bhaktivedanta Swami Prabhupāda. Prabhupāda was certainly merciful to me, who was undeserving of his kindness. I tried to escape his mercy many times during his presence on this planet, but at each turn, he grabbed me by the hair and pulled me back. He is thus the glorious master mentioned in the *Caitanya-caritāmṛta.* I aspire to become a worthy and eternal servant of such a glorious master.

Contents

Preface to the Revised Edition

My Glorious Master was written as an offering to Śrīla Prabhupāda in 1996, the year ISKCON celebrated the centennial anniversary of Prabhupāda's birth. The nine years I describe – 1968 to 1977 – start from my twenty-first birthday and end several months into my thirtieth year.

In 1994–1995, when I was writing this book, I was able to meditate on these earlier events in my life with enough distance that a drop of balance seeped into how I viewed them. But how my comments would change were I writing this book today!

This is a revised edition, but I chose to leave how I described the events and my comments on them from the '90s essentially as they were written because they accurately document my life at the time the events occurred and my thoughts on those events two decades later.

What I did change from the first edition: I added a number of previously unpublished photographs. I also edited some of the language used in the first edition to make some things clearer. I corrected several inaccuracies that had inadvertently slipped into the original text. And especially, I softened a few of my comments and attitudes that twenty years later now seem too absolute. On one occasion I deleted an event unessential to my story to soothe a disagreement between godbrothers.

I was helped in this revision, as always, by my wife, Jagat-tāriṇī Dāsī, who discovered a treasure of letters she had written to her mother in the '70s during the time she was in Los Angeles and we were together in Hong Kong. She also uncovered a transcript of the interview she gave Satsvarūpa Dāsa Goswami for his biography of Śrīla Prabhupāda. Both these primary sources, plus her critical reading of my book, proved helpful in the book's revision.

Reading again about events that happened almost forty years ago but remain foundational to my life today was sometimes delightful and sometimes confronting. As I reviewed the actions and thoughts of a less mature version of myself, I saw the complexity of my conditioning and my own simpleness, my arrogance and my innocence, my passion and my sincerity. But what most touched my heart was seeing again the guidance Śrīla Prabhupāda so benignly and consistently bestowed on this fallen soul. Remembrance of it brought me easily into his intimate, deep, affectionate presence.

Actually, this focused reminder of his presence in my life was the greatest benefit I received from revising *My Glorious Master*. I pray that as you read, you too will be touched by Śrīla Prabhupāda's compassionate concern, strength, and sweetness.

Preface

> The ocean of the pastimes of Lord Caitanya Mahāprabhu is immeasurable and unfathomable. Who can take the courage to measure that great ocean? It is not possible to dip into that great ocean, but its sweet mellow flavor attracts my mind. I thereby stand on the shore of that ocean to try to taste but a drop of it.
>
> – *Caitanya-caritāmṛta, Ādi* 12.94–95

My humblest obeisances to the pink and soft lotus feet of my Guru Mahārāja, His Divine Grace A. C. Bhaktivedanta Swami Prabhupāda, an empowered preacher-teacher-warrior. As the pastimes of Śrī Caitanya Mahāprabhu are like an ocean, so the pastimes of His confidential servitor, Śrīla Prabhupāda, are also oceanic. Prabhupāda fearlessly uprooted atheism, pseudo-theism, nihilism, and scientific "word jugglery," and boldly led countless souls back to Godhead.

The two holy *dhāmas* of Navadvīpa and Vṛndāvana descended with Prabhupāda. Within those *dhāmas* reside Śrī Śrī Gaura-Nitāi and Śrī Śrī Rādhā-Kṛṣṇa. Whoever met Prabhupāda also met his Lords, knew Their fragrance, and heard Their desire.

I sat with Prabhupāda in 1972 in Manila, the Philippines, when he was scheduled to speak in the Hotel Intercontinental's Grand Ballroom. As he waited to start, Prabhupāda toyed with a paper flag on a wooden stick. It broke. Prabhupāda laughed like a child, as if saying, "Just see the nature of this material world." He then told me: "My desire is that all living beings in the universe go back to Godhead. You please help me with this desire."

To fulfill his compassionate desire, Prabhupāda, depending on Kṛṣṇa's mercy, organized ISKCON, wrote books for worldwide distribution, and trained his students to preach. I was fortunate enough to be one of Prabhupāda's students. Many others had more association with Prabhupāda, but although my physical association with him was limited, the exchanges were intimate, because many took place with few other devotees present. In addition, Prabhupāda kindly gave me his shelter when I was in difficulty. That was his causeless mercy upon me and I thank him again and again for not kicking me away.

I hope the devotees find pleasure in reading these anecdotes about my exchanges with Prabhupāda. At the end of most anecdotes I have written a personal reflection to show some of what I learned from each exchange. I realize, however, that even the teachings he directed toward me are beyond my scope to deeply understand. Yet I, as his disciple, without claiming to predicate his mind, nevertheless felt the need to extract lessons from each episode, limited as my capacity might be. As for the Lord, so also for His empowered devotee:

ahaṁ hi pṛṣṭo 'ryamaṇo bhavadbhir
ācakṣa ātmāvagamo 'tra yāvān
nabhaḥ patanty ātma-samaṁ patattriṇas
tathā samaṁ viṣṇu-gatiṁ vipaścitaḥ

O *ṛṣis*, who are as powerfully pure as the sun, I shall try to describe to you the transcendental pastimes of Viṣṇu as far as my knowledge is concerned. As the birds fly in the sky as far as their capacity allows, so do the learned devotees describe the Lord as far as their realization allows.

– *Śrīmad-Bhāgavatam* 1.18.23

While writing my remembrances I referred to Prabhupāda as "Prabhupāda" and not as "Śrīla Prabhupāda." This was generally our habit when addressing or speaking about him, so I wrote it this way to maintain authenticity. To facilitate easier reading, I dispensed with proper etiquette, and generally referred to my godbrothers and godsisters without the more formal "Dāsa," "Dāsī," or "Prabhu," and to my wife simply as "Jagattāriṇī." The *Conversations* books also follow this standard.

I wrote mostly from notes I started compiling in 1985, and when my memory contradicted information found in the Vedabase program,* I deferred to the Vedabase. By the mercy of the Vedabase, I was also able to add segments of Prabhupāda's lectures and room conversations that were especially meaningful to me or that helped establish Prabhupāda's mood in a particular place. I lightly edited Prabhupāda's words when necessary to make his spoken words flow more like written text,

Also, I added information that did not directly refer to Prabhupāda when it clarified circumstances or described the transitions in my life. Since Prabhupāda had to deal with those transitions, I thought them relevant.

This book does not retell, except in passing, many great and well known incidents in Prabhupāda's preaching. Rather, it narrates apparently insignificant incidents wherein Prabhupāda compassionately worked to save an insignificant soul by his actions, example, and words. Although I have recorded these few incidents, we could have written an entire book on each day of Prabhupāda's association, because each was a continuous flow of meaningful events. As Kṛṣṇadāsa Kavirāja Gosvāmī related about Śrī Caitanya Mahāprabhu: "Even Anantadeva, who possesses thousands of mouths, cannot fully describe the ecstatic transformations that Śrī Caitanya Mahāprabhu experienced in a single day. What can a creature like me describe of those transformations? I can only give a hint of them, as if showing the moon through the branches of a tree." (*Caitanya-caritāmṛita, Antya* 17.64–65)

---

*The complete database of Prabhupāda's books, conversations, lectures, walks and letters.

If, in fulfilling my desire to glorify Prabhupāda, I have offended any Vaiṣṇavas, I beg their forgiveness, for I depend on the tolerance and mercy of the Vaiṣṇavas. I wrote these vignettes to purify my heart and to feel closer to Prabhupāda, and I will consider this book successful if the reader experiences through it the compassionate association of Prabhupāda, my glorious master.

Acknowledgments

Many devotees shared their experience and offered practical guidance in publishing this book. Others inspired me and gave me courage. Still others donated valuable time and worked hard in conceiving, writing, polishing, and preparing *My Glorious Master* for publication and distribution. We pray that Śrī Caitanya Mahāprabhu and Śrī Nityānanda Prabhu are pleased by their contributions to the glorification of Śrīla Prabhupāda.

Kaiśorī Devī Dāsī of Gīta-nāgarī Press helped with extensive editing, proofreading, and advice. Her eye for clarity and the ability to ask the right questions helped me say what I wanted to say.

Tattvavit Dāsa acted as our consulting editor, answering hundreds of technical questions. Brajajana Dāsa also edited during the initial stages of production.

Lalita Mañjarī Devī Dāsī, my daughter, entered portions of the manuscript into the computer and I thank her. Mahāmāyā Devī Dāsī patiently entered diacritical marks and offered many helpful suggestions. Maithilī Devī Dāsī also entered corrections. Puruṣottama Dāsa answered questions on diacritical marks. Kālindī Devī Dāsī proofread and, with a marathon effort, deciphered and entered manuscript changes into the computer. Viṣṇu Mūrti Dāsa and my old friend Śyamānanda Dāsa offered sagacious advice after critically reading the manuscript. Vegavatī Devī Dāsī proofread.

Thanks go to Jita Girīśa Dāsa for allowing us to include his descriptive account of Śrīla Prabhupāda's visit to Auckland, and to Śatadhanya Dāsa for his remembrances of Prabhupāda's "*śloka* classes" in Japan.

Yamarāja Dāsa, who designed the cover for *The Art of Teaching,* also designed an attractive cover and went to great trouble to lay out *My Glorious Master's* photo section. The Bhaktivedanta Archives, always helpful, located many of the photos. Durāśaya Dāsa, an old Hong Kong preaching veteran, and Savitrī Devī Dāsī uncovered the magazine and newspaper articles used in the book.

Svarga Devī Dāsī, Sundarānanda Dāsa, and Ananda Vṛndāvanesvari Devī Dāsī helped the publishing from Vṛndāvana, and Aniruddha Dāsa helped from Australia.

Dina Bandhu Dāsa, Puṇḍarika Vidyānidhi Dāsa, Jīva Dāsa, Bindu Mādhava Dāsa, Jambavān Dāsa, Mārkaṇḍeya Dāsa, Veda Vyāsa Dāsa, and Lal Krishna Dāsa all provided computer-related assistance.

Vraja Vihārī Dāsa, while responsibly carrying out his other important duties, underwent unlimited anxiety and toiled hard to do the layout and act as production coordinator to insure *My Glorious Master* would be a suitable offering to Śrīla Prabhupāda's lotus feet.

My final thanks to Jagattāriṇī Devī Dāsī, for her sensitive suggestions as I prepared this manuscript, and for her "through thick-and-thin" support during most of my Kṛṣṇa conscious life.

Without the association, support, and affection of so many kind Vaiṣṇavas, how could we go on?

New York City, 1968

Beginning the Journey from Buffalo to Disciple

Jim Kurtain and I hitchhiked down from Buffalo, New York to New York City. Our purpose was clear: we wanted to see Swamijī – A.C. Bhaktivedanta Swami – the founder-*ācārya* of the International Society for Krishna Consciousness. We were both students at the State University of New York at Buffalo and had both begun chanting at a free university course given in mid-January of 1968. Now we had become interested enough to thumb our way to New York City.

Swamijī had just returned from India, where he had gone to recover from a heart problem. He landed first in San Francisco and then traveled on to New York. He had only been there for a few days when Rūpānuga, our teacher at the free university course, suggested we travel to New York to meet him.

The early March weather was cold, and snow had blanketed the fertile upstate farmland. We left on a Friday morning and covered most of the 250 miles to New York City by late afternoon. Our final ride dropped us at the upper tip of Manhattan, so we jumped aboard a subway, headed downtown, and jumped off in

Greenwich Village, the West Village. We knew that Swamijī's Friday night *kīrtana* and class began at 7 P.M. and as we were already late, we ran crosstown to the East Village and arrived at "Matchless Gifts," 26 Second Avenue.

Kīrtana had already ended by the time we arrived and Swamijī was speaking from the raised platform the New York devotees had built for him. I stepped into the storefront, sat down, and stared. It was the first time I was seeing my spiritual master.

* * *

Several months before making this trip to New York City, I went to visit my parents in Rockaway, New York. A letter arrived from a university friend named Eric, who told me he had enrolled me in the Bhakti Yoga Meditation course that started in January 1968. I became quite happy while reading his letter, for I considered myself a seeker of truth.

A few days later, I watched a bearded devotee – either Rāyarāma or Hayagrīva – on television describe how he had met Prabhupāda. He said he was walking down Second Avenue one day and had met the Swami. I thought, "Things like that never happen to me." But my own time was approaching.

Then again a few days later, while visiting a friend, I watched Les Crane interview Swamijī in San Francisco. The devotees chanted Hare Kṛṣṇa with arms raised in the air. Then Les Crane asked Swamijī if he was liberated. Swamijī replied, "Yes." He then waved his hand toward his Haight-Ashbury band of disciples, who sat on a carpet at his feet, and added, "And all my disciples are also liberated." Les Crane's final question to Swamijī was about his age. Prabhupāda smiled widely and said, "Seventy. And I still have all my teeth."

After I returned to Buffalo, I found myself chanting Hare Kṛṣṇa in a meeting room in Norton Hall, the student union. It wasn't the first time I had chanted Hare Kṛṣṇa – but this was different from the 1967 "Be-in" in a park in Buffalo where I had drummed on a guitar case and sung the mantra. The incense and candles burning on the altar, the Persian carpet, and the forty university students sitting in various postures on the floor added an Eastern flavor, but the real difference was Rūpānuga, an initiated disciple of Swamijī, who was bringing Kṛṣṇa consciousness to our university. After Rūpānuga led us in chanting, he began his lecture. I agreed with his philosophical thrust that material gain cannot satisfy us, and I decided to take up chanting Hare Kṛṣṇa as he advised: fifteen minutes twice every day, morning and evening. Before leaving that first class I reflected, "I wanted meditation and I got religion instead. Just my luck."

Despite my luck, by the next class I thought of myself as a devotee. The Hare Kṛṣṇa *mahā-mantra* had incredible potency, and it prompted me to compare all my previous attempts at self-realization to a dog's chasing his tail. A voice prompted me from within, "You've never completed anything. Keep chanting Hare Kṛṣṇa and complete this." As the weeks passed, I bought beads and switched over to a diet of *prasāda*.

Rūpānuga told me, "Whatever you like to do, you can do in Kṛṣṇa consciousness."

"What about listening to records?"

"You can listen to Kṛṣṇa conscious records," he said. Interested, I inquired how many Kṛṣṇa conscious albums were out. His confident reply: "One."

"One! I have a hundred and fifty albums that I play one after another!"

I nevertheless purchased the "one" album and played it continuously. In the privacy of my attic apartment, I flipped the album again and again. Amazingly, this one album satisfied me. Gradually I began to decipher Swamijī's Indian accent: "On the cover of the record album..." and, "There is no need to understand the language of the mantra... even a child can take part... and dance in ecstasy."

By the time I arrived at 26 Second Avenue that March and was face to face with Swamijī, I fully understood his accent. "I already knew him," was my initial reaction to his presence. Seeing him was like meeting someone familiar, like a grandfather.

Serving the Devotees

I was not able to concentrate on Swamijī's words, and I remember nothing of his lecture. Yet I glimpsed his great power. I lived in the temple that weekend, slept on the floor, and woke at 5:30 a.m. with the other devotees. The devotees engaged me in exotic but odd tasks, like writing out longhand the *Easy Journey to Other Planets* manuscript so it could be edited, getting gesso and other art supplies for Jadurāṇī, and searching the East Village gourmet food stores for Tiger's brand milk for Swamijī. The errand to purchase milk for Swamijī especially filled me with happiness. I chanted as I walked through St. Mark's Place and felt a deep, previously unexperienced joy.

A First Feast

That Sunday, Swamijī held a feast, an initiation, and an installation of Jagannātha deities. I sat in the temple room and chanted with the devotees. It was the first time I had ever heard a *mṛdaṅga*. As the *kīrtana* continued, Robert, one of the devotees to be initiated, carried in a huge Jagannātha Deity and placed Him on the altar. I was shocked. First African drum beats and now a totem! What kind of group *was* this? But as I looked at Jagannātha's smiling face, I relaxed and smiled with Him.

Swamijī initiated three new disciples: Bob became Vāmanadeva Dāsa, Jay became Jayādvaita Dāsa, and a second Jay became Jaya Nārāyaṇa Dāsa. In addition, Haṁsadūta and his wife Himavatī sat in on the fire ceremony to consecrate their marriage. Swamijī both performed the ceremony and lectured.

During his lecture, Swamijī explained that he was a *sannyāsī*, a renunciant, and traditionally should have nothing to do with marriages and marriage ceremonies, but he was duty-bound to perform his disciples' weddings because they were completely dependent on him.

* * *

I observed these esoteric, culturally un-American events taking place on Second Avenue with amazement. I felt simultaneously aloof, as one feels when watching a documentary about a distant land, and intimate, for I had already tasted results from chanting Hare Kṛṣṇa. I imagined myself sitting shaven-headed and cross-legged before the sacrificial fire and receiving initiation from Swamijī. But I knew I wasn't ready; I needed something more.

Jaya Nārāyaṇa, as it turned out, was writing a school paper on Swamijī and the Hare Kṛṣṇa devotees. His initiation experience was part of his paper. The following morning, his purpose fulfilled, he disappeared onto Second Avenue and was never heard from again. Jayādvaita Dāsa Brahmacārī and Vāmanadeva Dāsa fared much better.

Transcendence and Goodness

Swamijī's lecture continued. He spoke about Prahlāda Mahārāja and told the story of the boy devotee who was harassed by his atheistic father and later saved by Lord Nṛsiṁhadeva. At the end of his lecture, I raised my hand and asked Swamijī my first question. It was not submissive. "In your class you mentioned that devotees were in the mode of goodness. I thought that devotees were transcendental to the mode of goodness." Prabhupāda's answer was to the point: "Yes, devotees are transcendental. But they generally act in the mode of goodness."

* * *

I had only been chanting for several months and neither understood the meaning of "transcendental" nor "the mode of goodness." Yet I already thought myself learned and therefore offered my understanding to Prabhupāda. His straightforward answer satisfied me. Later, I understood that surrender places a devotee under Kṛṣṇa, not under the modes of nature, but that does not allow him to act whimsically in the name of being transcendental. Rather, when not required to act otherwise, pure devotees act naturally in the mode of goodness. Thus rather than rejecting the mode of goodness as an impure product of *māyā,* they embrace the mode of goodness as the platform from which to step off to transcendence.

Flowers into Water

After the lecture, initiation, marriage, fire ceremony, and Sunday feast, I was asked to dispose of the holy flower remnants in the East River. Although I didn't relish the thought of walking through the slums to the river, I accepted the service.

Before throwing the flower remnants into the murky water, I offered my obeisances on the nearby pavement. Then I threw the flowers in and watched them ebb and flow in the water. I then returned to 26 Second Avenue, chanting during the entire walk. Again I felt joy in chanting Hare Kṛṣṇa and depending on Him.

To Bow or Not to Bow?

The following morning, as Jim and I were about to begin our trip home, Brahmānanda asked us if we would like to accompany Swamijī on his morning walk. We both agreed.

We were told to wait for Swamijī outside the storefront. Suddenly, the vestibule door opened and Swamijī, effulgent and bundled in warm clothing in the morning coolness, stepped onto the dull, and dirty, glass-speckled sidewalk. Swamijī looked me in the eye and I bowed to offer my obeisances. I perceived in Swamijī's glance his desire that I not bow down on the filthy New York street, but I wasn't bold enough to heed my perception.

To Stop or Not to Stop?

The four of us – Swamijī, Gaurasundara, Jim, and I – headed silently uptown on Second Avenue. The streets were nearly deserted.

Swamijī walked briskly along Second Avenue, not heeding the red lights, but simply glancing left, then right before crossing.

* * *

I had been curious to see how Swamijī would deal with the street lights: would he follow the letter of the law and "stop on red," or be practical and cross as traffic permitted? Without a moment's hesitation, Swamijī chose the practical course. I was satisfied to see this and understood that Kṛṣṇa consciousness is practical.

Democrats and Republicans

Our walk continued in silence toward Eighth Street, St. Mark's Place. Swamijī then headed east several blocks to Avenue B, turned into Tompkins Square Park, and began walking the circular walkway opposite St. Bridget's Church. After completing the round several times, Swamijī headed back toward Second Avenue, pulling his three young followers in his wake. On Second Avenue, close to the temple, Swamijī chose to break the silence. Turning across the avenue toward a wall lined with Democratic Party posters for the upcoming 1968 presidential elections, Swamijī stopped, pointed his cane, and looked at us, "What are these Democrats and Republicans?"

My mental reaction was typical of the '60s: "There's no difference between these parties. They are both cheaters." But I remained silent, unsure of how to answer. Gaurasundara began explaining the difference between the parties based on their stance on the Vietnam War. I remember feeling foolish as I realized I was twenty-one years old and had no idea as to the difference, even on a superficial level, between Democrats and Republicans. Years later I understood that feeling a fool before one's spiritual master is appropriate and that my spiritual master was personally instructing me, even during this initial morning walk.

Back to Buffalo

Swamijī resumed his silence for the rest of the walk, and we arrived back at 26 Second Avenue.

Jim and I stood and watched as Gaurasundara opened the door. This allowed both Swamijī and him to pass through the anteroom and the courtyard to Swamijī's second-story apartment. Nothing of external significance had occurred during the walk. Swamijī had uttered only six words the entire time, but by the time we got back to 26 Second Avenue, I had decided to become his disciple.

Jim and I offered our obeisances, went in and ate our breakfast of "heavenly porridge," picked up our bags, and left for Buffalo.

Montreal, June 1968

A Matter of Choice

I had been chanting Hare Kṛṣṇa since January, and in April 1968 I was the first to move into our newly acquired Buffalo temple. The temple, ISKCON's seventh, was a rickety, white, two-story house on La Salle Street, near the university. When university classes were just about to end in April, I received a letter from a girlfriend suggesting we go to Cape Cod together for the summer. I informed Rūpānuga that I would be leaving for Cape Cod with my girlfriend, but that I would be back in September. Rūpānuga sat me down, looked me in the eye, and told me that it was time for me to make my choice: did I want to become a devotee or not? I quickly decided to stay with the devotees and I wrote my friend explaining that I was unable to accompany her.

Later that summer, Rūpānuga approached me as I pulled weeds in the temple garden. Swamijī was now in Montreal and was holding an initiation ceremony on Sunday. Rūpānuga asked if I wanted to become initiated. I said I would think about it.

At that time, I had no idea of the commitment involved in accepting a spiritual master. As I pulled weeds, a voice inside advised that initiation would help me continue chanting Hare

Kṛṣṇa and stop me from leaving Kṛṣṇa consciousness. After five minutes of deliberation, I informed Rūpānuga that I would like to take initiation.

I had a few dollars to put toward my bus fare. Rūpānuga gave ten more, a few friends chipped in a bit, and the remainder came from the temple's collection box. I was ready to go.

* * *

Prabhupāda had been unable to obtain permanent residency status while physically residing in the U.S., so he had flown to Montreal, Canada, where his disciples had recently established a temple. As soon as Prabhupāda arrived, devotees began visiting him, and, as several aspiring disciples were ready for their vows, Prabhupāda decided to hold an initiation ceremony. Brahmānanda, acting as Prabhupāda's secretary, phoned Rūpānuga from Montreal and asked whether or not I was ready for initiation. Rūpānuga had passed on his question to me.

Good Advice for Avenue du Parc

Although Kīrtanānanda had opened the Montreal temple, it was now being managed by Haṁsadūta and Himavatī. The temple was in an old, second-story bowling alley on Avenue du Parc, and by the time I arrived, most of the bowling lanes had been removed and the wood reused to construct Prabhupāda's *vyāsāsana,* an altar, and room dividers to separate the hall into several makeshift rooms. The temple room was quite large. Its walls were decorated with Brijbasi prints imported from India and purchased on Saint Mark's Place in New York's East Village. There were also paintings of Viṣṇu, Rādhā-Kṛṣṇa, Pañca-tattva, and Lord Caitanya's *saṅkīrtana* – all done by New York's ISKCON's art department. A large, blue banner with the Hare Kṛṣṇa *mahā-mantra* sewn in gold letters was hung prominently. Several devotees – Śivānanda, Puruṣottama, Harināma, and others – had already arrived to visit Swamijī.

I remember seeing Pradyumna standing before a mirror, meticulously applying *tilaka* and then exclaiming softly to himself, "*Vaiṣṇava!*" Jaya Patāka would be the first wake, at 4:30 A.M. and he would let the others sleep until 6:00. Gopāla Kṛṣṇa (then Gopal), would come straight from work every day, still wearing his business suit, and offer respects by bowing down to each picture in the temple room.

Swamijī stayed in an apartment a few blocks from Avenue du Parc. Someone asked me if I would be willing to wash Swamijī's clothes. I immediately agreed. Each day I walked to his apartment, took his saffron *dhotī, kurtā,* and top piece, and hand-washed them in the bathtub.

* * *

Rūpānuga had offered me good advice before leaving: "Take every opportunity to personally serve Swamijī." I was ready, therefore, and when the chance came, I grabbed it.

Swamijī and Prabhupāda

One day, Puruṣottama, Prabhupāda's secretary, took me aside and told me that "Swamijī" was not a first-class name. He said that "Gurudeva" was third-class, "Swamijī" was second-class, and "Prabhupāda" was first-class. Before long, we were all calling Swamijī "Prabhupāda." Although it took some getting used to, "Prabhupāda" soon began to sound correct.

* * *

I wasn't sure where Puruṣottama had gotten this information, but Swamijī accepted our calling him "Prabhupāda." Within a few months, an article appeared in *Back to Godhead* magazine explaining the meaning of Prabhupāda as "one at whose feet all masters sit," and explaining that Swamijī had graciously accepted our gesture of affection by allowing us to address him by that title.

Not Unto Kṛṣṇa

Prabhupāda spoke on *Bhagavad-gītā* in the Montreal temple every Monday, Wednesday, and Friday night. Tuesday and Thursday evenings were more intimate, with Prabhupāda meeting the devotees in his apartment. We sat on the floor before his low desk and Prabhupāda, dressed in a pink turtleneck, was effulgent, peaceful, powerful, and tireless.

At one meeting, Prabhupāda read the last verse of chapter nine, *man-manā bhava mad-bhakto mad-yājī māṁ namaskuru:* "Always think of Me," Kṛṣṇa says, "and become My devotee. Worship Me and offer Me your obeisances." As he read, he suddenly appeared angry.

Prabhupāda's own *Bhagavad-gītā As It Is* had not yet been published, so he was reading from Dr. Radhakrishnan's edition. Prabhupāda said that Dr. Radhakrishnan had translated the verse properly, but his commentary was a Māyāvāda interpretation and stood in contrast to Kṛṣṇa's own words in the verse. Dr. Radhakrishnan had commented that "It is not Kṛṣṇa to whom one must surrender," but that Kṛṣṇa was directing Arjuna, and all living entities, to surrender to the "unborn, unmanifest within Kṛṣṇa."

* * *

Prabhupāda did not view the philosophical wrangling of Māyāvādīs, materialists, or atheists with intellectual distance and detachment. He deplored their philosophical "word jugglery" because it misled innocent souls from the lotus feet of Kṛṣṇa and tangibly damaged their spiritual lives. Strong criticism of opposing philosophies was more a deep personal concern for Prabhupāda than an intellectual exercise.

The Perfect Teacher

While lecturing, Prabhupāda called for Pradyumna, who had begun studying Sanskrit, to locate a verse in the *Bhagavad-gītā* he carried for reference. "I think it is in chapter seven," Prabhupāda said.

Pradyumna replied, "I think it's in chapter four."

Prabhupāda didn't say anything, but when Pradyumna called out that he had found the verse, and after Prabhupāda had him read both the Sanskrit and the English translation, Prabhupāda asked softly, "What chapter was it in?"

"Seven," Pradyumna sheepishly replied.

* * *

Kṛṣṇa could have directly informed Indra that He was his master, the Supreme Personality of Godhead, but instead He chose to indirectly instruct Indra about His position by allowing him to witness the lifting of Govardhana Hill. Similarly, Prabhupāda wished to curb the scholar Pradyumna's freshly blossoming pride by allowing him to first search for the verse in the wrong chapter.

Entering the Sacrificial Arena

One hour before the initiation ceremony I was tying a *dhotī* around my waist for the first time. My fear that it would fall off did not stop my self-conscious walk across the temple room, through the loud *kīrtana* of *mṛdaṅga* and *karatālas,* to offer my obeisances to Prabhupāda, who sat on the floor before an earth mound decorated with colored zigzag designs. The wood for the fire, a pot of ghee, and a ladle sat by his side.

Brahmānanda tied the reddish wood neckbeads around our necks and devotees read from *śāstra* in Sanskrit or English from the four corners of the sacrificial arena.

A Dog's Good Quality

Prabhupāda lectured on the meaning of our neckbeads, which he likened to a collar signifying us as Kṛṣṇa's dogs. "A dog,"

Prabhupāda said, "has one good quality: he is loyal to his master."

* * *

Prabhupāda generally did not praise dogs, but he found their quality of loyalty ideal.

The Temples of Vṛndāvana

Prabhupāda then spoke about Vṛndāvana. I had already heard of Vṛndāvana from the *Śrīmad-Bhāgavatam*. He said that the temples in Vṛndāvana that had been started by the Gosvāmīs were now in the hands of rascals who did not maintain them properly. He said, "We should get them back and care for them."

* * *

Prabhupāda, as a long-time resident of Vṛndāvana, had seen the poor standard of temple maintenance, and had even witnessed temple caretakers selling the Deity's property. His instruction was to right the wrong of these improprieties.

An Early Request for Relief from Management

"I am an old man," Prabhupāda said, "and I can leave at any moment. You young men please take responsibility to manage this Kṛṣṇa consciousness movement and push it throughout the world."

* * *

As early as 1968 Prabhupāda wanted relief from the management responsibilities of ISKCON. He wanted his disciples to take up that burden. The assurance that ISKCON would continue, even in those early days, was dependent on the sincerity and cooperation among Prabhupāda's disciples to properly manage his mission.

Becoming a Viṣṇujana

The lecture was over and Prabhupāda chanted on our beads before the fire, before the Vaiṣṇavas, and before our eyes. When he finished chanting on one devotee's set of beads, he called that devotee forward and requested him to recite and promise to follow the four rules. He then showed with his own hands how to chant on the beads, teaching us to hold the beads between our thumb and second finger, to chant one mantra per bead, and to avoid chanting on the head bead. He then handed us our beads and gave us our spiritual names.

"Your name is Viṣṇujana Dāsa," Prabhupāda said to me as he handed me my beads.

* * *

Prabhupāda wore my beads around his neck as he chanted on them, and he held them in his hand before he placed them into my outstretched hands. When I received my beads from him they were still warm from his touch.

I retained the name Viṣṇujana for about an hour. A devotee then came to me with this message: "Prabhupāda said there's already a Viṣṇujana. Your name is Bhūrijana."

Three other *brahmacārīs* were initiated: Dayal Nitāi Dāsa, Ananta Dāsa, and Nayanābhirāma Dāsa.

Guru-dakṣiṇā

Prabhupāda performed the fire sacrifice, and when it was over, I noticed Nayanābhirāma offer Prabhupāda a delicately carved, silver drinking glass. A devotee then explained to me that a new initiate was required to offer a gift of appreciation to his spiritual master as guru-*dakṣiṇā*. It was the first time I had heard that information, and I was embarrassed because I had nothing to offer. I then thought of my $20 return bus fare and offered that money as *dakṣiṇā* at Prabhupāda's lotus feet.

Hearing the Name

On an ensuing evening, the devotees gathered in Prabhupāda's apartment for *Bhagavad-gītā* class. At the end of the class, Prabhupāda dropped a piece of fruit into his mouth and distributed a piece of the remaining fruit to each devotee. One by one the devotees left, but I stayed behind, making it look as if I had not yet received my piece of fruit. Prabhupāda looked at me questioningly. I said, "I'm not sure of my name."

"Bhoo-ree-jan."

With my heart pounding, I quickly offered my obeisances and left.

* * *

I had stayed behind because I wanted to hear my new name pronounced directly by my spiritual master. I received the impression, however, that Prabhupāda did not think my sentiment necessary.

Of Worms and Māyā

Prabhupāda maintained his usual format of *kīrtana*-lecture-*kīrtana* during both morning and evening lectures in Montreal. He sang the Hare Kṛṣṇa mantra each morning before his lecture. Sometimes he also chanted "*govinda jaya jaya, gopāla jaya jaya, rādhā-ramaṇa hari, govinda jaya jaya.*" The devotees would dance to his sweet singing with their arms raised in the air.

At the end of his lectures, he usually called for questions. I asked two questions on that visit to Montreal. The first one was about worms and their particular characteristic of taking up two separate lives when cut in half. "How is it possible that one living entity can become two?" Prabhupāda's answer was simple: a second spirit soul enters the cut-off part of the worm.

The second question alluded to the philosophical fact that a spirit soul cannot avoid his constitutional position of service to Kṛṣṇa. He either serves directly in the spiritual world or indirectly through *māyā* in the material world. I asked Prabhupāda why we should bother endeavoring to serve Kṛṣṇa if we are already serving Him through His *māyā* energy. Prabhupāda replied that serving Kṛṣṇa directly of our own will brings the soul happiness, and that serving Kṛṣṇa indirectly and unwillingly through His *māyā* brings only misery.

* * *

Although I had previously read it, I did not remember that Prabhupāda had already answered my question about direct and indirect service in his purport to *Śrīmad-Bhāgavatam* 1.3.38:

> Only the pure devotees can know the transcendental name, form, and activities of Lord Kṛṣṇa due to their being completely freed from the reactions of fruitive work and mental speculation. The pure devotees have nothing to derive as personal profit from their unalloyed service to the Lord. They render incessant service to the Lord spontaneously, without any reservation. Everyone within the creation of the Lord is rendering service to the Lord indirectly or directly. No one is an exception to this law of the Lord. Those who are rendering service indirectly, being forced by the illusory agent of the Lord, are rendering service unto Him unfavorably. But those who are rendering service unto Him directly under the direction of His beloved agents are rendering service unto Him favorably. Such favorable servitors are devotees of the Lord, and by the grace of the Lord they can enter into the mysterious region of transcendence by the mercy of the Lord. But the mental speculators remain in darkness all the time. As stated in *Bhagavad-gītā*, the Lord Himself guides the pure devotees toward the path of realization due to their constant engagement in the loving service of the Lord in spontaneous affection. That is the secret of entering into the kingdom of God.

Neither of my questions were very philosophical, penetrating, or practical. They were simply the doubts of a struggling conditioned soul whose intelligence was grappling with apparent philosophical contradictions caused by his birth and education in Western culture. Prabhupāda answered both questions to my satisfaction.

Humility

Once, as Prabhupāda sat on his *vyāsāsana* after class, an Indian gentleman dressed in suit and coat stood before him. He asked Prabhupāda which languages he knew. Prabhupāda listed Hindi, Bengali, and English. "Prabhupāda, you also speak Sanskrit," I offered. Prabhupāda looked at me and replied, "No. I don't know Sanskrit."

* * *

Prabhupāda was a published author and scholar, but he was extremely humble about his accomplishments. Yet when required, he could be the proudest of warriors on behalf of his Guru Mahārāja and Śrī Caitanya Mahāprabhu.

Back to Buffalo and a Letter

I went back to Buffalo after a week in Montreal. Since I had given Prabhupāda my return bus fare as guru-*dakṣiṇā,* I had to hitchhike back. A few weeks after my return, I wrote Prabhupāda a letter in which I asked over twenty questions. I wanted to know why Jesus said, "Father, why have You forsaken me?" at the crucifixion. I wanted to know what a devotee should do if he misses Ekādaśī. I asked whether the Supersoul was the same as the Holy Ghost of Catholicism and whether we should fast totally on Ekādaśīs or only from grains. And I asked why we observe Ekādaśī at all.

He answered some of the questions in a two-page letter, which I subsequently lost. He complimented me on my intelligence and admonished the senior devotees for being unable to satisfy my inquiries.

Prabhupāda said that we observe Ekādaśī because it is the eleventh day of the moon. The proper observance of Ekādaśī, he said, is to maximize chanting and reading. And, he said, it is better to completely fast, but added that if that was too difficult, then we should eat as little as was practical.

He mentioned that there is no such thing as a Holy Ghost – all ghosts are unholy – and that Ekādaśī should be observed on the following day if we accidentally miss it.

The letter also contained some esoteric points, but I no longer remember their context. Prabhupāda mentioned that rain falling on the head of a serpent during the *svāti* constellation would cause the appearance of a jewel on a serpent's head and that the Sanskrit language is called *devanāgarī* because Sanskrit is spoken by the demigods.

Rūpānuga accepted Prabhupāda's admonition that senior devotees should be able to answer such questions as a personal reprimand. Yet he and everyone else were excited about Bhūrijana's letter from Prabhupāda, especially about the part concerning jewels on the heads of snakes. As was the standard in those early days, my letter was retyped and carbon copies were sent to each of the six other ISKCON centers.

New York City, Late Summer, 1968

Again in New York

In late August 1968, I took advantage of the school break to visit my parents in New York City. My grades had improved since I had become a devotee, and as my parents thought my newfound Kṛṣṇa consciousness was a passing fad, they reluctantly accepted my changed lifestyle. They didn't like me burning incense in the house, and I kept my door closed to the unholy odors of their cooking. Outside of these inconveniences, they had nothing tangible to complain about.

I used to visit the 26 Second Avenue temple from my parent's home, sometimes staying overnight. On one visit I met Mukunda, Gurudāsa, Śyāmasundara, and their wives. They had come from San Francisco via Montreal and were on their way to London to open ISKCON's first center there.

During their visit we heard good news: Prabhupāda had been given permanent residency by the American Immigration office and would soon be arriving in New York. We felt the expectancy and joy of children freshly informed that Christmas, with holidays and gifts, had just been rescheduled for the following week. The devotees painted over the "Matchless Gifts" signboard that still adorned the entrance to 26 Second Avenue, transforming it into "The International Society for Krishna Consciousness." Prabhupāda's imminent arrival inspired me to shave my head for the first time.

* * *

A devotee's personal inspiration and commitment to advancement in Kṛṣṇa consciousness is his wealth. Rūpānuga, the leader of our fledgling Buffalo temple, did not once express that my spending time with my parents would cause me to "bloop" or fall down. Rather, he trusted my inspiration to become a devotee and my own commitment to Kṛṣṇa consciousness. Similarly, Prabhupāda never pushed me or forced me to shave my head. Rather, he inspired me to please him. Based on his inspiration, shaving my head followed naturally.

Yet Kṛṣṇa consciousness and surrendered service to our spiritual master is not limited to our inspiration or our being dealt with in a congenial or respectful way. We must also serve when we are not feeling inspired. An advanced disciple is prepared to serve his guru unhesitatingly, without personal consideration, regardless of any difficulties. Selfless service to the spiritual master is a prerequisite for attaining selfless service to Śrī Śrī Rādhā and Kṛṣṇa.

Prabhupāda's Arrival in New York

Prabhupāda entered the 26 Second Avenue temple and lectured to the devotees who had gathered to greet him. He began by relating his travel experience in coming to New York – it had taken him one hour to fly from Montreal to New York, and then two hours to battle the traffic from New York's JFK airport to the Lower East Side – and he mocked the so-called advancement of modern civilization.

* * *

We all laughed along with Prabhupāda at the foolishness of the modern materialists, the "*karmīs*." They were always making technological advances, but they could never foresee the repercussions that only caused greater inconvenience or even danger. Prabhupāda worked to detach us from our conditioned view of "advanced," contemporary society.

Rādhā and Kṛṣṇa and Prabhupāda in Brooklyn

Rādhāṣṭamī fell on a Sunday during Prabhupāda's visit. The devotees planned to go with Prabhupāda to the Brooklyn Botanical Gardens and hold *kīrtana*. Indirā Dāsī and her sister, Ekayaṇī Dāsī, were to be dressed up during the outing as Rādhā and Kṛṣṇa. "We should treat them just as we would Rādhā and Kṛṣṇa," the temple president told us.

Prabhupāda arrived by car while most of the devotees rode the subway. (I wasn't sure how "Rādhā and Kṛṣṇa" made their way, but later I found out that they too took the subway.) The overcast sky suddenly cleared as Prabhupāda arrived and illuminated the park with his presence.

The devotees sat around Prabhupāda, and Rādhā and Kṛṣṇa sat nearby on a blanket. Prabhupāda led the *kīrtana* and the devotees chanted and danced with their hands in the air.

I brought my 35mm Kowa SLR camera, but I had no film. I was bubbling with anxiety. I really wanted to take pictures, so I left the *kīrtana* to scour the New York streets for a shop open on a Sunday that sold film. I ran and ran, finally found the film, and rushed back. I had been gone half an hour and the *kīrtana* was going strong. I snapped some photos. One was included in the original *ISKCON Handbook* – Prabhupāda chanting with Indirā and Ekayani behind him dressed as Rādhā and Kṛṣṇa – published in 1969 by ISKCON Press.

* * *

Prabhupāda took part in the entire Rādhāṣṭamī festival without saying a word about "Rādhā and Kṛṣṇa." The devotees even offered them food and accepted their remnants as *mahā-prasāda*. Months later, I heard that Prabhupāda said it was not bona fide and that we should not do such things.

Disciples Speak

After the *kīrtana,* Prabhupāda requested his senior disciples one by one to preach. Brahmānanda, Rūpānuga, Dāmodara, Jadurāṇī, and others stood and spoke.

* * *

Only devotees were in listening range, so we understood that Prabhupāda was examining his students. I watched Rūpānuga stand and speak, his hands folded in sincerity, and I daydreamed what I would say if Prabhupāda called on me. I decided I would walk to the young black couple standing a hundred yards away, watching us curiously, and invite them to come and meet Prabhupāda. But Prabhupāda didn't call on me. I wasn't sure if I was relieved or disappointed.

Prabhupāda at the Movies

One afternoon the following week, we learned that Prabhupāda would come down from his apartment and watch Dāmodara's 8-mm movie of our Rādhāṣṭamī expedition. A single chair was placed in the temple room for Prabhupāda and a movie screen was set up. Prabhupāda sat and watched the uncut, unedited, silent movie. After smiling and enjoying the movie with his disciples, he went back upstairs.

* * *

A parent smiles with pleasure at a child's first attempts to walk or speak. Prabhupāda was similarly pleased at 26 Second Avenue.

And as childish antics are no longer pleasing to a parent when the child has grown up because the parent expects more, similarly, Prabhupāda gradually expected more from his disciples.

Prabhupāda's early pastimes at 26 Second Avenue had long ago ended, yet Prabhupāda still reciprocated easily with his disciples' simple attempts to please him. His mood was congenial, and he accepted whatever the devotees offered. Gradually, however, as the movement gained strength and the devotees began to mature in their Kṛṣṇa consciousness, Prabhupāda pushed his disciples to advance, distribute more books, and to spread Kṛṣṇa consciousness throughout the world.

Around this time, Prabhupāda also told his filmmaker disciple, Dāmodara, to make a movie of the *Bhagavad-gītā.* He said if Dāmodara would make such a film, he would personally direct it.

The Good Old Days of Kṛṣṇa Consciousness

Using whatever excuse I could think of, I managed to bypass two sets of guards and enter Prabhupāda's 26 Second Avenue apartment while he was speaking with several devotees. Kīrtanānanda Swami, Hayagrīva, Umāpati, and Gaurasundara sat on the floor. Prabhupāda sat behind his low desk on a woolly, Nepali carpet.

UMĀPATI: This is just like the old days, Prabhupāda.
PRABHUPĀDA: There are no old days in Kṛṣṇa consciousness.

* * *

Prabhupāda's words made everyone laugh, but it was, in fact, a heavy statement. A disciple may enjoy the sweet and even transcendental remembrances of the past, but the increased organization, rules, and regulations that Prabhupāda places on his disciples does not allow them to sit back and muse nostalgically about "the good old days." The new days may not be entirely to our liking, but we should nevertheless somehow keep serving Prabhupāda.

Umāpati remembers this same incident with one addition: Prabhupāda added "We are all eternal" to his comment.

Dr. Frog, RIP.

On Prabhupāda's request, Gaurasundara brought out an 11x16 inch card on which he was inking the story of "Dr. Frog." Everyone present, including Prabhupāda, laughed at Gaurasundara's comic rendition of Dr. Frog attempting to estimate the size of the ocean from his well by puffing out his chest: "Do you mean the ocean is three times the size of my well?"

* * *

A standard piece of ISKCON jargon is "puffed up." Its derivation can be traced to a frog puffing himself up inside his well and finally bursting. We all laughed at Dr. Frog's antics, but our tendency to be "puffed up" did not burst with the demise of Dr. Frog, Ph.D.

Gaurasundara Dāsa's comic strip was later printed in *Back to Godhead* magazine.

Folk Wisdom from Prabhupāda

During this meeting Prabhupāda mentioned two gems of folk wisdom, both of which I heard him say:

1. If something is auspicious, do it immediately. If something is inauspicious, put it off. 2. Something is better than nothing.

* * *

Following the first gem guarantees that we won't miss opportunities to better ourselves to help others. A second point of this gem applies when circumstances force us to act inauspiciously. When such a situation arises, we should delay as long as possible, hoping for a favorable change. The second gem teaches that even a slight gain is better than no gain at all. I have found both sayings helpful in both material and spiritual dealings.

Medium Cows

While Prabhupāda was in Montreal, Kīrtanānanda and Hayagrīva, after having left ISKCON for some time, returned and offered him their newly acquired land in West Virginia. Prabhupāda named it New Vrindaban. Now Prabhupāda began advising them how to develop it.

KĪRTANĀNANDA: What kind of cows should we get? Should we get the best quality cows? Or cows of the lowest quality?
PRABHUPĀDA: Medium.

* * *

The devotees were inexperienced in tilling land and caring for cows. Prabhupāda therefore advised a middle of the road approach. A few months later Prabhupāda visited New Vrindaban and gave further instructions on how to develop the land. He wanted New Vrindaban centered on worshiping Kṛṣṇa in seven temples, caring for cows, and farming – simple living and high thinking.

A Personal Instruction for Happiness

Our *darśana* ended and the devotees offered their obeisances and left. I remained behind because I wanted to say something privately to Prabhupāda. When all the devotees had gone and I too was near the door, I turned and asked Prabhupāda how I could serve him. I longed for a personal instruction.

"Take this Kṛṣṇa consciousness and be happy. *Jaya.*"

* * *

The word "*jaya*" seemed to flow from Prabhupāda's mouth slowly, like thick honey. I have added this instruction to others Prabhupāda gave me that I have yet to fulfill. I therefore beg the Vaiṣṇavas to please bless me that I can one day fulfill all of Prabhupāda's instructions, including this one.

Soon after this meeting with Prabhupāda in his 26 Second Avenue apartment, I returned to Buffalo for my final university semester. Prabhupāda also left New York, stopping briefly in Santa Fe and then traveling onward to preach in Seattle.

Buffalo to Chapel Hill, 1968–69

Rūpānuga's Empowered Preaching

I lived in the temple and attended classes during the final semester of my senior year at the University of Buffalo. Every evening after studying in the university library, I would go home to the temple and be greeted by Rūpānuga, his wife, their five-year-old son, and the other students or friends who had joined. *Prasāda,* especially the hot *dāl,* always tasted incredible after a day at school. Later, we would all gather around the big gas stove outside the temple room and savor "banana nectar" – milk with mashed bananas, spiced with cinnamon, cloves, coriander, and vanilla beans sizzled in ghee before being added. We *brahmacārīs* would then carry our sleeping bags into the temple room, crawl in, and fall asleep.

* * *

Rūpānuga's Buffalo preaching success was unique and outstanding. Our La Salle St. temple was lively, with university students dropping by for morning *Śrīmad-Bhāgavatam* classes, thrice-weekly evening *Bhagavad-gītā* classes, and our Sunday feast. (It was my service to telephone all the people listed in our guestbook and invite them to the feast.) On Tuesdays and Thursdays we held a Bhakti-Yoga Class at the student union.

Rūpānuga continued his program for years. By the time I left Buffalo, Trivikrama, Jagadīśa, and Prahlādānanda had joined. Rūpānuga's accredited course on the *Bhagavad-gītā* attracted Bhagavān and Kṛṣṇa Bhāmini Dāsī to join. Guṇagrāhi and Kuśakratha soon followed, and Romapāda had already received his first BTG. Ayodhyapati, Laxmimoni Dāsī, Narottamānanda, Nityānanda, Tejīyas, Madira Dāsī, Satyavrata, Muktakeśa, Lokavarṇottama, and many others joined the Buffalo temple after I left. In addition, two other successful temples were either started (Detroit) or had their preaching fortified (Toronto) as a direct result of Rūpānuga's Buffalo preaching success.

The mood in Buffalo, and throughout the movement at this time, was to follow Prabhupāda's fearless preaching spirit. Prabhupāda had directly inspired us by his example and words. He wrote to Brahmānanda in 1967:

> I have read your statements regarding opening centers. I am not in agreement with Mr. Altman that we are expanding very thinly. In my opinion, a single sincere soul can maintain a center. You know I started the center at 26 Second Avenue alone. I took the risk of $200 per month for the rent. At that time there were no assistants. Mukunda was at that time a friend, but there was no responsibility for him for maintaining the center. Gradually Kirtanananda and Hayagriva joined, but they did not take any responsibility. Still I was maintaining the establishment simply depending on Krishna and then Krishna sent me everything – men and money. Similarly, if a sincere soul goes out and opens a center in any part of the world, Krishna will help him in all respects. Without being empowered by Krishna, nobody can preach Krishna consciousness. It is not academic qualification or financial strength that helps in these matters, but it is sincerity of purpose which helps us always. Therefore, I wish that you will remain in charge of New York, let Satsvarupa be in charge of

Boston, let Mukunda be in charge of San Francisco, let Janardana be in charge of Montreal. Let Nandarani and Dayananda be in charge of Los Angeles, and let Subala das be in charge of Santa Fe. In this way you will follow my example as I did in the beginning at 26 Second Ave. That is preaching, cooking, writing, talking, chanting, everything one man's show. I never thought about the audience. I was prepared to chant if there was no man to hear me. The principle of chanting is to glorify the Lord and not to attract a crowd. If Krishna hears nicely then He will ask some sincere devotees to gather in such place. Therefore, be advised that thousands of centers may be started if we find out a sincere soul for each and every center. We do not require more men to start. If there is one sincere soul, that is sufficient to start a new center....Let us remain sincere to Krishna and His bona fide representative and we are sure to carry out our mission successfully. Hope you are well.

Your ever well-wisher,
A.C. Bhaktivedanta Swami

A Kīrtana for Prabhupāda's Pleasure

Kṛṣṇa consciousness was thriving in Buffalo. Trivikrama, Jagadīśa, and I took jobs as taxi drivers to support the temple. We would often drive all night, when there was less traffic and most of the fares were long distance rides. Trivikrama made friends with Mr. Montana, the owner and radio dispatcher, and we would all say "Haribol" to him on the air and hear his broadcasted reply, "Haribol." Hearing "Haribol" again and again on the radio encouraged us, and we'd talk about spreading Kṛṣṇa consciousness by setting up our own taxi company complete with saffron cabs.

Attending university classes also took on a preaching dimension, and many students wanted to know about "the far out thing I was into" that had caused me to change my habits, give up listening to rock music, and shave my head. By the time I graduated, the Buffalo temple was well-established.

We Buffalo devotees taped one of our *kīrtanas* and sent it to Prabhupāda with a letter. The *mṛdaṅga* and *karatālas* were soft and the melody sweet. The devotee men sang first as a group and the women responded. The *kīrtana* began slowly, sped up, and again slowed. A guitar accompanied us. Prabhupāda replied to my letter:

> My Dear Bhurijana,
>
> Please accept my blessings. I am in due receipt of your letter of January 13, 1969 along with the kirtan tapes and pictures of the Buffalo temple. I cannot tell you how very much I enjoyed listening to this wonderful tape recording. All of the super excellent qualities of kirtan were present on this tape and it was thus a great joy to hear it. On this tape Rupanuga has set an example for all householders because there was singing on this of Hare Krishna by all of his family members. It was all sounding very nicely, and I am going to show this tape to the Sankirtana Party here in Los Angeles so they may take example from such nice kirtan.
>
> I am very pleased that you are graduating from college in a few days and are anxious to engage your labors in spreading this Krishna consciousness movement. Also, I request you to study carefully the Bhagavad-gita As It Is because there is so much important service that an intelligent boy such as yourself can do in preaching work and spreading our movement around the world. You have a very good example from your Godbrother, Rupanuga, and so continue to help him as you are doing, and it shall be very successful for you.
>
> So thank you again for your nice letter along with the tape. I hope this meets you in very good health.
>
> Your ever well-wisher
> A.C. Bhaktivedanta Swami

* * *

Prabhupāda liked our *kīrtana* tape! "All of the super excellent qualities of *kīrtana* were present." As Prabhupāda felt joy listening to our *kīrtana,* we felt joy in Prabhupāda's pleasure.

Prabhupāda glorified Rūpānuga for spearheading the Buffalo preaching and for engaging his wife and son in chanting the *mahā-mantra.*

Prabhupāda also encouraged me to use my energy in preaching, and he told me to purify my intelligence by studying *Bhagavad-gītā As It Is.*

From Student to Student-Teacher

I appeared for my graduation ceremony wearing cap, gown, and *tilaka.* My school performance had drastically improved after becoming a devotee, and I had made the Dean's honor list for both of my final semesters. My parents could not help being satisfied.

Just after graduation, I heard that Patita-Uddharana's mother had offered ISKCON the use of her home for three months to get the preaching started in Chapel Hill, North Carolina. With Rūpānuga's permission, I went to open ISKCON's thirteenth center. I informed Prabhupāda of the plan in a letter, and he replied as follows:

> My Dear Bhurijana,
>
> Please accept my blessings. I am in due receipt of your letter dated February 3, 1969, and I'm so pleased and encouraged to note the contents. Your idea of going to North Carolina is excellent because there are so many students there, and you are a college graduate, so I think that you are just the devotee to do the job nicely. The only thing is that I do not think it is necessary for you to go there alone, so immediately you may contact Tosana Krishna in Santa Fe temple, and he is also willing to go there to be your assistant. If the two of you find the place suitable, then for some time myself and Purusottama will go there to make the center fortified. So you may write immediately to Tosana Krishna in this connection, and the both of you may start on this important new endeavor.
>
> Regarding the seeds which you have sent, yes, they are genuine tulasi seeds.

Thank you again for your most encouraging letter, and I shall be awaiting further news from you in this matter.

Your ever well-wisher
A.C. Bhaktivedanta Swami

* * *

We had sent Prabhupāda some seeds to make sure they were actually *tulasī*. We asked Prabhupāda about almost everything, because we knew nothing. Prabhupāda was always willing to respond to our appeals.

Prabhupāda's Simple Preaching Success Formula

I flew to North Carolina within a few weeks of my graduation, six months after initiation, and one year after first contacting the devotees. Due to Prabhupāda's fanning efforts, he had the movement's preaching spirit ablaze. The devotees, thinking that the entire world would soon be Kṛṣṇa conscious, were revolutionary missionaries in Prabhupāda's service. Just after I arrived in Chapel Hill, Prabhupāda wrote me:

My Dear Bhurijana,

Please accept my blessings. I am very happy to be in receipt of your nice letter of March 6, 1969, and thank you very much for it. Yes, you are two ideal ones for preaching there, and I can understand that things are going very nicely. This is very much encouraging to me. Hold kirtanas and serve prasadam, and gradually people will come, more and more. That is the program. You are both sincere students and very intelligent boys, and Krishna will supply you all facility for your preaching work if you try sincerely.

Your ever well-wisher
A.C. Bhaktivedanta Swami

* * *

Prabhupāda gave Toṣaṇa Kṛṣṇa and I the simple formula for preaching Kṛṣṇa consciousness: *kīrtana* and *prasāda*. After preaching for two months from Patita-Uddharana's mother's house, we rented a house closer to the University of North Carolina. We would stand every day on Main Street in Chapel Hill, chant Hare Kṛṣṇa, and distribute sweets. We supported our preaching by working as house painters, construction workers, bricklayer's assistants, and other odd jobs. We also formed a university-sponsored Bhakti-Yoga Club and held a weekly (and popular) Saturday night feast. Toṣaṇa Kṛṣṇa silkscreened some posters, and we hung them around the university. Our preaching based on Prabhupāda's instructions expanded.

Māyā Strikes Back

But soon disaster struck. It was the 1960s and the Vietnam War was raging. I had just graduated from university and was therefore now eligible for the draft. When the letter came from the United States Government – "Greetings" – I was ordered to appear for a pre-induction physical. I immediately wrote Prabhupāda and he replied quickly:

> My Dear Bhurijana,
>
> Please accept my blessings. You will be pleased to know that one devotee, Karttikeya, has already received his 4-D ministerial status from the draft, and I am enclosing herewith carbon copy of the letter I have sent to your draft board. So we shall save you from the draft. If you stick to the study of our books and continue as a preacher, there will be no difficulty for you to get 4-D classification.
>
> Your ever well-wisher
> A.C. Bhaktivedanta Swami

* * *

Kṛṣṇa and the Draft Board

My local draft board was in old-fashioned Durham, North Carolina, home of Pall Mall, Duke of Durham, and Raleigh cigarettes. The entire town reeked of tobacco. Prabhupāda's letter requesting that I be given ministerial exemption from the draft was not accepted by the conservative local draft board, but I had my own plan how Kṛṣṇa would save me. Many of my uncles and cousins were doctors, and they provided me with letters explaining my myriad of illnesses, including a chronic cough, bronchitis, and asthma. My feet were flat, my eyesight poor, and one of my legs was shorter than the other. I was also anemic.

They read my letters when I went for the physical, but the doctors didn't seem impressed. I began to get nervous. They saw my short-cropped hair, neckbeads, and chanting beads. After thrusting a needle into my arm and pulling out some blood they said, "Blood count sufficient." They considered my legs, lungs, feet, and eyes. Not great, but good enough. The other young, jockey-short-clad draftees were marching through the array of doctors and passing the medical examination. My anxiety increased. I had no more letters left – nothing to help me. Bhūrijana Dāsa, Hare Kṛṣṇa devotee, in the army and shipped off to Vietnam!

They weighed me, measured me, peeped into my mouth to check my teeth. "This is ridiculous," I thought. "I'm passing the physical. Is Kṛṣṇa going to help me?" The chief doctor, standing with a military man on his right, read through my file. He tapped the purple stamp pad and raised the official stamp of approval in his hand. The words, "You passed, son," were about to escape his mustached mouth. "Kṛṣṇa, help!" I was screaming internally. Thinking that fortune favors the bold, I began to rant and rave. "You can't take me! I'm a Hare Kṛṣṇa! I'm not fit for the army! I'm a vegetarian! It's against my religion! I demand to see a psychiatrist! I demand to see a psychiatrist! I demand to see a psychiatrist! You're not taking meeeee!"

The doctor stared at me and ordered me to step out of line. "I demand to see a psychiatrist." Reluctantly, he agreed, and my appointment was set for the following Tuesday.

On Tuesday, I did not go alone. I shaved my head and wore my robes. The army corporals acting as orderlies outside the psychiatrist's office were impressed. They smiled as I walked through. I also smiled. I carried Lord Jagannātha, Baladeva, and Subhadrā in my bag.

The psychiatrist sat balding over his glasses in a swivel chair at a desk. When I walked into the room, he motioned toward a couch and suggested I lie down and relax while he asked me some questions.

"No, I will sit on the floor," I said, plopping myself down on the carpet. His eyes widened as I pulled a brocade cloth from my bag and carefully set it out before me on the carpet. By the time I had extracted my small carved deities of Jagannātha, Subhadrā, and Balarāma, I had captured his full attention. I pulled out a pair of *karatālas* and started singing:

nama oṁ viṣṇu-pādāya kṛṣṇa-preṣṭhāya bhū-tale
śrīmate bhaktivedānta svāmin iti nāmine

śrī-kṛṣṇa-caitanya prabhu nityānanda
śrī-advaita gadādhara śrīvāsādi-gaura-bhakta-vṛnda

hare kṛṣṇa hare kṛṣṇa kṛṣṇa kṛṣṇa hare hare
hare rāma hare rāma rāma rāma hare hare

When I thought the doctor had benefited sufficiently from the *mahā-mantra*, I sang, *jagannātha swami nayana pathagame bhavatu me*. Then I put away the *karatālas* and pulled out my *japa* beads Sitting before the deities, back straight, eyes closed, I chanted loudly on my beads: Hare Kṛṣṇa, Hare Kṛṣṇa, Kṛṣṇa Kṛṣṇa, Hare Hare/ Hare Rāma, Hare Rāma, Rāma Rāma, Hare Hare.

The psychiatrist leaned forward. He rubbed the first and second fingers of his left hand together as if fingering invisible beads. "I see you are chanting on beads. You know that when you go into the army – and they are going to take you into the army – they are going to take away your beads." Then he repeated it again, for emphasis, "You know they will take away your beads."

This was my cue: "No! They will not take away my beads." I spoke strongly, keeping my voice loud, flat, and mechanical. Then I repeated, "They will not take away my beads."

The psychiatrist studied my face for a few moments. Pointing to Jagannātha, Baladeva, and Subhadrā, he inquired about their identity. "That is God," I replied. The psychiatrist squinted, as if trying to scan my mind. I put my hand back in my bead bag and softly chanted *japa*. He stared at me for another two minutes, jotted some notes on the papers on his desk, and said finally,"All right, you can go. Take a seat outside."

The orderlies were still smiling. They were clearly on my side. A bell rang and one uniformed orderly raced into the psychiatrist's office. He quickly returned with some papers and waved me over. He whispered, "He's written that there's nothing wrong with you, but that you're not suitable for the army."

* * *

Prabhupāda and Kṛṣṇa saved me from the draft!

Drops of Nectar in Chapel Hill

During my stay in Chapel Hill, I received several instructive letters from Prabhupāda. Here are some excerpts:

Observing Gaura-Pūrṇimā

Dear Bhurijana,

Please accept my blessings. Regarding Lord Caitanya's birth date, it is March 4, and you may celebrate it as elaborately as is possible for you. Immediately you should contact Brahmananda in New York, and ask him to send you a few chapters of Teachings of Lord Caitanya which you will return afterwards. So on this day you may read from these chapters. To celebrate you should have a picture of Lord Caitanya on the altar and decorate Him with flowers very nicely. Chanting and lecturing may go on. In these lectures you should explain very carefully Lord Caitanya's teachings that we are eternal servitors of Krishna, and it is not that we are ourselves the Supreme Lord.

Your ever well-wisher
A.C. Bhaktivedanta Swami

* * *

Teachings of Lord Caitanya had not yet been published. The simple Gaura-Pūrṇimā ceremony as recommended by Prabhupāda was complete and fully satisfying.

Remaining Brahmacārī

Dear Bhurijana,

Please accept my blessings. I am pleased to note that you have decided to remain as brahmacari because it will be the most "undiverting" for your Krishna consciousness. Actually this is correct. If one is able to remain as brahmacari, that is first class because so much botheration of household life is immediately avoided. But Krishna consciousness is not limited that one must be brahmacari to execute, or one must be sannyasi to execute. Spiritual means that there is no conditions whatever, so in any position one may be in, he can chant Hare Krishna, preach Krishna consciousness, and pray to Krishna to engage him more and more in His transcendental loving service.

Your ever well-wisher
A.C. Bhaktivedanta Swami

* * *

When I decided to remain *brahmacārī*, I was twenty-two years old. Prabhupāda, however, as the expert and experienced teacher, somehow extracted a pure motive from my immature decision to remain undiverted in my Kṛṣṇa consciousness. He also accurately understood that I was too young to make such a lifelong decision. Therefore, he encouraged me by explaining the benefits of *brahmacārī* life, but he also carefully explained that Kṛṣṇa consciousness is fully transcendental and not limited by time, place, circumstance, or *āśrama*.

Questions about Jagannātha Masks and Lotus Feet

Dear Bhurijana,

Please accept my blessings. Regarding the Jagannatha mask, it is not bona fide. The footprint of Krishna is all right. You can keep It by the throne and while taking care of the Deities, you also wash the Foot, wipe It, and put It back. Generally this is done with a little sandalwood pulp. There are markings on the chest and feet of the Personality of Godhead. That is the distinction between Him and ordinary living entities. Just like in our palms there are certain marks for a particular person indicating his fame and fortune. Similarly the Supreme Personality of Godhead has got certain signs on His Lotus Feet which are unique for Him only, and they are not to be found in ordinary living entities. In Vaikuntha all the inhabitants have exactly the same bodily features as Narayana, but Narayana is made distinct by the marks on His chest and lotus feet. The Goddess of Fortune recognizes Her husband by these symptoms. That is the version of devotees.

Your ever well-wisher
A.C. Bhaktivedanta Swami

* * *

We had received the masks and the foot impression from a young American traveler who had recently returned from India. Prabhupāda's discrimination was our only insurance to avoid mistakes while worshiping Kṛṣṇa.

An Adventure at Woodstock

Toṣaṇa Kṛṣṇa, Vṛndāvana Candra (who had recently come to assist us), and I heard about Woodstock, the upcoming giant music festival, and decided to attend and preach.

We hitchhiked from North Carolina to New York City and then on to Woodstock. We had no idea what to expect when we arrived.

Tens of thousands of young, hip citizens of East Coast America had converged on Woodstock's barren farm fields. Although tickets were sold for the event, no one was prepared for the size of the turnout. The promoters gave up demanding payment or checking tickets. They were moved by the spirit of the '60s and they opened the gates to all. Throngs of young men and women channeled through and became part of the "happening." This was *the* event, and they were part of it. Countless gaily dressed hippie pilgrims milled around and danced, or sat absorbed in the intoxications of the moment and the music from the main stage.

They had traveled on Kali's call to Woodstock. Their mood was accepting, so they accepted us with our shaved heads and Indian dress. We held *kīrtana* in the evenings, and many joined in the chanting. During the day, we handed out incense and peacock feathers and asked for donations. We also looked for opportunities to preach.

One evening, I attempted to chant on the main stage by disguising myself as a follower of Swami Satchidananda, the bearded and trendy uptown New York hatha-yoga guru. As he and his followers marched up the ramparts to the stage, I followed behind waving my bundle of peacock feathers up and down, looking like the final member of their entourage. But my attempt was foiled at the last moment by a *yoga* student, and I was ordered off the stage. (Years later, I met Swami Satchidananda in Hong Kong, and he showed a movie of his exploits in the West. The screen filled with a shot of the Swami and his students walking onto the Woodstock stage. Behind his head, I could clearly see my bundle of peacock feathers waving up and down. "Hey, that's me," I proudly told him.)

We were determined to chant Hare Kṛṣṇa onstage. On the final evening, we were given permission to chant side-stage at the "Hog Farm." The weather was threatening and it was already dark. The rock group's electric guitars were screaming heavy metallic blues. The lead singer called to the crowd, "You are moving the sun! You are moving the moon!" The blues notes bent, the bass guitars thumped, the drums thundered, and the crowds went wild in the dimly lit, cloud-covered night. Dancing with abandon, eyes turned upward, and with and without partners, the audience clapped and approved of the band's reminder that human beings are God.

We were the next act. In that moment of demonic insanity we walked onstage with *karatālas* and our simple message: "Chant Hare Kṛṣṇa and be happy. We'd like you all to chant with us." Our chant began, and a few from the audience joined in.

Suddenly we heard loud, antagonistic yells of "Shut up! Stop chanting!" The fever of the protests increased, but we continued. "Shut up! Stop that chanting! Rock is our soul!" We heard and recognized the black leather jackets of the "Mother-F______s," a New York City radical, anarchistic street gang, as the leaders of the dissent. We kept chanting and they stepped up their protest. We chanted faster. We saw gang members standing up and moving toward the stage. "How can we stop chanting," I wondered. "But how can we continue?"

"Hare Kṛṣṇa, Hare Kṛṣṇa, Kṛṣṇa Kṛṣṇa, Hare Hare," we sang into the microphone. Our eyes scanned the crowd in the darkness, and our ears weighed the sounds of responding chanters against the calls of angry protesters. Suddenly, just as the tension began to peak, the generator exploded and the power died. Darkness fell like a curtain over the stage. Our act was over.

That night a heavy rain fell, halving the Woodstock fever. The crowds were drenched and the festival began to wind down. We three tired, aspiring servants of Prabhupāda, happy but sick from the damp, began our return journey to New York City late the following morning.

Part of our gain from our weekend's preaching was a trunk full of small coins. When we arrived at our 61 Second Avenue temple in New York, we discovered that we had collected almost $600! ISKCON was poor in those days and we were astounded by the size of our three-day collection. We decided to send part of the collection to Prabhupāda.

Our letter offering Prabhupāda $200 was sincere, but not in

touch with the actual worth of $200. It began with flowery pomp: "My dear Srila Prabhupāda, please accept our humble obeisances and this donation of $200 for your book fund. Please use this money to publish *The Nectar of Devotion* and thus save all the university students throughout the land."

Prabhupāda, as his reply shows, accepted the spirit of our donation and overlooked its amount:

> My Dear Bhurijana, Tosana Krishna and Vrindavana Candra,
>
> Please accept my blessings. I beg to thank you for your sending me the check for $200 for my book fund, and I think of it as a big contribution of $2,000,000. I have come to your country to carry out the wishes of my spiritual master, and you are kindly cooperating with me. Certainly Krishna will be pleased to bless you with all spiritual benediction.
>
> I shall be glad to hear from you about your other progress in the matter of Sankirtana Party and selling BTGs. That is our main strength for preaching work. Thank you very much.
>
> Your ever well-wisher,
> A.C. Bhaktivedanta Swami

* * *

If we had thought more carefully, we would have distributed *Back to Godhead* magazines at Woodstock rather than only incense and peacock feathers. *Back to Godhead* distribution was becoming the backbone of Prabhupāda's preaching formula.

New Vrindaban, 1969

Hearing the Tape

Prabhupāda visited New Vrindaban during the summer of 1969. Toṣaṇa Kṛṣṇa and I took turns hitchhiking from Chapel Hill to see him.

When I was dropped off at Route 250, I saw the "ISKCON New Vrindaban" sign pointing down the twisting, uneven, dirt road and I began the hike. A small mountain stream cut across, following the road through a shallow valley to the right. Prabhupāda himself, at 73, had just weeks before walked the entire two miles to the farmhouse temple.

As soon as I arrived, I was invited by Prabhupāda's secretary into Prabhupāda's room. I climbed the steep stairs and offered my obeisances. Prabhupāda sat smiling and effulgent behind a metal trunk-desk in an almost bare, second-floor room.

Prabhupāda's first words were, "Have you heard the tape?"

"No," I said, and he turned on a tape recorder. *Taṁburā* vibrations and *mṛdaṅga* rhythms filled the room. Viṣṇujana was singing, his voice deep and resonant. He offered respects to guru, Gaurāṅga, and the eternal associates of Kṛṣṇa in Goloka: *"vande 'ham śrī-guroḥ śrī-yuta-pada-kamalaṁ śrī-gurūn vaiṣṇavāṁś ca."*

Other devotees climbed the stairs and came in to listen. The atmosphere was thick and sweet, and I stood up and danced to the taped *kīrtana*.

* * *

Rādhā and Kṛṣṇa reside in Prabhupāda's pure heart. Everywhere Prabhupāda went was transformed into a *dhāma,* a holy place of pilgrimage.

Kali-yuga and Ghee

In 1969, New Vrindaban was impoverished. When it came time for my second initiation, the temple could only afford two pounds of butter to turn into ghee for the fire sacrifice. Half of that small amount spilled as the devotee carrying the ghee pot slipped on his way to the sacrificial arena.

Prabhupāda simply shook his head when he was handed the pot with its tiny amount of ghee. "In Vedic times," he said, "tons of ghee was spared for a single *yajña*. But now, just see!"

* * *

I remember wondering if the small amount of ghee was an inauspicious omen for my initiation into brahminical life, but Prabhupāda performed the *yajña* himself, despite the inconvenient and inappropriate amount of ghee, and that was all-auspicious.

Lessons on Practicality

The day prior to the ceremony, I surrendered to helping the devotees rip down a house in Wheeling to get lumber for construction at New Vrindaban. I then spent the morning before the initiation searching for my beads. By the time the ceremony was about to begin, I was tired and I dozed while Prabhupāda lectured.

I was sitting directly in front of him and he spoke sharply to me, "You are inattentive!"

* * *

Surrender must be tempered with practicality, and I should have rested sufficiently before the initiation ceremony.

Dispassionate and intelligent searching for missing items is practical, but frantic and passionate searching only creates anxiety. I vowed from that day on not to waste time looking over and over again in the same place for missing beads (or anything else). Experience has shown that if lost items are to reappear, they do so on their own, as my beads did, when Kṛṣṇa desires. If He is not disposed, frantic searching doesn't help.

My Brahminical Initiation Test

Amid the *kīrtana* and readings, Prabhupāda called me to his side and softly intoned the Gāyatrī mantra into my ear. Then he demonstrated how to count ten mantras on my right hand. "Now you do it." Unsure, tired, inattentive, and frightened, I started counting from one to ten on the creases and tips of my right hand, praying that Kṛṣṇa would guide me on the correct path from one to ten. Only by His mercy did I succeed.

Time, Place, and Circumstance

Prabhupāda was walking alone one morning on a dirt road. He suddenly turned and, carrying a *loṭa,* headed out into the fields. I had my camera with me and enthusiastically followed Prabhupāda. I called out from behind, "Prabhupāda, they asked me to take pictures for BTG."

He turned, paused for a moment and said, "Yes, but not now."

* * *

Few devotees at this time had been to India, and none had any experience of Indian village life. No one, therefore, knew the meaning of a man with a *loṭa* walking out alone into the fields.

How many details about living a simple, ideal human life Prabhupāda wanted to teach us! In order to do so, Prabhupāda wanted to establish a Kṛṣṇa-centered Vedic village at New Vrindaban. Prabhupāda tolerated our ignorance just as an affectionate father tolerates the immature behavior of his children.

The Power of Kṛṣṇa – the Power of the Scientists

Each afternoon, Prabhupāda sat on a hill under a persimmon tree. Resting his hands on a makeshift wooden table, he spoke casually to whoever gathered to hear him. One afternoon he waved his hand dramatically across the lush, green valley and spoke about the scientists' limitations.

"The scientists can drop a bomb. Then all the leaves from these trees will be finished." He paused as the devotees watched his hand move again to span the valley, "But they cannot bring the leaves back."

"Kṛṣṇa is so wonderful," he continued, "with so much more power than any scientist. He can make all the trees leafless in winter and again bring back all the leaves in summer."

* * *

We were satisfied just sitting with Prabhupāda and hearing him speak simple *kṛṣṇa-kathā*.

Speaking from Below, Being Heard from Above

I gave a morning *Bhāgavatam* class from the First Canto. I sat on the simple pillow *āsana* and glorified Śukadeva Gosvāmī, declaring that Śukadeva's giving up Brahman realization for Bhagavān realization clearly proves the superiority of Bhagavān realization. As I lectured, Prabhupāda listened from his room above.

When I finished speaking, Devānanda challenged, "Why does Śukadeva's acceptance of Bhagavān necessarily mean Bhagavān realization is superior? Perhaps it is simply his preference."

I responded dutifully: "Śukadeva was not alone in his rejection: the four Kumāras also rejected Brahman for Bhagavān."

Devānanda wasn't satisfied. Other devotees joined in and argued; some of them even became angry: "How can someone in impersonal Brahman have a personal preference?"

"The scriptures say that we can't stay in Brahman, but that we must fall from that position."

"We accept what Prabhupāda says and Prabhupāda says Bhagavān is best!"

After pounding Devānanda into submission, we all filed up the winding stairs to Prabhupāda's room. I reached the top first. Prabhupāda looked at me and smiled, "So, they have put the question to you." I nodded my head, realizing that Prabhupāda had been listening to my lecture.

"Prabhupāda," one devotee ventured, "is it that impersonalists *must* fall down, or is it that only *most* of them fall down?"

Prabhupāda replied, "All of them fall down."

"Why?"

Prabhupāda was silent for several seconds. His silence accentuated the dim light that mixed with the dawn sun and illuminated his golden face.

"Because – " and he seemed to be thinking deeply how to explain this esoteric point to his children, "they get lonely."

* * *

An expert teacher knows his material so thoroughly that he can explain the most complicated subject simply and clearly.

Faith in Śāstra

One afternoon while Prabhupāda sat under the persimmon tree, Trivikrama approached him. Trivikrama asked Prabhupāda about the contradiction between the shortened Kali-yuga lifespan predicted in *Śrīmad-Bhāgavatam* and modern science's claim that lifespans are increasing.

Prabhupāda denied the scientists' claim. When Trivikrama responded that the scientific records prove it, Prabhupāda's answer was simple and to the point. "We accept the authority of the *Śrīmad-Bhāgavatam.*"

* * *

Logic and direct experience, although useful in proving śāstric conclusions, are in and of themselves imperfect methods of uncovering absolute conclusions and cannot lead us to the Absolute Truth. When logic and experience conflicted with *śāstra,* Prabhupāda always accepted the śāstric conclusion.

The Best Choice Was Also Digestible

That same afternoon, Prabhupāda's servant brought him a tray of freshly cut fruit – mangoes (which were Prabhupāda's favorite), oranges, apples, and grapes. Prabhupāda ate a few pieces of the fruit, and his servant then carried the tray away. As the servant walked back to the farmhouse, he stopped and offered me some of Prabhupāda's remnants. Prabhupāda watched.

I looked at the golden mango slices, the sweet grapes, the succulent orange sections, and chose the orange peel that had touched Prabhupāda's mouth. Prabhupāda saw me reach onto the plate and take the orange peel. He broke into a huge smile. Laughing as I placed it in my mouth, he said, "It is digestible."

* * *

Dust from a pure devotee's feet, water that has washed his feet, and remnants of his food are the most holy items. Prabhupāda appreciated that I chose the remnants that had touched his lips over the apparently more delectable items on the tray. "It is digestible." No adverse effects accrue from proper choices in Kṛṣṇa consciousness. I later found out, while living in Hong Kong, that orange peels are not only digestible but medicinal.

A Choice: Practicality or Spiritual Sentiment

Brahmānanda sat with Prabhupāda under the persimmon tree and discussed Prabhupāda's old apartment at 26 Second Avenue. The devotees had already relocated from the original 26 Second Avenue storefront to 61 Second Avenue. Brahmānanda asked Prabhupāda whether we should keep the old apartment because the rent was $150 per month and the New York temple was poor.

Prabhupāda considered the question only from the practical viewpoint. The temple was poor and therefore it was impractical to keep the apartment. He told Brahmānanda to drop the lease.

Argument as Offense

Rāyarāma came from New York to discuss *Back to Godhead* magazine with Prabhupāda. Prabhupāda had complained that Kṛṣṇa had not looked beautiful on the two-tone brown cover of the previous issue. He also objected to the hippie-culture advertisements Rāyarāma carried in the magazine.

Rāyarāma sat with Prabhupāda in his upstairs room. Prabhupāda reprimanded him. Amazingly, Rāyarāma argued back. At the bottom of the steep, spiraling stairs stood Gargamuni, listening both attentively and with apparent relish. I walked over to the stairs and also began to listen.

Prabhupāda said, "If you wish to argue with your spiritual master, then what can I do to help you?"

Gargamuni turned to me and gestured that I should leave. "This is only for big devotees."

* * *

Ādau guru-pādāśrayaḥ, as Śrīla Rūpa Gosvāmī states in his *Bhakti-rasāmṛta-sindhu*, is the beginning of spiritual life: "One must first accept shelter at the lotus feet of a spiritual master." We are certainly allowed to present our viewpoint before our guru, but we must ultimately surrender to his desire. The guru's desire is Kṛṣṇa's desire, and a disciple must always defer to his spiritual master with respect and faith.

Rāyarāma's inappropriate attitude was actually a symptom of the lust and doubts that were wreaking havoc in his spiritual life. Soon after this conversation with Prabhupāda, Rāyarāma left the association of devotees and returned to his previous, sinful lifestyle.

Gargamuni's comment which forbidding a beginner like me from witnessing a senior disciple arguing with Prabhupāda was more or less justified, yet the instruction gathered from the episode is certainly instructive for both beginners and "big devotees."

Of course, the "big devotee" is the one fully surrendered to his guru, beyond attraction to sense gratification, and well on his way to realizing his eternal relationship with Kṛṣṇa.

Not for BTG

Prabhupāda sat outside the temple-farmhouse on a mat in the hot sun. Devānanda massaged his soft body, which now glistened with mustard oil. Prabhupāda was jolly as he spoke to the devotees present.

I listened for a while and then got my camera. I focused and snapped. Prabhupāda turned to me and smiled, "This picture is not for BTG."

* * *

Official or publicly published pictures of exalted personalities who propagate the serious mission of reclaiming souls from pain and death should not be casual or intimately personal. Rather, they should reflect the seriousness of the mission. I understood this same point when I heard from Gurudāsa that Prabhupāda had objected to the photo of himself published on the back of the first edition of *Kṛṣṇa* book. He said it was too informal. The BBT used a more formal photo for the second edition.

Moments with Prabhupāda in Darśana:

The Basic Principle of Sādhana.

Brahmānanda, Hayagrīva, Kīrtanānanda, and others sat upstairs with Prabhupāda as Prabhupāda gave *darśana*. He told us, "The secret of Kṛṣṇa consciousness is to arrange your day so you cannot forget Kṛṣṇa for a moment." Prabhupāda turned to Brahmānanda, "You have been with us for some time now. It is not difficult, is it? You are able to arrange like this?"

Brahmānanda smiled and attested to the simplicity of the principle and the bliss that results from successfully executing it.

* * *

The *Viṣṇu Purāṇa* states:

smartavyaḥ satataṁ viṣṇur
vismartavyo na jātucit
sarve vidhi-niṣedhāḥ syur
etayor eva kiṅkarāḥ

"The essence of all the rules and regulations is to always remember Kṛṣṇa and never forget Him. All other rules and regulations are meant to assist this primary one."

Expert and More Expert

Prabhupāda then turned the conversation to Hayagrīva. Hayagrīva was editing Prabhupāda's *Bhagavad-gītā* and had come with technical editing questions. With his professorial voice, Hayagrīva explained how he removed the italics from Sanskrit words that were now common in the English language, such as *brāhmaṇa* and guru. He asked Prabhupāda's approval for this.

Hayagrīva continued questioning and Prabhupāda laughed, seeming to toy with Hayagrīva and his technical questions of style and usage. Hayagrīva didn't seem to notice. Ultimately, Prabhupāda allowed Hayagrīva to proceed as he desired. After all, Hayagrīva was expert both in editing and the English language.

* * *

Prabhupāda did not interfere with the work of his "experts." Rather, he acknowledged their skills and encouraged them to engage their talents fully in Kṛṣṇa's service.

The Proper Ear to Hear Proper Chanting

As devotees sat and spoke with Prabhupāda, others would listen at the bottom of the stairs or come up and join in the discussion. Arundhatī Dāsī sat at the bottom of the stairs, chanting *japa*. Prabhupāda noticed her chanting and asked who it was. A devotee replied "Arundhatī," and Prabhupāda asked her to come up.

She climbed the stairs and offered her obeisances. Prabhupāda said, "Very nice chanting!"

* * *

Every Western devotee walking through Vṛndāvana's Loi Bazaar immediately hears the motives behind the shopkeepers' chanting of "Hare Kṛṣṇa! Haribol, Prabhu! Come!" It is the quality of the chanting that is important. We can attract Kṛṣṇa by chanting His names if we chant with quality. Both Kṛṣṇa and Kṛṣṇa's devotee can hear the difference between chanting that is motivated or inattentive and chanting that is pure. Prabhupāda explains the importance of the quality with which one chants Kṛṣṇa's names in a purport to one of the prayers Kuntīdevī offers Lord Kṛṣṇa:

janmaiśvarya-śruta-śrībhir
edhamāna-madaḥ pumān
naivārhaty abhidhātuṁ vai
tvām akiñcana-gocaram

My Lord, Your Lordship can easily be approached, but only by those who are materially exhausted. One who is on the path of [material] progress, trying to improve himself with respectable parentage, great opulence, high education, and bodily beauty, cannot approach You with sincere feeling.

PURPORT: Being materially advanced means taking birth in an aristocratic family and possessing great wealth, an education and attractive personal beauty. All materialistic men are mad after possessing all these material opulences, and this is known as the advancement of material civilization. But the result is that by possessing all these material assets one becomes artificially puffed up, intoxicated by such temporary possessions. Consequently, such materially puffed up persons are incapable of uttering the holy name of the Lord by addressing Him feelingly, "O Govinda, O Kṛṣṇa." It is said in the *śāstras* that by once uttering the holy name of the Lord, the sinner gets rid of a quantity of sins that he is unable to commit. Such is the power of uttering the holy name of the Lord. There is not the least exaggeration in this statement. Actually the Lord's holy name has such powerful potency. But there is a quality to such utterances also. It depends on the quality of feeling. A helpless man can feelingly utter the holy name of the Lord, whereas a man who utters the same holy name in great material satisfaction cannot be so sincere. A materially puffed up person may utter the holy name of the Lord occasionally, but he is incapable of uttering the name in quality.

– *Śrīmad-Bhāgavatam* 1.8.26 with purport

The Greatest Scholar

Prabhupāda then glorified Śrīla Jīva Gosvāmī. "Jīva Gosvāmī was a boy when his father died. He wanted to go to his uncles,

Rūpa and Sanātana in Vṛndāvana, but he thought, 'What service can I do? I'll just be a burden.' He then went to Benares to study and became the greatest scholar the world has ever seen. It has been said that there has never been a scholar as great as Jīva Gosvāmī, nor in the future will there be a scholar as great as he."

* * *

We had heard of Jīva Gosvāmī even in those days, but we only knew of him as one of the Six Gosvāmīs of Vṛndāvana and the nephew of Rūpa Gosvāmī and Sanātana Gosvāmī. I immediately became attracted to Śrī Jīva Gosvāmī because of Prabhupāda's glorification. Years later, while living in Vṛndāvana, I was fortunate enough to glimpse from a great distance the piercing sharpness of Śrī Jīva's śāstric and logical exposition of Gauḍīya Vaiṣṇava philosophy. Jīva Gosvāmī's knowledge of the *Bhāgavatam* is so complete that it has been compared to a man holding a walnut in the fist of his hand.

Two Incidents of Answering from Hearing and Reading

Prabhupāda asked a simple question: "What is the name of Śrī Caitanya Mahāprabhu's eight written stanzas?" The room was quiet. I called out "*Śikṣāṣṭaka,*" pronouncing it "*she-kas-tak.*" I was imitating Prabhupāda's Bengali pronunciation, which I had heard on a tape that had been distributed to the temples. Pradyumna, who also sat nearby, then answered, "*Śikṣāṣṭakam,*" pronouncing it, "*shik-sha-sta-kam,*" as if transliterated from Sanskrit.

* * *

Prabhupāda understood my pronunciation and accepted my answer, but the other devotees couldn't understand what I said because they had only seen the word written, not heard it pronounced by Prabhupāda.

Prabhupāda then mentioned how Brahmā had first heard Gāyatrī directly from Kṛṣṇa. He again questioned the devotees: "Which Gāyatrī mantra did Kṛṣṇa bestow on Brahmā?" No one answered. I called out, "Kāma Gāyatrī." Prabhupāda nodded in approval and replied, "You may utter it." Then I became confused and recited the Brahma Gāyatrī by mistake. Prabhupāda shook his head.

* * *

Prabhupāda had described Lord Brahmā's initiation by Kṛṣṇa into Kāma Gāyatrī in *Teachings of Lord Caitanya* and had even mentioned the mantra. That book was published in 1969 and I had already read it. I was thrilled to be able to answer Prabhupāda's question, but I lacked the surety to reply with the proper mantra. I remember at this time feeling inspired to deeply hear, study, learn, and remember the scriptures in preparation for Prabhupāda's future examinations.

Just Like Narendra Mullik

A branch of the Kṛṣṇa consciousness movement began spontaneously in Atlantic City, New Jersey, in 1968. One youth had met the devotees in New York City, chanted with them, gone home to Atlantic City, and started all his friends chanting. As a result of his spontaneous attraction to Kṛṣṇa's name, many devotees joined ISKCON, but he never joined.

Prabhupāda asked Brahmānanda about this boy, with whom Brahmānanda had been in contact from 26 Second Avenue. When Brahmānanda explained that the boy could not adopt a Kṛṣṇa conscious lifestyle, Prabhupāda said it reminded him of his own past.

Prabhupāda relaxed, leaned back, and gracefully moved his right arm over the top of his head until his hand touched his left ear. He explained that because he had seen so many cheating sādhus as a youth, he had no interest in *sādhus* as a young man, but his friend, Narendra Mullik, literally forced him to meet Śrīla Bhaktisiddhānta Sarasvatī Gosvāmī Mahārāja.

Prabhupāda concluded, "Although I did not take initiation from my Guru Mahārāja for six years after this first meeting, I always thought of him from that first meeting onward." Then he added, "Just like Narendra Mullik brought me to my Guru Mahārāja but he himself could not take his shelter, this boy has brought so many others but he himself could not join."

* * *

Prabhupāda's mood as he drew the parallel between Narendra Mullik and the Atlantic City boy was attractive, sweet, and mysterious. Hearing him speak made me think about my own case: "Why me and not others?" Many of my friends had begun chanting but then quickly dropped Kṛṣṇa consciousness for other pursuits. Why? Many were more intelligent and seemed more sincere in their quest for the "truth" than me. Why does one soul stay and another leave?

The Nectar of Devotion describes that devotional service is cultivated through many lives. Each soul has his own unique Kṛṣṇa conscious history. By the mercy of the Vaiṣṇavas, a soul makes his Kṛṣṇa conscious start by hearing the holy name, seeing a holy Vaiṣṇava book, taking *prasāda,* or performing service, even unknowingly, to a Vaiṣṇava. Thus a Vaiṣṇava connects a soul with the Lord's internal energy.

From that point a soul can only move forward. His Kṛṣṇa conscious credit is eternal and will increase. One soul may be hearing about Kṛṣṇa for the first time whereas someone else, apparently coming to Kṛṣṇa consciousness at the same time, may actually be further along the path.

Compassionate devotees should therefore loudly chant Kṛṣṇa's holy names and distribute *prasāda* and books as widely as possible without being attached to the results. Kṛṣṇa conscious piety will be bestowed on many, many hearts, and when a soul's time comes, his fortune will manifest by attraction to serve Śrī Śrī Rādhā and Kṛṣṇa and Their devotees.

A Kiss on a Lotus

One morning after the *japa* period had ended and the *kīrtana* had begun, Prabhupāda came down the stairs from his second- floor room to give the *Śrīmad-Bhāgavatam* class. As Prabhupāda entered the temple room and walked toward his *vyāsāsana,* all the devotees bowed down. I offered my obeisances and then quickly sat up. Prabhupāda paused just before Kīrtanānanda Swami's bowed head. Kīrtanānanda Swami raised his head and kissed Prabhupāda's foot.

* * *

I was stunned. "Am I supposed to do that?" I wondered, noting that Prabhupāda had accepted Kīrtanānanda's gesture of reverence and affection.

The Roar of Thunder

In the class that morning, Prabhupāda spoke of the hand gaining strength by its supplying food through the mouth to the stomach. If the hand tries to eat independently, it will weaken and perish. Prabhupāda used this simple analogy to show that the soul must serve Kṛṣṇa to be happy. Then Prabhupāda called for questions.

New Vrindaban was famous for sheltering crazy fellows who had often taken too many drugs before joining the movement. One of them, Maṅgala, raised his hand.

"Yes?" Prabhupāda acknowledged him.

Maṅgala explained that using the hand to feed the stomach is not the only way to be nourished. "In fact," he said, "when people are sick, they can be fed through the anus."

All the devotees turned and stared at him. What a peculiar question. Actually, it sounded more like a challenge. Prabhupāda thundered his reply: "What you have said, that is for diseased persons! We are speaking of how a normal person eats and gets nourished. That way is the hand feeding the stomach! We should accept the standard system!"

* * *

In a Vyāsa-pūjā lecture, Prabhupāda once spoke of the great austerities Śrīla Bhaktisiddhānta Sarasvatī Ṭhākura had performed to initiate his preaching. Prabhupāda's own austerities were uniquely formidable. Perhaps one of his greatest austerities was dealing with the drug-crazed youths of the '60s.

A Foundation for the Future

I worked as a bricklayer's assistant to support the Chapel Hill temple. I made money at it, but I also learned how to lay bricks. I thought it would be something I could teach others. "With an army of bricklayers," I thought, "we could develop New Vrindaban." I informed Prabhupāda of my idea when I saw him at New Vrindaban.

He approved. Then he described the Indian system of making bricks. "First, the clay is shaped into a brick. When they have many bricks, they place them on dried wood and light a fire under them. By the time the fire has died, the bricks are baked strong."

I was inspired by Prabhupāda's directions. I walked into a field, found some local clay, and formed a small brick. I then threw it in the cooking fire. When I returned a few hours later, the clay had hardened.

When I showed it to Prabhupāda, he took the brick in his hand and scrutinized it. I couldn't penetrate his mood. "Should I continue learning to lay bricks?" I asked.

"Yes," Prabhupāda said. "This is our philosophy: learn something and teach others."

* * *

I was an ISKCON devotee, the president of a new temple, and a philosophy graduate from the University of Buffalo. Not only was I laying bricks, but I was thinking of it as a possible Kṛṣṇa conscious career. Prabhupāda accepted my enthusiasm, and although he didn't directly comment on my choice of vocation, he left me with a sparkling jewel: "This is our philosophy: learn something and teach others."

"Learn something and teach others." Simple, yet packed with the sentiment of Vaiṣṇava *sevā* and the power of preaching. "Learn something and teach others": the key to practical study. "Learn something and teach others": the mood of a devotee as teacher. "Learn something and teach others" became grafted to my consciousness by Prabhupāda as a fundamental principle of my Kṛṣṇa conscious life.

The Pains of Unsimple Living

In the name of efficiency, the New Vrindaban devotees bought a second-hand wringer washing machine. I was one of the devotees delegated to transport it from the main road to the farm house, a two-mile hike.

The machine was old-fashioned, built to last, and heavy. A few of us hoisted it onto our shoulders. We would carry it a few hundred feet before its weight forced us to put it down. We then hung it between thick wooden poles and, with more devotees helping, again heaved it onto our shoulders. We strained, walked a few hundred feet, and again had to put it down. We spent hours hoisting, thrusting, pulling, and pushing. Finally, we got the washing machine to the well directly in front of the farmhouse. We were all exhausted.

We ran an extension cord from the farmhouse to the washing machine, but where would the water come from to fill the tub? We realized that we were going to have to move the washing machine down the valley to where a small stream tumbled from a waterfall into a pond. But what about electricity?

As the devotees tossed around possible solutions, someone told Prabhupāda about it. His reply? "Just see."

* * *

Prabhupāda envisioned "plain living and high thinking" as the working principle for New Vrindaban. He knew all our work-saving plans would only result in more work. He saw all our muscle straining and ensuing problems as opposing the principle of New Vrindaban. "Just see."

A Garland of Affection

My two-week visit to New Vrindaban passed quickly in Prabhupāda's association. When it was time to return to Chapel Hill, a few devotees and I who were headed back to the New York temple climbed the stairs to Prabhupāda's room to offer him our respects. We then picked up our bags and started walking down the farm road to the main road.

Suddenly we heard a voice from behind us, "Uddhava, come up!" We turned. Prabhupāda was calling from the upstairs window. Uddhava immediately ran back up the stairs. A few minutes later, Uddhava returned, smiling and garlanded with Prabhupāda's garland.

* * *

Prabhupāda offered Uddhava his garland as an affectionate parting gesture. I remember the twinge of envy that pierced my heart. When I reflect on this incident along with its uncomfortable feeling of envy, I preach to myself: A spiritual master deals with each disciple personally and individually, and one should beware of envying his dealings with other disciples. Do not imagine that his dealings are based on superficialities – likes or dislikes. Dealings between guru and disciple are deep and are meant for the disciple's welfare. In addition, it is not possible for a disciple to understand the depth of consciousness that motivates his spiritual master's actions.

Uddhava left the association of devotees three years after his visit to Prabhupāda in New Vrindaban.

Send Photos

I received the following letter soon after I returned to Chapel Hill:

Dear Bhurijana,

Please accept my blessings. I remember when you were in New Vrindaban with me, you took some photographs with your camera. Please send these pictures to Brahmananda in New York for our Back to Godhead. In future issues we will be featuring many such photographs of our activities. I hope this will meet you in good health.

Your ever well-wisher,
A.C. Bhaktivedanta Swami

* * *

I had already sent BTG the pictures I took at New Vrindaban How amazing it was that Prabhupāda remembered my taking pictures. Prabhupāda's remembering us fixed our minds on him

Prabhupāda speaking in the Montreal temple room, 1968. (p. 10)

Temple at 26 Second Avenue, New York, 1968. Back (left to right): Rāyarāma, Puruṣottama, Hari Vilāsa, Ṛṣi Kumāra, Uddhava, Paramānanda, Dāmodara, Madhusūdana, Jayādvaita. Middle (left to right): Jagadānanda, Nayanābhirāma, Bhūrijana, Umāpati, Advaita, Jayarāma, Rohiṇī Kumāra. Front (left to right): Satyabhāmā, Indirā, Brahmānanda, Ekayāṇi, Balāi. (p. 22)

Prabhupāda at the Brooklyn Botanical Gardens
("Rādhā and Kṛṣṇa" in the background),
summer 1968. (p. 23)

Teaching *bhakti-yoga* at the University of Buffalo. (Rūpānuga in jacket and tie; Jagadīśa playing guitar.) (p. 30)

Kīrtana on the lawn at the University of Buffalo, 1968. (Kṛṣṇabhāmini, standing at left, Trivakrama, sitting at left in profile; Jagadīśa playing drum; Rūpānuga sitting at right playing *karatālas*.) (p. 30)

Bhūrijana passing out peacock feathers, Woodstock Music Festival, 1969. (p. 41)

Prabhupāda at New Vrindavan, 1969. Photos (this page and the top of the next page) taken by the author for *Back to Godhead* magazine, no. 29. (p. 63).

As Prabhupāda returns from bathing, he passes by devotees and the washing machine, New Vrindavan, 1969. (p. 61)

Bhūrijana receiving second initiation from Prabhupāda, New Vrindavan, 1969. (p. 47)

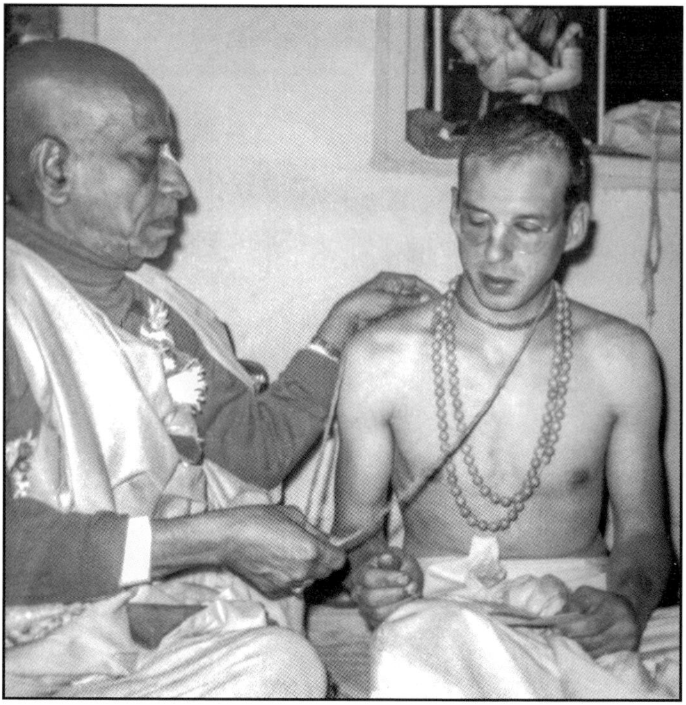

First All East Coast *saṅkīrtana* gathering in New York City, 1969. This photo, taken by the author, was on the cover of *Back to Godhead* magazine, no. 29. (p. 66)

Kīrtana at the Ginza, Tokyo, 1970. (Sudāmā playing harmonium; Cintāmaṇi, *karatālas;* Bhūrijana, *mṛdaṅga.*) (p. 67)

Cintāmaṇi distributing Japanese *Back to Godhead* magazines in Tokyo, 1970. (p. 67)

Bhūrijana preaching in the Ginza, Tokyo, 1970. (p. 67)

Public program in Tokyo, 1970. (p. 68)

Bhūrijana and Jagattāriṇī chanting in Hong Kong, 1971. (p. 78)

The Asia Magazine photo of Prabhupāda in the Park Hotel, Hong Kong, 1972. (p. 101)

Asakawa-Cho temple during Prabhupāda's visit to Tokyo in 1972. Left to right: Sudāmā, Bhūrijana, Bhānu, Satyadeva (standing at right). (p. 114)

Waiting for the Bullet, Tokyo train station, 1972. (pp. 139–140)

Prabhupāda sitting on the vyāsāsana in the San Juan temple with Siddha-svarūpānanda (above) and Jagattāriṇī (bottom), Manila, 1972 (pp. 161–62)

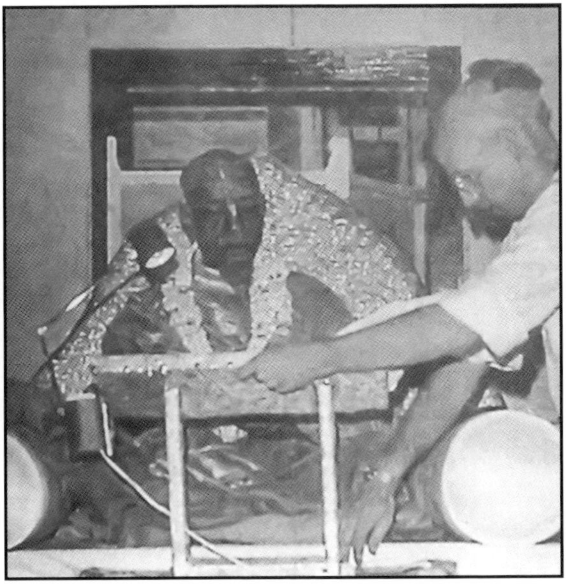

Adjusting the frail bookstand, Manila, 1972. (pp. 166–167)

Chanting in western clothes, Hong Kong, 1974. (p. 175)

Prabhupāda in Bombay wearing the gold bracelet Bhūrijana gave him in Hong Kong, 1974. (p. 189)

Prabhupāda speaking at the Hong Kong Hilton, 1974. (pp. 208–209)

Airport arrival, Melbourne VIP lounge, 1975. (p. 250)

Japan, 1970

A Surprise Order to Go East

Despite our moments of enthusiasm and our occasional successes, the Chapel Hill center did not do well, and we closed it toward the end of 1969. We then moved to New York to help with the preaching there. One day I received an aerogram from Prabhupāda. His letter was short: he requested that I join Bali Mardan and Sudāmā in Tokyo to help them pioneer the preaching in Japan. My head spun. Beyond a visit to Mexico as a college student, I had never ventured outside North America. I had visions of crowded muddy streets, rickshaws, and bright neon lights. Tokyo? "I don't even have any money."

Still, Prabhupāda's order filled my mind. After I recovered from the initial shock, it occurred to me where to find the money. I left the temple and took the subway to my parents' home in Rockaway.

I begged my parents for the few thousand dollars in savings bonds they had accumulated for me. They stared at me in disbelief. They had been saving the bonds to give to me at my wedding, but what could they do when confronted by an independent-minded, shaven-headed member of the Hare Kṛṣṇa movement who wanted his own money to go off on a mission to Japan? They gave me the money.

I can only imagine what my parents thought after I left. I was intent on saving Japan on Prabhupāda's order, so I didn't stay to discuss it with them. I caught the A train back to our Second Avenue temple.

The temple president was overjoyed to see the savings bonds, especially because there would be money left over after the cost of my ticket. He told me that the extra money would be sent to Prabhupāda's book fund. Then he accompanied me to the bank, allowing me to turn neither left nor right. He stood next to me at the bank teller's window while the transaction was completed, fearing, I guess, that I would "bloop" once the money was in my hands.

* * *

I'm glad that the extra money was sent to the book fund, but I would have preferred to give the donation voluntarily rather than having it offered on my behalf through intimidation.

During my stay in New York, a giant peace march protesting U.S. involvement in the Vietnam War was held in Washington, D.C. Devotees from ISKCON temples throughout the East Coast gathered, and after the huge *kīrtanas* we held in Washington, we all again gathered to chant Kṛṣṇa's names up and down Fifth Avenue in New York City. I snapped several photos of the "*mahā-harināma*" and sent them to BTG. One even found its way onto the cover.

Preaching in Japan

In the last week of December 1969, I flew into Tokyo's Haneda Airport, cleared immigration, and hailed a taxi, handing the driver my copy of the temple address in Meguru-ku. The address proved to be obscure, and it took hours to locate it. Finally, at 9 P.M., I saw a shaven-headed, dark-skinned Westerner taking out the garbage.

"Haribol!" I yelled out. It was Sudāmā. After paying the driver we carried my luggage up three flights of stairs to a tiny flat.

Within a month of my arrival we shifted from Meguru-ku to an old-fashioned, Japanese-style tatami-matted apartment in Shibuyu-ku, and for the next six months we rotated our preaching between Meguru-ku, Shinju-ku, the Ginza, Shibuya, and other sophisticated suburbs. On Prabhupāda's recommendation we dressed in fine silk robes and wore flower garlands. Sometimes we would travel by subway to the Ginza, where we would chant and distribute literature. At other times, Sudāmā's wife, Cintāmaṇi Dāsī, and I would chant alone or distribute pamphlets, Rādhā-Kṛṣṇa Temple record albums, and Japanese *Back to Godhead* magazines. If no devotees were available to chant as we distributed, we played taped *kīrtanas* on our big Aiwa reel-to-reel tape recorder.

Our Sunday feasts were sparsely attended, but they were always joyful – Sudāmā was an excellent cook. He had spent time as Prabhupāda's personal servant and had learned to cook directly from Prabhupāda. He taught me how to make *halavā* (soaked in ghee and sugar), *samosās* (with cauliflower and peas), and *gulāb-jāmuns* (with powdered milk and no flour) exactly as Prabhupāda had taught him. I learned to enjoy cooking, and would cook often. On Ekādaśīs I would fast all day but still cook for the devotees.

At one point, Sudāmā and Cintāmaṇi left Japan and traveled to Korea to renew their visas. Alone, I would distribute magazines each day at the Ginza. One day as I distributed, I heard a loud "Haribol!" Surprised, I looked up and saw huge Brahmānanda rushing toward me in blue baggy pants, his arms outstretched to envelop me in his embrace. His mission in Tokyo was to produce *Kṛṣṇa* book with the Dai Nippon printing company. He stayed for more than a month, and when Sudāmā returned, we would spend hours sitting and discussing Prabhupāda in our lonely Tokyo temple.

Bali Mardan had left Tokyo to open ISKCON's first temple in Sydney, Australia, soon after my arrival. A few months later, just after Brahmānanda's visit, reinforcements – Amogha and Satyavrata – were sent from Los Angeles. We visited Kyoto, the Zen holy city, for a guest appearance on a television show. We also held a Ratha-yātrā in a Meguru-ku park, chanting Hare Kṛṣṇa as we carried Jagannātha, Baladeva, and Subhadrā on a palanquin. We held our "big" *harināma* every Friday evening in Shinju-ku, the most upbeat suburb in Tokyo.

One day, as we chanted in front of a Shinju-ku bank that was closed for the weekend, a huge protest march filed past us on the street. Thousands of protesters, most wearing red or white bandanas and carrying huge banners, shouted slogans as they marched past. Suddenly, the Japanese police arrived with their gas masks and shields, and began to beat the protesters with clubs. We kept chanting as a dangerous riot erupted like a movie scene right before our eyes. In our innocence, we simply kept chanting Hare Kṛṣṇa and Kṛṣṇa protected us.

Kṛṣṇa sent quite a few Japanese boys and girls to visit our temple and attend our public programs. It was austere preaching to them because they mostly came to practice English, not study Kṛṣṇa consciousness. We continued, regardless, on Prabhupāda's order.

Prabhupāda's Unexpected Visit to Japan

Prabhupāda arrived unexpectedly in Tokyo in mid-August, 1970, accompanied by a party of six of his most senior disciples. Four of them were *sannyāsis*. Sudāmā, Cintāmaṇi, Satyavrata, Amogha, and I greeted him at the airport. Prabhupāda looked different. "Was Prabhupāda sick?" I wondered. Prabhupāda looked much older than when I had last seen him at New Vrindaban.

* * *

Except for Sudāmā, no one knew anything about the difficulties Prabhupāda had been undergoing and which had prompted his sudden visit. Later, we heard that Prabhupāda had left America due to a "conspiracy" among his disciples. Prabhupāda's mail was being filtered in Los Angeles and his movements restricted. ISKCON's letterhead no longer listed him as the founder-*ācārya* of

ISKCON but simply as the founder. Prabhupāda's worry and loss of sleep showed in his face.

These problems appeared as a defeat to Prabhupāda's preaching, but Prabhupāda used the "defeat" to initiate his preaching in India, the biggest preaching field in the world. Thus Prabhupāda's transcendental intelligence turned bad to good, unfavorable to favorable, and defeat to victory.

Yet ISKCON's difficulties did affect Prabhupāda. After arriving in Tokyo, he wrote to Haṁsadūta:

> Your first letter was duly received, but during the last few months I was very much mentally depressed. I do not wish to discuss those points, but simply request all the members of the Governing Body Commission to organize this institution very uprightly.

Then in the same letter, Prabhupāda discussed his plans for preaching in India:

> Now I am staying in our Japan center looking after the publication of books, dealing with Dai Nippon Printing Co., and I have already placed order with them for different books and magazines to the extent of $52,000. Most of these books will be carried to India for making propaganda there on or before the World Sankirtana Party reaches there.

The Conspiracy Thickens

We were shocked by a telephone call from New Vrindaban a few days later. The callers asked us to inform Prabhupāda that the "conspirators," to whom Prabhupāda had just awarded *sannyāsa,* had attended a festival at New Vrindaban and preached that Prabhupāda was actually Kṛṣṇa! A few of the devotees had become confused, but some senior devotees had defeated the *sannyāsīs*.

* * *

Before leaving America, Prabhupāda had given the "conspirators" *sannyāsa* and ordered them to travel and preach. In that way, he said, they would become purified and free of their offenses. Instead, they caused more trouble and crossed Prabhupāda's line of tolerance. Prabhupāda was not going to allow his fledgling society to become threatened or contaminated by their philosophical deviation. When he heard this news, he cut them off from ISKCON.

Prabhupāda's tolerance toward his young disciples was unlimited, but he limited it to protect his society. ISKCON's mission was too important. He was still concerned, however, for the spiritual lives of the "conspirators." He made it clear that they would be again welcome in ISKCON when they rectified their mistake. The *sannyāsīs* quickly returned to ISKCON and to Prabhupāda's service.

Vyāsa-pūjā Day, 1970

Prabhupāda stayed in his Tokyo apartment on Janmāṣṭamī of 1970. He spent the day with some disciples reading *Kṛṣṇa* book, starting at the beginning and attempting to complete the first volume by midnight.

The following day was Prabhupāda's Vyāsa-pūjā, and he agreed to celebrate it at our small suburban temple in Shibuya-ku. We spent the morning cleaning, cooking, and decorating. Prabhupāda had not yet visited the temple, and I had not seen him since his arrival.

Toward noon, Sudāmā drove Prabhupāda to the temple in our white, rented Toyota van. Prabhupāda entered the wood-paneled compound, left his shoes on the Japanese-style porch, and stepped up to the hallway. He passed through the narrow passage and stared for a moment at his own picture, upside down, which had been removed from the *vyāsāsana* to make room for him to sit. He entered the temple room and observed its old wood walls and *tatami* mat floors. He saw our decorations of yellow, pink, and white carnations on the altar.

Prabhupāda was grave. He took his seat on the *vyāsāsana*. I began to offer *ārati* to Prabhupāda as Kīrtanānanda Swami, Madhudviṣa Swami, Devānanda Swami, Tamal Krishna, and the local Tokyo devotees performed *kīrtana*.

Prabhupāda stopped the *ārati*. "Where is the *puṣpa?*" he demanded. No one understood that Prabhupāda was calling for flowers. Devānanda Swami ran to the kitchen to prepare *puṣpa* rice, thinking that was what Prabhupāda meant.

Anxiety filled the room. Prabhupāda wasn't satisfied.

Prabhupāda looked gravely at the devotees and called for Tamal Krishna. He slowly stepped up to the *vyāsāsana*. Prabhupāda spoke to him in a hushed, heavy voice. We could barely hear his words.

"Why you don't know how to perform the Vyāsa-pūjā? Were you not there in Los Angeles when I performed it for my Guru Mahārāja?"

"Yes, Prabhupāda," replied Tamal Krishna.

"Then where are the flowers? Where is the offering of *prasāda*? So many *sannyāsīs* are here. Why a junior man is performing the *ārati*?"

Prabhupāda continued, "And why my picture is outside in the hall? It has been turned over as well. The poison has also spread to here!"

* * *

Prabhupāda was angry. He expected intelligence – we should have learned how to worship the spiritual master by his example – and we failed to meet his expectations.

Prabhupāda expressed his disappointment to Tamal Krishna. He viewed our Vyāsa-pūjā attempt, and the upside-down picture in the hallway, as an another example that he was being minimized by his disciples. "The poison has also spread here."

Tamal Krishna felt terrible and apologized to Prabhupāda. He begged Prabhupāda for a second chance, and Prabhupāda allowed us to try again the next day. Prabhupāda then instructed Tamal Krishna on how to properly celebrate Vyāsa-pūjā.

Years later, I heard that Prabhupāda told a devotee who had offered him an ill-fitting *kūrta* and then adjusted it and re-offered it: "To rectify your mistakes as soon as possible is a sign of intelligence."

Vyāsa-pūjā Day, 1970: Take Two

The next day we observed Vyāsa-pūjā according to Prabhupāda's instructions. Kīrtanānanda Swami, the most senior *sannyāsī*, offered the *ārati.* We each offered flowers at Prabhupāda's feet as he sat on the *vyāsāsana,* and then read him our written homages. Finally, Prabhupāda was offered a feast.

* * *

Prabhupāda told us that each devotee should offer him flowers three times. *Kīrtana* was going on, and after each offering of flowers, the devotee paid his *daṇḍavats.* After I offered flowers three times, he took a yellow flower and placed it in my outstretched palms.

Prabhupāda even specified the order in which the devotees should approach him to make their flower offerings: first *sannyāsīs,* then *gṛhastha* men with their wives, then *brahmacārīs.*

Waste Not, Want Not

Prabhupāda had brought his Rādhā-Kṛṣṇa deities with him to Japan and had set Them up in a closet in his apartment. We bought carnations for Them every day and Kārttikeya, Prabhupāda's servant, decorated Them. One day, Prabhupāda told Kārttikeya to string the discarded carnation stems, with the long stems hanging down, as a decoration across the top of Rādhā and Kṛṣṇa's altar.

* * *

The stem decoration was neither standard nor gorgeous, yet

Prabhupāda insisted that Kārttikeya use them. Prabhupāda did not waste Kṛṣṇa's energy. He insisted that everything be used creatively in Kṛṣṇa's service.

A Thank You

When I entered Prabhupāda's apartment to deliver carnations on the day following the successful Vyāsa-pūjā, Prabhupāda smiled at me and said, "Thank you very much."

* * *

I had happily danced during the *kīrtana* on our first attempt to celebrate Prabhupāda's Vyāsa-pūjā. "After all," I thought, "Prabhupāda is here with us." My affection, even in the midst of our disaster, caught Prabhupāda's attention and, it seemed to me, he was now thanking me. How refined was Prabhupāda's teaching expertise! He used one incident to teach many devotees according to their individual requirements. Thank *you*, Prabhupāda.

Tolerance

Brown ants were on the march into our temple room, across the floor, up Prabhupāda's *vyāsāsana*, along the painting of Śrīla Prabhupāda, across his face, down the back of the painting, off the *vyāsāsana*, and out the old-style, sliding multi-windowed door. Prabhupāda came into the temple room and motioned that he didn't want to sit on the vyāsāsana. Fearfully, a devotee shooed the ants from Prabhupāda's picture, but Prabhupāda stopped him, "Don't bother. They are not disturbing."

Prabhupāda Leaves for Calcutta

Prabhupāda stayed in Tokyo for more than two weeks before he left for Calcutta on August 29, 1970. During his stay, he took his daily morning walk in the well-kept Tokyo parks. Usually he walked only with Sudāmā or one or two *sannyāsīs*. On one of those walks, he commented that because the Shinto temples had no deities, they were dead. He also said the fruitless trees were impious.

During this visit Prabhupāda negotiated to print some of his books, including a Hindi *Back to Godhead* magazine, with the Dai Nippon Printing Company. He was preparing for his Indian preaching tour, and he wrote letters to his disciples in America who were dealing with the "conspiracy" crisis. Mostly Prabhupāda was waiting for confirmation from Acyutānanda and Jaya Patāka in Calcutta that the visas were complete and other preparations made to receive him and his party upon his arrival.

Actually, Prabhupāda's party increased from six to seven during his Tokyo stay. He personally convinced a Canadian *bhakta* of Japanese descent to accompany him to India. Bruce Enomoto was chanting sixteen rounds a day, studying Japanese, and living outside the temple. Bruce traveled to India with Prabhupāda and later became Prabhupāda's initiated disciple, Bhānu Dāsa.

We regular members of the small Shibuya-ku temple saw Prabhupāda at the temple only a few times other than the two celebrations of Vyāsa-pūjā. We had little idea of his problems, struggles, or plans. Each day, the *sannyāsīs* who were not personally attending to Prabhupāda and the four local devotees would go on *harināma* and magazine distribution at the Ginza in downtown Tokyo. I never thought to ask Prabhupāda if I could go to India with him. He left for Calcutta on schedule, and we simply went on with our duties.

Hong Kong, 1972

In Prabhupāda's Service; In Kṛṣṇa's Hands

Preaching on Prabhupāda's order in Tokyo offered me a surprise opportunity. Bali Mardan, who had just returned to Tokyo from Sydney, asked me, in early October 1970, to start a new center in Hong Kong. I agreed and began collecting the fare. The temple president took my first week's collections, but I had enough by the second week to sail from Tokyo to Okinawa to Taiwan and then on to Hong Kong.

The sea voyage was a pleasant change from routine temple life. I spent my time reading, chanting, and relaxing as the small cargo boat dipped and turned in the South China Sea. I arrived in the middle of the night and felt quite at home: Hong Kong was lit as brightly as New York City.

The next morning I took a taxi to the local Gurudvara-Sikh Temple and met up with Bali Mardan, who had been in Hong Kong for a week. We lived at the Sikh temple for two weeks, sleeping on the rope beds and accepting their *capātīs* and hot *sabjī* once a day. During the day I collected donations from the local Indian community and informed them of ISKCON's plan to open a Hare

Kṛṣṇa temple. Two weeks later, Bali Mardan was ready to sail to Malaysia to open a new center. The day before he left, Jagattāriṇī Dāsī (at that time, Janne), arrived from Los Angeles.

During my stay in Tokyo, Sudāmā had one day asked me if I wanted to get married, and I had nonchalantly agreed. He opened correspondence with the Los Angeles temple president and, under Prabhupāda's direct arrangement, a match was made for me. She was not yet initiated and her name was Janne. We began exchanging letters. Somehow I never really thought the marriage would take place, so I was surprised when she in fact arrived in Hong Kong.

Janne had been an Australian actress who had casually chanted Hare Kṛṣṇa at the first Pott's Point temple in Sydney. On her way to London for the premier of *Ned Kelly,* the film in which she co-starred with Mick Jagger, she stopped for a short "pilgrimage" in Hollywood. There, Kṛṣṇa arranged for her a stark view of material reality, and she fearfully took shelter of the temple on Watseka Avenue. Prabhupāda was there, Viṣṇujana Swami was leading the devotees out onto Hollywood Boulevard for *harināma* every day, and Gargamuni was managing the temple. The atmosphere crackled with excitement. She moved into the temple that day, telephoning Michael Love of the Beach Boys to drop her luggage off at 3764 Watseka Ave.

Six months later, Janne's American tourist visa ran out. The temple authorities arranged for her to travel to Hong Kong, marry me, and assist in the Hong Kong preaching. One morning we received a phone call from the Hong Kong airport. She had arrived. Bali Mardan picked her up, leaving me to cross to the Kowloon side of Hong Kong Harbor and rent a guest room in Chung King Mansions. Bali Mardan performed our marriage ceremony in the Kowloon Hindu temple that afternoon and left for Malaysia the following morning.

Later, Janne's mother sent her a Melbourne newspaper clipping. The headline read: "Weird Cult Forces Famous Actress to Marry Japanese Monk."

Hong Kong ISKCON was Janne and Bhūrijana, actress and "Japanese monk" from Brooklyn, New York. We were young, idealistic, inexperienced, and thrust together by fate to preach in a capital city of Kali's kingdom. We both wanted to please Prabhupāda, so we remained in Hong Kong, but times were hard.

* * *

And what was Prabhupāda thinking as we struggled in his service in Hong Kong? Subhag Mahārāja later related that just after joining ISKCON, he was in England and was sitting with Prabhupāda while Prabhupāda was deep in thought. Suddenly a tear glided down Prabhupāda's cheek. After several minutes, Subhag asked him what he was thinking about that caused him to cry. Prabhupāda said he was thinking of his two disciples in Hong Kong who had sacrificed everything and who were suffering so much just to please him.

Hell with Electricity

Chung King Mansions, more a tenement than a mansion, was hell, but at least it had electricity. (As a devotee escorted Prabhupāda through a New York subway station in 1966, the devotee suggested that the subway was like hell. Prabhupāda's reply: "No, in hell there is no electricity.") It was damp, hot, inhabited by prostitutes, smugglers, peddlers, and a variety of low-class people of every nationality. We tried to move from our guesthouse room by renting a flat with the meager collections I had gathered. It didn't go through and our deposit, which was basically every cent we had, slipped from my hands. For the two weeks until the deposit was returned, we lived on four Hong Kong dollars, about sixty U.S. cents.

During those two weeks, all my anxiety about money stopped. How could I be anxious about money when I had none? Every day during those two weeks, someone from somewhere would arrive with vegetables, rice, and wheat flour. Or someone would bring cooked chickpea *prasāda* from a temple or invite us to take *prasāda* at their home. All our necessities were supplied.

Even our rent was paid by an Indian shop owner who had seen us chanting in a nearby park. We didn't ask him to pay the rent, but he asked us to allow him to do this service. Slowly the fact dawned on me: Kṛṣṇa was actually protecting us, His insignificant, naive, immature servants who were trying to please Prabhupāda.

On the day the deposit was returned, Kṛṣṇa cut off the supply, and from our returned $150 U.S. dollars, we had to again pay our way.

Our Hong Kong Visa Connection

Six months after our arrival in Hong Kong, Prabhupāda initiated Janne as Jagattāriṇī Dāsī, servant of "one who is capable of saving the entire universe." Our preaching was beginning to increase. We preached wherever we found an opportunity: chanting in Chinese sections of the city, visiting Hong Kong University and Hong Kong's International School, and holding Sunday school classes for the children of the Hong Kong Indian community. But our time in Hong Kong was running out. I had come on a three-month tourist visa and had already extended it by six months. We applied for a missionary visa but received no reply.

Prabhupāda wrote us and described his experience with the American immigration officials. He told us that governments don't like to change the purpose of a visa while the person is still living in their country.

Prabhupāda recommended we approach influential men, especially Westerners, and ask them for letters of recommendation. We didn't know many people in Hong Kong and could not think of even one influential person we could ask. Suddenly, we remembered Mr. Gindraux, the managing director of TWA Airlines in Hong Kong. Mr. Gindraux had spent time in India and had visited and taken a *prasāda* feast with us at Chung King Mansions. We had tried to help his teenage son with his drug problem. "Yes," we decided, "we should see Mr. Gindraux and get a letter from him as Prabhupāda suggested."

We memorized Prabhupāda's letter as we traveled to the Hong Kong side of the harbor and TWA's office complex. Mr. Gindraux immediately called us into his office and we repeated Prabhupāda's words to him, emphasizing Prabhupāda's suggestion and our need. We then asked him for a letter.

Mr. Gindraux leaned back, first smiled, and then laughed. "I can do even better than that," he said. "I'm going to a party tonight. I will be seeing my friend, Mr. Watson, the head of the immigration department. I'll talk to him and try to get your work done."

* * *

We were granted a permanent Hong Kong visa within a few weeks.

A Surprise Telephone Message

By 1972, we had rented a small, second-floor flat on Cameron Road. Jagattāriṇī decorated the walls with pictures of Kṛṣṇa surrounded by cloth, beads, and peacock feathers. Prabhupāda was supposed to visit us in Hong Kong, but our GBC had canceled his visit. Jagattāriṇī was feeling somewhat desperate, so went to Sydney when she heard Prabhupāda was there. She spoke to him about whether or not we should stay in Hong Kong. Meanwhile, quite unexpectedly for me, Prabhupāda's secretary Śyāmasundara called me in Hong Kong from New Zealand, where Prabhupāda had gone after his Australia visit. Prabhupāda would soon be arriving in Hong Kong on a one-day stopover, he said. We would then all travel together to Tokyo. "Prabhupāda is insisting," Śyāmasundara said, "that he stay at the Park Hotel."

"Why?" I asked.

Śyāmasundara explained that Prabhupāda's one day in Hong Kong was considered a stopover, and the airline was providing the hotel room at no charge.

* * *

This was Prabhupāda's first visit to Hong Kong. To be frugal with Kṛṣṇa's money, Prabhupāda accepted the airline's arrangement. Śyāmasundara also explained that Prabhupāda and his entourage would accept the airline-provided transportation from the airport to the Park Hotel.

A Swan's Entrance into the Land of Dragons

A large gathering of the interested, curious, and devoted mingled in the Park Hotel's penthouse function room. The room was decorated with flowers, and the hotel couch was covered with a cloth. The air was filled with expectancy. About thirty Indian children and one hundred Indian adults waited along with our few Chinese followers.

A *kīrtana* began. It was nearing the time when Prabhupāda would emerge from the hotel's top floor, walk up the one flight to the meeting room, and greet his Hong Kong Hare Kṛṣṇa devotees.

Suddenly Prabhupāda appeared, effulgent in saffron dress and flower garlands and smiling sweetly. The *kīrtana* increased in intensity, "*Jaya* Prabhupāda! *Jaya* Prabhupāda!"

I fell to the ground in obeisance and quickly jumped up to lead Prabhupāda to his sitting place. I had begged some gladiolas, and was spreading them at Prabhupāda's feet as he walked. By the time Prabhupāda reached the couch, the *kīrtana* was in full swing. The children chanted and the *mṛdaṅga* and *karatāla* players jumped up and down. Even the staid Indian businessmen were swept into Prabhupāda's enthusiastic welcome.

One by one, admirers of Prabhupāda's worldwide preaching came forward to offer garlands of Hong Kong's indigenous flowers laced with gold and silver tinsel. They touched his feet as everyone chanted Hare Kṛṣṇa.

An Inappropriate Offering and a Test

I offered the remaining gladiolas near Prabhupāda's feet. Prabhupāda frowned as he whispered softly to me, "They are spoiled."

He then quickly smiled and added, "Oh, you have so many students!"

"No, Prabhupāda," I smiled back, "*you* have so many students."

* * *

Patraṁ puṣpaṁ phalaṁ toyam: Kṛṣṇa accepts even a leaf, a fruit, a flower, or some water from a devotee if they are offered with devotion. Implicit in that phrase, "with devotion," is that the offering must be clean, carefully prepared, and suitable for the person to whom the offering is made. Common sense is helpful. Since this incident, I always examine the quality of my flowers before offering them, especially to Prabhupāda. Old, wilted, "spoiled" flowers are not acceptable.

Prabhupāda did not allow me to become discouraged by his comment about the "spoiled" flowers. He quickly followed it with, "Oh, you have so many students!"That statement did not enter my heart as a simple comment. It felt like a test. I momentarily paused, then responded with heartfelt confidence. These were his students, not mine. I was simply acting as his servant. Any other reply, I felt, would have been improper and inaccurate.

Prabhupāda on Gandhi

The *kīrtana* ended and Prabhupāda intoned the *prema-dhvani* prayers. The children and the few Chinese devotees present bowed down and replied, "*Jaya*!" to Prabhupāda's glorifications. All eyes then focused on Prabhupāda.

Prabhupāda thanked those present for offering such a warm welcome, and after a few minutes of explaining the importance of the Kṛṣṇa consciousness movement, he began criticizing Mahatma Gandhi.

"Of course, Gandhi is given so much respect for bringing India out of British control to independence. But it was Subash Candra Bose who actually forced the British to grant India independence. Gandhi held up independence for twenty years with his idea of nonviolence. Subash Candra Bose's Indian National Army was actually the thing that made the British leave India."

Prabhupāda spoke about Gandhi for some time and then called for questions. The Hong Kong Indians stared at Prabhupāda in shocked silence.

* * *

I remember thinking, "Why is Prabhupāda talking about Gandhi? What does Gandhi have to do with Kṛṣṇa consciousness? And why is he speaking of Gandhi during this first visit?"

Later, while we were alone, Prabhupāda explained to me the details of how Subash Candra Bose's Indian National Army (INA) had succeeded while Gandhi's attempt had failed. Prabhupāda prefaced his explanation, "I will explain in case they ask you."

Indian National Army

Subash Candra Bose had a pact with Germany, who agreed that all Indian soldiers captured fighting for the British would be given to Bose's army. This army, stationed in Burma, would first train and then, it was planned, attack the British in India. It was fear of this Indian National Army, not Gandhi's pacifism, that forced the British out of India.

Hearing Prabhupāda's explanation of bygone, seemingly inconsequential history was as sweet as nectar, and I didn't ask him why he had spoken about it to the Hong Kong Indians. I speculated that Prabhupāda wanted to attack their cherished conceptions of material reality in the hopes that they would respond and he would be able to preach to them. Or, perhaps Prabhupāda was showing that he was not coming to Hong Kong like most *sādhus,* to flatter and collect funds.

I never asked Prabhupāda directly though, and it wasn't until years later, when I looked back at the transcripts of the talk, that his reasoning became clear. As Subash Candra Bose had collected an overseas army of Indians to liberate India, Prabhupāda similarly wanted to collect such an overseas army of Indian Vaiṣṇavas to one day liberate their native country.

A Lone Question

Prabhupāda's call for questions received no response, so I stood up and addressed the audience, "Does anyone have any questions for Prabhupāda?"

Silence. Suddenly a young boy said, "Who started the forest fire?" It was Lalu, a ten-year-old boy from one of our children's classes. "Prabhupāda, who started the forest fire?" he repeated.

Prabhupāda accepted the question as serious and began preaching, "No one started the forest fire. *Saṁsāra-dāvānala-līḍha-loka-trāṇāya kāruṇya-ghanāghanatvam.* This material existence is a blazing forest fire of suffering – birth and death. We try so hard to be happy here, but we cannot. No one starts the forest fire of material suffering. No one wants this fire to burn, but it must burn us in every case."

* * *

Months before Prabhupāda's visit, I had read the story of Kṛṣṇa swallowing the forest fire to our Sunday school class. When the class ended, Lalu wanted to know who had started the fire. I remember smiling and saying, "Prabhupāda is coming in a few months. Why not ask him?" By the time Prabhupāda came, I had forgotten the incident, but Lalu had saved his question.

A Gift of Eternal Benefit

Larry Mak was a Chinese businessman working with our Spiritual Sky incense factory in America. I introduced him to Prabhupāda:

BHŪRIJANA: This gentleman takes care of the punk. He ships the punk to Los Angeles. He has a present for you.

PRABHUPĀDA: Oh.

BHŪRIJANA: This is Larry Mak. (Larry Mak opened a jewelry box and pulled out a gold bracelet. I clasped it around Prabhupāda's right wrist.)

PRABHUPĀDA: What is that? Oh, this is for *sannyāsī* or for ladies?

BHŪRIJANA: It is for the health.

* * *

Larry Mak wanted to offer Prabhupāda a gift. I suggested a gold bracelet because I had heard that gold was good for the health. Larry Mak bought an ornately carved, 18-karat gold ladies' bracelet. Prabhupāda accepted Larry Mak's gift, but he also commented on the inappropriateness of a *sannyāsī* actually wearing such an ornament. Prabhupāda again questioned me about the bracelet when we flew together to Japan. When I told him that it had cost $250, he appreciated Larry Mak's sentiment.

I heard that the bracelet was eventually melted down and used to make Prabhupāda a gold tooth, to Larry Mak's eternal benefit.

Food for Thought

Just before Prabhupāda stood up to leave the flower-and-cloth-covered couch, he asked me a question. Referring to the many young Indian boys and girls present he asked, "Who are the leaders? Call them." I searched the children's innocent faces and pointed, "Lalu, Suresh, Raju, come up." The three boys looked at each other and stood up. Prabhupāda gave them each a garland from around his neck. As they were about to sit down he instructed them to become serious in Kṛṣṇa consciousness. "Every day, you should eat one flower from your garland."

Prabhupāda then left the reception room and went to his room. My heart swelled as the children began spontaneously singing, "*saṁsāra-dāvānala-līḍha-loka...*"

* * *

Eat a flower a day! Prabhupāda's request was unique and merciful. If the children followed it, although none did, it would help them remember the most fortunate event of their lives. When I learned of their failure, I was so disappointed that I began to lose hope in the future of their Kṛṣṇa consciousness. The last remnant of hope finally evaporated during Prabhupāda's next visit in 1974. Lalu again attended Prabhupāda's lecture, this time at the Hong Kong Hilton. He even danced during the *kīrtana*. As he danced, a coin, ten Hong Kong cents, fell from his pocket. I tapped him on the shoulder and suggested he offer it at Prabhupāda's feet. Lalu nervously picked it up, refused, and put the coin back in his pocket.

In a Park Hotel Room

After the meeting, we gathered in Prabhupāda's room. I asked Prabhupāda if he would allow me to get him some of the all-purpose Chinese medicine, ginseng, which was legendary for its invigorating qualities. Prabhupāda looked at me and smiled. "I don't want to take any medicine. I have already told my disciples that if I am dying, don't call a doctor and don't take me to the hospital. Just place some *tulasī* leaves on my head and chant Hare Kṛṣṇa."

* * *

Hearing Prabhupāda speak of dying in 1972 was unnerving. We never thought of Prabhupāda leaving this world. But his instructions on how he wished to leave revealed his determined faith in Kṛṣṇa consciousness.

A Fall for the Better

Suddenly we heard a knock on Prabhupāda's door. It was Gulab, one of our Indian congregational members. His eyes searched the hotel room, and when they lighted on Prabhupāda's effulgent form, he dove at Prabhupāda's feet. He then asked Prabhupāda if he could take *sannyāsa*. Prabhupāda looked skeptical, "How can you take *sannyāsa?*"

* * *

Gulab was a worker in one of the many Ṣindhi cloth shops in Hong Kong. He chanted a few rounds every day and understood no philosophy. He spent his life toiling and suffering to support his wife and children, who still lived in Bombay. Prabhupāda immediately saw Gulab's lack of qualification for *sannyāsa* and understood that he was trying to avoid family responsibilities.

Yet seeing Prabhupāda and diving at his lotus feet cannot go in vain. Although Gulab was not ready at that time to attain Prabhupāda's shelter, later, by Prabhupāda's mercy, he achieved the mercy of Prabhupāda's disciple Tamal Krishna Goswami Mahārāja. He is now an initiated devotee, Gauravāṇī Dāsa, and lives in Śrīdhāma Māyāpur.

Karma in Every Culture

Early the next morning, Prabhupāda went for a walk in Kowloon Park. The smell of stinking garbage greeted him as he stepped from the hotel and made his way through Tsim Tsa Tsui's asphalt, concrete, and closed shops. The park was a green and luxurious haven from the stark Hong Kong pavement, and it was already filled with Hong Kong citizens doing their eerie ballet of rhythmic, slow-motion Tai Chi exercises.

Prabhupāda held his head high as he circled the flower beds and fountains. "Did you see her picking through the garbage as we walked here?" asked Prabhupāda. "So much prosperity and someone is forced to pick through the garbage for food."

As we walked, I tried to explain China's aversion to religion. When the British were attempting to subjugate China, they shipped crates of Bibles alongside crates of opium. Because of this, I explained, the Chinese government was now anti-religion. Prabhupāda's reaction was strong, "They do not know anything about religion." He said that the Chinese in Hong Kong were only interested in making money, "push-button money."

After fifteen minutes in the park, Prabhupāda headed down Cameron Road toward our small temple. The lift carried him up one flight, through the obnoxious fumes of the nonvegetarian restaurant next door, and into our temple room. Incense blocked out the horrendous neighborhood smells. A tape of Prabhupāda singing "*'Rādhā-kṛṣṇa' bol bol bolo re sobāi*" played softly.

* * *

The Chinese, or anyone's, aversion to religion shows a lack of understanding and common sense. Prabhupāda also defined the capitalists' desire to do no work other than organizing others to make money for them as "push-button money."

When he later traveled to India, Prabhupāda told how he saw one lady in Hong Kong picking through the garbage for food. Wherever he traveled, Prabhupāda spotted examples proving that the only shelter from material suffering was Kṛṣṇa consciousness.

Prabhupāda Visits Our Humble Temple

Prabhupāda examined our temple, noticing the elaborate and multi-colored bead decorations my wife had created, the orange-yellow linoleum floor, the brightly lit rooms, the incense, and the atmosphere created by our simple worship.

I asked Prabhupāda to sit in a carved wooden chair we had constructed for his *vyāsāsana*. He sat, his feet on the ground, and I offered him *ārati*. "*Ei śikhā diyā sab nadīyā phirche nece' gaura-nitāi,*" the tape continued as I offered water in a conch shell followed by the other *ārati* articles.

The music soon ended, and Prabhupāda's taped explanation of the song began. He motioned that I should end the *ārati* even before the final items were offered. Prabhupāda then spoke. A reporter from *The Asia Magazine* sat with us on the floor, waiting for his interview.

* * *

We were preaching in Hong Kong only for Prabhupāda's pleasure. I was satisfied to finally be able to offer Prabhupāda *ārati* in our little center. It was the perfection of two years of austere Hong Kong preaching.

Prabhupāda Speaks

PRABHUPĀDA:

'rādhā-kṛṣṇa' bol bol bolo re sobāi
(ei) śikhā diyā, sab nadīyā
phirche nece' gaura-nitāi

So *'rādhā-kṛṣṇa' bol bol bolo re sobāi, ei śikhā dīyā:* This is the teaching of Lord Caitanya. Bhaktivinoda Ṭhākura, the composer of this song, says that "you get out of all kinds of dangers if you simply take to chanting this Hare Kṛṣṇa mantra." *'Rādhā-kṛṣṇa' bolo, saṅge calo:* "Please cooperate with Me," Lord Caitanya says, "and chant Hare Kṛṣṇa." *Ei-mātra bhikhā:* "I am asking only this. I am begging."

So our mission is also like that. We are asking people without any argument or political purpose. Simply we are asking that you chant Hare Kṛṣṇa. That's all. Wherever we are opening our branches, our only business is requesting people to chant Hare Kṛṣṇa or Rādhā-Kṛṣṇa. We don't want anything else. We simply wish to spread the Hare Kṛṣṇa mantra because people are being washed away by illusion. They are being washed away and always in trouble. *Khāccho hābuḍubu, bhāi. Jīv kṛṣṇa-dās, e biśwās, korle to' ār duḥkho nāi:* "But if you try to understand that your position is eternal servitude to Kṛṣṇa, then your all troubles are over."

So you are all here. I think you should open a very nice center for preaching this gospel. And we have no discrimination. We accept anyone because we do not see the outward body. Just as a gentleman is not interested with the outward dress, he is interested with the person he talks to. Similarly, we are interested to see every person as spirit soul. *Paṇḍitāḥ sama-darśinaḥ. Paṇḍita* means learned. *Sama-darśinaḥ.*

vidyā-vinaya-sampanne
brāhmaṇe gavi hastini
śuni caiva śva-pāke ca
paṇḍitāḥ sama-darśinaḥ

"One who is actually learned, he sees everyone equally, either he is a very learned scholar or he is a dog or a *caṇḍāla* or an elephant." So how the learned scholar and dog can be seen on the equal level? Not that the dog and the learned scholar are equal, but seeing them equally means to see the spirit soul within the body. That is true vision. Outwardly, by the body, one is a learned scholar and another one is a dog. That is outwardly. But inwardly, everyone is spirit soul, Brahman. That is called *brahma-darśana.* So if people are taught this philosophy, then all these distinctions and creations of different kinds of problems – the Chinese or Communists, the Americans or capitalists, and so many differences we have created – will end. The problem now is fight coming from competition. There is enmity, enviousness. All due to ignorance. Or, in one word, it is due to lack of Kṛṣṇa consciousness.

Therefore we have taken this path for social improvement in human society. Let us cooperate.

* * *

Prabhupāda was speaking to our congregation – Chinese and Indians – who were, to varying degrees, interested in Kṛṣṇa consciousness. He knew that in order to cooperate and spread Kṛṣṇa consciousness they would have to remove the ignorance of bodily identification through Kṛṣṇa conscious realization.

Prabhupāda's Encouragement

PRABHUPĀDA: So this is nice place. You have decorated it nicely. Everything is nice so far the little place is concerned. How many rooms you have got?
BHŪRIJANA: This is it.
PRABHUPĀDA: Only one room.
BHŪRIJANA: And this little room in the back.
PRABHUPĀDA: That's very natural. It is costly here.

* * *

Prabhupāda noticed our simple living facility, which we had decorated to the best of our ability, and encouraged us.

Education: The Key to the Future

PRABHUPĀDA: But these children and their parents are also very much interested. So I think you should have a nice institution here to train the children in this country. And after their education, they may take to any line of livelihood. That doesn't matter. But the foundation...Just like in our Vedic system, first of all *brahmacārī*. Even Kṛṣṇa, God Himself, although He knows everything, but just to teach us, He also became a *brahmacārī* in the *gurukula*. Lord Rāmacandra, He also accepted a guru, Vasiṣṭha. That is our Vedic system. Anybody may be anything, but the process is *tad-vijñānārtham sa gurum evābhigacchet*. In order to learn the value of life, spiritual value of life, one must go to a guru.

* * *

Prabhupāda saw the seed of Kṛṣṇa consciousness in the children of Hong Kong and thus provided a vision that would allow that seed to grow and blossom.

A Universal Principle

PRABHUPĀDA: Similarly, everyone has to hear either from Kṛṣṇa or from His bona fide representative. That is *śrotriyam*. The result will be that after becoming a student of such bona fide guru, one will be firmly fixed up in God consciousness. That is the result, firmly fixed up. Now, these boys and girls from foreign countries, three or four years ago they did not know Kṛṣṇa. But now they are so perfectly devotee of Kṛṣṇa, and nobody can deviate them.

* * *

A warning to all of us: hearing attentively and submissively from a bona fide spiritual master firmly fixes a devotee in spiritual life. Acting against this principle is dangerous.

The Secret of Success

PRABHUPĀDA: If somebody says that "You give up this Kṛṣṇa consciousness and take something else." Now here is Śyāmasundara. His father is a very, very rich man. He is always canvassing Śyāmasundara, "You are my only son. You come, do business. You take millions of dollars, whatever you like." But he is not going. There are many like that. They cannot give up Kṛṣṇa consciousness. And you know our Jagattāriṇī, wife of Bhūrijana. She was a theatrical girl and earning millions of dollars. But she has given up everything. She is a nice girl, educated and qualified. But she is satisfied.

I asked her to go and marry Bhūrijana. She never saw him and did not know what kind of husband she would be accepting. But simply on my word, she came from Los Angeles and got married.

The only consideration is how to please Kṛṣṇa and His representative. *Guru-kṛṣṇa-prasāde pāya bhakti-latā-bīja. Bhakti* is just like a creeper, and the seed of that creeper can be obtained by the mercy of guru and Kṛṣṇa. That is Vedic injunction.

yasya deve parā bhaktir
yathā deve tathā gurau
tasyaite kathitā hy arthāḥ
prakāśante mahātmanaḥ

The Vedic knowledge becomes revealed to a person who has unflinching faith in Kṛṣṇa and guru. This is the system.

* * *

Years ago in Los Angeles, a devotee asked me how long I had been married. When I said twenty-one years, his jaw dropped. "To the same person?" It is perhaps amazing that my wife and I have been married for so long, because as in most marriages, ours has weathered rough periods. When young devotees ask for a success formula for a Kṛṣṇa conscious marriage I usually suggest they marry someone they respect, and that they view their commitment to their marriage as direct service to their spiritual master. Obviously, being deeply satisfied in one's own Kṛṣṇa consciousness helps. These principles, along with Kṛṣṇa's mercy and more than a pinch of good luck, have helped me maintain my marriage in Prabhupāda's service.

Prabhupāda's original point was that children need to hear from a guru, but then he expanded this point to make it relevant to the entire audience: everyone needs a guru. In Prabhupāda's preaching he would often speak about elements of self-sacrifice in his disciples, as he did with Śyāmasundara and Jagattāriṇī. His disciples were living examples of the philosophy.

An Interview with Prabhupāda

BHŪRIJANA: A reporter is here to interview you, Prabhupāda.
PRABHUPĀDA: All right.
REPORTER: The Hare Kṛṣṇa movement started in the United States. Why did it start in the United States rather than India?
PRABHUPĀDA: Because the United States, they are our best customer.

A businessman goes to a place...Just like you have come here. Why you have come here? Wherever there is best possibility of doing your business, there you must go. I went to United States because I know these people are not poverty-stricken.

Our Indian people have been trained to think that they are poverty-stricken. Actually, they are not poverty-stricken. The leaders have educated them: "You are all poverty-stricken." This is India's position. I knew that the Kṛṣṇa consciousness movement would not be successful in India. The government will not help. The public is educated in a different way. They are after technology.

And "familiarity breeds contempt." They say, "What is this Hare Kṛṣṇa movement? We have known it since a long time. What effect it will have?" Many Indian students in foreign countries, they say, "Swamijī, how will this Hare Kṛṣṇa movement benefit us? We want technology."

So that is the mentality of the Indians at the present moment. They have lost their own culture and therefore they are beggars. So I thought it wise to go to a country where there is no poverty.

* * *

Prabhupāda quickly recognized the reporter as having come to Hong Kong for the same reason that Prabhupāda traveled west. The reporter, whose name was Dom Moraes, was a published author of Indian, but not Hindu, origin. He had emigrated to Hong Kong from Bombay and had been living in Hong Kong for years. He was not a pious man. I was surprised at how candidly Prabhupāda answered his questions.

The Cause of Satisfaction

PRABHUPĀDA: When one has satisfied his senses, he is no longer interested in sense gratification. Perhaps you know C. R. Das from Calcutta. Fifty years ago, C. R. Das was earning fifty thousand rupees per month, but he was not satisfied.

One day, he and his wife were sitting together. His wife questioned, "Why do you look so morose? Everything is at your command. You have education, popularity. Still, you are unhappy. Why?"

Just then, by chance, C. R. Das saw one mendicant passing by on the street as a *sādhu*, a beggar. So he said, "I want to become like him."

Many other instances are there in history. Like Bharata Mahārāja. He was young man, twenty-four years old, and emperor of the whole planet. He had a young wife; he was a king, and he had everything. But he left everything.

Lord Buddha was a young prince and he was surrounded by dancing girls. But as soon as he went outside he saw an old man. "What is this?" "This is old man. Everyone has to become old like this." So he became immediately converted to a saintly person. "I must go and meditate and realize myself. Why shall I become old?"

* * *

Prabhupāda preached to the reporter rather than answering him with carefully worded statements.

Preaching on the Guru's Order

Reporter: How many disciples do you now have in the U.S.?

Prabhupāda: Although one cannot expect many disciples, still, there are two thousand. Not many come because I insist on many restrictions. And because people in general have forgotten Kṛṣṇa, forgotten God, Kṛṣṇa consciousness is difficult to understand. I am trying to remind them and bring them to Kṛṣṇa consciousness.

It is a very difficult job. I have to shed my blood three tons before I make one person convinced in Kṛṣṇa consciousness. That is my experience. Especially Europeans and Americans. They do not accept anything blindly. Questions, questions, questions. They are inquisitive, and they want to know, so I give them answers. Especially in Europe and America, when I make this condition that you cannot have illicit sex, you cannot have intoxication, you cannot eat meat, you cannot gamble...This is their daily habit. This is their life.

Even a British lord, Lord Zetland, refused these principles, "Oh, we cannot give up these things." So I strictly control my students, but still they are coming. So it is very difficult job, still, there are many thousands. And they are so sincere. If I ask them, like I have asked this boy [Sudāmā Vipra Swami], to go to Red China, they go even at the risk of their life.

* * *

Prabhupāda revealed the price a preacher must pay to turn a materialist into a devotee: "It is a very difficult job. I have to shed my blood three tons before I make one person convinced in Kṛṣṇa consciousness. That is my experience."

Koṭiṣv api mahā-mune. A devotee is a rare soul in degraded Kali-yuga. Yet Prabhupāda was so powerful that he inspired thousands to give up material life, worship Kṛṣṇa, follow Kṛṣṇa's instructions in the *Bhagavad-gītā,* and selflessly preach – even at the risk of their lives – the message of Kṛṣṇa consciousness.

Thus by Caitanya Mahāprabhu's order and by Prabhupāda's mercy souls trapped in *māyā's* kingdom are becoming dear to Kṛṣṇa:

ya idaṁ paramaṁ guhyaṁ
mad-bhakteṣv abhidhāsyati
bhaktiṁ mayi parāṁ kṛtvā
mām evaiṣyaty asaṁśayaḥ

na ca tasmān manuṣyeṣu
kaścin me priya-kṛttamaḥ
bhavitā na ca me tasmād
anyaḥ priyataro bhuvi

> For one who explains this supreme secret to the devotees, pure devotional service is guaranteed, and at the end he will come back to Me. There is no servant in this world more dear to Me than he, nor will there ever be one more dear.
>
> – *Bhagavad-gītā*, 18.68–9

How dear preacher-devotees are to Kṛṣṇa! How dear to Kṛṣṇa must Śrīla Prabhupāda be!

Preaching to Indians with Westerners

PRABHUPĀDA: It is the duty of the Indians to spread this Kṛṣṇa consciousness movement, but I am training these foreigners. They are doing this duty. But it is the duty of the Indians. It is their culture. But in India, a young Indian man is satisfied if he gets a nice wife and a little bit of money. Then he says, "My life is successful."

Therefore I went away. I previously approached many gentlemen. "Please, you have got four sons. Give me one son. I shall make him a real *brāhmaṇa.*" But there was no result because they do not know the value of Kṛṣṇa consciousness.

Now with Western disciples, Kṛṣṇa has given me a chance to preach in India. A very good chance. Now they are appreciating. When I go to India they become surprised, "Swamijī, how you have done this thing?"

Success Without Pride

REPORTER: Your home base is in Los Angeles.
PRABHUPĀDA: Yes, my headquarters is in Los Angeles. Now we have made very big headquarters in Bombay, Juhu. Twenty thousand square yards. We are constructing a very nice temple there. And similarly, we have got another headquarters at Lord Caitanya's birthsite, Navadvīpa. There also we are constructing a very big temple.

REPORTER: What about England? London? How is your movement doing?

PRABHUPĀDA: Yes, in London we have a very nice temple near the British Museum, 7 Bury Place. And all Europeans, they come to see our temple from Germany, from France. Because we have been advertised in cooperation with the Beatles. The Beatles, George Harrison. You know his name? He is a very famous man. Yes. So we have produced some records in cooperation with George Harrison's organization. Because the records are produced through George Harrison, we have got a very, very big sale. And that has advertised Rādhā-Kṛṣṇa Temple, London. So people come from all parts of the world to see what is our Rādhā-Kṛṣṇa temple.

Why Criticize Others?

REPORTER: Do you have any connection with the Maharishi?

PRABHUPĀDA: No.

REPORTER: What do you think of the Maharishi?

PRABHUPĀDA: Why shall I speak of others? Then people will be angry. At least, my position in foreign countries is far better than any Swami's up to date. Vivekananda went to America about eighty years ago, 1893. So Ramakrishna Mission has got about four or five centers in America. But I have got centers in America and Europe, about forty centers, and so many students. In the Ramakrishna Mission you won't find so many American boys as followers. But we have got thousands of followers. And they are all young men and girls. So that is my hope, that even if I die – I am seventy-six now – these boys will conduct this movement. I am sure.

* * *

Practical advice for preachers speaking to reporters: reporters become thrilled – they have their story – but the public tends to become angry when religionists criticize others, especially other religionists.

In addition, Prabhupāda expresses his conviction that his disciples and their subsequent followers would sincerely and intelligently continue to maintain and expand ISKCON.

All Roads Lead to Vṛndāvana – and Book Distribution

REPORTER: Where were you born?

PRABHUPĀDA: I was born in Calcutta, 1896.

REPORTER: And what did you do?

PRABHUPĀDA: Yes. I was ordinary man. That's all.

REPORTER: Did you work?

PRABHUPĀDA: Yes. I worked as a manager of a chemical concern in my family life. I have got my family also, my wife and children, my grandchildren, in Calcutta. But I have nothing to do with them.

REPORTER: And when did you start on…

PRABHUPĀDA: I left home in 1960, practically.

REPORTER: You left Calcutta?

PRABHUPĀDA: Yes. Say, for last twenty-two years.

REPORTER: And where did you go when you left Calcutta?

PRABHUPĀDA: I retired to Vṛndāvana. So there I began to write books. When three books were finished I started for America. There also I wrote dozens of books. You have seen our books? Our *Kṛṣṇa* book is selling like anything in Europe and America.

We are practically maintaining ourselves by selling books. We sell our books all over the world, about 20–25,000 rupees daily. We spend seven to eight lakhs of rupees monthly. In Los Angeles alone we spend $20,000 per month. In New York we spend $10,000 per month.

* * *

We know of Prabhupāda's pleasure when his books, filled with transcendental knowledge, are sold, but here Prabhupāda mentions another point about book distribution: "We are practically maintaining ourselves by selling books." What a transcendental way to maintain ourselves: selling books by speaking about Kṛṣṇa all day.

Crooked Questions, Straight Answers

REPORTER: Doing what? How do you spend it?
PRABHUPĀDA: We have to maintain our establishment, the temple, the Deity, so many devotees. In each center we have got at least twenty-five devotees. At the most two hundred devotees. So their living costs, everything. But some way or other, Kṛṣṇa is giving us. But we have no fixed income, neither we have any bank balance.

* * *

Common materialists can never understand how a pure devotee is satisfied by working to please Kṛṣṇa. When viewing Prabhupāda and his movement, such a reporter can't help but apply his own materialistic and selfish tendencies and assume that ISKCON is a business with a boss on top who is "enjoying" the fruits extracted from the hard work of those whose sentiments he is exploiting.

The Root of a Problem

REPORTER: In the minds of some people, the sudden attraction of Western youth to Eastern religions...
PRABHUPĀDA: No. It is not Eastern. That is a wrong conception. God is for everybody. When I speak of Kṛṣṇa consciousness to Eastern people, they say, "What is this Kṛṣṇa? We know Kṛṣṇa. What we have to learn from Swamijī?" Again, "Familiarity breeds contempt."

But in the Western countries when we speak of Kṛṣṇa, they see the philosophy. They see the science and become attracted.

Kṛṣṇa is for everyone. Kṛṣṇa is neither Western nor Eastern. But Easterners, especially Indians, they have learned to reject. That is their education – immediately reject Kṛṣṇa.

This is their new culture – to reject everything. At least Jawaharlal Nehru began like that, "Anything Indian is bad. Everything London-made is good." That was his philosophy. And if one European would go to see him, immediately admission. And if an Indian goes to see him, three days he has to wait. So Jawaharlal made this impression, "Everything Indian is bad, and anything made in London..." Because he was made in London. He was educated in London.

In my household life, I did some business and I had to see Jawaharlal Nehru when he was a common man. I went to his house. I saw it is completely Europeanized, although he is in *khādī*. His father hated Indian medicine. Motilal Nehru. I was selling medicine, so I introduced him to one preparation and Motilal Nehru says, "Doctor, in case of medicine, please do not prescribe Indian."

You see? So this is our mentality. We have got all foreign mentality, but we are claiming that we have become independent. But we are not independent. We have been culturally conquered by the materialistic advancement of foreign countries. We have lost our own culture. This is our position.

* * *

Prabhupāda directly described the root cause of contemporary India's atheistic, anti-traditional leanings – the national leadership of India, beginning with Nehru, abhorred Indian culture and trained the people accordingly.

No Compromises from Prabhupāda

REPORTER: Thank you so much. I'm sure...

PRABHUPĀDA: So many Indian swamis, they requested me to dress myself with coat and pants. I never agreed. See all my pictures?

Why shall I take to coat, pant? What is use? Now my students, they are giving up coat, pant. And girls, they are taking to *sārīs*. There is now even a good demand for *sārīs* in Europe and America.

BHŪRIJANA: They were even telling me here that I should wear diplomat's clothes instead of *dhotī*. They were ashamed.

PRABHUPĀDA: Hare Kṛṣṇa. So we shall go now?

* * *

Although his example of "coat, pant" is simple, Prabhupāda's message of no compromise is essential for those who preach.

Dom Moraes went on to write his article for *The Asia Magazine*, which was sent out in newspapers throughout Asia. The article came out a month later, with pictures of Prabhupāda's reception at the Park Hotel and excerpts from the interview. The article turned out neither sweet nor complimentary, and it received many angry letters of complaint from readers throughout Asia. I also visited the *Asia News* editor and complained. He agreed, saying, "Dom Moraes is too cynical. We should have sent someone else." But it was too late; the article had already been published. If at all possible, devotees lining up newspaper and magazine coverage should demand the right to approve articles prior to publication.

God's Doll House

Prabhupāda's visit to our temple ended with the reporter's interview. On his way out, Prabhupāda saw a handmade doll's house in the corner of the temple room. Jagattāriṇī had custom-designed and personally pieced together the cross-sectioned plastic doll's house. It had different rooms, and she had outfitted it with small furniture, velvet carpets, mirrors, and toys. Prabhupāda walked over and looked inside. In one small corner of the plushly decorated doll's house was an altar in a small temple room. On a throne sat Jagattāriṇī's Laḍḍu Gopāla Deity. When Prabhupāda saw the Deity, he seemed surprised, but then he joined his hands together before his heart in respect.

* * *

Prabhupāda did not seem to notice any peculiarity in a Laḍḍu Gopāla Deity being in a doll's house. He saw that a Deity of Kṛṣṇa was being cared for, and he simply offered his respects.

A Distasteful Blunder

As we walked down the stairs to the street, heading back to the Park Hotel to prepare for the flight to Tokyo, Prabhupāda instructed me to prepare *kicchari* for his breakfast.

"First boil three cups of water, then add one cup rice and one cup mung *dāl*. Add one teaspoon of salt, some turmeric, and let it cook for fifteen minutes."

I offered my obeisances and raced back to the temple. I went over the proportions and ingredients again and again in my mind. I put the water on to boil. Then it occurred to me that the other devotees would also need to eat, so I tripled the ingredients.

After ten minutes, I noticed that the *kicchari* wasn't cooking. "Three times the ingredients," I lamented, "but the same flame!"

The *kicchari* was only half-cooked – still hard. I added more water and tried cooking the *kicchari* longer.

Prabhupāda's departure time was fast approaching. His taxi was due to leave in fifteen minutes. Anxiously, I lifted the pot and raced to the Park Hotel. I burst into Prabhupāda's room and served Prabhupāda the steaming hot *kicchari*.

Prabhupāda, peaceful as always, ate one spoonful, then another, and pushed the rest aside.

* * *

I remember an old BTG article on the *Rāmāyaṇa*. Hanumān first located Sītā Devī, his assigned duty, and only after succeeding in that did he go further and burn Laṅkā for Rāma. If only I had learned this lesson from the example of Śrī Hanumānjī.

Sent by Kṛṣṇa's Mercy

There was little time to muse over my mistake. I helped Prabhupāda catch his taxi and then quickly went back to the temple to pack and ready myself to accompany Prabhupāda's party to Tokyo.

My *dhotīs* and *kurtās* found their way into my travel bag. Some money and some books followed. But where was my passport?

I stared at the clock. Overturning papers and clothes, I searched and re-searched everywhere. The recommended check-in time had already ended. Quickly passing through anxiety, frustration, anger, desperation, and hopelessness, I finally lost all anxiety and began to pray, "Kṛṣṇa, I can't find my passport and there's nothing I can do by myself. I surrender. If you want me to accompany Prabhupāda to Japan, You'll have to place my passport in my hand. I've looked and looked and I still can't find it."

I then looked again free from anxiety and in a dependent mood. Within seconds, I found my passport, said a quick goodbye to my wife, and was on my way to the airport. Once aboard, I passed Prabhupāda's seat on the way to mine. He looked at me with concern at my lateness. I smiled and said, "You must have some service for me in Tokyo."

* * *

I've mentally noted the following lessons from this incident. Hectic times are intense. Plan and prepare everything well in advance. Then, as the event looms closer, go over all important plans and preparations again and again. Count on arrivals and departures to be the most frantic. Above all, depend on Kṛṣṇa. Be surrendered as His servant and know that He will ultimately protect you according to His desire. Plan, plan, plan ahead, but depend on Kṛṣṇa.

Asking Questions

Prabhupāda was accompanied by Nanda Kumāra, (his cook), Śyāmasundara (his secretary), and Pradyumna (his Sanskrit editor). At first I sat next to Śyāmasundara, but Prabhupāda adjusted our seating arrangements because he wanted Śyāmasundara to take dictation of his letters. I later sat next to Prabhupāda.

I didn't have many questions to ask Prabhupāda as I sat beside him, but I did have one: Caitanya Mahāprabhu could speak *kṛṣṇa-kathā* with Rāmānanda Rāya, but you are surrounded by young disciples. Do you have anyone with whom you can speak *kṛṣṇa-kathā*?

I turned this question over and over in my mind, but never asked it. I just wasn't bold enough.

* * *

Remembering this incident, I find myself, like an uncle, suggesting to the disciples of godbrothers that they take advantage of opportunities to inquire from their spiritual master. If they have questions but fear them improper, they should nevertheless ask and trust that their spiritual master, who is their well-wishing friend, will inform them of any impropriety. Hesitating to ask, I fear, may one day leave them with the realization that the opportunity to inquire, which Kṛṣṇa had provided, has passed.

Chant! Chant! Chant!

"Keep your consciousness pure when you are in Prabhupāda's presence by always chanting and always praying for his mercy." This good advice came to me just before I went with Prabhupāda to Tokyo. I tried my best to follow it.

While sitting next to Prabhupāda I chanted and chanted and chanted. I chanted the *mahā-mantra*. I chanted every *śloka* and song I could remember. When I ran out of *ślokas* and songs, I returned to continuously chanting the *mahā-mantra*.

At one point, the passenger behind me called over the seat, "Stop that chanting!" Prabhupāda smiled. I lowered the volume, but continued chanting. I cut and served some fruit for Prabhupāda, but continued chanting. Prabhupāda dozed after that, but I chanted on.

Finally, just as the plane was preparing to land, and after Prabhupāda had taken out his mirror and applied fresh *tilaka,* he turned to me and said, "This is a nice habit you have, this always chanting. Nanda Kumāra, see how Bhūrijana is always chanting. You should also get this habit!"

* * *

Prabhupāda's instructive encouragement to always chant Kṛṣṇa's name is the essence of the path of *sādhana-bhakti.*

smartavyaḥ satataṁ viṣṇur
vismartavyo na jātucit
sarve vidhi-niṣedhāḥ syur
etayor eva kiṅkarāḥ

> "One should always remember Kṛṣṇa and never forget Him. All the rules and regulations should be understood as assistants to always remembering Kṛṣṇa and never forgetting Him."
> – *Padma Purāṇa*

In his *Upadeśāmṛta* Śrīla Rūpa Gosvāmī refers to constant chanting as the essence of all advice. I therefore embrace Prabhupāda's encouraging words as a most dear instruction, and I pray to him for the ability to always chant Hare Kṛṣṇa.

Tokyo, 1972

Samosās from Kārttikeya and Sudāmā

The Tokyo temple was now situated in a remote, rural district called Asakawa-cho. Next door to the temple was a restaurant that specialized in cooking meat in an open barbecue pit, and special buses would cart Tokyo residents two hours to reach it. Business was booming.

Prabhupāda heard about the restaurant during the long drive from the airport, and both positive and negative lessons about the "restaurant near our Tokyo temple" later appeared in Prabhupāda's worldwide preaching. On the positive side, he explained that people will travel from anywhere to our Kṛṣṇa conscious restaurants if the *prasāda* is of high quality. On the negative side, he commented on modern civilization's misuse of time wherein a man will waste two hours simply to get flesh to eat. "I have seen in Tokyo," he would add.

Immediately upon his arrival, Prabhupāda was escorted up the winding metal stairs to the temple room. The *kīrtana* ended as Prabhupāda sat down on the simple *vyāsāsana* before the assembled devotees and small deities of Rādhā and Kṛṣṇa.

PRABHUPĀDA: So what *prasāda* you have prepared?

CINTĀMAṆI: Um, Kārttikeya Prabhu?

PRABHUPĀDA: Kārttikeya Prabhu? Where is Kārttikeya? [*Kārttikeya comes from the kitchen. The devotees laugh.*]

DEVOTEE: There's some *rasgullās* and some fruit. We have some fruit and vegetables.

PRABHUPĀDA: I wanted some *samosā.*

DEVOTEES: Ah.

PRABHUPĀDA: Sudāmā Prabhu, can you prepare it?

SUDĀMĀ: Yes, Śrīla Prabhupāda.

PRABHUPĀDA: So do it.

* * *

Kārttikeya had served as Prabhupāda's servant. Later he became a *sannyāsī,* then left the *sannyāsa* order. Prabhupāda knew that Kārttikeya was in Japan assisting Sudāmā and, out of affection he had called for him. Sudāmā had also been Prabhupāda's servant and was an expert cook. When Sudāmā was serving Prabhupāda, Prabhupāda taught him to make *samosās* using peas and cauliflower. Prabhupāda was hungry. Other than a little fruit on the plane, all he had eaten that morning was a few spoonfuls of half-cooked *kicchari.* But he showed no signs of agitation or impatience. Rather, his mood, both when asking for Kārttikeya and requesting Sudāmā to make *samosās,* was personal and affectionate.

Next Business

Prabhupāda then spoke to Karandhara, the head of the Los Angeles temple and a BBT trustee. Karandhara was one of Prabhupāda's main managers. He had arrived the previous evening.

PRABHUPĀDA: Karandhara Prabhu, how do you like this place?

KARANDHARA: It's nice, Prabhupāda.

PRABHUPĀDA: Yes, for spiritual advancement it is a nice place.

* * *

Could Prabhupāda have been hinting that the temple, hidden in the remote Japanese countryside, hours from Tokyo, was peaceful and conducive for one's own Kṛṣṇa conscious advancement, but not practical for Japan's only preaching base?

Exchanges with Karandhara

PRABHUPĀDA: You have reached here last night?

KARANDHARA: Yes. Here are some gifts from the devotees in Los Angeles.

PRABHUPĀDA: Oh, what is this? Something sweet?

KARANDHARA: Yes, Prabhupāda.

PRABHUPĀDA: You open it. Open it. What is this?

KARANDHARA: That is sandalwood pulp.

PRABHUPĀDA: Oh, so many letters.

ŚYĀMASUNDARA: Checks. These are checks, Śrīla Prabhupāda.

PRABHUPĀDA: That's nice. When you bring checks, I am very glad. [*Chuckles.*] So how much you have deposited?

KARANDHARA: In which account?

PRABHUPĀDA: My account. So in Los Angeles is everything all right?

KARANDHARA: Yes, Prabhupāda. All the different envelopes are from the different departments – Spiritual Sky, Mail Order, ISKCON Media.

PRABHUPĀDA: So you keep it in this envelope. Then I shall see.

* * *

Prabhupāda appreciated the affectionate gifts of his Los Angeles disciples – sandalwood paste, *sandeśa,* and letters, but Prabhupāda appreciated most the offerings of money with which he could spread the Kṛṣṇa consciousness movement.

A critic may think that Prabhupāda's motive was to take money from his disciples, but Prabhupāda was interested only in spreading Kṛṣṇa consciousness around the world. He needed money. Prabhupāda never hoarded money or used it for his own benefit.

He was eager to recover money from *māyā* and use it in Kṛṣṇa's service.

Prasāda Distribution

PRABHUPĀDA: You distribute that *prasāda*. Give everyone.

DEVOTEE: Is this a *laḍḍu?*

PRABHUPĀDA: Yes. I will also take little. Now distribute. [*Pause.*] Oh, you take more. Why little, little? Give more. Give me also little more.

TRIVIKRAMA: *Jaya!*

PRABHUPĀDA: Mmm. It is very nice.

DEVOTEE: Prabhupāda distributes mercy to the world.

PRABHUPĀDA: Who has made it?

KARANDHARA: Dhruvānanda.

PRABHUPĀDA: Oh. He is good cook?

KARANDHARA: Yes.

PRABHUPĀDA: Mmm. He has made nice.

SUDĀMĀ: Shall I save one for later for you?

PRABHUPĀDA: No, no saving. [*Laughter.*] Give me immediately. [*Laughter.*] Give them.

ROMAHARṢAṆA: Prabhupāda? Your Divine Grace? I have a question. I was always under the impression or understanding from your teachings that one never eats in front of the Deities. Can you please explain that?

ŚYĀMASUNDARA: He says that he always understood that one should not eat in front of the Deity. What is the difference?

PRABHUPĀDA: Difference is generally we should not eat before the Deity. But there is another injunction: *prasādaḥ prāptir mātreṇa bhoktavyaḥ*. As soon as *prasāda* comes, you should immediately eat it.

All the devotees laughed as Prabhupāda ate the remaining part of his *laḍḍu*.

* * *

Caitanya Mahāprabhu and His associates were fond of taking *prasāda;* they tasted the sweetness of Kṛṣṇa consciousness by eating Kṛṣṇa's food remnants. Prabhupāda also relished *kṛṣṇa-prasāda,* and he immediately honored and appreciated the fine taste of the sweets Karandhara had brought from Los Angeles.

Romaharṣaṇa was an eccentric devotee living in Tokyo. The devotees were shocked by his question that seemed to indicate that perhaps Prabhupāda was acting inappropriately or even offensively by eating in front of the Deities. But Prabhupāda simply laughed and counter-quoted a verse from the *Padma Purāṇa.* When Prabhupāda popped the *laḍḍu* into his mouth after quoting the verse, the disturbance the devotees felt by the question vanished and they felt at once both satisfied and joyful.

To Go or Not to Go?

A few days later, Prabhupāda sat on the *vyāsāsana* and lectured. At the end of the lecture, he remarked that devotees should want to leave the material world and go back to Kṛṣṇaloka. When I heard this, I remembered Śrī Caitanya Mahāprabhu's prayer, *janmani janmanīśvare bhavatād bhaktir ahaitukī tvayi.* Lord Caitanya did not want liberation. He only wanted to perform devotional service birth after birth. Thinking these exalted thoughts, I said, "Prabhupāda, we don't want to go back to Godhead. We only want to serve you."

Prabhupāda looked up, "Don't make me stay here to accept your service."

"You're already there, Prabhupāda," I whispered to him.

* * *

Prabhupāda pierced my imitative allegiance to eternal service. He knew me. He knew I had not understood the depth of love for Kṛṣṇa that a devotee who has imbibed the eternal serving spirit experiences. Only based on that love does the experience of decrying liberation have true meaning.

A Service for Bhūrijana

Prabhupāda walked each morning from his small, rented, Japanese cottage to the nearby temple, his cane indenting the rocky soil. When he entered the temple room, he leaned his cane against the wall and walked toward his *vyāsāsana.*

I followed directly behind Prabhupāda and made sure that his cane didn't fall over. If it began to fall, I would smile, catch it, and stand it upright again.

* * *

I derived great happiness from this simple service to Prabhupāda's cane. I admit at times praying for it to fall just so I could catch it. I continued serving Prabhupāda's cane throughout his visit, even when we later visited Kobe. There, Prabhupāda would walk up the stairs to his apartment and drop his cane, without looking back, as he grabbed hold of the stair railing. I would catch it and carry it up the stairs.

How satisfying it is to serve with affection.

"Let Us Enjoy"

One day we sat with Prabhupāda while Śyāmasundara read him his mail. The first letter was from Devānanda, a devotee who had joined ISKCON after Prabhupāda's visit to the Morningstar Ranch in 1967. Devānanda later took *sannyāsa* and traveled with Prabhupāda in 1970 from the West Coast of America through Japan and to India. By the time Prabhupāda received this letter from him, he was confused and had again started taking intoxication.

Śyāmasundara tried to explain the gist of Devānanda's letter.

ŚYĀMASUNDARA: He's saying that he had an argument with the devotee sitting behind him and he explains what went on. But not much of it seems to make sense. Should I go on?

PRABHUPĀDA: [*Smiling.*] Yes, let us enjoy.

Śyāmasundara then read the letter, which rambled on as Devānanda described the details of a trivial and inconclusive argument he had had with another devotee. With Prabhupāda's permission, we laughed at Devānanda's letter, and Prabhupāda laughed along with us.

* * *

The old saying, "You've got to laugh to keep from crying," was appropriate here. Devānanda was not the first of Prabhupāda's leading disciples to fall victim to *māyā,* and Prabhupāda had on occasion shed tears at his disciples' leaving Kṛṣṇa consciousness. Joking about Devānanda's difficulties was a unique mood, and Prabhupāda allowed us to see how *māyā* had made a fool of Devānanda.

Although Prabhupāda had many times attempted to help Devānanda, now, thousands of miles away, Devānanda was again taking intoxication. Prabhupāda could do little but humorously place Devānanda's example before his other disciples as a lesson.

Who Should Surrender?

Prabhupāda left the temple room after class and made his way back to his cottage. A few disciples trailed behind. A cold rain fell as we walked in single file close to the temple building, watching water drizzle off its eaves.

I was walking directly behind Prabhupāda. Prabhupāda, still walking, said to me, "Trivikrama can go to the Philippines. What do you think?"

I thought fast. Prabhupāda was responding to my request that we find someone to accompany Sudāmā Vipra Swami to open a temple in Manila. Knowing the nature of the Philippines I didn't think it wise that a *sannyāsī* go alone, and since Prabhupāda didn't think much of my suggestion that Nanda Kumāra go, he made his own recommendation. But he asked my opinion.

"No, Prabhupāda, I don't think he's the right person."

"Why?"

"With two swamis, I think they would have trouble deciding who would surrender to whom."

Prabhupāda thought for a moment. "It doesn't make a difference who surrenders to whom."

* * *

I was surprised at my own boldness in responding to Prabhupāda's suggestion, but since he had asked, I had to answer according to my realization. Because both *sannyāsīs* had strong personalities and neither could be intimidated, there would be problems. Certainly Prabhupāda could have reprimanded my boldness or simply overruled my objection, but he took my doubt seriously and later suggested a different devotee to help establish ISKCON in Manila.

Prabhupāda's final comment, however, was the actual philosophical conclusion: "It doesn't matter who surrenders to whom," as long as the service goes on and both guru and Kṛṣṇa are satisfied.

Shivering in the Cold

In Asakawa-cho, far from the city of Tokyo, the temple windows were paper and the matted *tatami* floor was cold. As we chanted before Prabhupāda during *maṅgala-ārati* our breath turned to vapor.

Prabhupāda sat on the red velvet *vyāsāsana.* He looked at me, wrapped in a blanket, dancing and shivering. His soft eyes met mine and he hunched his shoulders in sympathy, "It is so cold, isn't it?"

* * *

I could understand that as I was inconvenienced by the cold, he was too. Of course, I cannot say that Prabhupāda's experience was the same as mine; he was an exalted devotee and I was "my body," but Prabhupāda didn't like cold weather either.

Prabhupāda's dislike of the cold expanded my understanding of the mood a great devotee maintains while serving: he will tolerate cold or any other unpleasant circumstances in the service of guru and Kṛṣṇa. This sincere and dutiful serving mood is neither mechanical nor automatic. It is a product of devotion and it gradually blossoms into love.

Stealing a Heart

During Prabhupāda's transit through Hong Kong, I had heard that he was dissatisfied with ISKCON leadership and had therefore temporarily disbanded the GBC. With boyish naivete and the desire to encourage him, I bought him a 24-karat gold ring and engraved it with the words, "*Jaya* ISKCON." I presented this ring to Prabhupāda in Hong Kong before we traveled together to Tokyo. Now as I sat with Prabhupāda in Tokyo during his massage, Sudāmā carefully rubbed mustard oil onto Prabhupāda's chest, back, legs, and hands. Sudāmā then noticed Prabhupāda's golden "*Jaya* ISKCON" ring.

"Prabhupāda," he asked, "you have a new ring."

"Yes."

"Who gave it to you?" Sudāmā asked, as he massaged the back of Prabhupāda's neck.

Prabhupāda slowly lifted his head and stared at me. Only the three of us were in the room, and I felt softened by Prabhupāda's glance.

"Who gave you the ring, Prabhupāda?" Sudāmā repeated.

Prabhupāda kept looking at me and said softly, "Oh, someone."

* * *

Prabhupāda could have told Sudāmā that I had given him the ring. Instead he replied, "Oh, someone." When he said those two words, my heart melted and flowed to his lotus feet in the intimacy of our simple and loving secret.

A Gift of a Name

While massaging Prabhupāda, Sudāmā mentioned that Prabhupāda had named the Japan *yātrā* "New Gāyā," after the town in Bihar, India, where Buddha gained enlightenment. Hearing this I joked, "Prabhupāda, if you don't give our Hong Kong *yātrā* a name, I will get envious." Prabhupāda looked at me and laughed. "You can call it New Ki Ki Tah. That is a province of Gāyā."

* * *

Prabhupāda reciprocated and granted my request. I think I was less interested in a name for the Hong Kong *yātrā* than the gesture of asking Prabhupāda for its name. The name New Ki Ki Tah somehow remained overlooked for the Hong Kong *yātrā*.

Moments Lost and Gained – a Double Loss

Prabhupāda initiated a Japanese boy and gave him the name Tukārāma. Tukārāma was weak, and he immediately wanted to leave the temple and go home. Thinking that a Japanese devotee was rare, I decided to go with him. We traveled to Tokyo and distributed books together. We then shared noodles on the *tatami* mat in his small room in Shinju-ku. I wanted to help him, so I spent the night there and then returned to the temple by midday. Prabhupāda noticed my absence during the morning *Bhāgavatam* class. "Where is Bhūrijana?"

"Preaching," was the message I had requested Sudāmā to pass on to Prabhupāda.

* * *

Tukārāma never returned. I felt like the Hindu who ate a sparse meal in a Muslim's home – his belly was still empty and his caste was lost. I neither succeeded in helping Tukārāma nor associated with Prabhupāda. Both the young devotee and the holy moments with Prabhupāda escaped me.

A Gift of a Moment

Romaharṣaṇa lamented his lack of personal association with Prabhupāda. We went to Prabhupāda's cottage together and sat silently praying under his closed window. Suddenly, the curtains parted and Prabhupāda faced us through the glass window. "Who is that?" he called.

"Your dogs barking for mercy," I replied.

The cottage doors slid open and Prabhupāda invited us in. He immediately gave me an assignment to locate his secretary.

* * *

Romaharṣaṇa's lamentation proved miraculously fruitful. Prabhupāda noticed our prayers, called us in, and then sent me away, leaving a tearful disciple alone with his spiritual master.

A Lost Moment

Nanda Kumāra was massaging Prabhupāda in the morning sun. I walked by, watching from a distance, and offered my obeisances. Then I noticed Nanda Kumāra waving to me. I stared, interpreted his signal, and walked away.

Later Nanda Kumāra questioned, "I was calling you. Why didn't you come?"

"Oh no," I lamented. "I was coming, but I thought you were telling me to go."

* * *

Another eternal moment stolen by ignorance.

The Nicest God

Trivikrama Swami was showing me a letter from his younger brother, a Christian, when we heard the buzzer. "Prabhupāda's calling us," he said. We both rushed for Prabhupāda's room.

Prabhupāda sat behind his low desk, smiling and peaceful. Trivikrama Swami took out his letter and showed Prabhupāda the tract his brother had enclosed called "A Hindu Turns to Jesus."

Trivikrama read: "While many Westerners are turning to Hare Kṛṣṇa, here's a Hindu with a Ph.D. who's been saved by Jesus." The tract then quoted the ex-Hindu's criticism of Indian religion. "They believe in the caste system and that an eternal soul changes from body to body. This is against Christianity and the words of the Holy Bible. Hare Kṛṣṇas, like most Hindus, also worship stone idols of Kṛṣṇa, giving the stone the same respect as God."

Prabhupāda listened silently. Trivikrama finished and asked Prabhupāda what he thought. Prabhupāda replied, "He is a big Ph.D. and still has not learned anything." He then reached for a large manila envelope and slipped out an 8x10 inch photo. Keeping its back to us, Prabhupāda looked at the picture with devotion. Then he turned the picture over to show us exquisitely adorned Rukmiṇī-Dvārakādīśa. He said proudly, "Anyway, our God is the nicest God!"

* * *

Prabhupāda buzzed for us simply to share a gift he had just received from Los Angeles. How could he take the tract's criticisms seriously when he was taking *darśana* of the "nicest God" – Rukmiṇī-Dvārakādīśa of Los Angeles?

The Intoxication of Māyā

When I was in Prabhupāda's association, at times I felt practically liberated. At other times, however, I felt miserable and even more entangled in *māyā* than usual. I asked Prabhupāda why this happened. He simply replied, "The intoxication of *māyā* is very strong."

* * *

An exalted devotee is powerful. His association may award us, despite our disqualification, with a semblance of transcendence. But until our attachment to Kṛṣṇa is mature, *māyā* is strong enough to pull us down. *Māyā* cannot touch us, however, if we somehow remain always in Kṛṣṇa's shelter.

kṛṣṇa – sūrya-sama; māyā haya andhakāra
yāhāṅ kṛṣṇa, tāhāṅ nāhi māyāra adhikāra

> "Kṛṣṇa is compared to sunshine, and *māyā* is compared to darkness. Wherever there is sunshine, there cannot be darkness. As soon as one takes to Kṛṣṇa consciousness, the darkness of illusion (the influence of the external energy) will immediately vanish. PURPORT: When a person is Kṛṣṇa conscious, he continuously hears about Kṛṣṇa, thinks about Him, worships Him and serves Him as a devotee. If he remains in Kṛṣṇa consciousness in this way, the darkness of *māyā* certainly will not be able to touch him.
>
> – *Caitanya-caritāmṛita, Madhya* 22–31

In Prabhupāda's association, being unsurrendered or on the mental platform was still more apparent and painful.

On the other hand, those who do not practice Kṛṣṇa consciousness fall victim to *māyā* and suffer regardless of the fortune of their circumstances. Prabhupāda explains in his purport to *Caitanya-caritāmṛta, Madhya* 10.65: "*Māyā* is so strong that Kālā Kṛṣṇadāsa left Caitanya Mahāprabhu's company to join gypsy women. Even though a person may associate with Śrī Caitanya Mahāprabhu, he can be allured by *māyā* and leave the Lord's company due to his slight independence. . . . One need only misuse his little independence. Once fallen and separated from the Supreme Personality of Godhead's association, one becomes a candidate for suffering in the material world."

Adding to the Bhāgavatam Class

Prabhupāda asked for a *Śrīmad-Bhāgavatam* volume from which to give his morning class. I ran to the temple library and from the few books present, chose the single Second Canto chapter, "Answers Citing the Lord's Version." Knowing that this chapter contained the four seed verses of *Śrīmad-Bhāgavatam,* I thought to please Prabhupāda by my choice of chapters. I also considered that hearing Prabhupāda explain these essential verses would be wonderful. I ran back to Prabhupāda and handed the thin volume to him. Prabhupāda accepted the book from my hand and smiled.

* * *

I was happy to do this service for Prabhupāda and I carefully (and quickly) considered the available books before choosing. At the time, I thought that Prabhupāda was pleased by my choice. In retrospect, however, I think that if Prabhupāda was pleased with anything, it was not my choice of *Bhāgavatam volumes,* but my attempt to make a conscious choice and my quick return.

Introducing the Daily Bhāgavatam Śloka

During Prabhupāda's visit to Japan in 1972, he introduced the system of devotees chanting the *Bhāgavatam ślokas* before class. This system is basically the same one we use everywhere in ISKCON today, but with two differences.

On his first day with us, Prabhupāda started with the first verse of the chapter. He read the *śloka* and taught it to us. His morning class covered the subject of this first verse. On the second day, he chanted the verse from the previous day line by line, and we responded in unison. Then he taught us the second verse. In addition, each devotee was also expected to chant the *śloka* for that day individually, while the rest of the devotees chanted each line responsively.

On the third day, Prabhupāda chanted the first two *ślokas* line by line, and we again responded in unison. He then taught us the third *śloka*. Day after day we chanted all the previous verses we had studied with Prabhupāda before learning the day's verse.

* * *

By chanting each Sanskrit *śloka* every day we naturally memorized them. To this day I more or less remember the opening *ślokas* of *Śrīmad-Bhāgavatam,* Canto Two, chapter nine, and the sound of all the *ślokas* that we covered in the chapter remains familiar. Śatadhanya Prabhu, who was also present, offers the following remembrances:

> One day, Prabhupāda was sitting on the *vyāsāsana*. He became very upset, and speaking loudly, described how he had gone through all the trouble to include the Sanskrit *ślokas* and transliterations in the *Śrīmad-Bhāgavatam,* but the devotees were neither showing any interest nor learning the correct Sanskrit pronunciation. In short, they were ignoring the Sanskrit he had placed in his books. He became adamant and said that from now on everyone in ISKCON must learn to pronounce correctly and understand the Sanskrit *ślokas*. For the next three weeks, every morning in *Śrīmad-Bhāgavatam* class, he called upon each devotee, requesting us to chant the *ślokas* aloud. The thing that made it unique was that Prabhupāda would take ten or fifteen minutes with one person and personally teach him how to pronounce every single Sanskrit syllable in the *śloka*. In that way Prabhupāda went around the temple room and personally taught the seven or eight people every day. We were studying the Second Canto, "Answers Citing the Lord's Version," and I remember, even to this day, the *ślokas* which Prabhupāda drilled into us intensely day after day. In fact, we would all get tutored by Pradyumna during the day so that the next morning we would not be embarrassed. We were finally able to correctly chant the *ślokas* in that chapter.
>
> Before Prabhupāda left, he announced there would be a final exam in the temple room. All of us came at class time, and

Prabhupāda called on each of us to recite the entire chapter in Sanskrit. Then Prabhupāda went through the trouble to make corrections and tell us how we did. This went on for hours, and he told each of us whether our recitation was good or we needed more work. Somehow I was last, because I was sitting on the side opposite the *vyāsāsana,* so when everyone had spoken I took my turn. I recited the whole chapter. Then Prabhupāda looked at me and said, "First prize."

Knees Down!

One morning as he spoke, Prabhupāda saw Śyāmasundara sitting with his knees up. Prabhupāda spoke sharply, "Sit properly!"

* * *

Sometimes I explain this incident to devotees sitting improperly during the *Śrīmad-Bhāgavatam* class. Inside I smile, remembering Prabhupāda through his "Sit properly!" instruction.

Morning Walks

Prabhupāda took his morning walks down a reddish dirt road, past his cottage, past the temple, and onward through a slightly uphill, wooded area. It was a forty-minute route.

Some morning walks were active, with Prabhupāda instigating debate and questions. Other walks were more meditative with only two or three devotees walking in silence, relishing the sound of Prabhupāda's cane digging into the earth as he walked.

Uncovering a Flaw

On one morning walk, Prabhupāda discussed an ISKCON controversy with Karandhara. Kīrtandnanda Swami had written

Prabhupāda suggesting that devotees only wear devotional clothing when distributing books. He spoke of his experiences that devotees wearing nondevotee clothing tended to fall into nondevotee behavior. Karandhara and others had taken the stand that Kīrtanānanda's suggestion, if implemented, would significantly decrease the number of books distributed. Prabhupāda was impressed by the figures put forward by Karandhara showing the expected rate of decrease in book distribution. As Prabhupāda and Karandhara discussed the points back and forth, Sudāmā, Trivikrama Swami, and I gathered closer to listen.

At one point in the discussion, Karandhara offered an alternative by which books could be distributed, but the amount of money collected would diminish. I interjected, "We're not interested in money." Prabhupāda immediately reprimanded me. "So we are not interested in money? Without money how can Kṛṣṇa consciousness spread? This is hippie philosophy. Money is Lakṣmī and is meant for Kṛṣṇa's service. This is nonsense."

* * *

Although I had meant to say that devotees are not interested in money outside of Kṛṣṇa's service, I could not hide from Prabhupāda a flaw in my consciousness. I remember one initiation where Prabhupāda named a disciple Rāmarañjana (one who brings Ramā, the goddess of fortune) and then ordered him to regain Lakṣmī, or Sītādevī, from the bogus spiritualists who, like Rāvaṇa, imitated holy men to steal her from Rāma. Prabhupāda was both fully spiritual and completely practical.

Prabhupāda concluded that while preaching and distributing books the devotees could continue wearing nondevotee dress – but the dress of gentlemen, not hippies. Prabhupāda explains his conclusions in these purports to *Śrīmad-Bhāgavatam:*

> In our Kṛṣṇa consciousness movement, the tactic of dressing oneself like an ordinary *karmī* is necessary because everyone in the demoniac kingdom is against the Vaiṣṇava teachings. Kṛṣṇa consciousness is not at all to the liking of the demons of the present

age. As soon as they see a Vaiṣṇava dressed in saffron garments with beads on his neck and *tilaka* on his forehead, they are immediately irritated.... The greater demons, like Hiraṇyakaśipu, are always prepared to chastise the Vaiṣṇavas, and they try to make arrangements so that Vaiṣṇavas will not come to sell their books and preach Kṛṣṇa consciousness. Thus what was done by Hiraṇyakaśipu long, long ago is still being done. That is the way of materialistic life. Demons or materialists do not at all like the advancement of Kṛṣṇa consciousness, and they try to hinder it in many ways. Yet the preachers of Kṛṣṇa consciousness must go forward – in their Vaiṣṇava dress or any other dress – for the purpose of preaching. Cāṇakya Paṇḍita says that if an honest person deals with a great cheater, it is necessary for him to become a cheater also, not for the purpose of cheating but to make his preaching successful.

– *Śrīmad-Bhāgavatam* 7.5.7

Sometimes the Kṛṣṇa consciousness movement sends its representative *sannyāsīs* to foreign countries where the *daṇḍa* and *kamaṇḍalu* are not very much appreciated. We send our preachers in ordinary dress to introduce our books and philosophy. Our only concern is to attract people to Kṛṣṇa consciousness. We may do this in the dress of *sannyāsīs* or in the regular dress of gentlemen. Our only concern is to spread interest in Kṛṣṇa consciousness.

– *Śrīmad-Bhāgavatam* 7.13.9

And in the *Caitanya-caritāmṛta:*

Sometimes members of the International Society for Krishna Consciousness – especially in the Western countries – find it difficult to approach people to distribute books because people are unfamiliar with the traditional saffron robes of the devotees. The devotees have therefore inquired whether they can wear European and American dress before the general public. From the instructions given to King Pratāparudra by Sārvabhauma Bhaṭṭācārya, we can understand that we may change our dress in any way to facilitate our service. When our members change their dress to meet the public or to introduce our books, they are not breaking the devotional principles. The real principle is to spread this Kṛṣṇa consciousness movement, and if one has to change into regular Western dress for this purpose, there should be no objection.

– *Caitanya-caritāmṛita, Madhya* 14.5

A Morning March with Prabhupāda

On another morning walk, about fifteen devotees waited by the temple to join Prabhupāda. As he walked past, Prabhupāda met the assembly's greeting of "*Jaya* Prabhupāda!" and obeisances with a silent glance. Suddenly, Sañjaya turned on a portable tape recorder and, like marching music, Yamunādevī sang *govindam ādi-puruṣaṁ tam ahaṁ bhajāmi.*

Prabhupāda stopped, turned, and planted his cane firmly on the ground. "There is one Bengali proverb." He paused as everyone stopped walking. The tape recorder was silenced. "Eat alone, study in twos, and walk in threes." Prabhupāda turned and continued his walk.

* * *

All the devotees wanted Prabhupāda's association, yet he obviously wanted a casual and peaceful morning walk. I lagged behind and thought of turning back, but then I realized that I was the only one who wouldn't be with Prabhupāda.

Prabhupāda appreciated our desire to be with him, so he tolerated the entourage tagging along, although he continued the walk in silence. After that day, though, few devotees went on walks with Prabhupāda. No one wanted to inconvenience him.

A Snake, a Rope, a Scorpion, or a Crab?

One morning as Prabhupāda, Śyāmasundara, and I walked, a small creature crawled across the road. Prabhupāda pointed at the crab-like creature with the tip of his cane. "A scorpion. Be careful."

We continued walking, as Śyāmasundara turned and whispered in my ear, "It's a land crab."

* * *

A scorpion or a crab? A snake or a rope? I had never seen a scorpion, but this creature looked quite like a crab. Prabhupāda explains the perfection and knowledge of an exalted devotee, a spiritual master, as being on a completely different level than scorpions, crabs, or spectacles-free eyesight in the following conversation, which took place during the 1975 Gaura-Pūrṇimā festival in Māyāpur.

PRABHUPĀDA: Yes. Pure devotee does not aspire anything, simply to be engaged in loving service to the Lord, wherever it may be. It doesn't matter.

JAYĀDVAITA: They know everything and they are perfect in everything. But sometimes, from our material viewpoint, we see some discrepancies. Just like we think that...

PRABHUPĀDA: Because material viewpoint. The viewpoint is wrong; therefore you find discrepancies.

JAYĀDVAITA: So we should think that we have the defect.

PRABHUPĀDA: Yes. *Ācārya* is explained, *bhakti-saṁsanaḥ:* "One who's preaching the cult of devotional service, he's *ācārya.*" Then why should you find any discrepancy?

JAYĀDVAITA: Because we see...For instance, sometimes the *ācārya* may seem to forget something or not to know something, so from our point of view, if someone has forgotten, that is an imperfection.

PRABHUPĀDA: Then you do not understand. *Ācārya* is not God, omniscient. He is servant of God. His business is to preach *bhakti* cult. That is *ācārya.*

JAYĀDVAITA: And that is the perfection.

PRABHUPĀDA: That is the perfection. Hare Kṛṣṇa.

JAYĀDVAITA: So we have a misunderstanding about what perfection is?

PRABHUPĀDA: Yes. Perfection is here, how he is preaching *bhakti* cult. That's all.

SATSVARŪPA: Prabhupāda, in one purport in the *Bhagavad-gītā* you write that a disciple of a bona fide spiritual master is supposed to know everything.

PRABHUPĀDA: Yes, if he follows the spiritual master.

SATSVARŪPA: But how could he know?...What does that mean, "everything?"

PRABHUPĀDA: Everything means whatever his guru knows he should know, that much. Not like God, everything. Within his limit, that's all. If he tries to understand whatever his guru has said, that much is "everything." Otherwise, "everything" does not mean that we know everything, like God, like Kṛṣṇa. That is not possible. If he regularly chants and follows the regulative principles, follows the orders of guru, then he knows everything. That's all. Not very much...knows everything, then what is the use of reading books when he knows everything? You cannot expect anyone to know like Kṛṣṇa, everything.

JAYĀDVAITA: Kṛṣṇa says in the *Bhagavad-gītā* that one who knows Him knows everything.

PRABHUPĀDA: Yes. Because if he knows that Kṛṣṇa is the Supreme Personality of Godhead, then he knows everything. That's all. Not that he should know as Kṛṣṇa. *Yasmin vijñāte sarvam eva vijñātam*...If he accepts Kṛṣṇa, the Supreme Personality of Godhead, the Absolute Truth, then he knows everything. That is finished.

JAYĀDVAITA: That knowledge itself is complete.

PRABHUPĀDA: Yes.

SATSVARŪPA: If there's some material information that such a person doesn't know, that's not really knowledge anyway.

PRABHUPĀDA: I did not follow.

SATSVARŪPA: If he doesn't know how many people live in...

JAYĀDVAITA: Just like Gaurakiśora could not write. So it appeared that he did not, there was something that he did not know, although he knew Kṛṣṇa.

PRABHUPĀDA: Yes. He knows everything. Otherwise how Bhaktisiddhānta accepted him as guru? He knows Kṛṣṇa. That's all.

NALINĪ-KĀNTA: What the spiritual master says, that is also perfect?

PRABHUPĀDA: Yes. Because he does not say anything concocted. Whatever he says, he says from *śāstra* and guru.

A Moment Alone

One morning as Prabhupāda, Śyāmasundara, and I were nearing the temple after a morning walk, Śyāmasundara split off to make a telephone call. Prabhupāda and I continued walking toward his cottage. Prabhupāda stopped. We stood together, surveying the rugged Japanese landscape with its scrub, barren, reddish earth, and pine trees on the small hills. The moment was sweet and silent; the two of us were alone and my heart filled with affection for Prabhupāda. "I just want to serve you, Prabhupāda," I spoke softly.

Without speaking, Prabhupāda's glance focused straight on me for a few seconds. "Did he hear? Did he understand?" I wondered. Prabhupāda continued his silence and we walked toward his cottage.

* * *

Words spoken in a sweet and intimate moment must bear the test of time.

Kobe, Japan, 1972–Part I

Our Morning Program of Praise

Prabhupāda's stay in Tokyo was broken by an engagement in Kobe, 270 miles south of Tokyo. In Kobe, Prabhupāda lived in the third-floor apartment of our host, the president of the Kobe Hindu Association. Every morning we held a quiet morning program. Prabhupāda sat on a cloth spread over the upholstered couch and chanted the *Gurv-aṣṭaka* prayers followed by a soft *kīrtana*. Once, he played the *mṛdaṅga* as he chanted the *Gurv-aṣṭaka* to his Guru Mahārāja, his eyes closed, the early morning sun brightening his golden complexion.

* * *

Prabhupāda was grave, in an internal mood, during these morning hours. After the *Gurv-aṣṭaka* prayers, we were inspired to chant "*Jaya* Prabhupāda, *Jaya* Prabhupāda" to praise him. Prabhupāda's response was to also chant "*Jaya* Prabhupāda, *Jaya* Prabhupāda" to glorify his own Guru Mahārāja.

Walking Past Hypocrisy

The devotees present – Śyāmasundara, Bhānu, Pradyumna, Sudāmā, and I – went on several morning walks through the Kobe suburbs with Prabhupāda. On one morning walk, he saw a sign for the Kobe SPCA and asked us what SPCA stood for. Sudāmā answered, "The Society for the Prevention of Cruelty to Animals." Prabhupāda retorted, "No, it means the Society for the Promotion of Cruelty to Animals!"

* * *

Prabhupāda condemned the hypocrisy of a Society whose professed purpose was to eradicate cruelty to animals, but who neither insisted on a vegetarian diet for its members nor opposed the organized murder of animals in slaughterhouses.

The Chopping Technique

Some of Prabhupāda's morning classes were less formal and more like preaching-conversations. The topics varied. One morning he said that many apparently sophisticated women who had big dogs as pets were actually engaging in sex with their dogs. He used this as an example to show the degradation of modern society. He said that syphilis had entered human society through women having sex with animals. Other topics were more standard, with Prabhupāda crushing our reliance on modern material scientific concepts.

* * *

Prabhupāda was often extremely heavy when describing modern civilization and the so-called advancement of modern technology. Invectives such as "rascal," "cheater," and "nonsense" abounded in his appraisal of society's leaders. He called his preaching style "the chopping technique" and said his Guru Mahārāja had also used it. Once Prabhupāda mentioned that some of his godbrothers had criticized his Guru Mahārāja's preaching style. "Those who criticized fell down," he added.

Crushing Chance

God's Way: Chance Comes from Necessity

During one conversation, Prabhupāda argued with the devotees that chance does not really exist. He explained how a man's necessity arises, and the needed article comes to a deserving man, if he works. The process that induces the article to come is not chance but Kṛṣṇa's supervision as Supersoul. Because the ultimate cause is not directly perceivable by a materialist, they foolishly name chance, not God, as the cause.

PRABHUPĀDA: If the chance comes as soon as the necessity is there, then we have to admit immediately God.

ŚYĀMASUNDARA: Yes.

PRABHUPĀDA: Because in the *Bhagavad-gītā* we hear *mattaḥ smṛtir jñānam apohanam,* that God is in everyone's heart as Supersoul. Now, I am thinking of getting something. So God knows immediately that "He wants to have this," so He gives me the necessary thing which appears to me as chance, without knowing God. The things are supplied by God because He is giving me all facilities to enjoy this material world to my heart's content by supplying all the ingredients. That is the material condition. So these foolish persons are taking it as chance, but it is not chance. God is omnipotent. As soon as He understands that I want this, He gives me some facility so that I get it. So it is not chance. It is by arrangement of superior authority. But because they are atheists, they have no sense of God consciousness, they are taking as chance, that necessity creates that chance; automatically it is coming. Not automatically, but all of a sudden it falls...Just like I am hungry, I want some food. So Kṛṣṇa knows it that you want...Some way or other, the food comes to me. So it is the arrangement of Kṛṣṇa, but I see it is chance: "I was hungry and by chance the food has come." That is my less intelligence. It is not chance; it is plan. Otherwise you cannot adjust the meaning of chance in that way, that as soon as there is necessity, immediately the opportune chance comes before us.

ŚYĀMASUNDARA: They say, "Well, it's my luck," or, "My bad luck."

PRABHUPĀDA: Yes, they say. So this "luck," as soon as you say "luck," there must be somebody who is giving you the luck, good luck or bad luck.

ŚYĀMASUNDARA: One man may desire something very badly, and his whole life long he will not get it. He will always say, "I am so unlucky."

PRABHUPĀDA: Because he is not fit to get it, so God does not supply it. So we do not take anything as chance. We take everything as plan. But because God's omnipotency is so subtle, we can't see how things happen. Therefore we say,"It is a chance, chance of physical arrangement." Just like in the airport, as soon as I step on the door it becomes opened. It is not chance. A child will see it is as chance: "Oh, how it is? I wanted to go and the door is already open." He takes it as chance. That is poor fund of knowledge. There is arrangement, nice arrangement, electrical arrangement. So to a poor fund of knowledge it becomes a chance, and to the mind it is not chance; it is arranged by higher authority.

* * *

Earlier during Prabhupāda's stay, while he was in his small cottage in Tokyo, Trivikrama Swami entered Prabhupāda's room when Prabhupāda was alone. Prabhupāda was quietly reading *Kṛṣṇa* book. "See what I do when I am free?" Prabhupāda remarked. Prabhupāda was a devotee of Kṛṣṇa. He had a great attachment to direct *kṛṣṇa-kathā*. Then why did he spend so much of his time poking holes in contemporary thought?

Faith in guru and *śāstra* is the foundation of *kṛṣṇa-bhakti*. Simultaneously maintaining faith in modern, materialistic science and technology and advancing in Kṛṣṇa consciousness is impossible. Prabhupāda had to demolish the forest of our unquestioned beliefs, our cultural conditioning, before the *bhakti* seeds he had planted in our hearts could grow and blossom.

Under Kṛṣṇa's control

PRABHUPĀDA: That plan is Kṛṣṇa's. That is said in the *Bhagavad-gītā, mayādhyakṣeṇa prakṛtiḥ sūyate sa-carācaram:* "Under My plan, under My superintendence, the nature is working. The changes of the world are going on for that reason." *Hetunānena kaunteya jagad viparivartate:* "All these changes are taking place on account of My supervision." So there is no question of chance. It is all planned by the Supreme. *Daiva netreṇa,* by superior arrangement.

ŚYĀMASUNDARA: Doesn't necessity mean plan?

PRABHUPĀDA: Necessity means for a foolish person like me, I want something. That is my necessity and God supplies me. "Man proposes, God disposes." And that reception, or that achievement, without it being explained by me, I take it as a chance. Because I cannot explain it. Just like the same example: the flower is fructifying. We are saying chance because we do not see how the working is going on.

ŚYĀMASUNDARA: You defined miracle like that once before.

PRABHUPĀDA: Yes. So there is nothing like miracle. Everything is done in so subtle way that we cannot understand. We take it as chance. The same example: just like a child steps before the door and it opens. He thinks, "Oh, by chance the door is opened." But it is not by chance. It is a plan.

* * *

After chopping down our blind faith in chance being the ultimate causal principle, Prabhupāda next established the more reasonable premise that ordered events occur not by chance, but by arrangement.

The Architect of Fortune

PRABHUPĀDA: The proprietor is living there. The servants are living there. The cats and dogs are also living there. The trees and plants are also living there, and insects and microbes and snakes and rats. So many living entities in the same building. Why they are different? What is the answer? They have been given the same chance of living in the same house, born in the same house. As the proprietor's son is born in the same house, these also, they are also taking birth the same place. Why they are denied the same advantage? And if they are denied, who has denied it? What is the answer to this question? They are all living entities.

BHŪRIJANA: The difference is that the human living entities have higher intelligence because of their body.

PRABHUPĀDA: That is the question, that "Who has given you high intelligence and not to the rats and cats?"

PRADYUMNA: You said in one place, "Man is the architect of his own happiness and distress."

PRABHUPĀDA: Yes. Yes, that is an axiomatic truth even by the modern man. Yes, that "Man is the architect of his own fortune." So as soon as there is work to make your fortune, then there must be a person to decide to give you a fortunate position. Just like in an establishment, so many men are working, but there is a president. He is considering the work file, "How this man has worked?" And he is being promoted, his salary is being increased, and somebody is degraded, no promotion, rather, transferred to some other place. The natural conclusion is when there are so many varieties of life in our presence and, although in the same place, they haven't got the same facility, so there must be somebody who decides on this point. So how you can deny God? Our point is the Supreme Person, the president, who decides on this fact, He is God. What is the opposite answer?

PRADYUMNA: They would say that you are in your position and they are in their position just by chance, just like…

PRABHUPĀDA: That is nonsense. This is sheer nonsense. There is nothing by chance. What is that chance? By chance one is becoming millionaire, and by chance one is becoming a cockroach. What is that chance? Explain that chance. It is evasive. It is most foolish reply, "chance." We have got this nice apartment. Is it by chance?

PRADYUMNA: No.

PRABHUPĀDA: Then?

BHŪRIJANA: There's never an example of chance.

PRABHUPĀDA: This is all nonsense. People are befooled by all this philosophy.

BHŪRIJANA: Albert Einstein said, "I cannot believe that the highest material principle is chance." He's a material scientist. He said, "I cannot believe..."

PRABHUPĀDA: Yes. Actually, if one is learned, scientific, he must admit. He must admit, unless he is a lunatic, rascal. He will say all these nonsense things, "chance." Why chance? What is taking place within your practical experience by chance? If by prearrangement we did not come here, then who would care for us? Even on the street we could not lie down. Nobody would allow. The police will arrest. "Who are these men?" How do you say chance? Everything is done by prearrangement. Chance is an explanation given by the rascals and fools. They are not sane men. There cannot be anything by chance. We got up on the train, and the train is running, and it is all chance? There is a huge management behind the train. Therefore we are comfortably seated, and we come to the destination right on time. All these are chances?

ŚYĀMASUNDARA: Their answer is that there was a necessity to go to the city, so we would have tried hundreds of different ways to come here, and by chance, eventually we would have found...

PRABHUPĀDA: No. We have not tried hundreds of others. There was a plan.

SUDĀMĀ: But even where does... In my mind, if I hear the word "chance," where does chance, how does chance come about, if there is such a thing?

PRABHUPĀDA: No. The rascal says that I am trying in so many ways; one of them succeeds by chance. But I am not working in so many ways. We had a plan: to come here to preach.

So according to that plan, we arranged with this man, and it is not chance. It is all prearranged. Where is that "I am trying this way or that way?" We are going to preach. There is a plan. So our men go before my reaching there and they make nice arrangement, nice apartment. Then they receive me. These are not chances. This is all prearranged plan.

* * *

To bring the argument from "plan" to the necessity of a "planner" who enforces that the plan is a logical step. My next comment brought out a doubt. I was a casualty of Kali-yuga's educational system and I thought that evolution's basic principle was change, not chance. Things necessarily change and that change is done by chance. I offered this argument to Prabhupāda.

Chance, Change, or Kṛṣṇa?

BHŪRIJANA: But they don't acknowledge the plan.

PRABHUPĀDA: Why they don't acknowledge? Everything is being done by plan. The rascal who is speaking like that, he is educated by a plan, by his parents. And therefore he is able now to talk nonsense and get the Nobel Prize. His education was planned.

SUDĀMĀ: Just like his book was planned, so now he is given the Nobel Prize. He won't say, "By chance I won."

PRABHUPĀDA: Yes. His plan to misguide the people, that is his plan.

BHŪRIJANA: They say that change is the principle. They say that change is the highest principle and out of so many different changes...

PRABHUPĀDA: No, how the change takes place? You are changing. You are changing from your childhood to boyhood, boyhood to youthhood. So there is a plan. Unless there is plan, why one child does not by chance become immediately old? What the nonsense will reply? Let the rascal reply to this. That here is a chance, that one child immediately becomes old man, by chance. Why there is process? This is plan. So you should have depth of knowledge, otherwise you will be carried away by these rascals. We cannot be carried away by these rascals. We never so easily believed that they are going to the moon planet. You see? We have to scrutinize everything. Yes. That is brahminical qualification. A *brāhmaṇa* will not accept anything simply because it is said by some rascal. A *śūdra* will accept because he has no intelligence. That is the difference between *brāhmaṇa* and *śūdra*. It is not a caste system. It is class – *guṇa-karma vibhāgaśaḥ*, division of high qualities and actual activities according to that quality. They misinterpreted. Because by the influence of Kali-yuga everyone is *śūdra*, so he does not know what is the actually brahminical qualification. Therefore there is competition: "Why this man? I am as good as he is, so why he should be called *brāhmaṇa*? Why he should be given greater facility?" So actually it has happened. A so-called *brāhmaṇa*, caste *brāhmaṇa*, he is working his intelligence like *śūdra*, and he is claiming, by birthright, *brāhmaṇa*. There must be protest. This has happened. Otherwise, that division is perfect, *guṇa-karma-vibhāgaśaḥ*. Anyone who comes to brahminical quality, he becomes *brāhmaṇa*. That is the injunction of the *śāstra*. Kṛṣṇa says *guṇa-karma-vibhāgaśaḥ*. You have no qualification, you do not work according to your quality, and why you are claiming to be *brāhmaṇa*? That is self-evident. *Guṇa-karma-vibhāgaśaḥ*. He never said by birth, never said. *Kalau śūdra-sambhavaḥ:* "In this age, Kali-yuga, all *śūdras*." Therefore they accept everything cheaply and at once, the *śūdras*.

ŚYĀMASUNDARA: Cheaply and at once?

PRABHUPĀDA: At once. Yes. The newspaper said that "Mr. Such-and-Such went to moon planet." Oh, immediately believe. See? A newspaper, a ten-cent newspaper. And in the *Bhagavad-gītā* Kṛṣṇa says, *yānti deva-vratā devān:* "One can go to the demigods' planets by worshiping them. You can go, *yānti deva-vratā devān*, as others have gone. Similarly, one can come to Me by worshiping Me." *Mad-yājino 'pi yānti mām*. So they never worshiped Candra, and how they can go to Candra's planet, the moon planet? Then Kṛṣṇa is false. Kṛṣṇa is imperfect. They become perfect. They are defying Kṛṣṇa's instruction. They have gone to moon planet. Then our whole propaganda, Kṛṣṇa consciousness, becomes bogus. Therefore I always protest.

SUDĀMĀ: They have not gone.

PRABHUPĀDA: They have not gone. We have got our tests. I am speaking from the very beginning, "They have not gone." And practically you see, even if they have gone, what utility they have made? They are simply planning, again planning. "We shall get petrol from there. We shall have defense from there." Simply bluffing, simply bluffing. The Americans will go to the moon planet to defend his country from the Russians. Just see. And we have to believe all these nonsense proposals. What defense they will do from there? Is it not the proposal?

* * *

Prabhupāda's reply was simple: change is not random, it is also by plan. He thus was training his disciples in independent, clear thinking. He didn't want us to remain faithful, foolish believers in the tenets of modern science. If we were to be of use to him and make advancement in this life, we would have to see beyond the trickery of modern science and faithfully preach the Vedic viewpoint.

At the time, I couldn't deeply accept Prabhupāda's arguments, but later when we returned to our Asakawa-cho temple, Prabhupāda continued to dismember our blind faith in evolution. One morning, Śyāmasundara and I walked with Prabhupāda. To our left, the dirt road dropped off in a steep decline; to the right a hill rose, topped with rows of pine.

"Just see," said Prabhupāda, pointing with his cane. "All trees are facing the sun." He stopped to observe and allow the point to sink in. "There is nothing that is chance in creation." Prabhupāda continued, "Evolutionary theory is nonsense. If chance is law, then why at least one tree is not pointing away from the sun?"

Prabhupāda's simple and clear example destroyed my conditioned faith in the theory of evolution.

Kobe Part II: Like a Lion in the Chase

Our Prabhupāda, Our Hero

Our journey to Kobe contained a dramatic pastime in which Prabhupāda was the hero. I've written it into a short play (below). Unfortunately, I wasn't able to find a recording of the lecture Prabhupāda gave in Kobe, so I edited one in a similar mood from *Back to Godhead.* I also changed a few time sequences and added detail and dialogue to make the story read better as a play, and added some of Prabhupāda's words and anecdotes that had happened elsewhere, such as a description of the faults of Māyāvāda philosophy spoken in New Vrindaban in 1969. Other than these minor additions and changes, this play is an accurate description of Prabhupāda's amazing pastime.

Scene One, 1972: Tokyo Train Station

[*Bhānu and Bhūrijana enter the train from left.*]

BHŪRIJANA: Here are seats 86–89. They're ours. When's Prabhupāda coming? The train's supposed to leave in ten minutes.

BHĀNU: Don't worry. I asked Prabhupāda to wait with Sudāmā until we found the seats. He should be here any moment.

BHŪRIJANA: When will we arrive in Kobe?

BHĀNU: It's about 270 miles and it'll take about three hours. We should be there by about two o'clock this afternoon.

BHŪRIJANA: From Tokyo! That's *fast.* [*Looks around.*] This train even *looks* like an airplane.

BHĀNU: The Japanese call this train "The Bullet," the Shin-kan-sen. It goes about 100 miles an hour. It won't even stop before Kobe.

BHŪRIJANA: Here comes Prabhupāda now. With Sudāmā – and not a moment to spare. *Jaya* Śrīla Prabhupāda!

[*Prabhupāda enters wearing a garland.*]

BHĀNU: *Jaya* Prabhupāda!

PRABHUPĀDA: Hare Kṛṣṇa. Thank you. Which seats?

[*Bhānu directs Prabhupāda and the other devotees into a compartment in which two sets of seats face each other.*]

BHĀNU: You please sit here, Prabhupāda. I'll sit here. Sudāmā over here, Bhūrijana, quickly. The train is due to leave now.

[*Conductor enters.*]

CONDUCTOR: Tickets, please. Please sit down. Due to the high speeds, no one is allowed to stand for the entire ride.

[*Conductor moves on. The train begins moving.*]

BHĀNU: Leaving right on time.

SUDĀMĀ: Prabhupāda, the Japanese technology is so advanced that a train like this can reach a speed of about 100 miles an hour.

PRABHUPĀDA: Yes, they are going fast, but where are they going? That is the question. Just like the story of the poet Kālidāsa. He is sitting on the end of a tree branch sawing. One passerby approaches him to warn him, "You will fall if you keep up your sawing." "Go away and stop criticizing. Mind your own business." Kālidāsa keeps sawing and... and what happens?

BHĀNU: Of course he falls.

PRABHUPĀDA: Yes. The rascal falls and runs and says, "How did you know I would fall? Are you an astrologer?" That is the definition of a rascal. He is going so fast, but he does not know where he is going.

SUDĀMĀ: Prabhupāda, you are like the passerby who tried to help.

PRABHUPĀDA: Therefore I say this rascal modern civilization based on cow-killing and technology is doomed. It will fall.

BHĀNU: And they won't listen to you.

PRABHUPĀDA: This world based on technology is ruining everything. Technology and Māyāvāda philosophy. Because of technology, people have given up their simple living style. Everyone is moving to the city for sense gratification. And because of this nonsense the Māyāvādīs have preached, "I am God. You are also God. All is one. It does not matter what I do. All paths are the same." [*Pauses.*] All nonsense. If we have bought a ticket to Kobe, will we arrive in Calcutta? No. Everyone has become foolish by this rubbish Māyāvāda philosophy. It is nonsense and we must preach strongly.

BHŪRIJANA: *Jaya* Prabhupāda.

PRABHUPĀDA: You young boys should also preach strongly. You must learn the truth – *mamaivāṁśo jīva-loke* – and preach strongly, as I am doing all over the world. Preach the truth just as Kṛṣṇa is speaking in *Bhagavad-gītā* and *Śrīmad-Bhāgavatam,* and do not compromise Kṛṣṇa's words.

BHŪRIJANA: Our mission is so difficult, Prabhupāda. No one wants to listen.

PRABHUPĀDA: But still we have taken so much risk and have left Vṛndāvana at such an advanced age... traveling constantly all over the world... just to save them.

[*Bhānu gets up and stands to the side.*]

BHĀNU: Prabhupāda, I think it will be more comfortable for you if you put your lotus feet up on the seat. I don't mind standing.

[*Prabhupāda puts his feet up.*]

SUDĀMĀ: Everyone else your age has long ago retired.

PRABHUPĀDA: Yes, I am an old man, [*Laughing.*] and still...

BHŪRIJANA: Seventy-six already.

PRABHUPĀDA: But I still keep traveling and preaching. I must. To save them and to train you.

SUDĀMĀ: Uh, Prabhupāda?

PRABHUPĀDA: Yes?

SUDĀMĀ: Before, when you said that Māyāvāda philosophy has ruined the world...

PRABHUPĀDA: Yes?

SUDĀMĀ: Well, Prabhupāda, that reminded me that I forgot to tell you something.

PRABHUPĀDA: You can speak.

SUDĀMĀ: The program for the Hindu community in Kobe, you know the one that you'll be speaking at tomorrow night?

PRABHUPĀDA: Yes?

SUDĀMĀ: [*Hesitatingly.*] Well, by mistake, I mean...uh, on the same program...the same night, I foolishly allowed the Hindu community leader, Mr. Mahesh, to schedule a...

PRABHUPĀDA: Speak up.

SUDĀMĀ: A Māyāvādī *sannyāsī.*

PRABHUPĀDA: What?

SUDĀMĀ: Yes, a Māyāvādī *sannyāsī* will be speaking the same night as you.

BHŪRIJANA: The same night? Sudāmā, you didn't!

BHĀNU: Before the entire Kobe Hindu community! At the same program as Prabhupāda? You didn't.

SUDĀMĀ: [*Apologetically.*] I did. I didn't mean it, but I couldn't help it.

BHĀNU: Prabhupāda will never tolerate hearing Māyāvādī philosophy. Imagine Prabhupāda sitting there and a Māyāvādī *sannyāsī* preaching, "You are all God."

SUDĀMĀ: I couldn't refuse. That Mr. Mahesh said that if all the members of the Hindu community were satisfied with Prabhupāda's program, he would consider donating to us one of his apartment buildings for a temple.

BHŪRIJANA: Sudāmā, I think you have made a great mistake.

PRABHUPĀDA: Satisfy the Hindu community? I will satisfy Kṛṣṇa. [*Laughing.*] But don't worry, Sudāmā has tried his best. You are all still young boys and make mistakes, but you have given up everything, so how can I take offense by your little mistakes?

BHŪRIJANA: But it's a *Māyāvādī* that's speaking.

PRABHUPĀDA: We shall see what is Kṛṣṇa's plan. We shall see.

[*Conductor walks past and sees Bhānu standing up.*]

CONDUCTOR: You cannot stand. The train is moving too fast. You must sit down immediately. Take your seat.

[*The devotees all nudge Bhūrijana to be the one to request Prabhupāda to move his feet.*]

BHŪRIJANA: Prabhupāda, the conductor is asking Bhānu to sit down. Could you please move your lotus feet?
PRABHUPĀDA: So the lotuslike devotee can sit down…Hare Kṛṣṇa.
ALL: *Jaya* Prabhupāda!

Scene Two, Kobe, the next morning

[*Prabhupāda is sitting on the couch in an apartment playing mṛdaṅga. Sudāmā and Bhūrijana are sitting on the floor. Prabhupāda is leading the Gurv-aṣṭaka prayers – "yasya prasādād bhagavat-prasādo." After chanting, Prabhupāda says the prema-dhvani prayers and is handed a volume of the Śrīmad-Bhāgavatam.*]
PRABHUPĀDA: Continue reading from the *Bhāgavatam.*
BHŪRIJANA: *Oṁ namo bhagavate vāsudevāya.* Reading from *Śrīmad-Bhāgavatam,* Canto Two, chapter nine, verse 35:

yathā mahānti bhūtāni
bhūteṣūccāvaceṣv anu
praviṣṭāny apraviṣṭāni
tathā teṣu na teṣv aham

Lord Kṛṣṇa is speaking: "O Brahmā, I Myself exist within everything created, and at the same time I am outside of everything." Should I keep reading the purport, Prabhupāda?
PRABHUPĀDA: Yes, keep reading. This is very important.
BHŪRIJANA: Purport by His Divine Grace A.C.Bhaktivedanta Swami Prabhupāda.

"The impersonalists perceive that the Supreme Brahman is all-pervading, and they conclude there is no possibility of His personal form. But the mystery of understanding transcendental knowledge is love of Godhead, and one who is surcharged with such transcendental love of Godhead can, without difficulty, see the Personality of Godhead, Kṛṣṇa, in every atom and every object. And at the same time he can see Kṛṣṇa, the Supreme Personality of Godhead, in His own abode, in Goloka Vṛndāvana. This vision can be revealed as follows:

premāñjana-cchurita-bhakti-vilocanena
santaḥ sadaiva hṛdayeṣu vilokayanti

[*Buzz buzz buzzzz. Doorbell rings.*]

SUDĀMĀ: I'll get it. [*Offers obeisances and gets up.*]
BHŪRIJANA:

yaṁ śyāmasundaram acintya-guṇa-svarupāṁ
govindam ādi-puruṣaṁ tam ahaṁ bhajāmi

SUDĀMĀ: [*From off stage.*] Oh, Mr. Mahesh. So nice to see you. And Mr. Santanam. Yes, Mr. Mahesh, your chauffeur was waiting when the train arrived last night. Thank you. Yes, Śrīla Prabhupāda's here. Come and meet him.

[*Sudāmā enters with two smiling, wealthy-looking Indians wearing suits and ties. They offer praṇāmas.*]

SUDĀMĀ: Mr. Mahesh and Mr. Santanam, this is Śrīla Prabhupāda, the founder-*ācārya* of the International Society for Krishna Consciousness.

MR MAHESH: So pleased to meet you, Swamijī.

PRABHUPĀDA: Hare Kṛṣṇa. Please sit down. [*To Bhūrijana.*] Continue.

BHŪRIJANA: "I worship the original Personality of Godhead, Govinda, whom the pure devotees, their eyes smeared with the ointment of love of Godhead, always observe within their hearts. This Personality of Godhead is known as Śyāmasundara, Govinda, or Kṛṣṇa, and He possesses all-attractive transcendental qualities."

PRABHUPĀDA: One must strictly follow the process of Kṛṣṇa consciousness, then one will get spiritual knowledge and will one day see Kṛṣṇa face to face. At the present, our knowledge is limited to this body. It is material, and material knowledge means ignorance – the cause of fear and anxiety. But this ignorance can be removed by getting the right knowledge of the self by hearing from the *Śrīmad-Bhāgavatam.* We can then become free from material attachment and enter into the kingdom of fearlessness.

This material world means fearfulness. Just like prisoners are always fearful in a prison house. They cannot violate the jail rules and regulations, and if they do violate the rules, this means another term or extension of their prison life. Similarly, we in this material existence are always fearful. Fearful and full of anxiety. Everyone in the material life, in all species and varieties of life, is full of anxieties because they are stealing the property of God and using it as if it were their own. Because we are thief, we are always in anxiety. "When will my stealing be finished? When will I get caught?" Liberation, *mukti,* means getting relief from these constant anxieties.

This is possible only when we give up our nonsense idea that this world is meant for us to enjoy and we take to the devotional service of Kṛṣṇa and act as His servant. Otherwise, it is not possible. We can take up devotional service in the association of a learned philosopher who is actually self-realized and who knows Kṛṣṇa as He is. Hare Kṛṣṇa. Any questions? [*Pause.*]

MR MAHESH: Swamijī, we have been hearing about you from Sudāmā.

SUDĀMĀ: Mr. Mahesh is the President of the Kobe Hindu Association and he owns many cloth factories. He is even the owner of this apartment building.

MR MAHESH: I am nothing. Everything is the grace of Lord.

PRABHUPĀDA: So, where does your cloth come from? It is also the grace of the Lord?

MR MAHESH: Certainly, everything is from Bhagavān.

PRABHUPĀDA: Oh, you are stealing from Bhagavān? [*Everyone laughs.*]

MR MAHESH: Swamijī, I am not just taking, I am also giving charity.

PRABHUPĀDA: Oh, you are just little thief. [*Everyone laughs.*]

SUDĀMĀ: And Mr. Santanam is the President of the Kobe branch of the Bank of India.

PRABHUPĀDA: *Jaya.*

MR. SANTANAM: Swamijī, I have been wanting to meet you for many years. I am knowing Sudāmā Dāsa since he first came to Tokyo.

PRABHUPĀDA: Thank you.

MR. SANTANAM: Swamijī, I am born *brāhmaṇa* and…

PRABHUPĀDA: [*Cuts him off.*] No. *Kalau śūdra sambhavaḥ.* Everyone in Kali-yuga is born *śūdra.*

MR. SANTANAM: No, your disciples are better than me, even though I am born *brāhmaṇa.* You can see my thread.

PRABHUPĀDA: No. Everyone in Kali-yuga is born a *śūdra.*

MR. SANTANAM: But I have a sacred thread.

PRABHUPĀDA: One thread costs a few *paisa.* Thread is not the test of a *brāhmaṇa.* Everyone in Kali-yuga is born a *śūdra,* still anyone can buy thread. But one must become trained by qualification to become a *brāhmaṇa. Bhagavad-gītā* says: *cātur-varṇyaṁ mayā sṛṣṭaṁ, guṇa-karma-vibhāgaśaḥ.* Kṛṣṇa says *guṇa-karma,* by qualities, not *janma-karma,* not by birth. *Śamo damas tapaḥ śaucaṁ.* These are the qualities of a *brāhmaṇa.* It is not by birth; it is by qualities. [*Pause.*]

SUDĀMĀ: Prabhupāda, Mr. Mahesh is considering donating this building to us for us to use as a temple.

MR MAHESH: Yes, I am considering, but there are so many factors involved.

PRABHUPĀDA: Your building is very nice. It would make a nice temple. What is the difficulty in giving this building for Kṛṣṇa's use?

MR MAHESH: Actually, this building is where my niece and elder brother are staying. All three floors are presently occupied. But, um, we can speak about this matter tomorrow. [*Pause.*] About the program tonight. We have rented one big hall and many Kobe families will be there. And one favorite Swamijī is also speaking. Most of our local families can speak English and Hindi, so you can speak as you like.

PRABHUPĀDA: My disciples do not know Hindi, so I will speak in English.

[*Bhūrijana pays obeisances and exits.*]

MR MAHESH: The other Swamijī, Swami Kaivalya, does not know English. You have heard of Swami Kaivalya?

PRABHUPĀDA: No. What is his philosophy? He is Vaiṣṇava?

MR MAHESH: Hmmm, I think he is not Vaiṣṇava. But actually, in our Hindu religion, all paths are same and all is one.

PRABHUPĀDA: All is one? So we can just take your building?

MR MAHESH: Um. Actually, Swamijī, there are many Hindu families here in Kobe. They are all interested in seeing you. All have heard of the famous Hare Kṛṣṇa Swamijī. And everyone will be coming tonight. If the program is successful, they can support one Hindu temple for your devotees to run in Kobe.

PRABHUPĀDA: What is this Hindu? Hindu means hodgepodge. All is one. This is nonsense. Where is the word "Hindu" mentioned in *śāstra?* In *Bhagavad-gītā*? In *Vedas*? Anywhere? Where is this "Hindu" mentioned even one time? Anyplace? One place?

MR MAHESH: Um.

PRABHUPĀDA: [*To Mr. Santanam.*]: You are born in a *brāhmaṇa* family. Any one place? No, this Hindu is a name given by Mohammedans. They cannot pronounce Indus River, so they are calling those on the other side Hindus in their own pronunciation. You know this? [*Pause.*] You don't know. But you can learn. To learn, one must approach a bona fide spiritual master and hear from him. This is the process. *Tad viddhi praṇipātena paripraśnena sevayā.* We must serve him and inquire from him. Then he will train us to see the truth. By training we can develop.

MR. SANTANAM: Swamijī, who is real guru?

PRABHUPĀDA: A guru knows Kṛṣṇa. *Premāñjana-cchurita-bhakti-vilocanena.* His eyes are decorated with love of Kṛṣṇa. He can see Kṛṣṇa everywhere. Become trained by such a spiritual master, and then you will understand everything. We are not Hindus and we are not training these boys to become Hindus. We are training them to love Kṛṣṇa, God.

[*Bhūrijana enters.*]

BHŪRIJANA: Prabhupāda, excuse me. Your breakfast is ready in the next room.

MR MAHESH: [*Stands up.*] We must go now anyway, and we will meet again tonight at the program.

MR. SANTANAM: Yes.

[*Prabhupāda exits.*]

MR MAHESH: Swamijī is very strong.

SUDĀMĀ: He is seeing Kṛṣṇa, he must be strong.

BHŪRIJANA: Sudāmā, ask about the garland money.

SUDĀMĀ: Mr. Mahesh, we must get Prabhupāda a nice garland for the program tonight. You can please give us some yen to purchase flowers?

MR MAHESH: Yen for flowers? How much? Here, take one thousand.

SUDĀMĀ: That will get about two roses.

MR MAHESH: How much do you need?

SUDĀMĀ: At least 10,000 yen.

MR MAHESH: 10,000! So much? All right, here is 10,000 yen. But you must make one garland for Swami Kaivalya as well.

SUDĀMĀ: But that's not enough yen for two garlands. Flowers are so expensive that it'll hardly be enough for one.

MR MAHESH: That's all I can give you. And make two garlands. Swamijī should be at the hall at 7:00 for the program; you please come at 6:30.

[*Mr. Mahesh and Mr. Santanam leave.*]

BHŪRIJANA: Sudāmā, I've got an idea how we can solve the garland problem. But anyway, it looks like the program tonight might bring some problems of its own.

Scene Three, at the Rented Hall

MR MAHESH: [*Looks at his watch and says to himself.*] It is already ten minutes before 7:00 and Swami Prabhupāda and his Hare Kṛṣṇa devotees have not arrived yet. [*Looks around.*] So many have come to see the Hare Kṛṣṇa guru. [*Bearded, fifty-year-old Swami Kaivalya, dressed in saffron and wearing tri-punja Māyāvādī tilaka, enters.*] Ah, Swami Kaivalya, you have just come. So many people are here, isn't it?

SWAMI KAIVALYA: *Daṇḍavat,* Maheshjī.

MR MAHESH: Oh, I see the Hare Kṛṣṇa devotees. Please, Swamijī, please take your seat. [*Mr. Mahesh seats Swami Kaivalya in one of the folding chairs that have been set up in rows.*] We will be ready very soon. You are ready to lecture?

SWAMI KAIVALYA: *Haṅ jī.*

MR MAHESH: We should be starting soon.

[*Sudāmā and Bhūrijana enter.*]

Mr Mahesh: Ah, welcome, welcome. Swami is coming? I think he will be happy. So many of our Kobe Hindus have come to see him. Already 150 families are here and more are coming every minute. He is very popular. And of course our Swamijī Kaivalya is here too.

Bhūrijana: Oh, Swami Kaivalya is here. Where? I have a garland for him. Hold Prabhupāda's garland, Sudāmā.

[*Bhūrijana hands Sudāmā a long garland of roses and holds a second garland.*]

Mr Mahesh: Both are very nice garlands. You have done well.

[*Bhūrijana and Sudāmā approach Swami Kaivalya. Bhūrijana pays his obeisances and offers the garland he is holding to Swami Kaivalya, who returns praṇāmas.*]

Bhūrijana: [*To Sudāmā.*] He doesn't speak any English, does he?

Sudāmā: No, only Hindi. Anyway, how did you manage to get two garlands worth of flowers out of 10,000 yen?

Bhūrijana: [*Whispers.*] The 10,000 yen all went toward Prabhupāda's garland. Our Māyāvādī Swamijī is at this very moment getting full benefit from wearing Prabhupāda's remnants – the garland Prabhupāda wore yesterday.

Sudāmā: Pretty good, Bhūrijana.

[*Mr. Mahesh walks over.*]

Mr Mahesh: Now, Hare Kṛṣṇa. When your Swami comes, he can sit there, on the chair just next to Swami Kaivalya. Who is speaking first?

[*Sudāmā looks around.*]

Sudāmā: No, no, Mr. Mahesh. Prabhupāda shouldn't sit in an ordinary chair. You know how important he is. When was the last time you had such a large gathering of your local Indians?

Mr Mahesh: *Accha.*

Sudāmā: Prabhupāda should be sitting on a *vyāsāsana*, an elevated seat. He should sit on that big seat over there.

Mr Mahesh: That cannot be. That seat is for *Guru Grantha.* Our Sindhi tradition is that whoever reads the *Guru Grantha*, he must sit on this seat. Swamijī cannot.

Bhūrijana: Prabhupāda should sit on it.

Sudāmā: Prabhupāda *must* sit on it.

BHŪRIJANA: And we better get Prabhupāda's *vyāsāsana* ready fast because Prabhupāda will be here in just a few minutes.

[*Bhūrijana takes Prabhupāda's garland from Sudāmā and then exits. He returns with vases of flowers and places them on the vyāsāsana and he again exits.*]

SUDĀMĀ: Please, Mr. Mahesh. Prabhupāda is such an exalted soul. He's not an ordinary *sannyāsī*. Please. He should be shown all respect.

MR MAHESH: All right, all right. The lecturers can all sit on the *āsana*.

SUDĀMĀ: Don't you think Prabhupāda should speak first?

MR MAHESH: Why?

SUDĀMĀ: Prabhupāda is senior to Swami Kaivalya by a lot. And not only that, but...

MR MAHESH: All right, all right.

[*Bhūrijana excitedly enters from the right.*]

BHŪRIJANA: Prabhupāda's here!

[*Prabhupāda enters wearing the long rose garland.*]

SUDĀMĀ AND BHŪRIJANA: *Jaya* Prabhupāda! *Jaya* Prabhupāda!

[*They sing as they lead Prabhupāda from the side of the stage to the vyāsāsana. Prabhupāda walks up the steps and sits on the vyāsāsana.*]

PRABHUPĀDA: You can start *kīrtana* now.

SUDĀMĀ:

nama oṁ viṣṇu-pādāya kṛṣṇa-preṣṭhāya bhū-tale
śrīmate bhaktivedānta-svāmin iti nāmine

namas te sārasvate deve gaura-vāṇī-pracāriṇe
nirviśeṣa-śūnyavādi-pāścātya-deśa-tāriṇe

śrī-kṛṣṇa-caitanya prabhu nityānanda
śrī-advaita gadādhara śrīvāsādi-gaura-bhakta-vṛnda

hare kṛṣṇa hare kṛṣṇa kṛṣṇa kṛṣṇa hare hare
hare rāma hare rāma rāma rāma hare hare

RESPONSE: [*Only by Prabhupāda's disciples. The Kobe Indians simply stare.*]

hare kṛṣṇa hare kṛṣṇa kṛṣṇa kṛṣṇa hare hare
hare rāma hare rāma rāma rāma hare hare

[*Kīrtana continues for fiveteen minutes with the few ISKCON devotees chanting and dancing enthusiastically before the amazed audience of Kobe Indian families.*]

SUDĀMĀ: *hare kṛṣṇa hare kṛṣṇa kṛṣṇa kṛṣṇa hare hare*
hare rāma hare rāma rāma rāma hare hare

RESPONSE: *hare kṛṣṇa hare kṛṣṇa kṛṣṇa kṛṣṇa hare hare*
hare rāma hare rāma rāma rāma hare hare

PRABHUPĀDA: *Jaya oṁ viṣṇu-pāda paramahaṁsa parivrājakācārya aṣṭottara-śata śrī śrīmad Śrīla Bhaktisiddhānta Sarasvatī Gosvāmī Mahārāja Prabhupāda kī jaya! Śrī śrī rādhā-kṛṣṇa gopa-gopīnatha śyāma-kuṇḍa, rādhā-kuṇḍa, giri-govardhana kī jaya!*

All glories to the assembled devotees. All glories to the assembled devotees. All glories to Śrī Śrī Guru and Gaurāṅga.

BHŪRIJANA: *Jaya oṁ viṣṇu-pāda paramahaṁsa parivrājakācārya aṣṭottara-śata śrī śrīmad His Divine Grace A.C. Bhaktivedanta Swami Śrīla Prabhupāda kī jaya!*

PRABHUPĀDA: *Oṁ namo bhagavate vāsudevāya.* [*Three times. Only Prabhupāda's disciples respond.*]

We are reading from the *Bhagavad-gītā*, second chapter, verse seventeen:

avināśi tu tad viddhi
yena sarvam idaṁ tatam
vināśam avyayasyāsya
na kaścit kartum arhati

"That which pervades the entire body you should know to be indestructible. No one is able to destroy that imperishable soul." So here, Kṛṣṇa clearly says that consciousness, the symptom of the soul, is *avināśi*, imperishable. Previously He said to Arjuna, "You, I, and all these other kings existed in the past, we exist now, and we shall continue to exist in the future."

There is no truth to the rascal Māyāvāda idea that after liberation we all intermingle and become a homogeneous lump. Even after we attain liberation we remain individual particles of consciousness.

This Māyāvāda philosophy is false. We are individuals eternally. Kṛṣṇa will explain that later in the *Bhagavad-gītā: mamaivāṁśo jīva-loke jīva-bhūtaḥ sanātanaḥ*. "The living entities in this material world are My eternal fragmental parts." This is confirmed in the *Upaniṣads: nityo nityānāṁ cetanaś cetanānām,* "Of all the eternal conscious living beings, there is one who is Supreme."

Yesterday we consulted the dictionary about the meaning of the word "God," and one of the definitions was "the Supreme Being." So we are living beings, but we are not supreme; we are subordinate. God is also a living being, but He is the Supreme Being. That is the difference. It is a very simple thing. You cannot say, "I am the Supreme Being." Yet the rascals say, "I am God." How can you be God? Are you Supreme? As soon as we ask this question – "Are you Supreme?" – you must answer, "No." Then how have you become God?

Just try to understand how foolish they are. Will any sane man say, "I am moving the sun, I am moving the moon, I am moving the seas?" Will any sane man say that? No. Will anyone here say that you are moving the sun and the moon? Anyone? Who will say? Nobody will say this. And still these rascals are claiming, "I have become God. We are all God." This rascal atheistic philosophy has killed the whole world. So many so-called "incarnations," so many "gods" are preaching false theories only. So many gurus – all rascals. Take my word for it. Anyone who is speaking against the principles of the *Bhagavad-gītā* is rascal number one. That's all. Don't give him any credit. On every page of the *Bhagavad-gītā* Kṛṣṇa is referred to as Bhagavān, the Supreme Personality of Godhead. Ask anyone if they accept. Ask him to his face: "Do you accept Kṛṣṇa as the Supreme Personality of Godhead?" If he says, "No," tell him, "Then you are a rascal." That's all. There is no exception.

Know that Kṛṣṇa is God, the Supreme. *Īśvaraḥ paramaḥ kṛṣṇaḥ sac-cid-ānanda-vigrahaḥ*. Kṛṣṇa is accepted as God by all the *ācāryas* and by all the Vedic scriptures. And when He was present on earth He proved that He was God. Nobody was equal to Kṛṣṇa when He was personally present.

So let us utilize our minute consciousness to understand the supreme consciousness, God. Although I am conscious, I am not supremely conscious. I am not all-knowing, but God is. So there is always a difference between God and ourselves. We can never be equal to God. That is impossible. We can become His humble servant, but we cannot do so if we think that one day we will become God. Understanding this is real intelligence. Otherwise, it is all rascaldom. Don't be victims of the rascals. Hare Kṛṣṇa. Thank you very much.

SUDĀMĀ: Are there any questions? [*Long pause.*]
MR MAHESH: No questions. Now Swami Kaivalya, you please come.

[*Swami Kaivalya steps to the vyāsāsana with Mr. Mahesh and Mr. Mahesh offers his hand to Prabhupāda to help him down. Mr. Mahesh, again offers Prabhupāda his hand and then again, but Prabhupāda remains sitting on the vyāsāsana.*]
SUDĀMĀ: I think Prabhupāda isn't getting down.
SWAMI KAIVALYA: *Ṭhik, ṭhik.*

[*Mr. Mahesh unhappily leads Swami Kaivalya back to his chair. He then carries the microphone from the vyāsāsana and sets it up in front of Swami Kaivalya.*]
MR MAHESH: You can speak from here.

[*Swami Kaivalya sits down and Mr. Mahesh announces.*]
MR MAHESH: Now we request Swami Kaivalya to speak about his philosophy.

[*Swami Kaivalya stands up, offers praṇāmas to the audience, closes his eyes and begins lecturing in Hindi.*]
SWAMI KAIVALYA: *Oṁ... Oṁ... Oṁ.*
BHŪRIJANA: [*After a few minutes, to Sudāmā.*]: Look, I can't even tell if Prabhupāda's listening to the Māyāvādī speak. He's just sitting and chanting with his eyes closed.
SUDĀMĀ: We might as well chant too. We can't understand a thing.

[*Sudāmā, Bhānu, and Bhūrijana put their hands in their bead bags and softly chant, rocking back and forth as they imitate Prabhupāda's movements.*]

BHŪRIJANA: [*After a few minutes.*] I'm bored.

SUDĀMĀ: Prabhupāda doesn't look bored.

BHŪRIJANA: At least Swami Kaivalya is wearing Prabhupāda's garland. I wonder what he's ranting and raving about?

SUDĀMĀ: I can't imagine, but look at how intense Prabhupāda seems.

BHŪRIJANA: [*After a few minutes.*] It seems like he's been going on and on for about an hour already.

BHĀNU: No, he's been speaking thirty minutes. I've been timing him.

SUDĀMĀ: I wonder how much longer this is going to last. [*Pause.*]

BHŪRIJANA: Sudāmā, look at Prabhupāda. He seems disturbed by something. He's looking all around.

SUDĀMĀ: Prabhupāda *is* disturbed, isn't he?

BHŪRIJANA: What's going on?

SUDĀMĀ: What's the Māyāvādī saying?

[*Prabhupāda looks from one disciple to another.*]

PRABHUPĀDA: [*Suddenly and strongly.*] Stop him!

[*Bhūrijana and Sudāmā are shocked and don't quite know what to do. Bhūrijana's body tenses, and he begins fingering the strings of the karatālas in his hand. Prabhupāda looks at his disciples intensely, and then looks Bhūrijana right in the eye.*]

PRABHUPĀDA: Stop him! [*Two-second pause.*] Start *kīrtana*! Immediately!

[*The devotees jump up and begin loudly chanting Hare Kṛṣṇa. They bang their karatālas and dance.Swami Kaivalya looks around and without much ado, makes praṇāmas, says daṇyavat, and sits down. Mr. Mahesh stands up, looks at Swami Kaivalya, looks at the devotees and at Prabhupāda, and walks off.*]

Scene Four, Prabhupāda's room in the apartment

[*Prabhupāda is sitting on the floor behind a low desk in a dimly lit room. He peacefully sips hot milk. Bhānu is attending him.*]

PRABHUPĀDA: Have the others come yet?

BHĀNU: No, Prabhupāda. They stayed after the *kīrtana* to distribute your books.

PRABHUPĀDA: That is good.

BHĀNU: Would you like some more milk?

PRABHUPĀDA: No, this is sufficient. What is that sound? See if Sudāmā and Bhūrijana have come.

[*Bhānu leaves and comes back after a few seconds.*]

BHĀNU: Yes, they've just arrived and they say Mr. Mahesh has come with them.

[*Sudāmā and Bhūrijana enter and offer their obeisances.*]

SUDĀMĀ AND BHŪRIJANA: *Jaya* Prabhupāda!

PRABHUPĀDA: So the people appreciated our program? Did they take books?

BHŪRIJANA: Some bought books, Prabhupāda, but most really couldn't at all understand what happened.

SUDĀMĀ: And to tell you the truth, Prabhupāda, neither did we. The Māyāvādī spoke in Hindi, so we couldn't understand anything. You let him speak for thirty minutes and then suddenly you stopped him. What happened?

BHŪRIJANA: We just wanted to come to see you as fast as we could.

SUDĀMĀ: We ran up the three flights of stairs.

[*Mr. Mahesh enters.*]

MR MAHESH: Swamijī, so many people could not understand why you have done that.

PRABHUPĀDA: [*Laughs.*] My Guru Mahārāja used to describe his preaching style as a chopping technique. [*Prabhupāda "chops" his right hand a few times into the open palm of his left.*] I have also adopted it. [*Laughs.*] These Māyāvādīs think of themselves as Vedāntists. *Dānta* means teeth and *vi* means no. So in front of the Vaiṣṇava *ācāryas,* all their big, big arguments have got no teeth. Just like they say: "We are all God but have forgotten." God has forgotten? How is that? How forgetfulness has covered God? That means forgetfulness is greater than God. No sane man will accept this.

SUDĀMĀ: *Jaya* Prabhupāda!

PRABHUPĀDA: So we should not tolerate their toothless arguments.

This Māyāvāda philosophy is just atheism. "We are all God." Nonsense! They are actually saying there is no God!

MR MAHESH: No, no, no. They are saying that truth is one. There are many paths and one truth.

PRABHUPĀDA: Just atheism. It has spoiled the world. Just see. People have given up worshiping God. They are practically not humans. They are killing cows. They are killing their own children in the womb. And they call this advancement of civilization. They are condemned. They are thinking as soon as the body dies, everything is finished, so let me now enjoy. But this is ignorance. They will not die. *Dehino 'smin yathā dehe.* They will live. *Na hanyate hanyamāne śarīre.* They will live for so many lifetimes and suffer – birth after birth – if we do not help them. [*Pause.*] So you have made yourself a successful businessman. Do you think Māyāvāda philosophy is good business? What do you think?

MR MAHESH: I think everything in our Hindu religion is one of tolerance to other paths. All religions bring us nearer to the God.

[*Prabhupāda gets very serious, and the corners of his mouth seem to extend down almost to the edges of his chin.*]

PRABHUPĀDA: Hmm. They are misguiding people away from Kṛṣṇa.

MR MAHESH: They are trying…

PRABHUPĀDA: … to make everyone forget Kṛṣṇa. "Not to Kṛṣṇa," they say. "Do not surrender to Kṛṣṇa. Surrender to the unborn, unmanifest within Kṛṣṇa." They don't know Kṛṣṇa is Absolute. He is the same in and out. They don't know and still they speak. That means they are cheaters.

MR MAHESH: So many opinions about truth are there.

PRABHUPĀDA: Yes, opinions. But from *śāstra* no one can avoid accepting Kṛṣṇa as the Supreme Personality of Godhead. It is insanity to avoid. All the Vedic literature. *Ṛg Veda* says: *oṁ tad viṣṇoḥ paramaṁ padam. Upaniṣad, Purāṇas, Gītā.* They all say Kṛṣṇa's form, His activities, everything is eternal.

MR MAHESH: Why just Kṛṣṇa?

PRABHUPĀDA: Why *not* Kṛṣṇa. The *śāstra* says Kṛṣṇa. *Īśvaraḥ paramaḥ kṛṣṇaḥ sac-cid-ānanda-vigrahaḥ. Śāstra* says, so we are also saying.

MR MAHESH: But Swamijī, *śāstra* also says God is everything.

PRABHUPĀDA: Oh, God is everything. If God is everything, why don't you worship Kṛṣṇa? Simply envy, that is all. Worship everything, but not Kṛṣṇa. Don't worship Kṛṣṇa's form. Don't hear of His activities. No face. No eyes. Practically you want to mutilate Kṛṣṇa. This is Māyāvāda philosophy.

MR MAHESH: Form is there, but one can go beyond to see.

PRABHUPĀDA: No! There is no beyond Kṛṣṇa. Kṛṣṇa says, *Ahaṁ sarvasya prabhavo:* "I am the source of everything." *Mattaḥ parataraṁ nānyat.* No "beyond Kṛṣṇa." We accept Kṛṣṇa's words. We don't tolerate this Māyāvādī nonsense. We are right. Everyone who disagrees with Kṛṣṇa is wrong.

MR MAHESH: [*Gets up and starts walking out.*] I think my apartment is not suitable for your Hare Kṛṣṇa temple. It has too many stories for walking up. Local people will not come.

[*Mr. Mahesh leaves. Three-second pause.*]

SUDĀMĀ: So much for our Kobe temple.

PRABHUPĀDA: [*Laughing.*] Never mind, one day he will appreciate how we have chastised him for his rascaldom. [*Pause.*] Actually, he is simply attached to his apartment house. He can become a mouse in his next life and live here, if he is so attached. [*Laughs and makes a chopping gesture.*] [*Pause.*]

BHŪRIJANA: Prabhupāda, you never told us why you listened to the Māyāvādī for thirty minutes and then stopped him.

PRABHUPĀDA: First, the Māyāvādī's preaching was all right, but then he began explaining *pañcopāsanā.*

SUDĀMĀ: *Pañcopāsanā?*

PRABHUPĀDA: *Pañcopāsanā* is when they recommend worship of five kinds of demigods. First worship Sūrya, then Gaṇeśa, then Durgādevī, Śiva, and Viṣṇu.

SUDĀMĀ: So that's what he was saying.

PRABHUPĀDA: Yes, so he was explaining this *pañcopāsanā*, their worship system, and then he started to say, "But one must ultimately go beyond this worship and one must give it up – because the Supreme is beyond worship. The Supreme is Brahman, formless." [*Pause for two seconds.*] And I could not tolerate that.

SUDĀMĀ: Whew.

PRABHUPĀDA: How could I tolerate this blasphemy? No, I could not. And neither could my Guru Mahārāja – "*rūpānuga-viruddhāpa-siddhānta-dhvānta-hāriṇe.*" He would not tolerate any statement against the authority of Śrīla Rūpa Gosvāmī.

BHŪRIJANA: You are a perfect servant of your Guru Mahārāja, Prabhupāda.

PRABHUPĀDA: These Māyāvādīs, they talk: "All is one," "The Supreme has no form," "All is illusion," but then when they get a little success, they build some hospital. Just see.

BHŪRIJANA: If everything is illusion, a dream, why cure a disease that a person is only dreaming? Better to wake him up.

PRABHUPĀDA: Yes, so they build hospitals and show that they have fallen from their own philosophy. They cannot themselves follow this Māyāvāda nonsense. Even the biggest Māyāvādīs fall down like this.

SUDĀMĀ: Or worse.

[*Two-second pause.*]

BHĀNU: Prabhupāda, must all Māyāvādīs fall down?

PRABHUPĀDA: Yes.

BHĀNU: Always?

PRABHUPĀDA: Yes.

SUDĀMĀ: Why, Prabhupāda?

[*Pause.*]

PRABHUPĀDA: Because they get lonely. [*Pause.*] The living entity must be active. It is his nature. Even in Brahman he longs for some activity. Always. So in Brahman he cannot stay inactive and he has no qualification to serve Kṛṣṇa in Vaikuṇṭha, so he must fall down. You can understand? This Māyāvāda is the last trap of *māyā*. Forget Kṛṣṇa, don't serve Kṛṣṇa, I am God, you are God. [*Laughs.*] But it is not attractive. And Kṛṣṇa is so attractive. His name, form, pastimes – with His cowherd boyfriends or Mother Yaśodā or the *gopīs*. So attractive. Anyone who comes in contact with Kṛṣṇa – even by hearing about Him – becomes mad after His association. [*Pause.*] So when Māyāvādīs hear from Kṛṣṇa's pure devotees, they also give up their nonsense loneliness and become devotees. [*Pause.*]

SUDĀMĀ: I think it's late Prabhupāda, and the train leaves early in the morning. We should take your leave and let you take rest.

PRABHUPĀDA: All right. Hare Kṛṣṇa.

[*All the devotees pay their obeisances and leave. Bhūrijana stays back.*]

BHŪRIJANA: You were like a lion at the program tonight.

PRABHUPĀDA: Yes, when I am out, I am like a lion in the chase, but when I am home with the devotees, I am like a lamb.

BHŪRIJANA: *Jaya* Prabhupāda!

[*Pays obeisances and leaves.*]

Manila, 1972

Preaching in the Philippines

Back in Hong Kong, several months after visiting Prabhupāda in Japan, I received an aerogram from Prabhupāda informing me of his plan to visit to the Philippines. He suggested I join him at our Manila temple. I was thrilled at his invitation and telegraphed Sudāmā Vipra Swami, the devotee who had begun the Filipino preaching. Sudāmā Vipra telegrammed back his surprise. Due to the recently imposed martial law, he hadn't received word of Prabhupāda's arrival.

A week before Prabhupāda was due, Jagattāriṇī and I flew to Manila and caught a taxi to our temple on Ortega Street in San Juan, a Manila suburb. We were shocked. The rented temple actually *was* a mansion. And it was bustling with both shaved-up and long-haired Filipino devotees. Our own small Hong Kong center was dead compared to this newly opened temple in Manila. There were so many happy Filipinos busy in Kṛṣṇa's service.

A devotee construction crew was assembling a new altar and a new *vyāsāsana* for Prabhupāda. The *vyāsāsana* was huge – "so

Prabhupāda would feel comfortable enough to speak for hours," Sudāmā Vipra Swami said. In the evenings, the construction noise stopped and the devotees would settle into a sweet *kīrtana*. What a contrast to the drab Hong Kong Chinese, whose mood was summed up in the Cantonese maxim, *mo chin mo gong* "no money, no talk."

The day before Prabhupāda's arrival, Sudāmā Vipra Swami pulled out the screens of the windows to allow air to flow in the humid Manila evenings, "the way Prabhupāda likes it." The next morning we picked up Prabhupāda and his entourage from the new Manila Airport (the old one had recently and mysteriously burned down after the anti-corruption wing of the police said they would investigate the airport manager's financial records). We drove Prabhupāda to his suite in the Manila Hotel Intercontinental, the best hotel in the city, because our rented temple in San Juan had no suitable facility. Smiling and always in Vṛndāvana, Prabhupāda gathered us on the floor around him while he sat cross-legged behind a round glass table.

Sudāmā Vipra Swami broached the subject of me moving from Hong Kong to the Philippines to assist him:

SUDĀMĀ VIPRA SWAMI: Prabhupāda, what about Bhūrijana staying in the Philippines to help with the preaching?

BHŪRIJANA: Hong Kong is such a materialistic place. Not many people are coming to our Hong Kong temple and so many are coming in Manila. It seems a better place for me to preach.

PRABHUPĀDA: But Hong Kong is so important city. It is the Chinese gateway. And one third of all the people of the world live in China.

BHŪRIJANA: But not many Chinese people are coming. Only Indians, and the Indians in Hong Kong are interested only in making money. They aren't serious about spiritual life. It takes the entire month for me to collect the rent for our apartment-temple!

PRABHUPĀDA: When a university class is going on, even if only one student is in attendance, it must not be closed.

BHŪRIJANA: But maintaining the temple is such a strain.

When I explained to Prabhupāda that we were now forced to spend 3,000 Hong Kong dollars (about 600 U.S.) on rent each month Prabhupāda became sympathetic and reluctantly agreed to our closing the Hong Kong temple in favor of us preaching in the Philippines.

* * *

Prabhupāda once told me that closing a temple was a disgrace. I held out for years in Hong Kong because of this, but the impenetrable materialism was discouraging, especially when contrasted with the lightness and receptivity of the Philippines. Prabhupāda looked at my case pragmatically, especially the amount of time it took me to collect the rent, and agreed to my request.

Guru's Words

Sudāmā Vipra Swami, Siddha-svarūpānanda Goswami, Śrutakīrti, Jagattāriṇī, and I sat around Prabhupāda's table, watching him as he ate fresh Filipino fruit – mangoes, bananas, and apples – for breakfast. Prabhupāda wanted milk, and sent Śrutakīrti out. Śrutakīrti was his new servant, and he was fresh from America. After ten minutes, Śrutakīrti returned pot in hand, complaining that the hotel staff wouldn't cooperate.

Prabhupāda insisted that he wanted hot milk and Śrutakīrti left again for the hotel kitchen. Ten minutes passed and Śrutakīrti again returned with cold milk. The staff wouldn't let him into the hotel kitchen.

Prabhupāda looked sharply at Śrutakīrti, "You are not serious!"

Sudāmā Vipra Swami, "Big Dave," heavy set, with a skull and crossbones tattooed on his arm, picked up the milk pot and walked out. He returned five minutes later with steaming hot milk. "Sometimes you have to yell, Śrīla Prabhupāda," he said.

Prabhupāda smiled.

* * *

A key to associating with Prabhupāda was to take all he said as weighty. No words or requests, even if spoken in a casual manner, were casual. My experience was that Kṛṣṇa reciprocated when we respected all of Prabhupāda's words with the utmost deference.

LSD Philosophy

Also sitting with us was Nilo Santos, a young member of the wealthy Manila aristocracy. Nilo liked to chant Hare Kṛṣṇa. Prabhupāda asked, "So what was your philosophy before you chanted Hare Kṛṣṇa?" Nilo smiled and said innocently, "LSD philosophy." Prabhupāda returned an even bigger smile, "Oh, so many of our students also followed that philosophy. Isn't that correct, Siddha-svarūpa?"

* * *

The Philippines had been transformed by the movie *The Godfather*. After it hit the Filipino movie theaters, gangs of imitation Mafia groups suddenly appeared, along with organized crime, real guns, and real killing. This fad lasted until the *Woodstock* movie was released in 1970. Then violence was out and drugs, love, and "LSD philosophy" were in. Yet although the mode had changed, countless souls were still being insidiously slaughtered. Prabhupāda once commented that because of Timothy Leary, "so many blossoming young flowers have become spoiled."

LSD philosophy had spread around the world. Prabhupāda's mercy had similarly spread to combat and cure it.

Drinking Hot, Honeyed Milk

Prabhupāda began to drink the hot milk Sudāmā Vipra Swami had brought. He dipped his spoon into a jar of honey and pulled it out half full. Then he dipped the honey-laden spoon into the milk. When he pulled it out, milk floated above the thick layer of honey still on the spoon. Prabhupāda sipped the milk off the top of the honey. He repeated this process several times until the milk had cooled.

* * *

Seeing Prabhupāda enjoy hot milk in this unique fashion brought us great happiness.

Hong Kong Mangoes

Prabhupāda then ate a long yellow mango. "These are not as good as the mangoes you gave me in Hong Kong," Prabhupāda said to me as his eyes twinkled. "Those mangoes also came from the Philippines," I replied.

A Mountain Surrounded by a Lake

Vijayadvaja, an American devotee serving in the Philippines, cooked for Prabhupāda both morning and noon. Each morning, Vijayadvaja followed Prabhupāda's recipe for *halavā:* one part semolina, two parts water, one part sugar, and one part ghee. The *halavā* looked like a small mountain floating in ghee. Yet Prabhupāda appreciated Vijayadvaja's cooking, especially his *halavā,* commenting, "The quality is sufficient."

Once, however, Vijayadvaja hoped to create a large quantity of remnants by loading up Prabhupāda's lunch plate with *prasāda.* Prabhupāda's comment: "When my plate is so full, I lose my appetite."

* * *

To please the Lord and His devotees is the pleasure of a devotee. Even a grain of selfishness in our attempt spoils the preparation.

Tolerance, Tolerance, Tolerance

Prabhupāda's suite in the Hotel Intercontinental was luxurious. A clay pot with a spigot at the bottom held fresh water. Prabhupāda drank from the pot on the first day because it kept the water cool "just like in India." But when the water was not changed the second day, Prabhupāda would not drink, although he neither complained nor mentioned the oversight.

* * *

In one circumstance Prabhupāda demanded hot milk and in another he tolerated unchanged water. How does a teacher know when to demand and when to tolerate? An expert teacher knows which of his own needs are essential and also knows when a response is required for the advancement of his student.

A Lecture that Filled Me with Fear

I am not a carpenter, but I was asked to construct a bookstand for Prabhupāda. He would use the stand to hold his *Bhagavad-gītā* while he gave the evening lecture. I set to work with borrowed tools and completed it just before Prabhupāda's class. It had a plywood base which tucked under his *vyāsāsana* cushion. Four wooden posts extended upward to support the angled wood stand on which the book rested.

During his first lecture, Prabhupāda preached strongly. As he spoke, he referred again and again to his *Bhagavad-gītā.* At times he held the stand as he rocked back and forth in the rhythm of his lecture. At other times he pushed forward on the bookstand while making his points.*

As soon as Prabhupāda began, I noticed strain on the book stand where the base met the posts. As Prabhupāda rocked back and forth, the posts also began to rock back and forth. I saw a glimmer of silver – the nails above the base. I became afraid. What if it collapses? What if Prabhupāda pushes against the stand and the posts come off? I was sweating. Prayers spontaneously erupted from my heart. I imagined Prabhupāda's enthusiastic preaching splitting the stand in two. Envisioning the stand's collapse, I heard Prabhupāda's voice in my mind demanding, "Who has done this? Who has built this?" I closed my eyes only to open them and focus on the widening gap between the base and the posts. The metal nails glinting in the temple lights seemed to sparkle a promise of my doom.

The lecture was eternal. I heard none of it. Sudāmā Vipra Swami, who was sitting next to me during my ordeal, commented, "Looks like Prabhupāda's lecture really hit you."

* * *

Kṛṣṇa pushed me to the limit. Directly after the lecture, I pounded tens of additional nails into the stand and made it strong enough to withstand the United States Marines. What did I learn? Better to be safe than sorry. Get things built, or at least checked, by experts. When planning for an event, always consider what could possibly go wrong and be ready for it. Be especially careful when serving your spiritual master and exalted Vaiṣṇavas. When a mistake is made, correct it as quickly as possible. Success and failure are ultimately in Kṛṣṇa's hands.

Bāla Kṛṣṇa, Balarāma, and Gaṇeśa?

Jagattāriṇī had grown attached to her Laḍḍu Gopāla Deity, which we began to call Bāla Kṛṣṇa. He was the Deity to whom Prabhupāda had offered his respects in the doll house in Hong Kong. Since then, Jagattāriṇī had added a slightly larger Laḍḍu Gopāla Deity as "Balarāma," and a tiny, one-inch Gaṇeśa deity. She had the three deities with her when we saw Prabhupāda in Manila.

When Jagattāriṇī showed Prabhupāda the group of deities, Prabhupāda encouraged her. "These are your deities. They are very beautiful." He turned to me, "Why Gaṇeśa?" I referred to

The Nectar of Devotion's recommendation that devotees worship Gaṇeśa to remove obstacles in their worship of Kṛṣṇa. Prabhupāda looked at me for a moment and said no more.

* * *

Prabhupāda knew we needed encouragement and companionship in Hong Kong. He always offered encouragement, even to the point of allowing Jagattāriṇī the companionship of personal deities, despite the informality of her worship and despite the worship of Gaṇeśa and his inclusion with Kṛṣṇa and Balarāma.

No Second Center

Jagattāriṇī began carrying the deities everywhere. During one of Prabhupāda's lectures at the temple, Prabhupāda climbed the high *vyāsāsana* steps and began to speak. Jagattāriṇī sat on the floor to the left of the *vyāsāsana* and placed her three deities before her on a velvet cloth. As Prabhupāda spoke, it occurred to her that it may be inappropriate to have the deities on the floor, so she carefully transferred them to the steps of Prabhupāda's *vyāsāsana.*

When the lecture ended and Prabhupāda was ready to climb down the steps, he saw the deities. Jagattāriṇī had been slow in removing them. He beckoned her forward. "When you are here, you can place the deities on the temple altar. You should not establish another center in the temple."

* * *

Prabhupāda waited for the perfect moment to instruct us about the general standard for devotees living in temples. Temples should have one center. Rather than individual devotees conducting independent worship, temple devotees should rally around the temple center, the temple deities.

Two Lotuses Near Kṛṣṇa and Balarāma

Jagattāriṇī followed Prabhupāda's order to keep the deities on the altar, but she still occasionally carried the deities with her in a box. On the final day of Prabhupāda's visit, we sat around Prabhupāda as he relaxed behind the round, glass hotel table. Jagattāriṇī placed the deities and their cloth on the table as Prabhupāda began his breakfast.

Prabhupāda viewed the deities as he took *prasāda*. When he finished and his plate had been removed, he moved to put his feet up on the table. Seeing the deities, he hesitated, then stretched his legs out on the floor. Later, as he continued speaking, he again went to put his feet on the table, but again saw the deities and stopped. Finally, he placed both feet on the table and continued speaking.

* * *

We were so foolish that we neglected to remove the deities even after Prabhupāda's two indirect requests. In our childish simplicity, we were satisfied to see Prabhupāda's lotus feet on the breakfast table near the deities. Jagattāriṇī, of course, quickly removed the deities, appreciating how Prabhupāda was completely relaxed and had acted without adding to her embarrassment.

Expertise

Sudāmā Vipra Swami arranged a lecture for Prabhupāda in the hotel's enormous, elegantly decorated banquet hall. Despite the government's ban on advertising, the news spread and the hall was packed. Five hundred Indians and Filipinos attended. Immediately after his lecture, Prabhupāda called for questions.

An Indian man stood up and said in a loud voice, "Isn't it true that the all-inclusive conception of the Absolute..." He rambled on. After about three minutes, the audience began fidgeting.

Prabhupāda leaned toward the microphone and asked, "Are you finished?"

"No," the man retorted, and he continued for another two minutes. Again Prabhupāda asked, "Are you finished yet?"

"No, let me speak." His monologue of disjointed, spiritual-sounding phrases continued. After another three minutes, the audience began to wax angry. Prabhupāda again gently spoke into the microphone, "Are you finished yet?"

"Yes, now I am finished."

Prabhupāda thundered into the microphone, "Then sit down!" The banquet hall filled with laughter and cheering.

* * *

Had Prabhupāda interrupted the man before he was able to "ask" his self-serving "question," the audience would have favored the man. Prabhupāda waited and allowed the man to parade his foolishness. When the audience had had sufficient time to realize the man's motives, Prabhupāda, with the full backing of the audience, demanded that the man sit down. Prabhupāda was expert.

Practical Bravery

We visited Prabhupāda in his room during the day. In the evening, we would see him during the *kīrtana* and lecture at the temple in San Juan.

On the first day, Prabhupāda traveled from the hotel to San Juan through the late afternoon traffic. The air was filled with smog, there was a traffic jam, and the Filipino drivers drove wildly. On the second day, a lorry almost smashed into Prabhupāda's car.

Prabhupāda went to the temple that second day, but he said the roads were unsafe and never went again.

* * *

Prabhupāda would tolerate unlimited personal inconvenience to help a disciple or to spread Kṛṣṇa consciousness. He was fearless. He had continued preaching in Calcutta even when his life was threatened by Naxalite extremists. Yet ISKCON and its worldwide preaching depended on him. Therefore he chose not to risk the Manila traffic just to give a lecture at the San Juan temple. Prabhupāda was always practical.

A Hong Kong Surprise

Prabhupāda flew on to India after staying in Manila for less than a week. Even though his stay was short, we were energized by his association. Thinking of my future preaching in Manila, I left for Hong Kong to wind up my affairs. A short tour of Hong Kong's intense materialism seemed bearable, and I set out to collect money and ship our temples' possessions to Manila. I also picked up from our Hong Kong publisher a newly printed Chinese edition of *Back to Godhead* magazine. Air-mailing five copies to Prabhupāda in India, I happily returned to Manila – my new preaching field.

But the relief of brighter preaching fields was not meant to be. After only one month of preaching in the Filipino mountain resort city of Bagio, it became clear to me that I belonged in Hong Kong. I returned and just after my first week back, I received a letter from Prabhupāda, written after he received the Chinese BTGs. His reply had been forwarded from the Philippines and it requested that I return to Hong Kong. I immediately telegraphed Prabhupāda my new Hong Kong address. Several days later I received his return telegraph: "May Krishna bless you more and more. Signed. A.C. Bhaktivedanta Swami."

* * *

I read Prabhupāda's telegram and understood that Prabhupāda was blessing me more and more and more and more for eternity. My understanding of the depth of his eternal blessing is shallow, but that does not limit the depth of his blessing. Nor does it limit the eternal good fortune it brings. My lack of spiritual strength, surrender, and determination only allowed me to remain in Hong Kong for another two years, but Prabhupāda's "more and more" blessing keeps afloat my ongoing attempts in devotional service.

Hong Kong, 1974–Part I

I have divided my telling of Prabhupāda's 1974 Hong Kong visit into two chapters. This chapter describes Prabhupāda's attempt to rectify and purify my consciousness.

Struggling and Going Under

We remained preaching in Hong Kong for Prabhupāda's pleasure. Our opportunities to occasionally see him and the letters we received from him gave us the strength to continue. But preaching in Hong Kong was lonely. We had no association with other devotees, since almost no one passed through our Far-Eastern preaching outpost. Those who did visit were often peculiar or rebels. Our ISKCON authority visited periodically, but his mood was hardly positive. Rather than leading or assisting our struggle to preach, he seemed to only either reprimand us or demand money. Our Indian supporters began relaying to us reports of unfavorable results of heavy-handed book distribution techniques in Australia and other parts of the world. We began to get critical of the devotees, thinking them passionate or fanatical in their attempts to spread Kṛṣṇa consciousness.

Jagattāriṇī had not even been initiated before she arrived in Hong Kong. She had flown starry-eyed into an arranged marriage, hoping to save the "unfortunate" Chinese of Hong Kong, but her stars quickly had turned to tears. She suddenly had no women devotee friends and she had a new husband whose New York "culture" and mannerisms appeared harsh to her. She had joined the exciting Los Angeles temple fresh from a budding film career, with months of ecstatic *harināma-saṅkīrtana* on Hollywood Boulevard with Viṣṇujana and sixty other devotees. Then suddenly she was alone in Hong Kong. I asked devotees in the U.S. to send us a householder couple as reinforcements. One wrote back, "Good devotees do not grow on trees." We had Prabhupāda's full support and encouragement, but little else.

We preached to the local Indian community, but discovered that company names like Radha-Krishna Enterprises, Krishna Kripa Exports, and Laksmi-Narayan Traders, did not indicate devotion. We approached wealthy Indian shopkeepers with *Back to Godhead* in hand and were refused its $1 cost. "But we are doing your work! This is the work of those born in India. We have taken it up. At least read our magazine." Their cold, blank stares cracked our hearts.

Prabhupāda then recommended we neglect the Indians and preach to the Chinese. Hong Kong was largely populated by Cantonese businessmen who had escaped from Communist China in the late 1940s. Their ideal was business; their tendency, atheism. In addition, they shared no love with the Hong Kong Indians and looked down on Indian culture. Their conception of Indian religion was "Right hand for eating, left hand for toilet."

Sudāmā Vipra Swami and Tuṣṭa Kṛṣṇa Swami became our friends. Tuṣṭa Kṛṣṇa Swami was successfully preaching in New Zealand, and I had met Sudāmā Vipra Swami when Prabhupāda had sent him to Hong Kong in an attempt to establish preaching in China before he opened the temple in the Philippines. Both Tuṣṭa Kṛṣṇa Swami and Sudāmā Vipra Swami had been followers of charismatic Siddha-svarūpānanda Goswami, then Sai, a 1960s spiritual leader from Hawaii. After Sai mixed Hare Kṛṣṇa chanting into his brew of natural living, meditation, and *kuṇḍalinī-yoga*, he surrendered his *āśrama* and his disciples to Prabhupāda. The Kṛṣṇa conscious style of these devotees, compared to the somewhat tense dealings with other ISKCON devotees, was refreshing, relaxed, friendly – and practical. At this time I did not know that tension existed between Siddha-svarūpa and his followers and Prabhupāda's other disciples.

I gradually adapted Siddha-svarūpa's ideas as an attempt to make our preaching successful in Hong Kong. With Prabhupāda's permission, I grew my hair and wore nondevotee clothes. Prabhupāda, however, insisted we wear *tilaka,* "even if applied thin." We moved our temple room to a smaller room in our flat, and converted the temple room into a typical living room with couches and chairs. We began cooking *prasāda* according to Chinese vegetarian tastes and held *kīrtanas* with *mṛdaṅga, karatālas,* and guitar. Gradually, Chinese people began responding to our *Back to Godhead* distribution and weekly "yoga" meetings at the Hong Kong City Hall, and guests began attending our Sunday Feast and *kīrtanas.* At times we would gather up a group and ferry from crowded Hong Kong to Dai Long Waan, a secluded local beach, take *prasāda*, and chant Hare Kṛṣṇa as the ocean waves rolled in. Chinese people were becoming devotees.

But along with adapting our preaching techniques we also slackened our Kṛṣṇa conscious practices – we began neglecting to hold *maṅgala-ārati* and would just wake up and chant our rounds. I became "too busy" to study Prabhupāda's books. Gradually, the weed of material enjoyment began to attach itself around my tender devotional creeper, and going to the beach to chant and wearing nondevotee clothes were beginning to assume other dimensions than as a preaching tactic. I imagined that Prabhupāda understood and was sanctioning all this due to our increased preaching success.

Real or Imagined Prabhupāda?

One day an aerogram arrived from Prabhupāda's secretary, Satsvarūpa Mahārāja, informing us that Prabhupāda would visit us in two weeks. His letter closed, "Hoping to see you again in Kṛṣṇa consciousness." My left eye twitched. Full of anxiety, I began to prepare for Prabhupāda's second visit to Hong Kong.

On the day of Prabhupāda's arrival, we arranged for a friend to carry the two luxurious rose garlands we would present to Prabhupāda. An acquaintance agreed to allow us the use of his Rolls Royce to drive Prabhupāda from the airport to the Hong Kong Hilton.

Jagattāriṇī and I traveled to the Kai Tak airport by taxi and waited for the garlands, the Rolls Royce, and Prabhupāda. Watching the black flight arrival notice board, I saw Prabhupāda's plane had arrived. Yet neither the garlands nor the Rolls Royce had appeared. I became anxious. "What if Prabhupāda steps out of customs and we don't have a garland for him? What if there's no car?"

After ten more minutes, the board announced that Prabhupāda's flight was clearing customs. I would be seeing him in only a few minutes. Where were the garlands and the Rolls Royce?

Then I saw passengers from Prabhupāda's flight walking down the ramp. A crowd gathered to greet the arriving passengers. My anxiety grew. Still no sign of the garlands or the Rolls Royce. "What will Prabhupāda think?"

My wife's eyes were glued to the gate. My eyes moved rapidly between the incoming passenger gate and the terminal doors. I prayed for a glimpse of rose garlands and a Rolls Royce.

I thought that Prabhupāda would be satisfied by the fine garlands and the luxurious transport. "He'll see that I'm following him properly," I thought. "But what will he think if..."

Suddenly I saw a glimpse of saffron behind the customs barrier. Then Prabhupāda, the guru of the entire world, my spiritual master, stepped from the gate. His deep eyes and countenance scanned the crowd. "I'm finished," I thought. "Prabhupāda's here and there's no garland and no car!"

At that moment Prabhupāda's eyes met mine. He was grave. As if on cue, my friend with the garlands arrived and the Rolls Royce chauffeur walked up a moment later. "Here are the garlands, Bhūrijana." "The car is ready by the south door."

"I'm in *māyā,*" I thought, and I fainted.

* * *

I had been imagining a Prabhupāda that allowed a compromise of purity and Kṛṣṇa conscious practices. When I was suddenly confronted by the real Prabhupāda, the illusory Prabhupāda dissolved like mist after sunrise. Prabhupāda, as he himself said, was "90% liberal," but that other 10% was strict.

Once Prabhupāda invited a disciple to sit with him as he translated *Śrīmad-Bhāgavatam* in the early morning hours. The disciple declined, saying, "I'm already sleeping only five hours a night." When Prabhupāda replied, "But I am sleeping less," the disciple squirmed. "Well, you are a *paramahaṁsa.*" Prabhupāda's answer was strong. "Why you are not *paramahaṁsa?*"

Yes, Prabhupāda was mellow and his association sweet, but please do not imagine that the Kṛṣṇa consciousness movement spread throughout the world by this alone. Prabhupāda also strongly and continuously pushed his disciples and insisted that they strictly follow the rules and regulations and sacrifice everything to satisfy the desires of Śrī Caitanya Mahāprabhu.

The Mercy of a Vaiṣṇava

The black Rolls Royce pulled out from the airport and made its way through heavy traffic from the Kowloon side of the harbor to Hong Kong. My wife and I rode with Prabhupāda in the car's plush back seat. Prabhupāda held his cane as he sat, garlanded with roses, looking like a royal ambassador from the spiritual world. Satsvarūpa Mahārāja sat in the front seat with the driver.

"So nice to see you, Prabhupāda," I smiled, trying to look and feel cheerful. Prabhupāda smiled and asked my wife about her parents, whom he had met in Australia.

Turning to me, he asked, "What is your morning program?"

"Well, Prabhupāda, we don't really have so many guests coming right now, so we usually don't have much of a morning program." My wife quickly closed the glass window between the front and back seats, separating Satsvarūpa Mahārāja from our conversation.

Prabhupāda continued, "Guests may or may not be coming, but why don't you have a morning program? Is your temple in ISKCON? Whose disciple are you?"

"Of course I am your disciple, Prabhupāda." I was getting nervous.

"Then why you don't have a morning program?"

Like a symphony opening with the clash of cymbals, Prabhupāda pointed out my deficiencies and misconceptions. My attempts to defend myself only increased Prabhupāda's attack. By the time the Rolls Royce had passed through the Harbour Tunnel and reached the Hong Kong Hilton, I was exhausted.

* * *

It is both the right and the duty of a spiritual master to criticize his disciples. By that criticism, says Cāṇakya Paṇḍita, good qualities develop. Therefore, at times we hear that it is glorious to be reprimanded by our spiritual master. It is glorious to have him weed the *anarthas* from our heart. But his reprimand is neither romantic nor pleasurable; it's intensely painful. The person we are working so hard to please is angry – even furious – with us. Nor can we rightfully, in defense, deflect the blame to others for our own faults and inabilities. Only by taking responsibility for our actions can we become rectified. Then good qualities can surface.

I can think of two analogies to describe how this mercy felt: open heart surgery without anesthesia and Adam's attempt to hide from God after he had sinned. I remember feeling I had no shelter and nowhere to hide.

Genuine concern for our spiritual lives caused Prabhupāda to act so strongly because he knew that our present path would in time leave no more "Hari Haribol!" We had mixed impurity, the enjoying spirit, into our Kṛṣṇa conscious practices and preaching. We had begun to drift. By asking "Whose disciple are you?" Prabhupāda drew the line: I was his disciple and I had to listen to him.

Despite my own inappropriate behavior, however, I was far

from aware of everything that was causing Prabhupāda's anger. For example, I didn't know that during the previous year, Gaurasundara, who had successfully pioneered the preaching in Hawaii since 1968, and who was also Prabhupāda's GBC representative for South America, had fallen victim to sex and intoxication. Months before his difficulties, Gaurasundara had begun allowing people to worship him as guru. Finally he fell down and sold ISKCON's Honolulu temple. He then disappeared, keeping much money from the temple's sale.

Prabhupāda had traveled to Hawaii from Los Angeles on his way to Hong Kong, yet Gaurasundara had remained aloof, avoiding Prabhupāda's association during his two-week stay. Prabhupāda was furious, and strongly condemned false teachers while he was in Hawaii.

PRABHUPĀDA: That is not our life, to become an impostor. It must be real person. By training, *yaḥ śāstra-vidhim siddhi,* by training under the teaching of a bona fide spiritual master, the *śāstra,* and then you'll automatically, the more you become a sincere, I mean to say, servitor of the spiritual master, the more you become qualified to become a teacher in the future. Otherwise where is your qualification? You may cheat others that you are teacher, but you are not actually teacher. You have no lesson, no education. A cheater is another thing. But practically to become a teacher...Just like in a school, teacher...A teacher is appointed. When the certificate is there that he has passed M.A. examination, and he has undergone the training, B.T., Bachelor training, then he's appointed: "Yes, you can be a teacher." And then a bogus man, he can be...He cannot be accepted as teacher. So that is going on. A bogus man, they're becoming teachers. Therefore the world condition is so degraded. A cheater is taking the place of teacher. Therefore the whole world is degraded.

DEVOTEE: If we have a desire to keep these promises, but we have a hard time to do it...

PRABHUPĀDA: As soon as you fail to keep your promise, then you're fallen. You have to rectify yourself. Immediately you're fallen.

> *Yaḥ śāstra-vidhim utsṛjya vartate kāma-kārataḥ, na sa siddhim.* That means you'll never get perfection. You'll fall down. You can cheat others that I am in dress of a devotee, so I am...What is your character? What is your actual value? That has to be judged. That is call bona fide teacher.

In addition, Siddha-svarūpa, who had been referring to Gaurasundara as his *śikṣā*-guru, had left ISKCON along with his followers. This had seriously affected or closed temples in Hawaii, the Philippines, New Zealand, and Australia. Strain and conflict between Siddha-svarūpa and other disciples of Prabhupāda had always existed over methods used in book distribution – "mellowness" versus a "somehow or other get it done for Prabhupāda" approach – dress, and the degree to which Siddha-svarūpa was revered by his followers. When differences erupted into hostility, however, Siddha-svarūpa left. Prabhupāda had been confronting these points for weeks prior to his Hong Kong visit:

HANUMĀN: ...and they had some temples in Rio de Janeiro and San Pablo, and they were followers of Gaurasundara and Siddha-svarūpa. And I think they're still there. And when I was there they were making *kīrtana,* and they were chanting Hare Kṛṣṇa. In the middle of their *kīrtana,* they would stop their *kīrtana,* and they would chant "*Jaya jaya* Siddha-svarūpa," and "*Jaya jaya* Gaurasundara." So I could not do anything. I told them it was all wrong and everything, and uh...But there is many, many innocent people who are following. They go there for the first time and they make them chant "*Jaya jaya* Siddha-svarūpa" and "*Jaya jaya* Gaurasundara," like this. So we were telling, we were talking with...

PRABHUPĀDA: There is no harm in giving "*jaya*" to Vaiṣṇavas provided they follow the Vaiṣṇava principles. Otherwise, to glorify Vaiṣṇava is not bad. [Pause.] No, no "*jaya*" to Mahāprabhu, Śrī Caitanya Mahāprabhu? They chanted?

SATSVARŪPA: Were they chanting, "*Jaya* Lord Caitanya, Nityānanda Prabhu?"

HANUMĀN: Yes, they were also chanting, "*Bhaja śri-kṛṣṇa caitanya.*"

Yes. But the point is that they were chanting the name of Siddha-svarūpa Goswami and Gaurasundara Goswami, uh, Gaurasundara Adhikārī.

PRABHUPĀDA: If one is Vaiṣṇava, then to glorify him is... that's not

HANUMĀN: So that's all right.

SATSVARŪPA: Just as long as that Vaiṣṇava is following the principles.

PRABHUPĀDA: But they should not attempt like that in the presence of their spiritual master. That is not good. When you found this?

SATSVARŪPA: When did you find they were doing this?

HANUMĀN: When I was there. I was in Brazil about three months ago. And the only books they had published is a book written by Siddha-svarūpa Goswami. They had published one book of him, and they were distributing this.

PRABHUPĀDA: What is the name of that book?

HANUMĀN: It was an introduction to Kṛṣṇa consciousness, question and answer.

PRABHUPĀDA: You have seen that book?

HANUMĀN: Yes, Prabhupāda. I have given to Karandhara.

PRABHUPĀDA: So is there anything awkward against our devotional life?

KARANDHARA: I can't read it. It's in Portuguese.

PRABHUPĀDA: Oh, it was in Portuguese language.

HANUMĀN: Gaurasundara has written some books, and so Siddha-svarūpa, answering the question, quotes from the book of Gaurasundara, and he mentions, "My professor, Gaurasundara, taught me," and he quotes many, many times. Practically more from the book of Gaurasundara than from your books.

And on dress in Hawaii

PRABHUPĀDA: Any questions?

DEVOTEE: Yes, one more.

GUEST: Is the exterior clothing important?

PRABHUPĀDA: Yes, important. Just like officially the policeman must dress, but a policeman sometimes in ordinary cloth also, that's

> his duty. But that is special case. But external, external dress is also required. In the dress of a police if he is a thief, that is very dangerous. That is very dangerous. Just like this dress of *sannyāsī,* saffron cloth, one will respect that "Here is a *sannyāsī.*" But if he is a thief in a dress of a *sannyāsī,* that is dangerous. That is dangerous.

Siddha-svarūpa and his followers had left ISKCON, but they maintained their relationship with Prabhupāda. I was vaguely aware of some of these facts, but Prabhupāda was fully aware of everything, although he was to mention little of the details of these worldwide occurrences to me during his stay. Yet the brunt of his displeasure landed with full force when he arrived in Hong Kong.

Preaching and Reading

Prabhupāda and his entourage rode the elevator to the top floor of the hotel. We had rented him the Thai Suite, the most luxurious rooms in the hotel. A group of about twenty young, interested Chinese waited inside.

Prabhupāda took his seat. He was pleased by the group of interested souls and he began *kīrtana.* His lecture criticized "those who preached but who were not reading." "Without *śravaṇa,* what is the *kīrtana*?" he asked the guests as he looked at me.

* * *

Devotees who are too busy preaching to read Prabhupāda's books should note this instruction. If we don't study, we may not be prepared to fight *māyā:*

> Men become strong and stout by eating sufficient grains, but the devotee who simply eats ordinary grains but does not taste the transcendental pastimes of Lord Caitanya Mahāprabhu and Kṛṣṇa gradually becomes weak and falls down from the transcendental position. However, if one drinks but a drop of the nectar of Kṛṣṇa's

pastimes, his body and mind begin to bloom, and he begins to laugh, sing, and dance.

PURPORT: All the devotees connected with this Kṛṣṇa consciousness movement must read all the books that have been translated (*Caitanya-caritāmṛta, Śrīmad-Bhāgavatam, Bhagavad-gītā,* and others); otherwise, after some time, they will simply eat, sleep, and fall down from their position. Thus they will miss the opportunity to attain an eternal, blissful life of transcendental pleasure.

– *Caitanya-caritāmṛita, Madhya* 25.278

Leading Others

Prabhupāda continued his forceful mood in front of the guests. "So how do you like our lifestyle?" Prabhupāda asked Jagattāriṇī. She paused, looked at Prabhupāda, and ventured, "I don't know." Her tentative answer evoked a heavy reply. "You don't know! You don't know! You are leading others and you 'don't know.'"

* * *

Prabhupāda's words rattled us to the core. Preachers have to practice what they preach. As Prabhupāda told the teachers in the Dallas *gurukula*, "Example is better than precept."

An Offering of a Smiling Face

As Prabhupāda spoke to the guests, he asked me to bring him a *Bhagavad-gītā As It Is*. I couldn't find one. Instant anxiety. Prabhupāda's movement is based on his books and none were at the hotel. I felt foolish. "We don't have any *Bhagavad-gītās* here now, Prabhupāda." He looked at me sternly. "What *do* you have? Only your face."

* * *

The Vedic literature orders us to approach the spiritual master with an offering of firewood, and the Deity with rice or a flower, fruit, or water. We should not approach the guru empty-handed. Our smiling face proudly paraded before him is not always sufficient to bring him pleasure.

Leaving Temples Behind

Later, when we were alone, Prabhupāda started again. "Why did you leave your old temple? It was small, but you had decorated it with so much devotion."

* * *

Our old temple was a small, rented flat in a crowded tourist district, Tsim Tsa Tsui, on the Kowloon side of Hong Kong. The temple walls, along with their cloth decorations, were blackened by the city smog, and the kitchen roof leaked badly. The flat itself was beside a nonvegetarian restaurant, and the fumes nauseated us.

Jagattāriṇī had painstakingly decorated that temple's walls with pictures of Kṛṣṇa. She artistically surrounded the pictures with peacock feathers and imitation jewels. No guest ever expressed appreciation of her work. Now two years later, Prabhupāda remembered the temple and its decorations. Prabhupāda had traveled the world many times since then and visited big American temples, opulent European temples, and seen the work of many powerful devotees. I was moved that Prabhupāda appreciated and remembered our humble devotional offering.

The Fall of Unqualified Gurus

Prabhupāda began criticizing his disciple, Gaurasundara, and his anger was as intense as the monsoon rains. "He wants to be guru, but he is not qualified. All of them, they want to be guru without qualification and they will fall victim to sex life." Prabhupāda then turned to me. "Your wife belongs to Kṛṣṇa. You cannot even enjoy one wife. They all belong to Kṛṣṇa." Prabhupāda continued preaching strongly, "All of them. Even that Swami Satchidananda has fallen down with some Western women."

* * *

I had met Swami Satchidananda, a popular impersonalist guru who had "done well" in the West, at Woodstock and then in Hong Kong. I had noted that his traveling companions were two vampish, dressed-in-black, Western secretaries. Prabhupāda's example of dealing with members of the opposite sex should be noted. As a *sannyāsī* he once refused to be alone in a room with his elderly and saintly sister. We should follow Prabhupāda's example and never challenge the laws of material nature by associating loosely with a member of the opposite sex.

Fortunate, Unfortunate, and Most Unfortunate

The next morning before leaving for his morning walk, Prabhupāda stood with us at the hotel elevator. He was grave, and as he looked straight toward the closed elevator doors, he spoke. "Those who come to Kṛṣṇa consciousness are fortunate. Those who do not come are unfortunate." Prabhupāda became even more grave. "But those who come and leave before they are mature..." He paused and turned to Jagattāriṇī and myself, "...they are *most* unfortunate."

The elevator arrived. Prabhupāda continued to speak from inside. "It seems that some have come to this movement to take." I immediately objected, "No, Prabhupāda, I don't think they have." Without a moment's pause Prabhupāda countered, "But we want them to take."

My head spun. "Yes." Prabhupāda continued, "We want them to take...our rules and regulations!"

* * *

Prabhupāda describes give-and-take in his purport to Mantra Four of *The Nectar of Instruction.* In this exchange, Prabhupāda expressed his consternation that he was freely giving and yet the exchange was incomplete because some did not fully accept his gift of the practices of *sādhana-bhakti.*

Envy and Falldown

Later, during his noon massage, Prabhupāda asked me, "Why they don't associate with the other devotees?"

"I think it is difficult for them because so many devotees are envious that Siddha-svarūpa has so many followers."

"Who is envious?" Prabhupāda challenged.

"Well," I stammered, and I mentioned one devotee's name.

Prabhupāda spoke almost in a whisper. "So he has fallen down. He has written me and told me that he was not able to follow the rules properly, and so he has said that he will leave. But because he feels repentant, he will come back."

* * *

Too often we eagerly correct others and yet remain blind to our own weaknesses. Prabhupāda taught me that criticizing others, even if the criticisms are justified, does not protect one from one's own shortcomings. One is often correct about the faults of others but wrong about his own.

Thinking "I am right (and sincere) and the other person is wrong (and insincere)" is dangerous. To protect our spiritual lives from offenses to other devotees, we should not be callous to their good intentions, and we should also beware of making criticisms that are neither spoken with affection nor truly meant to help. In addition, Prabhupāda implied in this exchange that a repentant attitude gives one a second chance.

Friends in Kṛṣṇa Consciousness

"And you? Man is by nature social. If you do not make friendship with the devotees, you will be forced to associate with someone. That will be forced by material nature. If you do not associate with devotees, you will make friendship with the nondevotees. If you make friendship with the nondevotees," Prabhupāda paused as he spoke, "you will not be able to follow the rules and regulations."

* * *

asat-saṅga-tyāga, – ei vaiṣṇava-ācāra
'strī-saṅgī' – eka asādhu, 'kṛṣṇābhakta' āra

A Vaiṣṇava should always avoid the association of ordinary people. Common people are very much materially attached, especially to women. Vaiṣṇavas should also avoid the company of those who are not devotees of Lord Kṛṣṇa.

– *Caitanya-caritāmṛita, Madhya* 22.87

This verse is Śrī Caitanya Mahāprabhu's definition of the essential behavior of a Vaiṣṇava. As we are social by nature, we must, while avoiding the association of nondevotees, satisfy our need for friendship through partaking in deeply affectionate and friendly association among the devotees. Śrīla Rūpa Gosvāmī instructs us how to do so:

dadāti pratigṛhṇāti
guhyam ākhyāti pṛcchati
bhuṇkte bhojayate caiva
ṣaḍ-vidhaṁ prīti-lakṣaṇam

Offering gifts in charity, accepting charitable gifts, revealing one's mind in confidence, inquiring confidentially, accepting *prasāda*, and offering *prasāda* are the six symptoms of love shared by one devotee and another.

Purport: In this verse Śrīla Rūpa Gosvāmī explains how to perform devotional activities in the association of other devotees. There are six kinds of activities: (1) giving charity to the devotees, (2)

> accepting from the devotees whatever they may offer in return, (3) opening one's mind to the devotees, (4) inquiring from them about the confidential service of the Lord, (5) honoring *prasāda*, or spiritual food, given by the devotees, and (6) feeding the devotees with *prasāda*.... Whenever there is a dealing of *prīti*, or love in intimate dealings, these six activities are executed. In the previous verse, Śrīla Rūpa Gosvāmī advised that one should renounce worldly association and keep company with the devotees *(saṅga-tyāgāt sato vṛtteḥ)*. The International Society for Krishna Consciousness has been established to facilitate these six kinds of loving exchanges between devotees.
>
> – *The Nectar of Instruction,* text 4

Invisible Headaches

"Prabhupāda, some devotees seem very Kṛṣṇa conscious, but they seem, on the other hand, to have displeased you."

Prabhupāda illustrated the situation with an example: "If the telephone is ringing and a man does not want to answer, he will say," and Prabhupāda pointed to his head and grimaced, "'Oh, I have a headache. I cannot come.' Can the actual situation be detected?"

* * *

Prabhupāda's example showed how internal, unverifiable symptoms of advancement cannot become the criteria for accepting a devotee as advanced or for accepting a devotee as one's spiritual master. An advanced devotee's qualification, however, can be directly observed by his behavior: he is fixed as a pure servant of his Guru Mahārāja and Kṛṣṇa. Requiring internal and esoteric qualifications opens the door for being cheated. Prabhupāda clarifies this in his purport to *Śrīmad-Bhāgavatam* 3.33.10:

> Sometimes doubts arise in the mind of neophytes about whether or not the spiritual master is liberated, and sometimes neophytes

are doubtful about the bodily affairs of the spiritual master. The point of liberation, however, is not to see the bodily symptoms of the spiritual master. One has to see the spiritual symptoms of the spiritual master. *Jīvan-mukta* means that even though one is in the material body (there are still some material necessities, since the body is material), because one is fully situated in the service of the Lord, he should be understood to be liberated.

Liberation entails being situated in one's own position. That is the definition in the *Śrīmad-Bhāgavatam: muktir...svarūpeṇa vyavasthitiḥ*. The *svarūpa,* or actual identity of the living entity, is described by Lord Caitanya. *Jīvera 'svarūpa' haya – kṛṣṇera 'nitya-Dāsa'*: the real identity of the living entity is that he is eternally a servitor of the Supreme Lord. If someone is one-hundred-percent engaged in the service of the Lord, he is to be understood as liberated. One must understand whether or not he is liberated by his activities in devotional service, not by other symptoms.

The Respect of a Vaiṣṇava

When Prabhupāda arrived, we had offered him a 24-karat gold ring with a raised "P" on it, a gold necklace with a "P", and a gold bracelet engraved with the full word, Prabhupāda. We had also arranged a Rolls Royce to carry him from the airport to his luxurious hotel suite. Prabhupāda appreciated our recognition of his position as the representative of Kṛṣṇa and told Satsvarūpa Mahārāja, "This is a great credit for the one who has made these arrangements."

* * *

I had asked Sudāmā Vipra Swami how to greet and honor Prabhupāda, and I made opulent arrangements according to his advice. When I heard both Prabhupāda's appreciation of our offerings and his strong criticism, I said, "Prabhupāda, I know you appreciated the arrangements we made for you. I learned this from Sudāmā Vipra Swami. So he helped me."

Prabhupāda's reply was dour. "That is nice. They may have helped you in the past, but they cannot help you anymore."

"Then how should I treat him and Siddha-svarūpa now?"

"You should treat them with respect," Prabhupāda replied. "A Vaiṣṇava treats everyone with respect, even an ant!"

* * *

Vaiṣṇava culture is steeped in etiquette. The practice of etiquette is neither superficial nor shallow, but it is meant to evoke the pleasure of Kṛṣṇa and His servants and to avoid offenses. A cultured gentleman would not have needed to ask how to treat someone else. Śrī Caitanya Mahāprabhu taught, "Give all respect to others and require no respect for yourself."

Final Instructions: Arrows on Tape

Early on the last morning of Prabhupāda's stay, Satsvarūpa Mahārāja told me Prabhupāda wanted to see Jagattāriṇī and I. I ran to Prabhupāda's room and offered my obeisances. My wife chose to remain outside the door and listen from there. Prabhupāda sat on a chair at a thin wooden desk. He was chanting softly to a large, black-and-white photo of "Gopāla Kṛṣṇa" framed on his desk.

"Play the tape," he said, and he pointed with his saffron bead bag to the dictaphone on a nearby table.

It was a tape of Prabhupāda's previous night's dictation of the Bhaktivedanta purports to *Caitanya-caritāmṛta, Madhya 19.151–57*. I turned the machine on and heard Prabhupāda describe the planting and protection of the *bhakti-latā-bīja.*

brahmāṇḍa bhramite kona bhāgyavān jīva
guru-kṛṣṇa-prasāde pāya bhakti-latā-bīja

The word *guru-prasāda* indicates that the spiritual master is very merciful in bestowing the boon of devotional service upon the disciple. That is the best possible gift the spiritual master has to offer...Endowed with the mercy of the Supreme Personality of Godhead, the spiritual master distributes the mercy to those who are elevated and pious. Thus the spiritual master trains his disciples to render service to the Supreme Personality of Godhead. This is called *guru-kṛpā.* It is *kṛṣṇa-prasāda,* Kṛṣṇa's mercy, that he sends a bona fide spiritual master to the deserving disciple. By the mercy of Kṛṣṇa, one meets the bona fide spiritual master, and by the mercy of the spiritual master, the disciple is fully trained in the devotional service of the Lord....

The methods, rules, and regulations by which one is perfectly trained in devotional service constitute the *bhakti-latā-bīja,* or the seed of devotional service. This is received from the spiritual master by the grace of Kṛṣṇa....The *bhakti-latā-bīja* can be received only through the mercy of the spiritual master. Therefore one has to satisfy the spiritual master to get the *bhakti-latā-bīja.* The *bhakti-latā-bīja* is the origin of devotional service. Unless one satisfies the spiritual master, he gets the *bīja,* or root cause, of *karma, jñāna, and yoga* without the benefit of devotional service. However, one who is faithful to his spiritual master gets the *bhakti-latā-bīja.* This *bhakti-latā-bīja* is received when one is initiated by the bona fide spiritual master. After receiving the spiritual master's mercy, one must repeat his instructions, and this is called hearing and chanting. One who has not properly heard from the spiritual master or who does not follow the regulative principles is not fit for chanting *(kīrtana).* One who has not listened carefully to the instructions of the spiritual master is unfit to chant or preach the cult of devotional service. One has to water the *bhakti-latā-bīja* after receiving instructions from the spiritual master.

One's devotional attitude increases in the association of a Vaiṣṇava.

tāṅḍera caraṇa sevi bhakta-sane vāsa
janame janame haya, ei abhilāṣa

By his personal example, Narottama Dāsa Ṭhākura stresses that a devotee must always remember to please his predecessor *ācārya.*

The Gosvāmīs are represented by one's spiritual master. One cannot be an *ācārya* (spiritual master) without following strictly in the disciplic succession of the *ācāryas*. One who is actually serious in advancing in devotional service should desire only to satisfy the previous *ācāryas*. *Ei chaya gosāñi yāra, mui tāra Dāsa*. One should always think of oneself as a servant of the servant of the *ācāryas*, and thinking this, one should live in the society of Vaiṣṇavas. However, if one thinks that he has become very mature and can live separate from the association of Vaiṣṇavas and thus gives up all the regulative principles due to offending a Vaiṣṇava, one's position becomes very dangerous....Giving up the regulative principles and living according to one's whims are compared to a mad elephant, which by force uproots the *bhakti-latā* and breaks it to pieces. In this way the *bhakti-latā* shrivels up. Such an offense is especially created when one disobeys the instructions of the spiritual master. This is called guru-*avajñā*. The devotee must therefore be very careful not to commit offenses against the spiritual master. As soon as one is deviated from the spiritual master, the uprooting of the *bhakti-latā* begins, and gradually all the leaves dry up.

While the *bhakti-latā* creeper is growing, the devotee must protect it by fencing it all around. The neophyte devotee must be protected by being surrounded by pure devotees. In this way he will not give the maddened elephant a chance to uproot his *bhakti-latā* creeper. When one associates with nondevotees, the maddened elephant is set loose. Śrī Caitanya Mahāprabhu has said: *asat-saṅga-tyāga – ei vaiṣṇava-ācāra*. The first business of a Vaiṣṇava is to give up the company of nondevotees. A so-called mature devotee, however, commits a great offense by giving up the company of pure devotees.

What follows are Prabhupāda's words directly as they were copied from the original transcript of his dictated tape. Thus some words are different from the edited purport currently published by the BBT.

The living entity is a social animal. If one gives up the society of pure devotees he must associate with the society of *asat-saṅga*, the association of nondevotees. By contact of nondevotees and nondevotional activities the so-called mature devotee becomes a victim of the mad elephant offense. Therefore whatever little growth there was of the devotional creeper is uprooted by such offensive activity. Therefore one must be very careful to defend the creeper with fencing by following the regulative principles and associating with pure devotees. If one thinks in the society there are many so-called devotees or there are so many nondevotees, still one should stick to the society, and if one thinks the society members are not pure devotees he can directly keep company or in touch with the spiritual master. If there is any doubt, he should consult the spiritual master. But without following the instruction of the spiritual master – the regulative principles given by the spiritual master and chanting and hearing of the holy name of the Lord – no one can become a pure devotee. By his mental concoction he falls down, and by association of nondevotees, breaks the regulative principles. Therefore he is lost.

* * *

Prabhupāda's recorded dictaphone tape purports felt like an arrow piercing my heart. This arrow carried the absolute message from Kṛṣṇa to me through His representative. What struck me most on the tape was Prabhupāda's tone of voice. His was not the voice of a professional translator; urgency poured from his heart. Prabhupāda's voice revealed a father's affection for a son he fears may leave his shelter. Laden with compassion, his words hit me, especially these: "Whatever (little) growth has taken place is quickly uprooted by such an (mad elephant) offense...." And, "If one thinks that there are many so-called devotees or nondevotees in the Kṛṣṇa Consciousness Society, one can keep direct company with the spiritual master, and if there is any doubt, one should consult the spiritual master."

The philosophy was now clear. Hearing Prabhupāda call out to his children touched my heart. Elated, miserable, ecstatic, and humbled, I understood the message was not meant for me alone.

I asked Prabhupāda if I could send a copy of the tape to Siddhasvarūpānanda Goswami, and he consented.

Concern

Prabhupāda was concerned about how I was withstanding the pressure of his purification. He inquired, "So, how are you doing?"

"I'm all right, Prabhupāda, but I'm afraid my wife isn't doing so well."

Prabhupāda looked worried and asked me to call her in. He also handed me his dictaphone tape and requested I give it to Satsvarūpa Mahārāja to type. I stepped outside and insisted that Jagattāriṇī go in and see Prabhupāda.

Jagattāriṇī had chosen not to be in Prabhupāda's room. She felt it too painful to be in her spiritual master's presence and yet feel so hopeless. Instead, she waited outside, wondering how such a terrible condition had come upon her so quickly. When the tape began, however, she listened earnestly and felt as if Prabhupāda was diagnosing and treating her condition and her questions were being answered.

A Special Ring

As we entered and offered our obeisances, Prabhupāda was grave. Slowly he removed a thin, gold wedding ring from his finger. He held it delicately between his thumb and forefinger and turned to Jagattāriṇī. "This is for you." Prabhupāda extended his arm and placed the ring into her outstretched palms. He appeared thoughtful, gentle, and soft like a loving father. Jagattāriṇī bowed her head and began to cry.

* * *

Medicine is at times bitter and difficult to digest. Prabhupāda, more careful than the most concerned doctor, was concerned for his "patient's" health. He knew that kindness was needed, and out of affection, he gave Jagattāriṇī a full dose.

"Just to Save Them"

Years later, I met a devotee who had been with Prabhupāda at the Honolulu airport before Prabhupāda's Hong Kong flight. He told me that he had dutifully warned Prabhupāda what to expect on his arrival.

When he told Prabhupāda that "Bhūrijana is in *māyā,*" Prabhupāda's reply was, "Yes, I know. I am going to Hong Kong just to save them."

* * *

Prabhupāda arrived in Hong Kong angry, yet his genuine concern was to save two fallen souls. As the founder-*ācārya* of ISKCON, Prabhupāda was preeminently busy and successful. Yet he not only had the ferocity of a lion as he corrected, but also the fully compassionate heart of a Vaiṣṇava. That combination, embodied in Prabhupāda, Kṛṣṇa's representative, had conquered the world. Prabhupāda also wished his followers to have both the courage of an Englishman and the heart of a Bengali mother. He spoke of the Vaiṣṇava preacher's heart in Hawaii just before his arrival in Hong Kong:

NITĀI: How does one become *"bhāgyavān?"*

PRABHUPĀDA: Bhāgyavān, opulent...If you earn money, you become *bhāgyavān.* The word has come from *bhagavān,* and *bhaga* means opulence, six kinds of opulence: *Aiśvaryasya samagrasya vīryasya yaśasaḥ śriyaḥ.* So one who possess all these things, not exactly like Bhāgavān, but partially, according to his position, he's called *bhāgyavān.*

NITĀI: But in this verse that you just quoted, *ei rūpe brahmāṇḍa brahmite kono bhāgyavān,* how does one come, become to the stage of...

Prabhupāda: We are making them *bhāgyavān*. We are giving them service, how to become *bhāgyavān*. We are spending our blood, gallons of blood, to make them *bhāgyavān*. This is the sacrifice of the devotees. Just like you are poor. Somebody, rich man, comes, all right, take one million dollars from me. You get immediately rich. So it is by the devotees' sacrifice that they're becoming...Just like Vāsudeva Datta. He requested Caitanya Mahāprabhu, "My Lord, You have come. Take away all these people, unfortunate people, back to home, back to Godhead. If You think they are so inglorious, they cannot be taken, then give all their sins to me. I shall suffer. You take them." That is Vaiṣṇava. They are sacrificing everything for these unfortunate rascals. Therefore they are becoming very, very dear to Kṛṣṇa. Kṛṣṇa says, *na ca tasmān manuṣyeṣu*. Those who are sacrificing everything for making these rascals fortunate, they become immediately very, very dear to Kṛṣṇa. Just like, if a rich man gives his money for public welfare, immediately he's recognized by the government. Yes. He's given some title. Why? Because he has given his possession for the benefit of the public. Similarly, the devotees, they are distributing their possessions to these unfortunate people. Therefore they are immediately recognized. That is the process. The devotee does not want any recognition, but he is satisfied knowing that "My Lord wants this rascal to go back to home, back to Godhead. So let me try my best." He knows the mind of the master; otherwise, why the master comes and canvasses, *sarva-dharmān parityajya mām ekaṁ śaraṇaṁ vraja?* He has no business, He wants that "These rascals are suffering in this material condition. They are My part and parcel, My sons. Let Me try." And the devotee understands that "My Lord wants it. So let me do it on His behalf." Therefore a devotee is so dear. Hare Kṛṣṇa, Hare Kṛṣṇa.

* * *

Prabhupāda's compassionate visit fixed my consciousness on him and his mission. For weeks, I dreamed again and again of Prabhupāda, and his instructions reaffirmed themselves as the guiding principles of my life. Prabhupāda, whose body at that time was seventy-eight years old, had traveled thousands of miles to save two fallen disciples.

Hong Kong, 1974–Part II

Meeting Our "Chinese Gentleman"

I mentioned to Prabhupāda that one Chinese gentleman wanted to see him. I was referring to Yeung Pak Hei, an educated, twenty-eight-year-old engineering supervisor for the Hong Kong Telephone Company. He was living at home, regularly attending our classes, reading Prabhupāda's books, and chanting Hare Kṛṣṇa. We were encouraging him to translate Prabhupāda's books into Chinese.

I left Prabhupāda's room and returned a few moments later with our Chinese gentleman. Prabhupāda, who was expecting someone elderly, asked, "When will the Chinese gentleman come?" I laughed and replied that he was here, and pointed to Yeung Pak Hei.

Prabhupāda looked at the serious young man before him. He seemed astonished at my use of the word "gentleman," but immediately accepted him as a gentleman. After I explained to Prabhupāda about Yeung's chanting and profession, Yeung asked Prabhupāda a relevant, personal question.

"I am chanting each day at home, but I don't have an inclination to move into the temple. We Chinese people are very attached to our families. Is this still satisfactory?"

Prabhupāda looked at him again, as if gauging how to respond. I expected a "safe" answer that would not pressure this rare soul or frighten him away, but Prabhupāda gauged differently. "It is not unusual that you are attached to your family. Chinese people are not the only ones who are attached. Even dogs and birds are attached to their families."

* * *

Prabhupāda kept his voice even, but his words pierced the peaceful atmosphere in his room. Yeung Pak was thoughtful, his furrowed brow betraying that he had heard, understood, and was analyzing Prabhupāda's reply.

A Press Conference

We arranged a press conference for Prabhupāda, and quite a few reporters came.

"Swamijī, you are an ascetic and you are preaching about renunciation of the material world. Yet you are sitting in luxury in the Hong Kong Hilton. Isn't that hypocritical?"

Prabhupāda started philosophically. "First you must understand what is renunciation. Nothing is ours. Everything belongs to Kṛṣṇa. What is the harm if Kṛṣṇa's servant uses Kṛṣṇa's opulence to glorify Kṛṣṇa?"

Prabhupāda noted that the reporter wasn't satisfied and took another tact. "Personally, I am not attached. I could live under a tree and be satisfied."

The reporter's interest increased with the mention of living under a tree. Perhaps he had a human interest story.

"But," Prabhupāda added, "if I was living under a tree and called a press conference..." Prabhupāda paused for a moment to allow the situation he was describing to capture the reporters' imaginations, "and if I invited all the reporters, would you have attended?"

* * *

Everyone laughed. Prabhupāda's example made yukta-vairāgya clear: using Kṛṣṇa's opulences in Kṛṣṇa's service was practical renunciation.

Passing the Question

A second reporter asked a typical and superficial question: "You preach nonviolence and are vegetarians, yet you have to kill the vegetables you eat. That is also violence."

Prabhupāda had heard this and other such questions hundreds of times, along with questions like, "What does the mark on your forehead mean?" "Why do you have a tuft of hair on the back of your head?" "Do you think dressing in robes and shaving your head alienates you from most people?"

Prabhupāda turned to me. "You answer."

* * *

I was caught off guard. Part of my "*māyā*" was not properly offering the food I was eating. I thought that using my energy in Kṛṣṇa's service was sufficient. Prabhupāda had caught me again, although this time, I had escaped detection by others. Like a student explaining a lesson in front of his teacher, I nervously but carefully explained to the reporter, before the watchful eyes of my spiritual master, the difference between unoffered vegetarian food and *prasāda*.

I cannot say for sure if Prabhupāda knew of my fault and was consciously using this opportunity to instruct me further, but I felt as though Prabhupāda was again weeding my heart.

"Tell Us about Guru Maharaj Ji"

A third reporter asked Prabhupāda a bombshell question: "One yoga group in Hong Kong is led by an Indian guru called Bal Krishna Yogesvara. His followers call him 'Guru Maharaj Ji.' This fellow says that he is Kṛṣṇa. Would you say something about Guru Maharaj Ji?"

Prabhupāda's eyes narrowed, but he declined to answer.

The reported rephrased his question. "Is Guru Maharaj Ji's group the same as your Kṛṣṇa consciousness group or different?"

Prabhupāda didn't seem interested in making a comparative study. He again avoided the question. "We don't know about other groups. If you wish to know about Kṛṣṇa consciousness philosophy, you can ask. We are not here to speak about others."

But Prabhupāda was becoming annoyed. The reporter sensed a story brewing and again pushed Prabhupāda. "What do you think about this Guru Maharaj Ji? His group is spreading quite quickly, isn't it?"

Prabhupāda suddenly decided to answer. His eyes opened wide. "This Guru Maharaj Ji is a cheat! Yes, he is a cheat, but Kṛṣṇa is God. He can be a bigger cheat!"

The reporters quickly scribbled in their notepads.

"Guru Maharaj Ji is a cheat, but he will get cheated by Kṛṣṇa," Prabhupāda continued, as he sat back on the plush couch, his hands defiantly crossed across his chest.

The reporters smiled. They had come for a story and they got one.

The next day the story broke in the *Hong Kong Standard,* a major Hong Kong newspaper, that the guru of the Hare Kṛṣṇa movement had publicly called Guru Maharaj Ji a cheater.

Prabhupāda smiled broadly when he saw the headline and had us purchase many copies. The story was later picked up by *Time* magazine, which ran it on February 11, 1974, under the title, "Trouble in Paradise."

> Trouble is stirring in Nirvana. A. C. Bhaktivedanta Swami of the Hare Krishna movement, at a news conference in Hong Kong last week

> denounced a rival guru: self-styled divinity Maharaj Ji, 16, now counseling his disciples in California. The ascetic swami, whose followers constitute a kind of saffron-robed Hindu version of the Salvation Army, began by saying, "You've got to decide whether he is God or a dog." Noting the young swami's luxurious lifestyle, the swami declared rather ominously, "He is cheating people, but he will be cheated in a bigger way. When God meets cheats He can be a better cheat than they."

Our press conference, I thought, was a success. Prabhupāda was pleased with the conference and as soon as it was over he asked his secretary, Satsvarūpa Mahārāja, for the recording of the meeting. But Satsvarūpa Mahārāja had neglected to record it. Prabhupāda waxed angry. "Such an important meeting and you did not record." I could see Mahārāja mentally vowing to always record Prabhupāda's talks from that time on. Prabhupāda dropped the issue and did not mention it again.

* * *

Was it *māyā* for me to feel a little satisfaction, knowing that at least I wasn't the only one Prabhupāda reprimanded?

Learning to Hear

Some Hong Kong residents did not agree that the press conference had been a success. Guru Maharaj Ji's followers were furious. They wrote a strong letter to the editor criticizing Prabhupāda for his intolerance. In addition, three members of the Indian community paid Prabhupāda a visit to discuss Guru Maharaj Ji's worthiness. I sat in. At one point, the men turned their criticism to Prabhupāda. I spoke out, "Of course Prabhupāda had to speak so strongly. After all, the man is cheating and so many people are becoming cheated. Is it right that he remain silent and let cheating go on?"

* * *

I remember feeling quite pleased as I rambled on. That is, until Prabhupāda caught my eye.

Through his eyes, Prabhupāda seemed to speak to me. "This is not the time to defend your guru's honor. I am here. Better you listen and learn."

Enemies to Friends

Quickly I sat down and listened to Prabhupāda preach. He spoke softly and continued arguing, jesting, quoting *śāstra,* and otherwise winning the three to his side. He also spoke strongly. "The rascal has gone to the hospital due to toothache and he never thinks, 'How is it that God must go to the hospital for toothache!'" They thanked Prabhupāda as they stood up to leave, and they expressed how they now could understand that his words, strong as they were, were correct.

* * *

One interesting result of this session was that because I carefully listened to Prabhupāda's words, I was able to respond strongly to a rebuttal letter to the editor written by Guru Maharaj Ji's followers.

> Guru Maharaj Ji is not God, nor can any living entity ever become God.... In a court of law, the judge carefully considers the existing law as well as the previous verdicts handed down from past authorities. He does not base his judgment on the opinion of the accused. Prabhupāda spoke strongly in the press conference not so much with the hope of convincing the foolish followers of Guru Maharaj Ji that they should give up their cheating leader. Nor are we so naive to write this letter with such an idealistic hope. We write to present to the nonbiased reader, who is not committed to following this cheater, that beliefs should be based on the words of the scriptures, the law books, rather than the baseless claims and concocted philosophy of Guru Maharaj Ji and his followers.

The letter was published and the Guru Maharaj Jis remained silent. Satisfied, I sent my letter to Prabhupāda. When I arrived in India several months later, Trivikrama Swami told me that Prabhupāda was so pleased with my letter that he had read it several times to his leading disciples and Indian guests.

Such is Prabhupāda's mercy. He does everything personally and then gives all the credit to his fallen servants.

Pushing Prabhupāda

Our preaching in Hong Kong was successful because we were using friendly and relaxed means to attract the local Chinese people. In our creative attempts at preaching, we held *kīrtanas* with guitars and *mṛdaṅgas*. I decided to ask Prabhupāda about it.

"Prabhupāda, we have been holding *kīrtanas* using guitars. Is that all right?"

"*Kīrtana* means *khol* (*mṛdaṅga*) and *karatāla*. That's all."

"But it is so difficult to preach in Hong Kong. And the Chinese people like *kīrtanas* better when they are soft and with guitars. They don't like loud *kīrtanas* with many instruments."

Prabhupāda acceded to my pushing and gave us permission to also use guitars in our *kīrtanas* along with the standard *khol* and *karatāla*.

* * *

Our spiritual master may sometimes agree to our requests because we present them forcefully, but that doesn't necessarily mean it is Kṛṣṇa's desire. We should be careful that our own enthusiastic vision does not cover our ability to recognize our guru's actual desires.

Compassionate Duty

Sunil Khemani was a mature, fourteen-year-old boy who chanted sixteen rounds a day and spent his free time at the temple. His family was favorable to his involvement in Kṛṣṇa consciousness, although his father was not a vegetarian.

Sunil brought his mother to visit Prabhupāda at the Hilton. After she took *darśana*, she asked Prabhupāda if she could cook for him. Prabhupāda agreed, and Sunil and his mother left. After they were gone, I informed Prabhupāda of the family's eating situation.

"Prabhupāda, Sunil's mother is sincere, but her husband eats meat and she cooks it for him. Do you want her to cook for you in her kitchen?" And, after a moment, I added, "In her pots?"

Prabhupāda looked at me as if he were weighing the situation.

"We can arrange others to do the cooking. Pradyumna can cook. Satsvarūpa Mahārāja can cook. You don't have to accept food from her if you don't want," I said.

Prabhupāda thought for some time. "It is my duty to accept. Otherwise how will they make any advancement?"

* * *

A *sādhu* should be careful where he eats and from whom he accepts food. In a *Caitanya-caritāmṛta* purport, Prabhupāda explains:

> The word *apavitra anna* refers to food that is unacceptable for a Vaiṣṇava. In other words, a Vaiṣṇava cannot accept any food offered by an *avaiṣṇava* in the name of *mahā-prasāda*. This should be a principle for all Vaiṣṇavas....If an *avaiṣṇava* offers food in the name of *mahā-prasāda*, it should not be accepted. Such food cannot be *prasāda* because an *avaiṣṇava* cannot offer anything to the Lord. Sometimes preachers in the Kṛṣṇa consciousness movement have to accept food in a home where the householder is an *avaiṣṇava*; however, if this food is offered to the Deity, it can be taken. Ordinary food cooked by an *avaiṣṇava* should not be accepted by a Vaiṣṇava. Even if an *avaiṣṇava* cooks food without fault, he cannot offer it to Lord Viṣṇu, and it cannot be accepted as *mahā-prasāda*. According to *Bhagavad-gītā:*
>
> *patra puṣpaṁ phalaṁ toyaṁ*
> *yo me bhaktyā prayacchati*

tad ahaṁ bhakty-upahṛtam
aśnāmi prayatātmanaḥ

"If one offers Me with love and devotion a leaf, a flower, fruit or water, I will accept it." (Bg. 9.26)

Kṛṣṇa can accept anything offered by His devotee with devotion. An *avaiṣṇava* may be a vegetarian and a very clean cook, but because he cannot offer the foodstuff to Viṣṇu, the food he cooks cannot be accepted as *mahā-prasāda.* It is better that a Vaiṣṇava abandon such food as untouchable.

– *Caitanya-caritāmṛita, Madhya* 9.53

The *Caitanya-caritāmṛta* states that a preacher should only accept *prasāda,* food offered to the Deities. Yet to give one *jīvātmā* a chance to perform devotional service, Prabhupāda's compassion overruled this injunction. I again understood the compassion needed for a preacher to become successful, but I also understood that a powerful preacher's instructions should be followed. We should understand and take to heart the principle – unselfishness and compassion – but we should nevertheless carefully and strictly follow his direct instructions.

Worshiping Lord Śiva

Hong Kong's large Indian population supported two Hindu temples, one on each side of the harbor. One morning, the head priest of the Hindu temple on the Hong Kong side came to visit Prabhupāda. After exchanging superficialities, he respectfully invited Prabhupāda to visit his *maṇḍira.* Prabhupāda nodded his head in acceptance and the priest, satisfied, left.

"Prabhupāda visit the Hindu temple?" I thought. "What will be the gain?" The friendly priest was a Māyāvādī. "Prabhupāda, do you really want to visit that temple?"

"Why shouldn't I? He has invited me."

"But they worship Lord Śiva in their temple," I fumbled.

"And do you tell them not to worship Lord Śiva?" Prabhupāda's eyes opened wide, his raised voice hinting that a thunderbolt may await me. It was a test.

"No. But Prabhupāda, they worship Śiva as the Supreme Personality of Godhead."

I spoke, by Kṛṣṇa's mercy, as fast as the wind, and the impending storm of Prabhupāda's anger immediately dissipated.

"Oh, then we should not go."

* * *

The second offense against the holy name is to consider the demigods, such as Lord Brahmā or Lord Śiva, to be equal to or independent of Kṛṣṇa. ISKCON devotees usually preach that the demigods should not be worshiped, but that is because most demigod worshipers see their deity as independently powerful. Ultimately, only Śrī Śrī Rādhā and Kṛṣṇa should be worshiped.

Demigod worshipers can become free from their offensive mentalities, however, without giving up their worship. Instead they can think of their worshipable demigod as a servant of Kṛṣṇa. Then they can offer *kṛṣṇa-prasāda* to the deity and worship Brahmā, Śiva, Gaṇeśa, or Durgā, with the hymns of the *Brahma-saṁhitā*.

Prabhupāda warned me in this exchange to beware of offending the demigods. They are empowered servants of Kṛṣṇa and should not be seen as separate from Kṛṣṇa. Even though we criticize improper worship of the demigods, we should never disrespect the demigods themselves.

For the Benefit of Others

Prabhupāda was scheduled to speak in the executive meeting room at the Hong Kong Hilton on the last evening of his stay. The hotel posted a black placard that read, "Tridandi Goswami A. C. Bhaktivedanta Swami Prabhupāda will speak on Krishna Consciousness."

In the plush meeting room, Prabhupāda sat on a makeshift *vyāsāsana* – a decorated chair – and received garlands from each of the almost one hundred children from our classes. Garlands covered Prabhupāda's shoulders, then neck, and threatened to cover his face. As more garlands were offered, we removed and distributed garlands as *prasāda*.

Prabhupāda lectured on the urgency of spreading Kṛṣṇa consciousness throughout the world. He also spoke about the *Bhagavad-gītā*, advising the children to memorize the entire scripture, beginning with the first verse.

During the final kīrtana, Prabhupāda motioned for me to comeup to the *vyāsāsana*. "You should take up a collection," he instructed.

I picked up a fancy silver bowl and approached each guest. Almost all the guests donated something, and by the time I placed the bowl by Prabhupāda's feet, it contained the equivalent of about $150 U.S. Prabhupāda was satisfied with the reciprocation.

* * *

I was acquainted with most of the guests. Mainly they worshiped Lakṣmīdevī and Śiva Śaṅkara for a few minutes in the morning to ensure a prosperous day. They had come to Hong Kong to make money, not to make spiritual progress. They were businessmen.

I understood two of Prabhupāda's purposes for reminding me to take a collection. One was to test the financial support of the Indian community. Prabhupāda was satisfied by the result.

The second motive was compassion. These guests had heard both Prabhupāda's lecture and the holy name of Kṛṣṇa, but they were doomed materialists. Prabhupāda was certainly not in need of $150, but they would get eternal benefit by offering Prabhupāda some of their hard-earned money. Prabhupāda was compassionate and wanted to give them the opportunity to render service.

7-Up

In honor of their distinguished guest, the Hong Kong Hilton management had placed flower bouquets throughout Prabhupāda's suite. They had also filled the small refrigerator in the suite with fruit and soft drinks. Prabhupāda had his servant bring him a 7-up. "It is a good taste, is it not?"

* * *

Prabhupāda drank 7-up once in Hong Kong. Prabhupāda also occasionally drank 7-up on airplanes. In 1976, he drank 7-up at the New York Ratha-yātrā.

Before that Ratha-yātrā in 1976, no ISKCON devotee, with the possible exception of devotees serving in India, would consider purchasing a soft drink, but when the devotees heard that Prabhupāda drank 7-up, 7-up instantly became "bona fide." As no logic could support why 7-up was special among soft drinks, any caffeine-free soft drink quickly became "bona fide" for ISKCON devotees. The path tracing history to present reality is, at times, amusing. At other times, it's frightening. At all times, it's intriguing.

Hotel Jalebis?

Hong Kong's January weather was cold. Prabhupāda decided he wanted hot *jalebis*. We searched the hotel's room service menu and saw that they offered *jalebis*. We asked Prabhupāda if he would accept those cooked in the hotel kitchen. Prabhupāda agreed to try them.

* * *

Jalebis, made with gram flour and cooked in ghee, add warmth to the body and are a tasty Indian home remedy for the common cold. Although Prabhupāda trained his disciples to refrain from eating food cooked in hotels or served on airplanes, Prabhupāda felt he needed *jalebis* and agreed to eat the *jalebis* cooked in the hotel kitchen. Although Prabhupāda was far above the instructions meant to train his disciples, he generally followed perfectly to set a good example.

The hotel never delivered our order of *jalebis*, and Prabhupāda never mentioned it again.

"Go and Live in Vṛndāvana"

In Prabhupāda's room was a double-canopied bed with lace frills and a silk cover, but for all its opulence, the room was cold. Prabhupāda asked me to find a heater, but the heater I found was weak, and I was left hoping its feeble warmth would spread. He then asked me to ready his bed for his rest. I carefully folded the silk bedspread and turned the covers back. Looking at the huge canopied bed, the little portion I prepared for Prabhupāda seemed so small.

Prabhupāda had called for Jagattāriṇī and me to offer us some intimate association. We spoke for a while and then he said, "After you have been preaching for ten years, you can go and live in Vṛndāvana."

* * *

Prabhupāda usually rested at 10 P.M. and awoke at midnight to translate. Sleeping on an opulent bed neither increased Prabhupāda's sleep nor stimulated his desire for enjoyment. He remained fixed in transcendence. For example, the day he arrived in Hong Kong, Prabhupāda's plane landed at 7:30 P.M. He arrived at the hotel by 8:30 P.M., held *kīrtana*, and spoke to guests. Then he preached to me until about one in the morning before he finally rested.

The rigors of continuous travel, soft beds, "old age," an "infirm body," and jet lag did not seem to affect Prabhupāda. He rose around 2 A.M. to translate even when he went to bed at midnight.

"After you have been preaching for ten years, you can go and live in Vṛndāvana." I had forgotten Prabhupāda's words until I was already living in Vṛndāvana. The timing of Prabhupāda's blessing was exact. Prabhupāda said this to us in 1974. I had already been preaching in Japan and Hong Kong for just over four years. I later headed up a *gurukula* at Gītā-nāgarī from 1976 –1982.

The Orient: January 1970–April 1974 = 52 months
Gurukula: August 1976–December 1982 = 76 months
Total 128 months, or 10 years, 8 months

I arrived at the shelter of Krishna-Balarām Mandir in 1983, and I now understand that my coming to Vṛndāvana was Śrīmatī Rādhārāṇī's fulfillment of Prabhupāda's blessing.

The Correct Side for Sitting

We had heard that Prabhupāda sometimes liked to sit in a rocking chair, so we bought a cane rocker and tied on it a red, Chinese silk cushion finely embroidered with colored flowers. Prabhupāda liked to sit on the chair, but before sitting he would turn the cushion over to the unembroidered side. We would turn it back over to the decorated side, but Prabhupāda clearly wanted to sit on the unembroidered side and would again turn the cushion over.

* * *

I don't really know why Prabhupāda preferred the unembroidered side. Perhaps he was expressing his lack of appreciation for Chinese artistry or his preference for simplicity. Or he may have been indicating that we shouldn't be enamored by the superficial niceties of Chinese culture.

Shivering from Cold on The Peak

Prabhupāda's morning walk was on The Peak, a high hill in Hong Kong. "It is like Darjeeling," he said. The foggy morning air and brisk wind were chilling and I feared Prabhupāda would become ill. "Should we go back, Prabhupāda? Are you cold?"

"No, and you?"

He was cold and I was sure of it, but he kept walking. I shivered and told him I was cold. He replied, "Then let us turn back immediately."

* * *

Prabhupāda allowed me a glimpse into his heart. The Peak was cold and his coat was thin. For his own reasons, however, Prabhupāda declined to turn back. As soon as he thought I was inconvenienced by the cold, however, he immediately wanted to return. Through this simple gesture, Prabhupāda indicated that a gentleman's acts are determined by the needs of others.

A Dog on The Peak

We returned to again walk on The Peak, with its lush green foliage and varieties of evergreen and deciduous trees. The view of Hong Kong and its harbor below (not yet awake to its passionate, grinding workday) was incredible.

As our small group of five walked beside Prabhupāda on the paved footpath, we saw a Chinese man with his large German shepherd. The dog was not on a leash, and it suddenly bounded playfully toward us.

The dog's master stood at a distance and called him back, but the dog seemed intent on smelling us and pawing our clothes. The Chinese man, still at a distance, dropped down on his knees and began clapping and calling the dog, "Come on, boy. Come here. Come. Come."

The dog finally left us and returned to his master. The man was jubilant. He affectionately patted the dog and repeated over and over, "Good boy, good boy. Good. Good." The dog slobbered, licked the man's hand, and pawed his chest. "Good boy, good boy."

Prabhupāda's demeanor was serious as he watched the scene. Finally, he turned to me, intoned an incredulous "Good?" and quickly resumed walking.

* * *

Prabhupāda didn't say anything about a human wasting his affection on a dog. "Good?" was all we heard. Prabhupāda's point seemed as clear, however, as if he had written a book: the concept of good in Kali-yuga has degraded to the level of doghood. Gone is the concept that good means austerity, cleanliness, truthfulness, mercifulness, and God consciousness. Now in Kali-yuga, an ordinary, slobbering, lowly dog is considered good. How fallen is contemporary civilization!

Kṛṣṇadāsa Kavirāja Gosvāmī defines eloquence as "truth spoken concisely." How eloquently Prabhupāda summarized Kali-yuga's devolution in that one incredulous "Good?"

At a later time I also heard Prabhupāda concisely express truth. In Melbourne in 1975, as Prabhupāda took his massage, I related to him elements from an exchange I'd had with a Christian. "Prabhupāda," I began, "a Christian man I spoke to defended meat-eating by quoting a Bible verse that says, 'It is not what goes into a man's mouth that degrades him; it is the words that come out.' "

Prabhupāda's six-word reply was truly eloquent: "You mean if you eat stool?"

Feet on the Ground

Prabhupāda pointed to a shiny object on the ground as we walked. I picked it up. It was an American dime. Prabhupāda indicated that I should keep it, so I happily put the coin in my pocket.

* * *

One university course I attended during my student life was taught by a well-known American philosopher. He used to quote a saying that stuck in my mind: "It's all right to have your head in the clouds as long as your feet are on the ground." I understood this to mean that we can be as philosophical and theoretical as we like, but unless we are practical, our philosophizing and theorizing are useless.

Prabhupāda was a learned and realized philosopher but was always practical. His feet were on the ground. He was experienced in the world, and he was meticulously observant. He used everything in Kṛṣṇa's service, even an insignificant dime that found its way into the pocket of a grateful disciple.

Swallowing Not Mustard Oil but Pride

Prabhupāda's servant told me he was out of mustard oil and that Prabhupāda needed it for his massage. I quickly left the hotel, found a shop selling Indian groceries, and bought a liter of oil. I got back just in time.

Prabhupāda was already dressed in his *gamchā* when I sat down to watch the massage. Before it started, Prabhupāda looked at the golden fluid with a steady eye. He then placed his palm over the opening and turned the bottle over, allowing a few drops to spill into his palm. Smelling the oil, he looked at me and announced, "This is not mustard oil."

"Yes, it is, Prabhupāda." I knew because I had just purchased it.

"This is not mustard oil," Prabhupāda said emphatically.

I told him how I went to the store, asked for mustard oil, and was given this oil. "This is what the shopkeeper gave me."

"That may be so," Prabhupāda said with finality, "but this is not mustard oil."

* * *

I had not yet been to India or experienced the clever dealings of Indian shopkeepers. Prabhupāda, however, recognized that I had been cheated. I felt foolish because he had immediately detected the defect in my purchase. Pride, no matter how many times it must be swallowed, never seems to lose its bitter taste.

Following Prabhupāda

Just before he and his entourage left Hong Kong, Prabhupāda asked me to bring some Chinese devotees to the Māyāpur festival. I agreed to try my best. As a gesture of affection, I bought Pradyumna, Prabhupāda's Sanskrit editor, a warm jacket, and I bought Prabhupāda a case of pure Australian ghee. We all then left for Kai Tak airport.

Prabhupāda sat in an airport chair waiting for his flight to be called. David, a young Chinese boy, came close to Prabhupāda and sat near his feet. "Prabhupāda, I love you," he said. Prabhupāda smiled affectionately at the boy and began to pat his head and stroke his face. Prabhupāda then looked up at me and motioned to David, "Then follow him."

* * *

Prabhupāda's instructing young, sentimental David to follow me thrust on me the heavy responsibility of properly representing Prabhupāda.

The ghee was for Prabhupāda's cooks – pure ghee is scarce in India – but when I arrived in Calcutta a month later, I saw many of the green ghee cans in Gargamuni Swami's room. I was furious, thinking that Gargamuni Swami had somehow or other commandeered them from Prabhupāda for his own use. Years later, however, I was satisfied to learn that Prabhupāda had sold the ghee to Gargamuni Swami.

Māyāpur, 1974

Mercy on Entry

I wrote Prabhupāda from Hong Kong and told him I would attend the Māyāpur festival as he desired. I also mentioned that I would bring several Hong Kong devotees, some of whom were Chinese.

We purchased the least expensive plane tickets to Calcutta – on Air Burma. There was a one-night stopover in Rangoon. It was easy to get transit visas for Burma, but we hit a snag with the one Indian visa we required. At that time, British Commonwealth citizens didn't require Indian visas. Four of us carried Commonwealth passports, and as an American, I could enter India for one month without a visa.

Yeung Pak Hei, however, carrying only Hong Kong identity papers, required an Indian visa. He applied to the Indian Consulate, but the Consulate, after a month of "call back tomorrows" did not comply. We decided that Yeung Pak Hei would try to enter India without a visa.

Our flight and stopover in Burma went well. The friendly and lackadaisical Air Burma officials in Rangoon didn't bother to check for valid Indian visas before we boarded our Rangoon-Calcutta flight. "Kṛṣṇa's mercy," I thought, but I wondered about the next and most crucial step.

We landed in Calcutta and stood in line. One by one, we refugees from Hong Kong's intense materialism passed through immigration. I stood behind Yeung Pak Hei. He handed his papers to the white-uniformed immigration official, who intently flipped through each page. He looked surprised and called over a second official. As they conferred, they jointly flipped through the pages of Yeung Pak Hei's papers. They then called over two officials from Air Burma, and all four again flipped through each page of his identity papers. Finally concluding that he had no visa, they prohibited his entry.

We had come so far. Could Kṛṣṇa possibly be allowing Indian immigration to refuse Yeung Pak Hei to see Prabhupāda, Śrī-dhāma Māyāpur, and Śrī Vṛndāvana-dhāma?

Yeung Pak Hei was Chinese, with almond eyes and straight black hair. He was dressed in a *dhotī* and *kūrta.* I said to an official, "Preaching Caitanya Mahāprabhu's message throughout the world is your duty, but we have taken it up. You should let him in. He is a devotee of your religion. See how he is dressed? See? He has *japa-mālā, kaṇṭhī-mālā, and tilaka.* He is chanting Hare Kṛṣṇa. He is a devotee of your Śrī Caitanya Mahāprabhu. You *must* let him in."

By this time, a host of white-uniformed immigration officials with black shoulderpads and an array of gold bars and stars had arrived. Several spoke loudly and others walked off in a huff and then quickly returned. Others stood at a distance, pointing at the two of us. Official after official flipped through each page of Yeung Pak Hei's papers, passing them from one to another.

I remembered the BBT newsletter that was sent to all temples from Los Angeles. Although the information was basically meant for Americans, it nevertheless advertised that landing permits would be granted on arrival. Visas were not required. I pulled out the paper and thrust it into the group of immigration officers, who passed it around, each holding the paper close and carefully reading, "Landing permits will be granted upon arrival; visas not required."

We argued our case again with fresh energy. "We have done nothing wrong. Why we should be penalized? We were simply following instructions. Please, we are requesting you."

The officials again spoke loudly among themselves. Their animated discussion continued, until the group gradually drifted into a nearby office.

We were then directed to a couch and asked to "wait for some time." Both Yeung Pak Hei and I chanted on our beads, wondering how Śrī Caitanya Mahāprabhu's mercy would be manifest. Could it be the Lord's desire that Yeung Pak Hei be refused entry? We could not say, but we sat, chanted, and tried to be patient.

Through the glass window in the immigration hall, we viewed a large group of devotees from the West. Their flights had arrived both earlier and later than ours, and they milled about, waiting for us to clear immigration so that the buses could leave for Māyāpur. I saw Jagadīśa, my old college friend from Buffalo, Jayatīrtha, whom I had met years ago in Los Angeles on my way to Japan, Kīrtanānanda Swami, who had arrived loaded with milk sweets for Prabhupāda from New Vrindaban, and tens of others. I felt like a ghost as I observed the devotees through the window – viewing life and possessing desires, but unable to interact with the real world and my fellow ISKCON devotees.

The bus drivers finally decided not to wait. "We will all meet soon in Māyāpur," I thought. We were now alone, dependent on Kṛṣṇa's mercy, waiting for Śrī Caitanya Mahāprabhu's decision to be delivered through the immigration officials.

We sat and chanted for hours. Finally, the two Air Burma officials walked toward us. They were smiling.

"They will let you in," the shorter and more official of the two began, "but they have one emergency fund that they keep in case some difficulty comes among them. They said they will appreciate if you could make some contribution to that fund."

"How much contribution?" I asked. "As you like," he replied. I quickly pulled out the two hundred-rupee notes I had acquired in Hong Kong and expressed that the officials had been so kind. Both Air Burma men shook their heads back and forth in appreciation and accompanied us through the immigration channel to freedom.

"India! We're home, Yeung Pak Hei!" I said, as I wondered about the peculiarity of our entry. We decided to spend the night in the Calcutta temple and travel to Māyāpur the following morning. We hailed a taxi and sped to ISKCON on Albert Road. As soon as we arrived in the small temple, we were informed that Prabhupāda was there – in his rooms. We raced passed the temple room and saw him sitting behind a low wooden desk. Cushions extended over the entire floor and were covered in clean, tight, white sheets. A middle-aged Indian man, a guest, sat opposite Prabhupāda. I offered Prabhupāda my obeisances from outside the door.

Prabhupāda saw me and immediately waved at me to enter. "How many have you brought?" he asked, his enthusiasm like that of a young boy.

* * *

Prabhupāda was pleased that we were successful in bringing devotees from Hong Kong to ISKCON's first major international Gaura-Pūrṇimā festival. He proudly informed the Indian gentleman that even the Chinese were becoming devotees.

Walk Along with Prabhupāda

Yeung Pak Hei and I journeyed to Māyāpur the following day. We had traveled from our lonely Far-Eastern preaching outpost in Hong Kong and suddenly found ourselves surrounded by hundreds of exuberant devotees from around the world. The following morning, after *maṅgala-ārati* and *japa,* for the first time we heard of greeting the Deities, which was accompanied by a tape of Yamunā Dāsī singing the *govinda* prayers. We then heard, also for the first time, of daily guru-*pūjā,* an *ārati* that devotees now offered to Prabhupāda as they sang *śrī*-guru-*caraṇa-padma.* Remembering that I had left the United States when no official ISKCON morning program had yet existed, I began to understand that I had been away for a long time.

One other morning I sat on the steps of the Māyāpur guesthouse feeling quite lonely amid the crowds of devotees. Prabhupāda suddenly appeared atop the guesthouse stairs with *sannyāsīs* and ISKCON leaders crowded around him for his morning walk. As soon as Prabhupāda saw me, he waved his hand as an invitation for me to accompany him.

A Fragrant Flower is Born

Yeung Pak Hei decided that he was ready to take initiation. When Prabhupāda called him to his *vyāsāsana* on Gaura-Pūrṇimā day, he instructed Yeung Pak Hei to offer his obeisances with his left side to his spiritual master and his right side to the Deities of Rādhā-Mādhava. Yeung Pak Hei recited the four prerequisite prohibitions: no meat-eating, no illicit sex, no gambling, and no intoxication, and Prabhupāda handed him his beads, requesting him to promise to chant sixteen rounds each day. He then gave him the name Yaśomatīsūta Dāsa. After Yaśomatīsūta offered his obeisances and was returning to his seat, Prabhupāda announced into the microphone, "Just as one sandalwood tree in a forest makes the whole forest fragrant, similarly, because of this one boy, the whole Chinese race has become glorious."

* * *

Prabhupāda had confided in me during a walk on the Hong Kong Peak that he wanted one Chinese boy to take initiation in Māyāpur during Gaura-Pūrṇimā. Even before that instruction, he had written and assured me that there was at least one boy in Hong Kong who would come to Kṛṣṇa consciousness. Prabhupāda's vision and blessing came to fruition on Gaura-Pūrṇimā day in 1974, when the first Chinese devotee, Yaśomatīsūta Dāsa, took Vaiṣṇava initiation from Śrīla Prabhupāda. Had I the vision, I would have seen demigods showering flowers of congratulations on both spiritual master and disciple.

Yaśomatīsūta served steadily over the years in Southeast Asia, especially in Hong Kong and Taiwan. He also translated many of Prabhupāda's books into Chinese.

Sweet Transcendental Sound

Just after his initiation, Yaśomatīsūta began translating the introduction to *Bhagavad-gītā As It Is*. We decided to bring it to Prabhupāda as soon as one page had been completed. Both of us entered Prabhupāda's room with the Chinese translation in hand and told Prabhupāda what Yaśomatīsūta had done. "Would you like to hear it, Prabhupāda?" I asked. Beaming, Prabhupāda asked Yaśomatīsūta to read to the Indonesian wood carving of Rādhā-Kṛṣṇa on the wall. After Yaśomatīsūta had read for several minutes, Prabhupāda turned to us, still beaming, "Is it not sweet?"

He then turned to the room full of aristocratic life members from Calcutta and said, "In Bengal, they are trying to turn others to become Communists, but we are going to China and making the Communists into Vaiṣṇavas."

* * *

Cantonese sounds guttural and harsh, even to the Mandarin-speaking Chinese, but in Prabhupāda's presence, in Śrīdhāma Māyāpur, and with the *Bhagavad-gītā* as the subject matter, all present could perceive Yaśomatīsūta's Cantonese rendering as sweet and special.

Prabhupāda smiled proudly at his first Chinese disciple. The life members were impressed by the truth of Prabhupāda's words and they gasped in amazement at one of Prabhupāda's preaching accomplishments – a "Chinese" Vaiṣṇava!

Vṛndāvana, 1974

By Prabhupāda's House

Just after the festival ended on Gaura-Pūrṇimā, our group traveled from Māyāpur to Calcutta, then Delhi, and finally Vṛndāvana. The Krishna-Balaram Mandir was then a construction site. The concrete pillars blossoming with steel rods looked like Kali-yuga lotus flowers. The devotees stayed at Fogal Ashram, while Prabhupāda lived in his own newly constructed house on the Krishna-Balaram Mandir property.

Once, as I sat behind Prabhupāda's house watching devotees feed the friendly peacocks, Satsvarūpa Mahārāja asked me to fan Prabhupāda as he took *prasāda*. I entered, offered my obeisances, and began fanning. Prabhupāda ate in silence. When he was almost finished his meal, Prabhupāda looked up at me and asked, "How do you like Vṛndāvana?" I replied that I liked it, but I liked Māyāpur more. Prabhupāda listened, but did not question or add anything further.

* * *

My appreciation of either Māyāpur or Vṛndāvana was that of a spiritual infant, and Prabhupāda accepted my words with a simple nod of his head.

Again, "Come and Live in Vṛndāvana"

Prabhupāda walked on Chatikara Road in the mornings and often lectured in the evenings at Fogal Ashram, but he spent his days at the Krishna-Balaram Mandir site. He even took his morning massage in a roped-off section at the construction site, in front of his newly built house.

Jagattāriṇī and I had some questions to ask Prabhupāda and we walked from Fogal Ashram to the Krishna-Balaram Mandir land, continuing through the wood, bricks, concrete pillars, and steel, to Prabhupāda's house. We sat down on the black marble entranceway and waited to ask Prabhupāda's secretary for a few moments with Prabhupāda. Satsvarūpa Mahārāja informed us that Prabhupāda was in his *gamchā* and taking his noon massage. "Seeing him now is therefore not possible." We sat disappointed and glum for a few moments, then with a sudden wave of inspiration, we walked to where Prabhupāda sat having his massage and slipped beneath the ropes.

Prabhupāda saw us and smiled. As soon as we raised ourselves from offering obeisances, he greeted us with, "So how do you like Vṛndāvana?" Jagattāriṇī answered quickly, "It's wonderful, Prabhupāda!" With eyes sparkling Prabhupāda responded, "Then you should come and live here." Jagattāriṇī laughed and said, "You have already sent us back to Hong Kong. How can we come and live here?" Prabhupāda paused and thought for a moment before replying. "Then," he said, "you can live here for some months each year."

* * *

Prabhupāda seemed eager to speak about the glories of Śrī Vṛndāvana-dhāma. When Jagattāriṇī expressed her appreciation, Prabhupāda immediately invited us to live in Vṛndāvana, although it was not yet practical for us to do so. Mathurā-Vṛndāvana-vāsa is also recommended by Śrīla Rūpa Gosvāmī in his *Bhakti-rasāmṛta-sindhu* as one of the five most potent forms of *sādhana-bhakti*.

Looking back, I think Jagattāriṇī did better than I when presented with the same question. She was able to spontaneously reciprocate with Prabhupāda's own affection for Śrī Vṛndāvana-dhāma.

Association on Our Terms

In his recent Hong Kong visit, Prabhupāda had clearly spoken about Siddha-svarūpānanda Goswami, but in Māyāpur, even while Siddha-svarūpānanda Goswami was present, Prabhupāda neither directly corrected him nor spoke as openly as he had in Hong Kong. This confused me, because I was not experienced in the subtleties of Prabhupāda's way of dealing. I asked Prabhupāda to again clarify Siddha-svarūpa's position. Prabhupāda replied, "At least he is now wearing *dhotī.*" I told Prabhupāda that he wore a *dhotī* in Prabhupāda's presence, but at other times he wore Western clothes. Prabhupāda's reply seemed a conclusive judgment: "Just see."

* * *

Prabhupāda, understanding my affection for Siddha-svarūpānanda Goswami, then gave me further instructions that would keep the association within the limits of his desires: "When he and his followers come to the temple in *dhotī* and with shaved head, you can associate with them."

Prabhupāda's answers satisfied me and I prepared to return to Hong Kong with my mind fixed on his instructions.

Melbourne, 1974

Leaving Hong Kong for Melbourne, Australia

Prabhupāda wanted me to remain in Hong Kong and preach, and I wanted to satisfy him. He gave me so much encouragement and mercy, but by the end of April 1974, after almost four years of struggle, I could no longer continue. Both Jagattāriṇī and I felt oppressed by Hong Kong's materialism, I was discouraged by the apathy of both the Chinese and the Indians, and I had been more or less alone in Asia without devotee association for four and a half of my six years as Prabhupāda's initiated disciple. It just became too much. I decided to leave.

Prabhupāda was shocked when I wrote him. He worried about the future of ISKCON Hong Kong as well as my spiritual life, but my mind was set. My wife and I would go to the West.

At first we thought we would go to America, but then we decided to go to Melbourne, the home of my in-laws. We left Devaprastha, an old college friend, in charge of the temple, and fled Hong Kong at the end of May. We traveled first to Thailand, then to Singapore, and finally on to Melbourne by mid-June. Prabhupāda was due to arrive in Melbourne a week later. Part of our reason for choosing Melbourne was to see Prabhupāda.

* * *

Failing to fulfill the order of one's spiritual master is extremely unpleasant, and Prabhupāda did not accept my offered list of reasons for leaving Hong Kong. I can offer no actual explanation for leaving but my lack of spiritual strength and determination to fulfill Prabhupāda's order.

A Hand from Above in Melbourne

The *kīrtana* began in the airport long before Prabhupāda's plane arrived. When Prabhupāda stepped from the passageway into the arrival lounge, the devotees went mad. Chanting, dancing, and crying, they crowded around Prabhupāda as clouds cover a mountain. Prabhupāda seemed to glide down the airport hallways. He and the devotees chanted and danced through the carpeted airport waiting rooms and passageways. Life suddenly descended into the staid Melbourne Airport. I couldn't approach Prabhupāda because he was surrounded by so many devotees, so I sped ahead down the stairs and waited at the bottom of a long escalator. "Prabhupāda has to ride this escalator to get downstairs," I thought, "and the devotees must allow him to go first."

The *kīrtana* grew louder and the devotees approached the escalator platform. After a moment's pause, Prabhupāda stood on a moving step, and began descending. He noticed a lone figure positioned near the bottom and smiled. I spontaneously reached out and he affectionately grasped my hand.

* * *

Where there's a will, there's a way. Prabhupāda's servant later informed me that Prabhupāda had remarked in the car, "Bhūrijana was there. Did you see him?"

Meat Prasāda

My wife and I were staying at her parent's home in East Brighton, a suburb of Melbourne. Prabhupāda's quarters, a small, one-story house near Brighton Beach, was nearby. At our first meeting, he demanded, "Why have you left? You were doing well. Don't be fooled. No one is there now. You are now not even living in the temple." In the course of my short replies, I mentioned that although we were not living in the temple, we were offering our food and eating *prasāda*.

Prabhupāda's retort was sarcastic: "What kind of *prasāda*? Meat *prasāda*?"

* * *

Prabhupāda manifested his concern for our spiritual lives with his piercing words. He also indicated the risk we accepted by living with and sharing cooking facilities with nonvegetarians, even though they were affectionate relatives.

Women Want Gold

While we sat in his room, Prabhupāda mentioned how modern materialistic culture destroys the finer sentiments of man. Husbands are not even able to properly maintain their wives, yet people are fooled into thinking that technological progress is increasing their standard of life. Prabhupāda then offered an example. "Women have a natural liking for golden jewelry. Now no one can afford. So the husband should provide his wife with nice gold jewelry. Then the wife will be satisfied and happy and will act as a good wife."

A few months before, I had, for the first time, purchased Jagattāriṇī gold earrings. I mentioned that fact to Prabhupāda, implying that I was pleasing him by properly taking care of my wife. Prabhupāda looked at me and dismissed my comment. "She is not interested in those things."

* * *

Prabhupāda describes life in more God conscious times in *The Teachings of Queen Kuntī:*

> The grains are abundant, the trees full of fruits, the rivers flowing nicely, the hills full of minerals, and the oceans full of wealth. What more could one want? The oyster produces pearls, and formerly people decorated their bodies with pearls, valuable stones, silk, gold, and silver. But where are those things now? Now, with the advancement of civilization, there are so many beautiful girls who have no ornaments of gold, pearls, or jewels, but only plastic bangles. So what is the use of industry and slaughter-houses?

An abundant life full of natural opulence satisfies the mind, but what satisfies a materialist has nothing to do with what satisfies a devotee. When Prabhupāda commented that Jagattāriṇī was interested only in Kṛṣṇa and not in gold earrings, she later told me her immediate mental reaction was "I'm not?" Although Prabhupāda had glorified the opulence of previous ages just seconds before, he was unimpressed by my purchase of gold earrings for my wife and insisted we acknowledge the ultimate standard – advancement in Kṛṣṇa consciousness.

Taking and Giving

Prabhupāda's strong words continued for another thirty minutes. By the end, I was crushed. When it was time to leave, I offered him my humble obeisances. He said gently, "If you think Kṛṣṇa has given you a little intelligence, you should act on it."

* * *

Prabhupāda, like a doctor administering medicine, shattered my confidence and then quickly restored it with the directive to follow my Kṛṣṇa-given intelligence. Prabhupāda thus presented me with a guideline for the immediate moment and for the rest of my life.

Guru's Affection

Prabhupāda had great affection for Tuṣṭa Kṛṣṇa Swami, who had served in Bombay and then opened a thriving ISKCON temple in Auckland, but was following Siddha-svarūpa. He had gone back to wearing Western clothes, changed his preaching style, and given up managing the New Zealand temple.

I sat with Tuṣṭa Kṛṣṇa Swami as he spoke with Prabhupāda. Tuṣṭa was a *sannyāsī,* but he was dressed like a nondevotee, with hair and a scraggly beard. Prabhupāda told Tuṣṭa Kṛṣṇa that he should dress as a *sannyāsī,* or at least like a gentleman. Prabhupāda then made a V gesture with his fingers, like a person smoking a cigarette. He held his other hand he as if he were holding a cup and drinking. Prabhupāda said, "But there should be no..."

After this conversation, Tuṣṭa, Jagattāriṇī, and I walked to the beach and discussed what Prabhupāda had said. The following day, the three of us again entered Prabhupāda's room. Tuṣṭa was dressed in a saffron wool sweater and wool tweed pants, also slightly saffron-colored. He had cut his hair neatly. He looked clean, respectable, and much more dignified.

As we sat together, Prabhupāda recounted the story of the great struggle had undergone to procure Hare Kṛṣṇa Land. Tuṣṭa Kṛṣṇa was the first devotee to see the Juhu property and contact Mr. Nair, and Prabhupāda retold the history from that point onward. After telling how Nair had cheated the devotees and fought against Prabhupāda to maintain control of the land, Prabhupāda narrated Nair's final defeat – his death by heart attack. Tuṣṭa Kṛṣṇa had also been the one to inform Prabhupāda of Nair's death when a Bombay devotee phoned Prabhupāda in New Zealand.

Tuṣṭa Kṛṣṇa seemed eager to reciprocate with Prabhupāda. He began recounting his remembrances of Prabhupāda's reaction after hearing of Nair's death. "Prabhupāda, you raised your hands in the air and called out 'Hare Kṛṣṇa!' You then folded your hands reverently and said, 'I am a saintly person and I know I should not have prayed for his death, but I could not help it. He was so offensive.'"

Prabhupāda and Tuṣṭa Kṛṣṇa spoke about Bombay ISKCON for some time, then Prabhupāda made his request. "You should go back to Bombay and be in charge.You were the first to find the land. You can even take back your wife, that Tulasī Dāsī. She is a nice devotee. You can go back and be in charge of Bombay."

* * *

Prabhupāda's affection and loyal sentiments toward devotees who had served him were steady and deep. He even suggested that a sacred tradition be broken – Tuṣṭa Kṛṣṇa Swami could return to his wife – as an attempt to save a beloved disciple.

Exacting a Promise

Another day, Tuṣṭa Kṛṣṇa, Jagattāriṇī, and I again sat with Prabhupāda, and again Prabhupāda spoke to Tuṣṭa Kṛṣṇa about his dress.

PRABHUPĀDA: Why your dress is not as a *sannyāsī*?

TUṢṬA KṚṢṆA SWAMI: The robes make people uncomfortable, Prabhupāda. They see you as different and can't relate. They won't relax enough to listen when I wear robes.

PRABHUPĀDA: But *sannyāsīs* must dress in saffron with robes and shaved head.

TUṢṬA KṚṢṆA SWAMI: I am following all the principles, but the dress is external and superficial. Why should we let it hamper the preaching?

PRABHUPĀDA: If the dress is superficial, why should you change your dress to please people who are so serious about the superficial? [*Pause.*] You understand my point? Superficial people become controlled by superficial and external things. Why do you dress to please superficial people? You should dress to please Kṛṣṇa.

TUṢṬA KṚṢṆA SWAMI: So you would like me wear saffron and shave up?

PRABHUPĀDA: Yes, I want you to promise this. Only wear saffron and keep your head shaved. This is *sannyāsī* dress. You should promise.

TUṢṬA KṚṢṆA SWAMI: Yes, Prabhupāda, I promise.

* * *

Watching Prabhupāda lovingly "checkmate" a misled son was moving. And how brilliantly had Prabhupāda turned Tuṣṭa's argument!

Surrender

Tuṣṭa Kṛṣṇa Swami and I sat with Prabhupāda on another occasion, and Prabhupāda preached to us about surrender.

"Our movement means that the beginning of spiritual life is surrender. If there is no surrendering, then there is no advancement. *Sarva-dharmān parityajya mām ekaṁ śaraṇaṁ vraja.* This is the beginning. If that thing is lacking, there is no beginning even, what to speak of advancement.... The word is disciple. Disciple means one who accepts discipline. If there is no discipline, where is the disciple? And 'disciplic succession?' Not that discipline is finished by one man. No. It will continue to go by succession. That is perfect. *Evaṁ paramparā-prāptam.* As soon as the discipline is broken, then everything is lost."

* * *

Kṛṣṇa did not instruct Arjuna until Arjuna submitted: *śiṣyas te 'haṁ śādhi māṁ tvāṁ prapannam.*

Using Flame or Smoke

Prabhupāda said that spiritual purity and spiritual strength are the results of surrender to the order of the spiritual master. If surrender, purity, and strict adherence to the guru's orders are absent, chanting will bring its effect only after a long time:

PRABHUPĀDA: But still we recommend, "Go on chanting." That will help you anywhere. It is exactly like that. If you ignite fire from wood, if the wood is dry, the fire takes place immediately. And if it is moist, then it takes time. Only smoke will come. So smoke is not required. The blazing fire is required.... If simply smoke comes, you cannot take any work out of it. As soon as there is smoke, there is fire. But that form of fire, smoke, is not useful. It is useful for troubling your eyes only.

What is smoke? Smoke is also fire, but you require blazing fire, not smoke fire. So blazing fire takes place if the wood is dry. Then it immediately takes place. Otherwise, you go on enjoying the smoke. Be satisfied.

* * *

Prabhupāda explained that the true benefit of chanting Kṛṣṇa's names, *kṛṣṇa-prema,* would not come quickly unless the "wood was dry," unless one first surrendered.

Cooking with Smoke

PRABHUPĀDA: So pure devotional service is flame. All other things are smoke. You must get the flame. Otherwise, your business will not get done. So naturally we fan when there is smoke, "Phat, phat, phat!" As soon as flame comes, there is no smoke. So again fan it. Let the flame come. Then everything will be all right. Otherwise be satisfied with the smoke. You are cooking with the smoke for three hundred years.

Cooking with Smoke: a Story

PRABHUPĀDA: There is a very humorous story about one man who was a *yogī*. He approached one big man. Generally, people are very inquisitive to see some yogic magic. So the rich man asked the *yogī*, "What you have learned about yogic perfection?"

YOGĪ: In the severe winter season, I can dip myself into the water and practice *yoga*.

RICH MAN: So, how long can you remain? All night?

YOGĪ: Yes, I can remain the whole night or as long as you like.

RICH MAN: All right. If you can remain within severe cold, within water, overnight, then I shall give you such and such presentation.

PRABHUPĀDA [*narrating*]: So the *yogī* agreed and he did it. In the morning when the man came, he said, "Oh, you are successful," but he did not want to give money. He asked his one advisor, "So what shall I do?"

ADVISOR (1): No, no, sir, you cannot give money.

RICH MAN: But how? What reason can I say?

ADVISOR (1): There was heat. He was using heat to protect himself from the cold in the water.

RICH MAN: So how there was heat?

PRABHUPĀDA [*narrating*]: You know in India they give *akāśa-pradīpa?* During Kārtika month it is our Vaiṣṇava principle. The lamp is there on the roof. On the roof there is a bamboo, and in the top of the bamboo there is lamp. So this man was in the lake and the advisor said, "You have seen that one lamp was there, and from the lamp heat was coming." [*laughing*] That lamp was three miles away and still he advised, "Yes, there was heat. Therefore, because of the heat you have tolerated." So what can the *yogī* say? He is only poor man. There was also another servant of that big man, so the poor *yogī* appealed to him that "See, I took so much trouble and he did not pay me anything."

ADVISOR (2): Don't worry. I shall see that you are paid.

PRABHUPĀDA [*narrating*]: Then there was an urgent business. The rich man said to his men, "Tomorrow I am going. You must go with me." Suppose he was to go at ten o'clock. Then at nine o'clock a messenger came to that servant who was helping the *yogī*: "You are ready?"

ADVISOR (2): No, I am cooking. When I shall finish my cooking, I shall take my meal, and then we shall go.

PRABHUPĀDA [*narrating*]: So after some time another messenger came and inquired. The answer was the same. "I am cooking and the cooking is not yet done." After more time, the rich man himself came. He was very angry. "So why are you making me late? Why you did not come?"

ADVISOR (2): I am just cooking. As soon as my rice is finished, I will take and then come.

RICH MAN: Where are you cooking?

PRABHUPĀDA [*narrating*]: Now, he has three tall bamboos, and on the top there was a rice pot, and he was giving fire at the bottom. That rich man saw. "What kind of cooking is this?"

ADVISOR (2): No, there is heat. It is going on.

RICH MAN: How have you done this? Such nonsense!

ADVISOR (2): No, if the temperature from the lamp on the roof of the sky could protect that man who was in the water all night, why won't my rice also be cooked?

PRABHUPĀDA [*narrating*]: The rich man could understand this is a reply, so that *yogī* was paid. This kind of progress, cooking, three miles above, a pot, a little fire, it will not act. There must be proper adjustment of cooking. Then you can cook food and eat. A little smoke or a little fire and three miles away the cooking pot, in this way, cooking is a useless attempt. One must be serious to cook. There is method how to cook. If you don't adopt that method and if you cook in your whimsical way, you will never be able to eat. If you say, "I shall cook in my way," and if you adopt that process, will it help? *Na sa siddhim avāpnoti na sukhaṁ na parāṁ gatim.*

* * *

Prabhupāda's message was to first surrender. Surrender dries the wood so the blazing fire of Kṛṣṇa consciousness can be ignited. In addition, we must "cook" by the standard procedure, which we learn from our spiritual master. We cannot expect cooked rice, love of Kṛṣṇa, to manifest by manufacturing our own process.

With dry wood and the necessary ingredients of rice, water, pot, and blazing flame, and by keeping the pot close to the fire of constant engagement in the service of guru and Kṛṣṇa, the rice will be quickly cooked and ready to relish.

Same Branch, Same Fruit, Same Taste

On another day, Prabhupāda spoke to Tuṣṭa Kṛṣṇa Swami very openly.

PRABHUPĀDA: If you want to start your own spiritual movement, then you have my permission.
TUṢṬA KṚṢṆA SWAMI: No, Prabhupāda. That's not my desire.
PRABHUPĀDA: There's no harm. Unless a tree has many branches it is not beautiful.

Prabhupāda then paused and spoke gravely. "But the taste of the fruit must be the same. The branch must bear the same fruit as the branch it has grown from."

* * *

This important instruction to Tuṣṭa Kṛṣṇa Swami shows both Prabhupāda's liberality as well as the limits he imposed on his disciples. Prabhupāda liberally said he would allow Tuṣṭa Kṛṣṇa, who was already preaching independently from ISKCON, to remain independent as long as he did not tamper with the process of *sādhana-bhakti*. Independent preaching, although not Prabhupāda's desire, could be acceptable, but concocting a system of "devotional service" other than the authorized method handed down in disciplic succession was not.

Go and Preach in Africa

Soon after I had arrived in Melbourne from Hong Kong, Prabhupāda told me, "You should go to Africa for preaching."

I had not been in a Western country for four years, but no sooner had I returned than Prabhupāda requested me to leave and go to Africa. Prabhupāda did not consider material factors for one who surrendered and desired to transcend.

My desire was obviously not strong enough at the time. I quickly thought of an excuse: "Prabhupāda, my expertise and training is dealing with the Chinese, not with Africans." Prabhupāda accepted and did not again mention preaching in Africa.

* * *

The spiritual master, like a doctor, carefully administers medicine just according to the patient's need. Sometimes he may apply medicine for a moment to judge whether it is suitable for a particular patient and his specific disease.

Like to Travel with Prabhupāda?

Neither Prabhupāda's servant, cook, nor Sanskrit editor had accompanied Prabhupāda from India to Australia. Satsvarūpa Mahārāja alone had come with him. I had no service. My plan was not to integrate myself with the Melbourne temple but to live separately. Prabhupāda made a suggestion to both help me and solve a need.

"Why don't you travel with me and assist?" he suggested to me one day. I was struck. Thoughts raced through my mind, the prime one being that if I traveled with Prabhupāda, he would strengthen me by his personal association and then send me back to Hong Kong. I would then neither be able to refuse nor be able to maintain in Hong Kong without him.

I could not express myself. "I don't have enough money to travel with you, Prabhupāda," I offered.

"Money is no problem," he answered. He then turned for confirmation to Tuṣṭa Kṛṣṇa Swami, who was also in the room. "Prabhupāda, Kṛṣṇa has so much money and He'll supply. There is no shortage." Prabhupāda looked back to me.

* * *

I would not agree to Prabhupāda's request that I travel with him. What wouldn't we give to again be presented with that chance? A golden opportunity given by Kṛṣṇa should immediately be taken lest it be lost forever.

Piercing Māyā

Jagattāriṇī and I walked into Prabhupāda's room in his small house near the beach. Prabhupāda had just awakened from his post-lunch nap and was again sitting behind his low desk. He did not look pleased.

He held up a stack of letters and pointed to the letter on top. "They write me," he began, "'Please accept my most fallen, insignificant obeisances. I have a great problem.' Just see."

* * *

Prabhupāda pierced the superficial humility of the letter writer, but it took me time to understand. How can someone fallen and insignificant have a great problem? An insignificant person can only have an insignificant problem.

Personally Training Disciples

Prabhupāda then looked at us with what I remember as extremely somber eyes. They seemed almost sorrowful to me. "I know no one is surrendering. I wish I could personally train all my disciples, but what can I do?"

* * *

Prabhupāda personally guided the original devotees who joined at 26 Second Avenue and those who joined ISKCON's second temple in San Francisco, but those days of seeing "Swamijī" every day did not last long. Prabhupāda's mission was expansive: to bring Kṛṣṇa consciousness to every town and village of the world, not to live with a few disciples in one or two centers. Prabhupāda was not only the guru of ISKCON, but the Founder-*ācārya* of the International Society for Krishna Consciousness.

Most disciples had little personal association with Prabhupāda, and few were directly trained by him. Some disciples never saw their spiritual master. Our training was that following Prabhupāda's *vāṇī* was real association, and he once told us, "Personal association is for fools."

But in the above exchange, Prabhupāda glorified the benefits of direct training by one's spiritual master. Certainly the great problem of an insignificant disciple would have been quickly placed in its proper perspective. We could have benefited from the opportunities to hear and watch an exalted Vaiṣṇava preach. Personal care from his pure heart would have soothed and softened the scars left by growing up in Kali-yuga and helped heal the rifts between young devotees competing for his blessings and attention.

We admit to being fools, and we lament like orphaned children because we have missed the opportunity to personally associate and be directly trained by Prabhupāda. As Prabhupāda asked, "What can I do?" Kṛṣṇa had a different plan.

Pilly Consciousness

Prabhupāda received another letter containing a report on the New York temple. The report stated that the devotees were regularly taking vitamin pills because they felt weak. Prabhupāda laughed, calling it "not Kṛṣṇa consciousness, but pilly consciousness."

"Wheat chaff and other unusable items are packed into vitamin pills and sold at high prices. There is a health fad," he explained, "and others are taking advantage and making money. This is all that is going on." He then explained the source of vitamins: "Just as cows eat grass and chaff and produce milk, vitamins were similarly coming from the fire of digestion."

* * *

Prabhupāda was skeptical about any positive effects coming from vitamins and other health food fads. Disease should be prevented by good diet, clean living, and hard work, not expensive and faddish "cures." Prabhupāda explains the basic principles of good health in a *Bhāgavatam* purport (1.1.10):

> The devotees of the Lord are always anxious for the spiritual improvement of the general public. When the sages of Naimiṣāraṇya analyzed the state of affairs of the people in this age of Kali, they foresaw that men would live short lives. In Kali-yuga, the duration of life is shortened not so much because of insufficient food but because of irregular habits. By keeping regular habits and eating simple food, any man can maintain his health. Overeating, over-sense gratification, overdependence on another's mercy, and artificial standards of living sap the very vitality of human energy. Therefore the duration of life is shortened.

A Devotee is Expert

Jagattāriṇī brought her brother David and an actress friend, Michelle, to meet Prabhupāda. We all went into Prabhupāda's room and offered our obeisances as Jagattāriṇī's brother handed Prabhupāda a bouquet of flowers. Prabhupāda began explaining how atheism is a foolish, illogical, and untenable philosophical stance. We all listened, and David voiced his appreciation of Prabhupāda's logic.

Prabhupāda had just received a new BBT publication, Svarūpa Dāmodara's *A Scientific Basis of Kṛṣṇa Consciousness*. Prabhupāda glorified the book and its author. "He is not an ordinary man," Prabhupāda said. "He has a double Ph.D. He is a scientist and he is writing about Kṛṣṇa. It is not just sentiment." Other devotees came into the room to listen. Prabhupāda glorified the new book before them as well.

Then a devotee offered Prabhupāda a new woolen sweater. Prabhupāda expressed his appreciation for the sweater's quality. Cāru, sitting nearby, commented to Prabhupāda on the temporality of material objects, including the sweater. Prabhupāda criticized Cāru's way of thinking.

"No, that logic is not very good. Because it is temporary we should see it as not good. No. These temporary things should be used in Kṛṣṇa's service. Just like this girl." Prabhupāda pointed to Michelle. "She is beautiful. Should we say she is not beautiful, or should she use her beauty in Kṛṣṇa's service? Your logic is faulty, saying that because it is temporary, it is not good."

Amogha then bounded into the room, offered his obeisances, and handed Prabhupāda a brocaded cloth as a gift.

"What is it?" asked Prabhupāda as Amogha laid the cloth out on Prabhupāda's desk. Amogha exuberantly explained that Prabhupāda could protect his *Śrīmad-Bhāgavatam* by putting this cloth on the floor under his *Bhāgavatam*.

Prabhupāda laughed, "Oh, this is for reading my *Śrīmad-Bhāgavatam* on the floor?"

"Yes," said Amogha.

Prabhupāda then picked up the cloth and held it out to Amogha. Smiling, he said, "Then this is for you. I don't read my *Bhāgavatam* on the floor."

* * *

Prabhupāda was so expert in dealing with devotees and guests. He effortlessly combined a reprimand of Cāru with the encouragement of a proud actress as he protected a philosophical point. Then he appreciated and reciprocated with Amogha's affection, but not with the practicality of his gift.

Celibacy

Prabhupāda sat with some disciples and spoke about the glories of celibacy. "If one remains celibate from the ages of sixteen to twenty-one, his brain becomes *so fertile* for spiritual realization." Prabhupāda stretched the "o" in the word "so" until it sounded four times as long. When he spoke the word "fertile," his eyes opened wide and moved slowly around the room. As his eyes met the glance of one devotee after another, each devotee's head dropped as he remembered his crippling, improper actions during those formative years. A long pause followed. "But," Prabhupāda continued, "if you chant Hare Kṛṣṇa, everything will be all right anyway."

* * *

Many devotees who come to the Kṛṣṇa consciousness movement arrive crippled, having spent years disturbing their consciousness through abortive attempts at sensual pleasure. As the lame cannot run, such devotees often feel themselves limping along, struggling to advance.

Prabhupāda was aware of this, but he had full faith in the potency of the holy name. Devotees who feel themselves crippled should follow Prabhupāda's instruction and unhesitatingly take shelter of Śrī Caitanya Mahāprabhu and the holy name in the mood of Narottama Dāsa Ṭhākura:

śrī-kṛṣṇa-caitanya prabhu doyā koro more
tomā binā ke doyālu jagat-saṁsāre

patita-pāvana-hetu tava avatāra
mo sama patita prabhu nā pāibe āra

My dear Lord Caitanya, You are most merciful! Who else within this world of birth and death can be as merciful as You? Your incarnation is to reclaim the most fallen souls, but You will not find a soul more fallen than me. My claim, therefore, is first.

Associating with Drunkards

Prabhupāda lectured in Melbourne's Town Hall and he seemed satisfied, although most of the seats remained empty. At the end of his lecture, Prabhupāda called for questions. A young man raised his hand. "How does one become sincere?"

"How does one become a drunkard?" Prabhupāda replied, and then paused. "If you want to become a drunkard, associate with drunkards. If you want to become sincere, associate with those who are sincere." He then pointed to the section of the hall where the devotees sat. "You should associate with them."

* * *

Even stalwart atheists like Hiraṇyakaśipu acknowledge association as essential for progress in every field of activity: "Association acts upon the heart as it does upon a crystal." As a crystal reflects and takes on the colors of its surroundings, so the heart takes on the qualities of those with whom we associate.

Prabhupāda used the graphic example of becoming a drunkard to present the importance of pure association. By pointing to his disciples as sincere, he both acknowledged their sincerity and reminded them of their responsibility to remain unmotivated, reliable servants of their spiritual master.

An Interfaith Dialogue

Bishop Kelley, the head of the Catholic Church in Victoria, visited Prabhupāda at his cottage. As usual, Prabhupāda sat on the floor. The bishop and his friend sat in chairs.

The bishop was elderly and pious, and Prabhupāda struck up an affectionate conversation with him. They spoke about the cold June weather and then about the loss of values in society. Prabhupāda asked the bishop to examine the book, *A Scientific Basis for Krishna Consciousness,* but the bishop didn't have his glasses. Prabhupāda then lent him his own glasses, and his prescription perfectly suited the bishop. Prabhupāda laughed, "Birds of the same feather."

They discussed the perfect but covered nature of the soul, the importance of hearing *śāstra* to remove the covering, and the possibility of communing directly with God. Prabhupāda clarified the bishop's fear that accepting the validity of subjective communication with God would increase the number of irreligious acts perpetrated in His name: "God told me to do it."

PRABHUPĀDA: There is individual instruction, but that is subordinate. The general instruction is that one should be fully surrendered to God. That is the general instruction. Now, if one is fully surrendered, in a particular case in particular circumstances, God gives him instructions what to do....According to circumstances He gives him. But general instruction is there, and that is recorded in scripture. That general instruction must be followed. One cannot say, "God is dictating through me something against the general instruction." That is not possible. The general instruction must be followed.

As their conversation continued, Prabhupāda requested that the bishop hear a tape of a recent class he had given, and as the bishop and his friend sat in their chairs and listened, Prabhupāda, with grace and dignity, rested his head on his arms on the table in front of him and appeared to doze.

The tape finished and the bishop expressed appreciation for Prabhupāda's message. Wishing Prabhupāda "Godspeed," the bishop and his friend, with *prasāda* in hand and in a jolly mood, left the cottage.

Later that evening Prabhupāda remarked to his secretary that the Christians should give up their meat-eating and then we could combine and preach with them. But first they must give up their meat-eating.

* * *

Prabhupāda seemed to consider the bishop sincere, so he expressed hope that a cooperative preaching effort – Kṛṣṇa consciousness and Christianity – might one day occur. Yet I recently heard why Prabhupāda may have played the tape for the bishop instead of speaking directly to him. After the bishop left, Prabhupāda revealed to the devotees that he had smelled alcohol on the bishop's breath and had decided against preaching to him any further.

Remaining a Fool

Prabhupāda sat at his low desk, satisfied and smiling. He spoke about the humility of advanced devotees. I was in a light, superficial mood. "My only qualification," I added, "is that I am a fool."

Prabhupāda looked at me sharply. "Yes, but you should not remain a fool."

* * *

Prabhupāda's answer cut through the superficiality of my childish comment. Actual devotees are humble, but they are never fools.

An Invitation

I drove up to Prabhupāda's beachfront cottage just as he and his entourage were leaving for the morning walk. I quickly parked my car, got out, and offered my obeisances on the pavement. Prabhupāda waved to me, gesturing that I too should join his walk.

* * *

It was exhilarating to receive an invitation directly from Prabhupāda to associate with him.

Prabhupāda's Only Criticism of the Devotees

Later, we sat at Prabhupāda's feet and listened to him preach. Material considerations were insignificant as long as we sat there. We wanted to become like he treated us. He treated us as if we were already sincere and compassionate devotees of Kṛṣṇa. By his association, we wanted to help a thankless world, a world that was caught up in fruitless trivialities and deadly misconceptions. We were neophytes, but Prabhupāda's association made Kṛṣṇa real to us and devotional service the glory of life. Prabhupāda spoke intimately with us, like comrades in battle.

"These books are for you," Prabhupāda said, as he pointed to several of the books he had written. "Do not make it an export business. They only buy and sell to others. For themselves they have no use." Prabhupāda imitated a devotee distributing his books, "Please take this book. It is very important." He then took the customer's role: "Oh, it is important? What is it about?" Prabhupāda again switched roles. "I don't know, it is for you!" We all laughed sheepishly. "My only criticism of the devotees is that they think my books are for distribution and not for reading."

* * *

Prabhupāda wanted his disciples to become philosophically strong by studying his books. Śāstric study grants us the ability to preach, fixes our intelligence, and purifies our hearts. At this time Prabhupāda also asked the devotees, "Why are we so interested in book distribution? Because it is distribution of knowledge. It is distribution of knowledge."

The Essence of Spiritual Life

During his visit, Prabhupāda asked me to go to Africa. He later agreed to my offer to preach in Singapore, where the government was unfavorable to the Kṛṣṇa consciousness movement and had recently even refused Prabhupāda permission to enter the country. Prabhupāda suggested I enter Singapore, wear nondevotee clothing in my preaching, rent an apartment, open a bookstore, and distribute his books. I went to Singapore after Prabhupāda left. Prabhupāda was pleased and sent me the following letter:

> My Dear Spiritual Son Bhurijana Dāsa:
>
> Please accept my blessings. I am very glad to receive your letter dated 8/7/74 from Singapore. I am very pleased that you have gone

to that place simply on my order, alone, to preach the message of Lord Caitanya. I like this kind of spirit in you very much. You know I went to your country also alone, in old age, because of the order given to me by my spiritual master. So I get great pleasure when I see my own disciples from America going to far off places leaving their rich nation with all facilities and their families, to preach. The secret of success in spiritual life is to satisfy one's spiritual master. This is the essence. You have captured this. So now go on in this way and do not falter. Follow the regulative principles and devotional practices I have given you. This will keep you fit. Be patient and determined, and ask everyone you meet to please chant Hare Krishna. I shall be very glad if you send me regular reports of your attempt.

I hope this meets you and also your good wife in best of health.

Your ever well wisher,
A. C. Bhaktivedanta Swami

* * *

We can sum up the success formula of spiritual life in a single, short sentence: one must satisfy one's spiritual master – *yasya prasādād bhagavat-prasādo*. The spiritual strength to do this is invoked by following the regulative principles and the standard devotional practices. Then on our guru's order, we can patiently and determinedly preach by asking everyone we meet to please chant *Hare Kṛṣṇa*.

Melbourne, 1975

Ready or Not, Prabhupāda is Coming!

After a few months of lone preaching in Singapore and Malaysia, I returned to Melbourne and took a job to support my family. My wife delivered our daughter on the day I returned to Australia. When I informed Prabhupāda, he wrote: "Now Krishna has blessed you with a daughter. The name Vrindaban Leela you have chosen is very nice." I gradually started a tapestry handbag business, which freed me from the torture of working for others. I was living as an independent householder at this time, and accepting that I would not be returning to Hong Kong or Singapore, Prabhupāda instructed me through letters how to properly execute the duties of my *āśrama*.

In 1974, ISKCON Melbourne was in a rented house in the down-and-out suburb of St. Kilda. The devotees searched for a new temple during Prabhupāda's 1974 visit, but they could not settle on one until after Prabhupāda had left. The new property, a historic building near South Melbourne, was at this time one of ISKCON's best properties outside India. Prabhupāda agreed to come for the official opening in 1975.

The devotees worked frantically day and night to lay the marble floor in the temple room, prepare Prabhupāda's quarters, and paint the building. As Prabhupāda's arrival approached, the building was nowhere near completion. The devotees asked Prabhupāda to "wait for some time" in Perth, Western Australia, until the building was ready. He complied, but when the "some time" proved too long, he decided to fly, ready or not, to Melbourne.

Foolish Questions, Perfect Answers

Prabhupāda's flight to Melbourne landed and he was escorted to a press conference in the airport's VIP lounge. A hundred jubilant devotees sat on the floor as reporters questioned Prabhupāda, who sat with Madhudviṣa on a raised dais. The questions were the usual:

REPORTER: What is your name?
PRABHUPĀDA: A. C. Bhaktivedanta Swami.
REPORTER: What do the "A" and the "C" stand for?
PRABHUPĀDA: If I say, you will not understand.
REPORTER: Please, I'd like to know what the "A" and the "C" stand for?
PRABHUPĀDA: You will not understand.
REPORTER: What do the "A" and the "C" stand for?

Prabhupāda then said "Abhay Caranaravindam." He pronounced "Abhay Caranaravindam" so fast that even I could not understand his words.

REPORTER: I'm sorry, I couldn't follow that. What did you say?
PRABHUPĀDA: Abhay Caranaravindam. [*Prabhupāda again quickly pronounces his name.*]
REPORTER: Could you repeat that again?
PRABHUPĀDA: I told you that you would not understand.

* * *

Prabhupāda was clearly unimpressed by the reporter's superficial question, and he playfully outmaneuvered him as easily as an adult outmaneuvers a child.

Sleeping Only Six Hours Each Night?

A second reporter began with a more pointed question.

REPORTER TWO: I've heard that your disciples work all day but only get to sleep six hours at night. I wanted to ask you how many hours each night you sleep?

PRABHUPĀDA: I generally go to sleep at ten o'clock at night and wake up at twelve. I then do my translating work.

MADHUDVIṢA: [*Interrupting, in a protective mood*] Prabhupāda doesn't sleep much at all. He sleeps less, not more than his disciples. He doesn't sleep more than four hours a night.

PRABHUPĀDA: No, not four hours. I go to sleep at ten and awake at twelve. How many hours is that?

* * *

The reporter should have recognized Prabhupāda as an elderly holy man traveling around the world on a God conscious mission. Instead, he was trying to expose that Prabhupāda was a "cult leader" and that he exploited his followers. These unfortunate and befooled followers, he was trying to imply, were working hard to support the luxuriant and easy living of their cult master. Prabhupāda revealed the opposite: although his disciples were working hard, he was not exploiting them for personal pleasure. Both he and his disciples were working hard for Kṛṣṇa's pleasure. Rather than using his disciples to finance his life of ease as the reporter was hoping to prove, he worked even harder than his disciples in the service of his Guru Mahārāja and Kṛṣṇa.

Support in Kṛṣṇa Consciousness

After the press conference, Prabhupāda went to the new Melbourne temple. When he saw the temple complex, he was impressed. One evening, I accompanied him as he walked from his room to the separate temple building. As we neared the temple room door, he turned to me and said, "You could have done this in Hong Kong."

I felt the sting of my spiritual master's disappointment. I fumbled and expressed to him my stock of excuses: "How could I? I was alone. The local Indians are materialistic and the Chinese are not interested and are atheists..."

Prabhupāda looked at me for a moment and then continued to the temple for his lecture.

* * *

Although I am from New York City, I easily rate Hong Kong as the most intensely materialistic city I have ever seen. As a preaching field, Hong Kong is far from a ripe fruit waiting to be plucked. It's a tough place to live.

Prabhupāda nevertheless knew that Kṛṣṇa consciousness could spread in Hong Kong. He knew that devotees could be made and a substantial temple established. He had hoped I could do this service, but I was unable. He was disappointed. Although I felt unqualified to do the service, he felt I was able.

Quite often it is a teacher's sustained faith in a student that empowers the student to reach his potential. When I reflect back on these words in particular, I am inspired by Prabhupāda's faith in me, which was even greater than the faith I had in myself.

Nonattachment to a Good Ring

Śrutakīrti vigorously massaged sandalwood oil into Prabhupāda's head. I suddenly noticed that he still wore the gold ring with the engraved "P" on it that I had given him when he visited Hong Kong in 1974.

"You still have the ring," I said in near surprise. "Yes," said Prabhupāda, "it is a good ring."

* * *

That Prabhupāda not only accepted but wore my offering for years thrilled me. I saw him wearing the ring many times. Because the gold was pure and soft and the ring size expandable, he would at times wear it on one finger and then move it to another.

Years after Prabhupāda's departure from this world, I learned what finally became of that ring. Prabhupāda's "son" had come to see him in Calcutta and had requested him again and again for money for bangles for his daughter. Prabhupāda finally give him the ring, and he left, satisfied. Prabhupāda then turned to his servant and said, "I am not attached."

Hearing Accurately

As Śrutakīrti continued massaging Prabhupāda, I handed Prabhupāda a stainless steel case with its top screwed on tightly. Inside was pure sandalwood oil, a gift passed from a devotee through me to Prabhupāda.

Prabhupāda lifted the metal case in his soft hands and said, "This case is for *kajal.*"*

"No, Prabhupāda," I replied, "it holds sandalwood oil." Prabhupāda insisted, "No, this case is for *kajal.*" Thinking that Prabhupāda may not have understood me, I again repeated that the case contained sandalwood oil.

Prabhupāda replied sharply, "There may be sandalwood oil inside, but the case is meant for *kajal.*"

* * *

Prabhupāda had understood my words perfectly, but I hadn't understood him. When I finally understood, I felt embarrassed and foolish.

Women, Widows, and Success

Śrutakīrti then rubbed mustard oil onto Prabhupāda's back. I moved to face Prabhupāda's front and was enjoying the sweet atmosphere that surrounded him. With his eyes closed, Prabhupāda spoke. "My godbrothers criticize me that I have allowed women to live in our temples. This is not done in India. Only *brahmacārīs* can live. But I have become successful because I have made this adjustment."

Prabhupāda opened his eyes and continued, "Although they criticize me, their Gaudiya Maths are empty. The only time they have people coming is during Gaura-Pūrṇimā to Māyāpur for *parikrama*. And who is coming for *parikrama?* Widows, women in white. Because I have made this adjustment I was successful."

Adjusting Principles

Śrutakīrti, as he moved to massage Prabhupāda's side, asked, "Prabhupāda, how can we tell the difference between making an adjustment and changing a principle?"

Prabhupāda's eyes closed and Śrutakīrti continued to massage. After a few moments, Prabhupāda opened his eyes and said, "That takes a little intelligence."

* * *

Śrutakīrti's question was penetrating. Clearly delineating between the adjustable and the nonadjustable, between a detail and a principle, is not easy. It requires intelligence. To foolishly mistake a nonadjustable principle for an adjustable detail will cause havoc in spiritual life, and to accept each detail as if it can never be adjusted is fanaticism. Fanaticism will cause havoc of a different nature.

If we have developed our spiritual intelligence, we can make distinctions between principles and details, but we should confirm our opinions with trusted friends or superiors. If we haven't developed our spiritual intelligence, we should take guidance from those who have. We should not act independently.

One Householder's "Good" Business

I spoke to Prabhupāda about my tapestry handbag business, which was doing well. I was able to send Prabhupāda donations every week. Still, I felt guilty that I was neither serving Prabhupāda in Hong Kong nor living in the temple.

I informed Prabhupāda about the items I was selling, describing them in an almost derogatory tone, but Prabhupāda was enthusiastic and he called the business "good."

I was surprised and asked, "I'm selling handbags. How is that good?"

Prabhupāda looked at me soberly. "One has to do something."

* * *

A householder living outside the temple must support his family. By Kṛṣṇa's mercy I both supported my family through a relatively sinless enterprise and was able to send weekly donations to Prabhupāda. Prabhupāda's appreciation of these small successes led him to term my business "good."

Free Books

Wishing to distribute books, but fearing the repercussions of the collecting techniques the devotees used, I asked Prabhupāda whether or not books could be purchased and distributed for free. His reply: "As far as possible."

* * *

Prabhupāda did not set up the Bhaktivedanta Book Trust to publish books and distribute them for free. Books were to be sold so the Book Trust could make a profit and publish more books. Prabhupāda generally extolled the glories of selling his books as opposed to distributing them for free. In 1968 he even said that anyone who turns his books into money would go back to Godhead. Collecting money through book distribution is practical. The exchange of energy – money for books – makes people take the books more seriously. Having paid for the book, they will be more likely to read it.

Secondly, devotees require money to maintain the temples and expand the preaching. Money from book distribution can fulfill ISKCON's needs for money while still allowing the devotee book distributors to speak all day about Kṛṣṇa.

Still, Prabhupāda also allowed us to distribute his books for free. Book distribution wherein a wealthy person buys books and distributes them in charity is successful both in India and Russia. Thousands of *Bhagavad-gītās* have been distributed to wealthy factory owners, who then present them to their workers.

A "Just See" Story

Stories often floated around about Prabhupāda. I had recently heard a fantastic story from several devotees, who obviously accepted it as true. I had my doubts and decided to ask Prabhupāda directly.

"Prabhupāda, some devotees told me a story that I wanted to ask you about. The story was that you were in your room with Viṣṇujana Mahārāja and he asked you about your *rasa*. The way I heard the story was that you started glowing brighter and brighter until Viṣṇujana Mahārāja crawled out of the room. Did that happen?"

Prabhupāda smiled, leaned back, and expanded his smile even further. "Just see," he said while shaking his head.

* * *

Prabhupāda's "just see" and his expression told it all. The remainder of the sentence – "the nonsense that people are speaking" – was clearly understood.

The Once-and-for-all Answer

Another time, as Prabhupāda took his massage, I asked him, "What is the position of devotees living outside?" Prabhupāda replied, "I shall answer this question once and for all times in the lecture tonight."

As usual, Prabhupāda's class that evening was attended by all the devotees, and as the devotees waited for Prabhupāda to arrive, an air of expectancy electrified the atmosphere. I was especially eager to hear Prabhupāda's lecture.

Prabhupāda proceeded with his class, and as I listened, I thought on several occasions that Prabhupāda was obliquely answering the question. At the end of the lecture Prabhupāda mentioned, "It is sometimes asked about living outside the temple for a devotee." He then began his answer. "Just as one does not have to be a member of the stock exchange to do business. He can do business without being a member. But if one is a member of the stock exchange, his doing business becomes easy because all of his associations are to do with business. Similarly, one can be a devotee and live outside the temple, but completing his devotional business is easier if he lives inside."

* * *

During these years devotees often asked Prabhupāda the "inside/outside" question. ISKCON's general view was clear and simple: those living in the temple were devotees and those living outside were demons. This did not represent Prabhupāda's idea, however. In the following excerpt from a morning walk (Hawaii, 1975), Prabhupāda thoroughly explains the inside/outside controversy:

DISCIPLE: It is very difficult to put everyone who is living outside the temple in one category. Some people, they are, many people that I know living outside are following strictly the regulative principles, and they are…

PRABHUPĀDA: Huh?

DISCIPLE: They are strictly following regulative principles and chanting their rounds and having morning *ārati* in their homes. And evening also, they are chanting. So instead of fighting, I think we should only try to encourage everybody to chant and follow the regulative principles.

PRABHUPĀDA: No, that is... Whether you live in temple or outside temple, the rules and regulation and the process must be followed. Then you are successful. It doesn't matter that you have to live in the temple. *Gṛhe thāko, vane thāko, sadā 'hari' bole' ḍāko.* Not that everyone has to live in the temple. If he does not agree with other godbrothers, friends, he can live separately, but he must follow the rules and regulations. That is wanted. But if you live with devotees, it will be automatically done.

DISCIPLE: Easy.

PRABHUPĀDA: Therefore it is recommended that you live with devotees. But you cannot make a new opinion so far the process is concerned. That must be followed. This is not good idea: "Whatever I do, it is my independence, and I will chant." So that is good in the sense that some day he will come to senses. Otherwise, for the time being, the chant is not very powerful. The fire in wet wood is not powerful. It will create some smoke. Although the fire is there. But if you put dry wood, immediately it will be blazing and your business will be quickly done. This is intelligence. There are many examples. A patient suffering from disease, a doctor said, "You should do; you should not do." So if we follow "You should not do," then it becomes quickly recovered. But if he becomes under the treatment of the doctor at the same time he does all nonsense, then how it can be successful? It will take time. That is stated in the *Caitanya-caritāmṛta. Pāpi jane aparādha āchāya pracūra.* Offenseless chanting is the ultimate goal. In the beginning we are not offenseless, but by chanting, chanting, by practice, we gradually become offenseless. But this is necessary, that you should be offenseless.

RAMEŚVARA: Śrīla Prabhupāda, it seems unfortunate that if the devotees cannot live in the temples, then they have to work for some *karmī* just to support themselves and then they do not have time to go on the *saṅkīrtana* party. So it is such mercy to be on the *saṅkīrtana* party. It seems very unfortunate that they do not have the time.

PRABHUPĀDA: No, then they should live in the temple if they want to give service in the *saṅkīrtana* party.

RAMEŚVARA: We always try to encourage them to come back to the temple.

PRABHUPĀDA: Yes. if he does not join the *saṅkīrtana* party, that does not mean his spiritual life is hampered. He has to follow the rules and regulations. He may not be able to join the *saṅkīrtana* party, but he must follow the process, rules and regulations. That is wanted. And because he is living outside the temple, therefore he will forget all rules and regulations and do whatever he likes – then it will ruin the whole thing.

DEVOTEE (1): Śrīla Prabhupāda, is it faster if one lives in the temple and goes on the *saṅkīrtana* party? Is it faster?

PRABHUPĀDA: That depends on him. Even in the temple, if his mind is in a different subject matter, then how it will help him?

BALI MARDANA: They like to preach that anyone who's living outside the temple is going to hell.

PRABHUPĀDA: Generally.

BALI MARDANA: But even devotees who are following. They like to preach that.

PRABHUPĀDA: No, that is not. That is not. Just like even in ordinary business, if you transact business in the stock association, you get good business. And outside the stock association you don't get. Because association is there, there are many purchaser and many seller. So if you have to sell, you get immediate purchaser, and if you have to purchase, there is immediate seller… Therefore the stock exchange is there. That is the way, that if we live together in the stock exchange of devotional service, then you can help me, I can help you. So our business will go on nicely. And outside the market, you can live three hundred miles away from the stock exchange. You will not get so much business. Like that.

DEVOTEE (2): You'll miss the opportunities.

PRABHUPĀDA: Yes, therefore it is helpful. if you want to do business, you must take the first opportunity, the greatest opportunity, do your business. That is intelligence. And if we think, "All right, I shall do slowly. In seven hundred lives I shall become perfect," that is another thing.

BALI MARDANA: It is riskier to stay outside.

PRABHUPĀDA: Oh, yes. Otherwise why you are opening so many centers and making arrangements: "We shall provide you with shelter, with food. These are the facilities. You live here, do whatever is your capacity. Don't sleep, but work." This is our teaching. *Satāṁ prasaṅgān,* this is also, and Rūpa Gosvāmī says, *sato vṛtteḥ sādhu-saṅge ṣaḍbhir bhaktiḥ prasidhyati:* "If you live with the association of devotee, then it will be quickly fruitful." And if you live with these ordinary men, then whatever you have got will be finished very soon. There is another verse. It is said there that it is preferred to live within a cage surrounded by fire than to live with the nondevotees. It is preferred.

Going Through the Gate First

Living outside the temple and being somewhat at odds with the local management, I was not allowed easy access to Prabhupāda. I was kept at a distance and neither invited for *darśanas* nor for morning walks.

Prabhupāda wanted me to return to Hong Kong because no steady replacement had been found, despite the year that had passed. I gained strength by reading the second half of the eighteenth chapter of *Bhagavad-gītā* and resolved, like Arjuna, to surrender. Although I was willing to return to Hong Kong, however, I realized that Jagattāriṇī could not. It was simply too difficult for her. While I would go, she could remain behind in Australia. I collected these thoughts and, not having the facility to speak with Prabhupāda, typed them into a letter. After *Bhagavad-gītā* class that evening I handed the letter to Prabhupāda as he stepped down from his *vyāsāsana.*

The next morning I rode my Suzuki motorcycle behind the motorcade of cars heading for the Melbourne Royal Botanical

Gardens. By the time I arrived, the devotees were already walking through the lush, green garden paths. They clustered protectively around Prabhupāda like bees around their queen. I could not get close.

Suddenly I remembered my "waiting at the bottom of the escalator" trick from Prabhupāda's 1974 visit to Melbourne. "When Prabhupāda leaves the gardens," I thought, "the devotees must allow him to walk first through the exit gate. I'll wait on the other side of the gate."

I rushed through the gate just before the walk was over and waited. The devotees soon came into sight. As they neared the gate, I watched Prabhupāda break from the cluster and walk through the gate. When he emerged, I greeted him with a smile and my obeisances. He looked at me and said, "I have received your letter. Come and see me at any time."

* * *

I was not strong in my Kṛṣṇa consciousness at this time. I mostly saw others' faults and neglected my own. We can just imagine how Prabhupāda must have viewed his young disciples, who at times were childishly divided into factions, thinking that they were more pure or sincere than others. Childish as they were, Prabhupāda maintained, counseled, and either directly or indirectly trained his disciples in spiritual life as long as they honored the sanctity of the relationship.

For the Future

Since Prabhupāda said I could see him at any time, I went to his room late one afternoon just as a social worker was leaving. Prabhupāda handed him a piece of *sandeśa prasāda* as the man mumbled something about a previously made appointment, offered his thanks, and left. Prabhupāda and the devotees – Madhudviṣa Swami, Ugraśrava, Amogha, and others – laughed.

Prabhupāda then looked at me. "I have read your letter. You should not take *sannyāsa* now." The devotees' laughter increased, thinking I had asked Prabhupāda permission to take *sannyāsa* in my letter.

"How old are you now?" Prabhupāda asked.

"Twenty-eight."

"How old is your daughter?"

"Only two."

Prabhupāda smiled and replied, "Householder is also an *āśrama*. It is also meant for spiritual advancement. You should remain a householder, and when you are fifty, your daughter will be twenty-four and can be married. Your wife can live with her. When you are fifty you can think about taking *sannyāsa.*"

* * *

In this conversation, Prabhupāda did not mention anything about my preaching in Hong Kong. Instead he ordered me not to take *sannyāsa* until I was fifty. I understood from his reply that I should not at present return to Hong Kong, but I was nevertheless puzzled after hearing his words.

Weeks later, as I walked down Flinders Street in downtown Melbourne, it hit me. Prabhupāda said I should continue in householder life until I am fifty. Then at that time, but not before, I can consider changing my household situation. Prabhupāda is instructing me now that when I am fifty, my situation and service may be changed, including the possibility of leaving my wife and family for preaching.

Interplanetary Eagles

During one evening lecture, Prabhupāda spoke boldly of giant eagles that fly from planet to planet, eat elephants, and hatch their eggs in outer space with the help of atmospheric friction. As he spoke, sitting tall and fully confident on the purple velvet *vyāsāsana,* his eyes blazed, challenging any doubters. "Any questions?" he asked at the end of his lecture. Silence.

One lone hand hesitatingly sprouted from the crowd of sixty-five devotees and guests.

RAGHUNĀTHA: Śrīla Prabhupāda, in your lecture you mentioned, um, um, giant eagles who, um, fly from planet to planet.
PRABHUPĀDA: Yes.
RAGHUNĀTHA: Well, um, it is, um, a little hard to believe.
PRABHUPĀDA: [*Sitting still taller, with his eyes almost defiant.*] What do you know? You are still within the womb of your mother!

* * *

The conditioned soul's conception of reality is incomplete and imperfect. We will readily admit that no two persons perceive the world in exactly the same way, yet we nevertheless consider our own perceptions reality.

Prabhupāda pointed out that Raghunātha's illusory perception of reality, which was limited by Australian cultural biases, finite intelligence, faulty cognizance, and spiritual babyhood, prevented him from understanding the goings-on within a material universe, what to speak of in Goloka Vṛndāvana.

An Open Darśana

Before my "you should not take *sannyāsa*" meeting with Prabhupāda, I had arranged through the temple authorities to privately meet Prabhupāda, but now that I had gone to see him on my own, I didn't need that appointment. Devotees begged me to be allowed to come during my scheduled meeting. My private *darśana* became an open *darśana,* and all the local devotees filed into Prabhupāda's room.

The parquet floor in Prabhupāda's room quickly became crowded with devotees, but still more entered. Prabhupāda sat on his plush, couchlike *āsana* as he watched his disciples enter. Madhudviṣa saw the devotees' enthusiasm and remarked, "Prabhupāda, it seems that the devotees want to get more of your association." Prabhupāda smiled affectionately. "I am also wanting that."

* * *

Prabhupāda's preaching mission required constant travel. Most of his disciples, therefore, lived in separation from Prabhupāda, although he remained the center of their lives. They rarely saw him more than a few days each year. Even during those few days, most devotees' association with Prabhupāda took place in his morning or evening classes. Empowered by the inspiration they derived during those times, however, the devotees continued throughout the year trying to please him by their services.

Still, the devotees always wanted more of Prabhupāda's association. Because Prabhupāda was attracted by their sincerity, he also relished their association.

Why Open Darśanas Were Rare

One young woman, who was neither initiated nor married, stepped up to Prabhupāda. She smiled and took out some drawings her five-year-old son had scribbled. Prabhupāda looked at the first one and the woman explained, "This is Kṛṣṇa with His cowherd boyfriends." Prabhupāda smiled lightly. "Very nice." She then pulled out a second scribbled picture: "Kṛṣṇa holding Govardhana Hill." The third, fourth, and fifth pictures followed in quick succession. Prabhupāda's appreciations turned from words to nods as his smile dropped toward a frown. The audience of devotees began to fidget and their eyes lowered in embarrassment as the woman continued producing picture after picture.

* * *

The devotees felt pain watching this woman take advantage of Prabhupāda's patience and tolerance. They knew the value of each moment of his time.

"Offer Me with Devotion"

The devotees in Melbourne had cultivated a flourishing *tulasī* garden in a round greenhouse near the back of the temple property. The *brahmacārī* "in charge" of the *tulasī* plants was an expert gardener, but he was eccentric. He also seemed to think his service was most glorious and that other services were inferior.

Madhudviṣa introduced him to Prabhupāda as several devotees sat at Prabhupāda's feet.

MADHUDVIṢA: Our *tulasī* gardener has a question for you, Prabhupāda.
PRABHUPĀDA: He should ask.

The devotee gardener, in an affected accent, asked Prabhupāda how many *tulasī* leaves should be placed on Kṛṣṇa's plate for the offering.

With his service as the center of the universe, his intonations and hand gestures revealed his vision of mountains of *tulasī* leaves on Kṛṣṇa's plate that would dwarf the tiny helpings of rice, *dāl*, *capātīs,* and sweets.

We expected Prabhupāda to praise the gardener for his ability to grow luxuriant *tulasīs,* but Prabhupāda simply looked at him for several seconds and then said, "One."

* * *

In the ninth chapter of *Bhagavad-gītā* Kṛṣṇa asks His devotees to offer Him a leaf, a fruit, a flower, and some water with love and devotion. Kṛṣṇa's mention of a leaf *(patram)* is in the singular. He is satisfied only by devotion, not the quantity or size of the offering.

Prabhupāda was reminding the devotee gardener that devotion is the essence of our accomplishments in the Kṛṣṇa consciousness movement.

A Chance Taken for a Gesture of Affection

The devotees accompanied Prabhupāda to the airport when he left Melbourne. Prabhupāda sat on the plastic chairs of the airport lounge, and tens of devotees sat on chairs and the carpeted floor near him.

Several devotees stepped forward to speak a few final words or offer a departure letter, apple, or flower. I watched everything from the back. I wasn't in good consciousness or spirits. I felt distant.

The boarding call for Prabhupāda's flight was announced. Prabhupāda stood up and the devotees offered their obeisances. A *kīrtana* started and the atmosphere filled with anticipation. From the crowd, I noticed that Prabhupāda's hat sat on his head at an awkward, almost comical angle. A thought raced through my mind. "What if people think it funny and laugh at Prabhupāda?" I tried to decide whether or not I should straighten his hat.

The internal dialogue began: "Prabhupāda doesn't care what others think. But it will be offensive for them to laugh. They should offer Prabhupāda all respect. How can I be the one who straightens it? Is it offensive to think others may look at Prabhupāda's tilted hat as comical?"

Prabhupāda walked slowly toward the gangway, allowing his disciples a few more moments of association. I stepped directly into his path. "Allow me to straighten your hat, Prabhupāda." He looked steadily at my face as my hands moved his hat from left to center on his freshly shaved head. I then quickly stepped back and Prabhupāda walked up the gangway to the sound of the *kīrtana.*

* * *

Prabhupāda did not acknowledge my "straightening," yet I immediately felt that I had acted properly. My analysis of the possibly unfavorable reactions of others may not have been accurate, but my motivation was simple – to protect Prabhupāda from an embarrassing situation. I had acted as his servant.

A Servant Serves

Due to the heavy judgment of ISKCON of the 1970s on devotees living outside the temple, and due also to my personal shortcomings, I found it difficult to associate with the devotees and do temple service in Australia. Yet serving Prabhupāda remained the only meaningful desire in my life. My first plan was to offer Prabhupāda $1,000. For weeks and weeks I tried to accumulate money for my offering, but money seemed to vanish as fast as I made it.

From the inception of my handbag business, I considered Prabhupāda its owner and myself its manager, so instead of saving to send Prabhupāda $1,000 in one lump sum, I began to send him checks each week.

My first offerings were only $25, but they gradually grew to $50, $100, and finally $250 a week. (Later, when Prabhupāda toured Australia during his final visit in 1976, I was able to fulfill my desire to give him $1,000.) Regardless of the size of my donation, each week's focus was my trip to the post office and my purchase of a money order in the name of His Divine Grace A. C. Bhaktivedanta Swami Prabhupāda. I would also write him a note expressing my affection and a prayer asking him to accept my insignificant offering.

* * *

Devotees doing business tend to make the financial success of their business a prerequisite to giving donations. I find this mentality counterproductive in my own circumstances, and in the circumstances of many devotees with whom I have spoken.

I learned that a donation – regardless of its size – must be offered for Kṛṣṇa's service each week. The size of the donation may vary according to the success of the business, but serving Kṛṣṇa has top priority, alongside paying for food, clothing, and shelter.

With every weekly check, I could think that at least some concrete service was completed, as opposed to hoping the business would one day be successful so I could one day serve.

By regularly offering donations to Prabhupāda and by thinking of the business as his, I was forced to work hard, depend on Kṛṣṇa, and consider my business devotional service. Prabhupāda appreciated my mood, especially the regularity of my offerings.

Letters from Prabhupāda

After a month or so, I started to receive letters of acknowledgment from Prabhupāda. One of Prabhupāda's replies instructed me that a disciple must somehow or other always serve:

> My dear Bhurijana Dāsa,
>
> Please accept my blessings. I am in due receipt of your letter dated September 12, 1975 with enclosed check for $127.68. In this way you are rendering very nice service and the more you render service, the more you advance. This is the only way. Therefore the Vedic regulation is that whenever one goes to see some saintly person or to visit a temple, he must offer something. That will help him. It is enjoined that one should first of all dedicate his life, and if it is not possible to do that, that one should dedicate his money. If he has no money, then he should utilize his intelligence how to spread Krishna consciousness. Or if he has no intelligence, then he should utilize his words that, "Yes, they are doing nicely. This is a nice movement." This is the process for advancement in Krishna consciousness. I hope this meets you in good health.
>
> Your ever well-wisher,
> A.C. Bhaktivedanta Swami

* * *

Practically speaking, the essential quality of a devotee, or of someone sincerely aspiring to become a servant of a devotee, is his serving mood. Regardless of external circumstances, therefore, a devotee always – somehow or other – renders service.

Devotees at times find themselves without service. Without service – and Prabhupāda indicated that service has a broad scope – thinking of oneself as a devotee has no meaning. One must always find some way to serve.

The "Best Useful" Service

My visits to the post office and the ensuing checks and letters to Prabhupāda continued week after week, month after month. Generally, Prabhupāda kindly acknowledged receipt of each letter and check with a letter of his own. In one letter to Prabhupāda, I had expressed that I was not able to serve him very well at the present, and I asked that he accept my donations until I could properly serve him.

Prabhupāda's reply encouraged me:

> I am in due receipt of your letters dated August 22, 29th, and September 5th with enclosed Dollars 50.00, 159.61, and 126.50. You say that someday you hope to be useful, but you are already useful – you are sending checks. This is the best useful. You are remembering me and chanting Hare Krishna. This is Krishna consciousness.

* * *

My insignificant donations may not have fully deserved Prabhupāda's generously terming them "the best useful," nevertheless, Prabhupāda expertly fanned the spark of my desire to serve.

The Responsibility of a Householder

One night I dreamed that I was walking with Prabhupāda on his morning walk. We were in Melbourne. Suddenly he stopped, turned to me, and asked me to buy a farm for the temple. The dream put me in anxiety, so I wrote to Prabhupāda and asked whether or not he considered it my responsibility to buy a farm. In his reply, Prabhupāda did not mention my dream:

My dear Bhurijana Dāsa,

Please accept my blessings. I am in due receipt of your letters dated September 19 and October 17, 1975 with enclosed checks for $100 and $500 respectively. So this is very nice that your checks are getting bigger. You are one of my older experienced students and I am always praying for your advancement in Krishna consciousness. As the husband of your wife, you should see that she is trained up nicely in Krishna consciousness. You also have a child, so this is your responsibility to see that your family no longer again has to come back and take a material body in this world of birth and death. This is the responsibility of a father in Krishna consciousness.

I hope this meets you in good health.

Your ever well-wisher,
A.C. Bhaktivedanta Swami

And in a later letter:

Naturally your daughter is chanting the transcendental Name of the Lord. It must be so, because unless one is pious in previous life, one cannot take birth in a Vaishnava family. Give her good chance to become Krishna Conscious more and more, and offer my blessings to your good wife Jagatarini.

I hope this meets you well.

Your ever well-wisher,
A. C. Bhaktivedanta Swami

* * *

A prime duty of a family man is to make his family Kṛṣṇa conscious. Mahārāja Ṛṣabhadeva describes this in the Fifth Canto of *Śrīmad-Bhāgavatam: pitā na sa syāt.* In Kali-yuga, this is easier said than done. Regardless of the outcome, however, we should do our duty with full conviction in the importance of helping our family members become Kṛṣṇa conscious.

Māyāpur, 1976

Entering Beautiful Māyāpur-dhāma

I arrived in Māyāpur-dhāma just before the Gaura-Pūrṇimā festival in 1976. Entering the holy *dhāma* by boating across the Ganges River soothed my mind and eyes. Māyāpur's rarefied spiritual atmosphere was apparent, and its beauty – the broad, rushing Ganges River and the vast lush, green fields – was stunning. Since my last visit, the devotees had begun constructing a long, double-storied building "as big as two trains," as Prabhupāda described it. I stayed in my one-man tent behind the temple.

* * *

I was inspired to visit Māyāpur and hoped to gain spiritual strength in Prabhupāda's association. I planned to chant sixty-four rounds a day, so I brought a tent, thinking that it would help me to spend more time alone chanting *japa* and less time socializing. I also hoped to avoid the festival fees.

Hearing as Never Before

In the mornings, Prabhupāda lectured on the teachings of Prahlāda Mahārāja. My life in Māyāpur centered on hearing his classes. At first I tried taping the lectures, but when my tape recorder failed, I took notes. I tried to write down each word.

Between my note-taking and chanting of sixty-four rounds a day, my hearing and concentration became acutely focused. Prabhupāda's words deeply penetrated my consciousness. I perceived that they came directly from the absolute platform. By Lord Caitanya's mercy, I was able to hear Prabhupāda better than I had ever heard him before.

Becoming a Servant: Excerpts from Prabhupāda's Lectures

In his lectures, Prabhupāda often spoke of the need to give up the mood of being master and to accept the mood of a servant.

PRABHUPĀDA: Disease is disease. Actually that is the fact. You say that, "We are suffering from malaria. It is better than to suffer from syphilis." No. Disease is disease. Similarly, either Brahmā or the ant, the disease is how to become master. This is the disease. Therefore, Kṛṣṇa comes to cure this disease. He says plainly, "Rascal, you are not master, you are servant. Surrender unto Me." This is the cure of the disease. If one agrees, "No more trying for becoming master," that is the cure of disease. Therefore Prahlāda Mahārāja says *nija bhṛtya-pārśvam:* "Engage me as the servant of Your servant." So this Kṛṣṇa consciousness movement means we have to give up this nonsense idea of becoming master. This is Kṛṣṇa consciousness. We have to learn how to become servants. Not only servant, but the servant of the servant. That is the cure.

* * *

Spiritual life means to change our mood and activities from enjoyer to servant. Maintaining the mood of master in spiritual life is as contradictory as lighting a fire under water. Engaging our "master" tendency in Kṛṣṇa's service may work for a limited amount of time, but it still skirts the essence of Kṛṣṇa consciousness – becoming a servant of God. We have to give up the idea that we are the master.

PRABHUPĀDA: Prahlāda Mahārāja said, "If You kindly want to give me some benediction, make me the servant of Your servant. " This is an actual benediction. One who has learned to become the servant of Kṛṣṇa's servant is perfect. Therefore Caitanya Mahāprabhu says *tṛṇād api sunīcena, taror api sahiṣṇunā.* A servant has to tolerate. Sometimes a master orders so many things, so the servant becomes disturbed. But still he has to execute and tolerate. That is perfection.

* * *

It is easier to agree to serve God than it is to serve God's servant. Serving the servant of God requires humility. We are truly fortunate if Kṛṣṇa sends us His representative and allows us to recognize and serve him.

PRABHUPĀDA: When Kṛṣṇa with His sixteen thousand wives went to Hastināpura, Draupadī was inquiring from each and every wife of Kṛṣṇa. Not actually all of them, but at least the principal queens. So every one of them was describing their marriage ceremony. Rukmiṇī explained that "My father wanted to hand me over to Kṛṣṇa, but my elder brother did not agree. He wanted to get me married with Śiśupāla. So I did not like this idea. I wrote Kṛṣṇa a private letter, that 'I have dedicated my life to You, but this is the situation. Please come and kidnap me.' So in this way Kṛṣṇa kidnapped me and made me His maidservant."

Every one of them were king's daughter. They were not ordinary person's daughters. But they wanted to become maidservant of Kṛṣṇa. This is the idea, to become servant and to become maidservant. Every woman should try to become maidservant of her husband, and every man should try to become a hundred times the servant of Kṛṣṇa. This is Indian civilization. Not that "Husband

and wife, we have equal rights." That, in Europe, America, movement is going on, "equal rights." That is not Vedic civilization. Vedic civilization means that the husband should be a sincere servant of Kṛṣṇa and the wife should be a sincere maidservant of the husband.

* * *

Prabhupāda pointed out that Western women would rather act as equals to their husbands than as assistants. He equated that mood with our dissatisfaction with the servant role and our impossible desire to become master. Although the wife should think of herself as a servant, the husband should not think of himself as her master. Kṛṣṇa is the master, and both husband and wife should peacefully adopt their appropriate roles as servants.

PRABHUPĀDA: There is no such thing to become master. It is useless. You cannot become master. *Jīvera 'svarūpa' haya – kṛṣṇera 'nitya-dāsa'*. Either man or woman, everyone is servant of Kṛṣṇa. We have to be trained up in that platform to become the best servant. Not only servants directly, but servants of the servant.

This is called *paramparā* servant. My spiritual master is the servant of his spiritual master, and I am also servant of my spiritual master. Similarly, we think, "servant of the servant." This is material disease. *Kṛṣṇa bhuliya jiva bhoga vancha kare, pasate māyā tare japatiya dhare.* As soon as we become puffed up – "Now I shall become master. I shall be simply giving order. I shall not follow anyone." That is *māyā*. So that disease is going on beginning from Brahmā down to the ant.

Our institution is for that purpose. If somebody comes here thinking this is a free hotel and free sleeping accommodation, then his coming to this association is useless. He must learn how to serve. If we take it that "Here is an institution where we can have free hotel, free living, and free sense gratification," then the whole institution will be spoiled. Be careful. All the GBCs should be careful that this mentality may not increase. Everyone should be very eager to serve and to learn how to serve. Then life will be successful.

* * *

Prabhupāda cautioned the devotees to beware the disease of getting a position in ISKCON and then imagining we have become the master instead of the servant. It is far better to always remain the servant of the servant of the *guru-paramparā*. A devotee must maintain this consciousness regardless of his external position.

PRABHUPĀDA: Everywhere you see it. People work day and night, but the purpose is how to become master. They cannot become master, but their ambition is how to become master. How to become the richest man like such-and-such big man. This is called the struggle for existence. Everyone is trying to become the master. Nobody is trying to become a servant. Ask anyone, "Why you are working so hard?" They will answer, "I shall get so much money, I shall become very wealthy, I shall have so many servants, so many workers, and I shall have control over them."

I am trying to become master instead of becoming a servant of Kṛṣṇa, but I have simply become the servant of my senses. So my position as servant is there. Is it not? I cannot change it. Just like a woman. If a woman dresses like a man, does it mean that she has become a man? No. A woman is still a woman. A man is a man. Simply by changing dress does not change the fact. Similarly, our constitutional position is to serve. And to serve whom? Kṛṣṇa. That is our constitutional position. But falsely we are trying to become master. Therefore, instead of becoming master, I have become the servant of my senses. This is our position.

The tongue is asking, "Why don't you come to this restaurant." "No, no, my belly is already filled up." "No, you must come." [*Laughter.*] You'll see. A man is coming from home after sumptuously eating. As soon as he comes to the street, immediately he enters a restaurant and drinks a cup of tea and a few biscuits. Why? What is the necessity? You are already filled up in your belly, and still, again immediately you are eating. "No, it is very palatable." So you are servant of your tongue. "Because it is palatable. Although my belly is already filled up, I must satisfy my tongue." So am I master? I'm not master; I'm the servant of my tongue.

You cannot understand by erudite scholarship what is Kṛṣṇa. It is not possible. Then Kṛṣṇa would have instructed *Bhagavad-gītā* to a great Vedāntist. No. Kṛṣṇa chose Arjuna to understand. Who was Arjuna? Arjuna was a *gṛhastha,* a *kṣatriya,* a soldier. A soldier is not expected to become a Vedāntist. Arjuna was not very qualified in that way to understand *Bhagavad-gītā.* But Kṛṣṇa said, "Yes, I will speak to you this *Bhagavad-gītā.* The *paramparā* is lost, so I shall again speak the old thing to you." "Why to me?" *Bhakto 'si priyo 'si me.* "Because you are My *bhakta.* You are My *priya.*" So by scholarship one cannot understand *Bhagavad-gītā.* That is not possible. One must become a servant of the servant of Kṛṣṇa.

* * *

We remain servants regardless of our masquerades. Even if we are able to avoid serving others, we fall to serving our own senses. No one succeeds at becoming the master, because the position is already filled by Kṛṣṇa, the Supreme Personality of Godhead.

Asking to Meet Prabhupāda

After being in Māyāpur for a few days, I decided to visit Prabhupāda. I saw Prabhupāda's secretary, Puṣṭa Kṛṣṇa, near Prabhupāda's second-floor room and asked him for an appointment. Puṣṭa Kṛṣṇa looked at me skeptically. We didn't know each other, and he was unaware of my service to Prabhupāda in Hong Kong. He said, "Look, five hundred devotees are at this festival and every one of them wants to meet with Prabhupāda." I became nervous, but I avoided the temptation to retreat.

"Maybe five hundred devotees want to meet Prabhupāda, but I'm the only one asking." Puṣṭa Kṛṣṇa acknowledged my point and left me to inform Prabhupāda of my request. He returned a minute later and said I could see Prabhupāda the following morning.

My meeting with Prabhupāda was short. I paid my obeisances and offered Prabhupāda two traveler's checks of $100 each and several bags of cashews, almonds, and raisins. He expressed his appreciation and well-wishes, and I left, feeling satisfied at having offered a little service.

The Dependence of the Disciple on His Guru

Prabhupāda continued to give the morning *Bhāgavatam* lectures and I continued to listen attentively. Prabhupāda spoke about the dependence of the disciple on his guru.

PRABHUPĀDA: Why the spiritual master's position is so great? Because he is very, very confidential servant of Kṛṣṇa. So this is the process. *Adau guru-pādāśrayam.* The first beginning of Vaiṣṇava life is to accept a guru, a spiritual master. Then other things. Because who will teach you? So we have to approach a pure Vaiṣṇava as a spiritual master and follow his instruction.

And what is his instruction? His instruction is as he was instructed by his spiritual master. The pure Vaiṣṇava does not invent anything new. *Yāre dekha, tare kaha 'kṛṣṇa'-upadeśa.* Caitanya Mahāprabhu says that "You all, every one of you become guru. Everyone. *Āmāra ajñāya* guru *hañā tāra' ei deśa.* Wherever you are living, it doesn't require that you have to travel all over the world. If you have no such capacity it doesn't matter. You remain wherever you are, but you become a guru. "How can I become a guru?" *Yāre dekha, tare kaha 'kṛṣṇa'-upadeśa.* Very simple thing. You instruct only what is instructed by Kṛṣṇa. That's all.

* * *

Becoming a guru first requires our becoming a pure servant of our own guru.

PRABHUPĀDA: Because we are bewildered, we are misdirected, so we have to follow guru. "How I can find out the real guru by whose words I'll be nicely directed and achieve?" That is not very difficult. You read *Bhagavad-gītā.* You'll understand. Just like Arjuna. When he was perplexed, he accepted Kṛṣṇa – guru. He said, *śiṣyas te 'ham:* "I now become Your disciple. We were talking as friends and our argument will not end, but I now become Your disciple."

Śiṣyas te 'ham. As soon as one becomes a *śiṣyas*... *Śiṣya* means under the order, regulation. A person cannot disobey the order of guru. Then he is *śiṣya.* if he argues, he's not *śiṣya.* Therefore Arjuna says, *śiṣyas te 'ham:* "I surrender. I voluntarily surrender to become your disciple. Now I shall not argue." That is called *śiṣya.* If you argue, then you are not a *śiṣya. Guru-mukha-padma-vākya, cittete koriyā aikya, ār nā koriho mane āśā.* This is *tapasya,* that "I shall not act anything which is not ordered by my guru." We will then be nicely guided and our existence will be purified. And as soon as our existence is purified, we will realize what is God, what is our relationship with Him, and what are our activities.

* * *

It is rare, especially in Kali-yuga, that two people fully agree on anything. If we wish to advance in spiritual life, we must suspend our tendency to disagree and surrender to a guru. Only then can we become a servant and purify our existence.

The Mercy of More Association

Prabhupāda again allowed me his association late one morning during his massage. Seeing Prabhupāda's golden skin glistening with mustard oil as he sat on the veranda made me feel like an intimate disciple. His servant worked the oil into Prabhupāda's body with strong movements as Prabhupāda sometimes remained silent and at other times spoke.

Nitāi, who had previously traveled with Prabhupāda as his Sanskrit editor, sat with me in front of Prabhupāda. Nitāi had recently gone to Vṛndāvana to organize the academics for the Bhaktivedanta Swami Gurukula and was now telling Prabhupāda of his plans.

Although I was not aware of the background, Prabhupāda clearly wasn't satisfied with Nitāi's proposal. He sat in the hot, mid-morning sun, his eyes closed, as his servant massaged his slender legs. "What is the use of making Sanskrit scholars? So many Sanskrit *paṇḍitas* are loitering on the streets with no engagement. No. We don't want our students to become Sanskrit scholars. We simply want them to become attached to the Vedic culture."

* * *

Prabhupāda had already reviewed Nitāi's curriculum plans and was now analyzing them as too academic. He did not approve. Prabhupāda's instructions on *gurukula* clearly indicate that his concern was that the students become devotees. Academic education is essential, but secondary to training in devotion. Prabhupāda wanted the children to have association with devotee adults and to follow the basic program for hearing and chanting.

Buying a Basket at Prabhupāda's Price

Prabhupāda began his morning walk surrounded by senior disciples. They walked towards the Jalāṅgī River on an embankment at the edge of a rice field, and I joined the group, walking in the field to the side of the path. Prabhupāda headed left when he reached the dirt road leading to Tarunpur. Soon, a farmer carrying a wicker basket of vegetables on his head passed and Prabhupāda stopped him. The farmer eased the basket from his head and allowed Prabhupāda to inspect the fresh *bindī* (okra). Prabhupāda and the farmer haggled back and forth in Bengali for a few minutes, leaving Prabhupāda smiling, for he had purchased the entire basket for twenty rupees.

* * *

Prabhupāda didn't like to see his disciples cheated by the local businessmen. He once remarked that whomever allowed himself to be cheated was as guilty as the cheater. Prabhupāda was expert in all dealings, and he expected us to follow his example.

I watched Prabhupāda enjoy his dealing with the farmer and then watched him direct the farmer to deposit the *bindī* at the ISKCON kitchen. Prabhupāda indicated that the farmer should be paid, and I seized the opportunity to serve Prabhupāda by handing the farmer twenty rupees.

Cultivating Goodness

I continued living in my tent, chanting sixty-four rounds a day, and listening attentively to Prabhupāda's morning classes. Prabhupāda spoke on several occasions from a practical viewpoint about the necessity of devotees cultivating goodness and resisting the domination of the lower modes of passion and ignorance.

PRABHUPĀDA: Just like I was rebuking you about the condition in that toilet. This is so nasty, *tamo-guṇa*. If I have no response to such *tamo-guṇa* place, that means I am also of that quality. Like fire and fire, there is no reaction. But in fire and water there is reaction. Similarly, *sattva-guṇa, sattva-guṇa,* there is no reaction. *Tamo-guṇa, tamo-guṇa,* there is no reaction. In English it is called incompatible. When different qualities mix, there is reaction, chemical reaction. Acid and alkaline, if you mix, there will be immediately effervescence.

If one is *sattva-guṇa,* then he cannot tolerate. Immediately obnoxious: "Oh, such a nasty condition." So I am very sorry there was no reaction in such a nasty toilet room. And you are getting sacred thread, which is for one with the quality of a *brāhmaṇa* – *sattva-guṇa.* It is very regrettable. Nobody reacted. So this is the position. We have to curb down *rajo-guṇa* and *tamo-guṇa.* Otherwise, there is no improvement.

If a person in Kṛṣṇa consciousness is found to have no reaction to *rajo-guṇa, tamo-guṇa,* then he is not improving. It is simply showbottle. So showbottle will not help. But if one actually develops Kṛṣṇa consciousness, then it is to be understood that he has surpassed *sattva-guṇa,* the brahminical qualification. Why do we offer sacred thread to a person who is coming from very, very low family? Because it is to be understood that by chanting Hare Kṛṣṇa mantra, by following the regulative principles, he has already come to the platform of *sattva-guṇa.* But if it is a false thing, there is no need of second initiation.

Our process is "Don't do this and do this: chant Hare Kṛṣṇa mantra sixteen rounds, and don't do this – no illicit sex, no meat-eating." That means he's becoming purified from the rotten condition of *rajo-guṇa* and *tamo-guṇa.* But if he does not become purified, then there should be no second initiation. This should be the rule.

* * *

Prabhupāda expected that the brahminically initiated should act to the brahminical standard of *sattva-guṇa.* He herein indicates that brahminical initiation should *only* be offered to those qualified by brahminical purity.

PRABHUPĀDA: This material world has three qualities, so there is always a struggle. If you want to remain in the *sattva-guṇa,* then the *rajas-tamo guṇa* will give you trouble. *Tadā rajas-tamo-bhāvāḥ kāma-lobhādayaś ca ye.* So we are trying to introduce this *sattva-guṇa* and above *sattva-guṇa, śuddha-sattva.*

Sometimes we experience that one person is elevated to the brahminical principle, *sannyāsī* principle, but all of a sudden he falls down. He becomes a demon. We have got experience. He becomes demon. This material world is so contaminated that even if you are on the *sattva-guṇa* platform, there is a chance of being contaminated by the *rajas-tamo guṇa.* The struggle is there. Therefore we have to become very, very careful.

But Kṛṣṇa will help. If you want to remain in *sattva-guṇa,* in purity, then Kṛṣṇa will help. Just like here, as soon as Brahmā was disturbed by the demons full of *rajo-guṇa* and *tamo-guṇa,* immediately the Lord came in His Hayagrīva *mūrti* incarnation.

If you remain a pure devotee, always surrendered to Kṛṣṇa, know very well that Kṛṣṇa will give you protection in any calamity. Don't be worried. Simply we must have faith. That is surrender. Surrender means *avasya rakhibe kṛṣṇa viśāsya pālanam.* You must be faithful that "I am engaged in Kṛṣṇa's service. I may go to hell or heaven. It doesn't matter. I am going to serve Him. It is sure that Kṛṣṇa will give me protection." So there should be no hesitation. If somebody is ordered, "Go to hell and preach Kṛṣṇa consciousness," he should remain faithful to Kṛṣṇa and Kṛṣṇa will give all protection. That is the principle.

* * *

Devotees who take risks on their guru's behalf quickly learn of Kṛṣṇa's personal protection. Prabhupāda encouraged the devotees to be bold and faithful in their preaching services on behalf of the Kṛṣṇa consciousness movement.

PRABHUPĀDA: All these books which we are distributing and publishing, what are they? They are Kṛṣṇa and His activities. That's all. So if you simply read our books very carefully, then immediately this disease of heart palpitation, anxiety, will cease because it is the dirty things, this *tamo-guṇa* and *rajo-guṇa,* that are disturbing us.

We are covered by the *tamo-guṇa* and *rajo-guṇa. Rajas-tamaḥ* means greediness and lusty desires. This is *rajas-tamaḥ.* So if we actually want to become free from anxieties, then first of all we have to come to the platform of goodness.

There are three platforms: *tamo-guṇa, rajo-guṇa, and sattva-guṇa.* So immediately we cannot come to the pure *sattva-guṇa śuddha-sattva,* the *vasudeva* platform. Just as Vasudeva is the father of Kṛṣṇa, so there is *vasudeva* platform also. Unless one comes to the *vasudeva* platform, there is no question of knowing Kṛṣṇa because only Vasudeva can beget Kṛṣṇa, or Vāsudeva. So we have to come to the platform of *vasudeva, śuddha-sattva.* But it is not immediately possible. Therefore, gradually, from the platform of *tamo-guṇa* and *rajo-guṇa,* we have to come to the *sattva-guṇa.*

In other words, we have to acquire the qualities of a *brāhmaṇa.* Therefore this initiation is to bring one to the platform of *brāhmaṇa. Cātur-varṇyaṁ mayā sṛṣṭaṁ guṇa-karma-vibhāgaśaḥ.* This is necessary. From this material platform to come to the spiritual platform one has to become a qualified *brāhmaṇa.* We first of all accept anyone who is prepared to chant and give him *hari-nāma.* What is the idea? The idea is that he'll gradually become *brāhmaṇa.*

This Kṛṣṇa consciousness movement is trying to raise the standard of the human society to become *brāhmaṇas* from their position of miserliness, *kṛpanā.* This is our attempt. It may be a tiny, humble attempt, but our aim is how these dogs and cats will become *brāhmaṇa.* This is our aim. We do not want to keep them in the position of cats and dogs and pigs. This is our attempt. So we may be successful or not successful, but our endeavor is very, very great.

* * *

Lord Rāmacandra engaged monkeys in His service. Similarly, Prabhupāda engaged his disciples who often came from backgrounds of complete *rajo-guṇa* and *tamo-guṇa.* His purpose was to exalt their consciousness to *sattva-guṇa* and finally to *bhakti.* Many disciples, even trusted servants and *sannyāsīs,* fell due to the difficult struggle with past conditioning. Prabhupāda had to display incredible affection, patience, tolerance, and determination as he pushed ISKCON forward. In the above lecture, Prabhupāda said that our materialistic culture is comprised of humans acting like cats, dogs, and pigs. Although his words pinched my false ego and attacked the pride of my American birth, I could not but agree with him.

Two Letters from Prabhupāda

One afternoon, Puṣṭa Kṛṣṇa casually mentioned that Prabhupāda had written me a letter that he had decided not to send. Naturally, I wanted to see that letter. Puṣṭa Kṛṣṇa opened his file and pulled out not one, but two recent letters to me from Prabhupāda. One was not to be sent; the other had been sent to my address in Australia, but I had not yet received it. I first read the letter Prabhupāda had written but not posted:

Letter one, service brings service

> My dear Bhurijana,
>
> Please accept my blessings. I have recently thought of a scheme to increase funds in our BBT account. I would like to send Indian goods to you for sales to the devotees and others. In the beginning I can have cloth sent, especially sarees. So many others are doing it successfully, we can also be successful. I will have the papers sent through Lloyd's bank as I have an account with them in London. So you can find out the Lloyd's branch there. You can deposit all monies received from sales of the sarees in the Lloyd's Bank. You may also keep a percentage of the sales for yourself. Please advise me if you are able to execute.
>
> Your ever well-wisher,
> A. C. Bhaktivedanta Swami

* * *

The project to produce and export cloth never manifested, but I was happy that Prabhupāda had remembered me. I was also proud that Prabhupāda was indirectly acknowledging my service of regularly sending him donations and that he had enough confidence in my business acumen to ask me to serve him in this way.

Letter two: love means service

Devotional service is not mechanical. Prabhupāda continuously and patiently instructed and inspired me to advance further in Kṛṣṇa consciousness. I felt the need to reciprocate with him through service. In the following letter, Prabhupāda confirmed my understanding of our relationship as correct:

> My dear Bhurijana,
>
> Please accept my blessings. I beg to thank you for your letter dated 16th January, 1976 along with the enclosed donation. Unless there is loving feeling, how is it possible for you to always make offerings to me? The spiritual master is always instructing his disciples and they in turn are always trying to serve their spiritual master. It is a reciprocal relationship of love.
>
> Your ever well-wisher,
> A. C. Bhaktivedanta Swami

* * *

This letter struck me deeply because Prabhupāda acknowledged my affection for him and my gratitude for all he was giving me. Without developing affection based on our appreciation of our guru's mercy toward us, our service to guru and Kṛṣṇa will neither deepen, nor expand, nor become *apratihatā*, "uninterrupted." Prabhupāda's words melted my heart.

A Darśana

Prabhupāda held open *darśanas* every evening, and his room filled quickly. One devotee showed Prabhupāda photographs of Nitāi-Gaurasundara from ISKCON Baltimore. Prabhupāda examined the photo with appreciation and expressed his desire to personally visit Baltimore and view these Deities.

* * *

Prabhupāda later fulfilled his desire when one morning, he "took his walk in a car" and drove from ISKCON Washington, D.C. to Baltimore during his final tour of the United States in 1976.

A female devotee informed Prabhupāda about her preaching attempts in Cleveland, Ohio. Prabhupāda listened. Although it sounded like her preaching was independent of the ISKCON center, he heard of her successes and encouraged her.

* * *

This *mātājī* was older than most of Prabhupāda's disciples and didn't take association from other devotees or from Prabhupāda's GBC representative for Cleveland. It also appeared that her philosophical understanding was not exactly correct. Still, Prabhupāda genuinely appreciated her independent attempt to encourage others to chant the Hare Kṛṣṇa *mahā-mantra* and to spread Kṛṣṇa consciousness in her home city.

Another *mātājī,* Candravāli, who was one of Prabhupāda's senior disciples and who had pioneered ISKCON's preaching in Mexico with her husband, voiced a complaint.

CANDRAVĀLI: Prabhupāda, we hear that in our philosophy the men should treat the women as mothers. But actually, the men, especially the *sannyāsīs,* don't treat the women as mothers. Instead they treat them as *māyā.* Their attitude, not the women, seems more like *māyā*! It doesn't seem proper.

Prabhupāda heard her complaint carefully. He smiled softly and began to reply. His words dropped from his mouth as if they were sweet ripe fruits falling from a tree.

PRABHUPĀDA: Yes, the men do not treat the women as mothers. Nor do the women act like mothers. Neither do they dress as mothers.

* * *

Prabhupāda answered this delicate question with directness, acknowledging the "butter and fire" nature in the dealings between men and women. Vedic culture compares men to butter and women to fire, not vice versa. In Kali-yuga, women seem determined to break from their traditional roles in social dealing. They seem to be thinking, "If the butterlike men are disturbed, then that's their problem, not ours. Why should we be penalized and our position restricted or minimized?" Prabhupāda, however, was not inclined to compromise the Vedic standard.

Identifying with our body, whether we are male or female, is spiritually incorrect. Still, we have to deal practically with the temporary nature of our physical condition to facilitate our spiritual progress and the spiritual progress of others. Both men and women should adopt the activities and restrictions of their bodily roles responsibly, despite the fact that those roles are temporary, and remain sympathetic (and not antagonistic) to the position and needs of others.

Developing Love for Rādhā-Mādhava

As Gaura-Pūrṇimā approached, Prabhupāda continued to lecture every morning and pointed us toward developing loving service to Śrī Śrī Rādhā-Mādhava.

PRABHUPĀDA: Without having a loving connection with Kṛṣṇa, it is not possible to see Him. You may practice this hatha-yoga or gymnastics yoga for many, many births, but you cannot see Kṛṣṇa. Kṛṣṇa can be seen when you smear love ointment in your eyes. *Premāñjana-cchurita-bhakti-vilocanena.* And that is possible through *bhakti*. Therefore, why not practice *bhakti-yoga* from the beginning if you want to see Kṛṣṇa? In our *bhakti-yoga* we can teach this art of seeing Kṛṣṇa within the core of the heart in one minute. It is so simple.

You are seeing Kṛṣṇa here [in the form of the Deity]. Let this make an impression and try to keep that impression within your heart always. Then you become a first-class yogi. Why so much gymnastics and pressing the nose? No. Take directly. If you are engaged twenty-four hours in the service of the Deity, you cannot see anything except the Deity. This *bhakti-yoga* practice is so simple.

Therefore it is the duty of guru to engage the neophyte devotee always in Deity worship.

śrī-vigrahārādhana-nitya-nānā-
śṛṅgāra-tan-mandira-mārjanādau
yuktasya bhaktāṁś ca niyuñjato 'pi
vande guroḥ śrī-caraṇāravindam

It is the duty of the guru to engage his disciples in Deity worship, in cleansing the temple, in dressing the Deity, in decorating the Deity, and in so many engagements.

So everyone should be engaged. If one is not competent to dress the Deity, he can simply wash the temple and cleanse it. That will also help. There is no difference between one who is cleansing the floor of the temple and one who is engaged directly in the Deity worship....There is no difference. They are all the same. Don't think, "I am engaged in cleansing the floor of the temple and he is engaged in decorating the temple. I should be envious." No, there is no question of one duty being better. Any kind of duty you are engaged...*Sva-karmaṇā tam abhyarcya*...if you cannot do something which is hard for you, you can do anything for Kṛṣṇa under the direction of the spiritual master. You'll get perfection. It is not that "I have to do this. I have to do that." No. Kṛṣṇa's service is manifold. If one is unable to take one kind of service, the spiritual master can give him another kind of service. Both services are accepted by Kṛṣṇa.

* * *

It is devotion that pleases Kṛṣṇa when one devotee shelters another; it is devotion that brings Kṛṣṇa happiness when we offer Him a donation; and it is devotion that awakens Kṛṣṇa's appetite when we offer Him food.

Humility

Prabhupāda: If you want to chant the Hare Kṛṣṇa mantra, then you have to take to the principle of *tṛṇād api sunīcena.* You have to become humbler than the grass. Grass is lying on the street. Everyone is trampling down the grass. There is no protest. *Taror api sahiṣṇunā.* And more tolerant than the tree. The tree is giving us so much help. It is giving us fruit, flower, and leaves. And when there is scorching heat, it also gives shelter, and you may sit down underneath. So beneficial, yet we still cut. As soon as I like, I cut it down. But there is no protest. The tree does not say, "I have given you so much help and you are cutting me?" No. The tree is tolerant. Therefore Caitanya Mahāprabhu has selected the tree: *taror api sahiṣṇunā.* And *amāninā mānadena.* For oneself one should not expect any respectful position, but the devotee should offer all respects to everyone. *Āmāninā mānadena kīrtanīya sadā hari.* If we acquire these qualifications, then we can chant Hare Kṛṣṇa *mahā-mantra* without any disturbance. These are the qualifications.

* * *

Śrī Caitanya Mahāprabhu listed these qualities as the prerequisite for constant chanting of the holy name. Humility and tolerance are present only in one cleansed of all sinful and pious reactions. Being fixed in these qualities is real fortune. Reaching this platform requires not only our earnest endeavor, but also Kṛṣṇa's mercy.

Fixed-up Thinking of Kṛṣṇa

Prabhupāda: Prahlāda Mahārāja says that the perfection of life is *tava kathāsu vaikuṇṭha-nātha:* one should be interested in *kṛṣṇa-kathā.* We are interested in so many *kathās.* We purchase a newspaper in the morning. Such a big volume, and so many *kathās* are there. And we read many material dramas and novels and fictitious stories and killing stories. We are very much attached to these. In all these *kathās,* stories, we are interested, but we are not interested in *kṛṣṇa-kathā.* This means that I am interested in *kathā,* that is my nature, but it has become perverted on account of being contaminated by this material world. This is our position.

Therefore Prahlāda Mahārāja said that the mind is full of dirty things. Within the core of heart are so many nasty, dirty things – material contamination. But it can be cleansed. *Ceto-darpaṇa-mārjanaṁ.* Caitanya Mahāprabhu has assured. The whole process of education and advancement of civilization is how to cleanse the dirty mind. Why it is dirty? Lusty desire and greediness. So we should always remember that the mind is both the best friend and the worst enemy. If it remains lusty and greedy, it is our worst enemy, and if it is Kṛṣṇa conscious, it is our best friend.

We have to control our mind. That is very easy, as Ambarīṣa Mahārāja did. We have to fix it up. This *arcana-vidhi* in the temple is meant for gradually making the mind think of Kṛṣṇa. You'll come to the temple, you'll see the Deity, you'll see Kṛṣṇa, and you'll think of Kṛṣṇa.

That is the system. Every man, every woman, used to go to the temple. This is our Vedic civilization – to make the mind Kṛṣṇa conscious, always Kṛṣṇa conscious. If you make your mind fixed up in Kṛṣṇa and think of Kṛṣṇa's activities, this lusty and greedy mind will be cleansed. Not only be cleansed, if you think of sex, you'll spit. This is the Kṛṣṇa consciousness movement.

* * *

Fixing our mind on Kṛṣṇa is the prime *sādhana* practice to purify the heart, but we products of Kali-yuga culture are not easily able to constantly remember Kṛṣṇa. The Deity worship, preaching, chanting, cleaning, studying, cooking, administrating, plus all the rules and regulations that we follow, are assistants to the prime practice of focusing our minds on Kṛṣṇa and never allowing it to deviate from remembering Him.

Pride with humility

PRABHUPĀDA: Prahlāda Mahārāja is feeling proud that "You are so affectionate to Your devotee." The Lord's name is *bhakta-vatsala*. He can offer His *bhakta* any position, even more than Himself. Just like Mother Yaśodā. She is *bhakta*, and the Lord has given her the position for punishing Him. Mother Yaśodā is threatening Kṛṣṇa that "Kṛṣṇa, You were very naughty. Now I shall bind You." So Kṛṣṇa, out of being afraid, was crying. Kṛṣṇa has given the position to the *bhakta* that "You chastise Me. I'll accept it."

This is a *bhakta*'s position. This is Kṛṣṇa's causeless mercy. He can do that. So Prahlāda Mahārāja is appreciating that "I am worthless. I have no qualification." That should be the position of the *bhaktas* always. Never we should think that "I have become a big *bhakta*." No. The author of *Caitanya-caritāmṛta* says humbly, "I am lower than the worm in the stool." Does it mean that he is actually low? No. But he's feeling like that. An advanced devotee is always so humble and meek. He always thinks of himself as worthless.

And still Prahlāda thinks, "The Lord is so kind and favorable. That is His causeless mercy. I am not qualified. I am not worthy of this facility." This is humility.

* * *

Prahlāda Mahārāja's pride is that the Lord had chosen him as an object of causeless affection, but because he feels that this is not due to any quality he possesses, his pride and his humility do not conflict.

Understanding Kṛṣṇa

PRABHUPĀDA: You have seen the picture of Lord Viṣṇu? He is very, very much decorated. But you'll see Kṛṣṇa decorated only with Vṛndāvana flowers. That is Kṛṣṇa's real form. He does not appear with many hands or many ornaments. No. Simple, as a boy. So *yaśodā-nandana braja-jana-rañjana yamunā-tīra*... What is that?

DEVOTEES: *Vana-cārī.*

PRABHUPĀDA: Yes. That is Kṛṣṇa. Kṛṣṇa is always Yaśodā-nandana. He is always ready to be chastised by Mother Yaśodā, by the *gopīs,* and sometimes by His friends. That is Vṛndāvana Kṛṣṇa. That is real Kṛṣṇa and that is real God. Even Brahmā, although such an exalted person who creates this universe, becomes bewildered seeing Kṛṣṇa as a cowherd boy. When Brahmā understood that "A cowherd boy in Vṛndāvana is said to be the Supreme Lord, Kṛṣṇa, my master," he wanted to examine whether Kṛṣṇa, that boy, was actually his master. He took away His calves and cowherd boys for a second and saw that Kṛṣṇa had expanded Himself into so many cows and calves and cowherd boys. Then he submitted. Similarly, Indra also wanted to examine Kṛṣṇa. So everyone, even Lord Brahmā, Lord Indra, and others – big, big demigods – they become bewildered in understanding Kṛṣṇa.

* * *

Lord Brahmā and Lord Indra tend to focus on the Supreme as the possessor of unlimited opulence and nothing else. Although we need to know Kṛṣṇa's opulence too, thinking of Him only in terms of His opulence disqualifies us from bathing in the sweetness of His Vṛndāvana pastimes.

In addition, Lord Brahmā and Lord Indra at times become skeptical about Kṛṣṇa's position as the Supreme Lord. If we attempt to practice self-realization based only on our own intelligence, or practice devotion mixed with fruitive desires, we too will become skeptical about Kṛṣṇa in His Vṛndāvana form.

The Result of Hearing and Chanting

Chanting sixty-four rounds a day and attentively hearing from Prabhupāda every morning for almost two weeks acted as a miraculous balm on my consciousness. The fetters of other desires began to loosen as my desire to personally serve Prabhupāda increased.

With my *japa* beads in hand, I chanted my way from my small tent, through the fields of chickpeas, to the Māyāpur *gośālā*. There I saw my old, eccentric friend, Bhaktījana, who had joined at 26 Second Avenue and whom I had met at our Buffalo temple just before Prabhupāda gave me initiation. We exchanged some pleasantries and he informed me that the temple's assistant treasurer had just been caught stealing. His *śikhā* had been cut off and he was driven from the temple with sticks.

Bhaktījana was tall and thin, with a long neck. Somehow his hair always looked about the same length, not long and not shaved, but always short and fuzzy. It gave him an otherworldly, impish appearance. But he had a penetrating intelligence.

As Bhaktījana brushed a cow, he explained how he had read in some obscure scientific magazine that flies were actually antiseptic and caused no disease. "I always guessed they didn't," agreed Bhaktījana, "because they're everywhere."

"Especially in this *gośālā*," I added, swatting several from between us. I decided to share with Bhaktījana the enthusiasm I was feeling in my Kṛṣṇa consciousness.

BHŪRIJANA: You know, I've been chanting lots of rounds since I arrived. On Ekādaśī I even got 108 done. And I've been really listening to Prabhupāda's lectures in the mornings and feeling more and more like increasing my service to him. What do you think I should do?

BHAKTĪJANA: Why not go and tell Prabhupāda?

Somehow or other, I had never considered directly revealing my mind to Prabhupāda. After all, Prabhupāda did have thousands of disciples and an increasingly large movement to oversee. The general mood of his disciples was to not approach him directly, but I was already more or less directly under Prabhupāda's personal care. Bhaktijana's advice struck my heart and a light went on. "Yes," I thought, "I'll go and tell Prabhupāda." I immediately headed back across the fields of chickpeas toward Māyāpur Chandrodaya Mandir.

I paused in front of the barricade outside of the corridor on the first floor. To the right were Prabhupāda's rooms. A guard made sure no intruders disturbed Prabhupāda, and Puṣṭa Kṛṣṇa Swami stood nearby. Black clouds were filling the sky and the atmosphere was becoming oppressive. A storm seemed imminent. Thunder and lightning suddenly began to lash the sky as the winds increased and the lights went out. I saw a devotee carry a kerosene lantern into Prabhupāda's room.

I walked over to Puṣṭa Kṛṣṇa Swami and told him I wanted to spend a few moments with Prabhupāda as soon as possible. He left to check with Prabhupāda, but returned to inform me that Prabhupāda's afternoon was already booked with meetings. My meeting was set for eleven o'clock the following morning. Considering the number of devotees at the festival, I was fortunate to receive an appointment for the following morning, but still, in my heart, I wanted to speak to Prabhupāda immediately.

I stood outside the barricade separating me from Prabhupāda's room. Devotees began scurrying for shelter from the storm. I closed my eyes and opened my heart to Prabhupāda. "O Prabhupāda, please let me serve you. My desire to serve you has increased. Please let me be your servant. Please let my service to you increase."

Suddenly, I felt a tap on my shoulder. It was Jagadīśa, my old school friend, who had originally visited our Buffalo temple just to talk me out of my involvement in the Kṛṣṇa consciousness movement, and who was now a GBC representative. He looked at me with his kindly smile. "This may sound like it's coming out of the blue, but how would you like to become the president of our temple in Laguna Beach, California?"

I looked at him, amazed. A smile expanded on its own and the ends of my lips felt as if they were nearing my ears. "Out of the blue?" I answered Jagadīśa. "I know which 'blue' this is out of."

"Well, what do you think?" asked Jagadīśa, looking somewhat confused by my answer. I thought for a few moments and answered, "I'm not sure. I don't have any objection, but I want to do what Prabhupāda wants me to do. I'll let you know tomorrow after I've spoken with Prabhupāda." Jagadīśa smiled and left me in silence to continue my prayers.

I entered Prabhupāda's room the next morning promptly at eleven. Prabhupāda was not present, but Tamal Krishna Goswami sat across from Prabhupāda's desk on a white, linen-covered mattress that spread from one corner of the room to the other. He looked at me and demanded to know the subject of my meeting with Prabhupāda. As I considered suggesting that it was none of his business, I saw that Prabhupāda had entered.

We both offered obeisances and Prabhupāda sat down behind his low desk. He was effulgent, humble, grave, light, elderly, timeless, and deep. By his presence, even the pure atmosphere of Māyāpur-dhāma seemed more rarefied. He gestured that I should speak.

I explained everything: how I had been in Māyāpur for two weeks and how I had increased my chanting to sixty-four rounds a day. I told him how I had been hearing his classes with rapt attention and that by carefully listening to his words, I felt purified and wanted to increase my service to him. I then explained that Jagadīśa had just asked me to become the temple president of the Laguna Beach temple. I told Prabhupāda that it wasn't that I wanted to become a temple president, but that I wanted to increase my service to him. I finally just asked him what I should do.

PRABHUPĀDA: It is my standing order to all my disciples that they should preach. If Kṛṣṇa gives you the opportunity to preach, you should take it. My Guru Mahārāja requested me to preach when I was a young man and it was so many years before I could take it up. Now I am an old man and am preaching, but it is still so nice.

Prabhupāda then leaned back upon his bolster backrest. His right hand moved atop his head and his left hand fell at his side. His face relaxed into a smile for several more seconds before he excused himself and left the room to care for his body. My heart was full, and with my order from Prabhupāda fixed, I offered my obeisances and left the room to find Jagadīśa.

Only Kṛṣṇa is the Independent Giver of Favors

Prabhupāda continued lecturing each day and I continued hearing attentively.

PRABHUPĀDA: *śrī-kṛṣṇa caitanya prabhu doyā koro more*
tomā binā ke doyālu jagat-saṁsāre

Actually we are all hankering after the favor of some big man – or some small man. That is the material world. But we should seek favor from the Supreme Personality of Godhead instead of going here and there.

That is the point. They have started so many humanitarian institutes to give favor to suffering humanity. But it is not possible. They cannot do it. It is a false attempt. There are so many instances. A father and mother are always ready to show favor to their children. There is no doubt about it. But does it mean that if one has got a very good and rich and able father and mother that therefore the children will be happy? Actually, if the child is destined to suffer, the good father and mother cannot give him shelter. That is not possible.

Suppose one is condemned by the court to be punished, capital punishment, to be hanged. The father may be a very rich man. If he pleads in the court, "Sir, whatever you want, I'll give you. Kindly do not condemn my son to be hanged." Is it that the hanging will be checked? No. Nobody can show another favor against the will of the Supreme. So we can ask favor from anyone, but we must know that nobody can favor us unless it is sanctioned by the Supreme Person. We must always know. It is not that one in a superior position can favor me. No, he cannot show favor unless it is sanctioned by the Supreme. Suppose we approach a rich man to favor us with some contribution or membership fees, but that rich man cannot favor us unless it is sanctioned by Kṛṣṇa. Kṛṣṇa is there within him and if he says "You give him this money," the man will give us. Suppose we request somewhere and he does not favor us. We should not be sorry. We should know that Kṛṣṇa did not dictate to him that he should donate. He is not so fortunate, therefore Kṛṣṇa did not dictate as such to him. So there is nothing over which to be sorry. This should be our principle.

So for anyone to favor another requires some extra endeavor, but Kṛṣṇa does not require anything extra. That is Kṛṣṇa. He can do anything He likes. He does not depend on others. Others depend on Kṛṣṇa's sanction but Kṛṣṇa does not require anyone's sanction.

* * *

Faithfully remembering that everything that occurs is sanctioned by Kṛṣṇa allows a devotee to live free of anxiety. Being dependent on Kṛṣṇa's mercy in all events as we serve Him allows us to live in His mercy, even in the material world. This key philosophical concept awards us a vision of Kṛṣṇa in every "material" transaction and keeps a faithful devotee safe in all circumstances.

Service as an Opportunity

PRABHUPĀDA: A devotee should not take up some business which requires very hard endeavor. No. We should take up only simple things. Of course, a devotee does take risks. Just like Hanumān, the servant of Lord Rāmacandra. Lord Rāmacandra wanted information about Sītādevī. So Hanumān did not consider, "How I shall go to the other side of the sea to Laṅkā?" He simply, believing in Lord Rāmacandra, calling "*Jaya* Rāma," jumped over it.

Hanumān jumped to Laṅkā, but Rāmacandra Himself had to construct a bridge. Of course, that bridge is also wonderful because the monkeys were bringing stones and throwing the stones into the sea. But the stones were floating. Where is the law of gravitation? Stones floating on the water? It cannot be done by the scientists. But Lord Rāmacandra desired, so the stone became able to float. Otherwise, how many stones we shall throw into the sea that it will come to the level of becoming a bridge? But Lord Rāmacandra wanted, "Let it be simplified for the monkeys. So let them bring the stones and they will float. Then we shall go."

Without stone He Himself could go, but He wanted some service from the monkeys. There were many other monkeys who were not capable exactly like Hanumān. Therefore they were also given some chance that "You bring some stone. You cannot jump over the sea like Hanumān, so you bring stones, and I will ask the stones to float."

* * *

We should accept service as an opportunity, whether we feel ourselves capable or not. Ultimately, if Kṛṣṇa desires, our service will be completed. our real success will be our sincere devotional attempts.

Two More Checks

I went to Prabhupāda's room and offered him two additional traveler's checks of $100 each. He smiled and exclaimed, "More checks! Another $200!"

* * *

Tamal Krishna Mahārāja and his Rādhā-Dāmodara Traveling Saṅkīrtana Party had recently offered Prabhupāda a donation of $20,000. Upon receiving that check, Prabhupāda said, "Only $20,000?" As Rāmacandra expected different services from his different monkeys according to their capacity, my tiny donation received a more positive response than Tamal Krishna Goswami's.

Gaura-Pūrṇimā, March 15, 1976

PRABHUPĀDA: Yudhiṣṭhira Mahārāja was asked by Dharmarāja, "What is the most wonderful thing in this world?" He answered, "The most wonderful thing is that every moment people are dying.

On every planet. Not that only on this planet there is death and that in other planets there is no death. No. Within this material world, on every planet, either Brahmā or the small insignificant ant, everyone must die. Everyone has to die. There is no excuse. Yet they are still planning a permanent settlement.

So Prahlāda Mahārāja and every Vaiṣṇava who is actually following the *paramparā* system of Vaiṣṇava duty, they are anxious. Prahlāda Mahārāja says they are *vimūḍha.* Why? Because, "They don't like You. They don't care for You: 'I don't care for God. I don't accept Kṛṣṇa.'" So all the Vaiṣṇavas, especially those who have taken to the Kṛṣṇa consciousness movement, have this mood. Prahlāda Mahārāja will speak later on that, "Sir, I am not inclined at all to go alone to Vaikuṇṭha. I must take them all with me. Otherwise I don't want to go."

Prahlāda Mahārāja is devotee. He can ask from Kṛṣṇa, "Give me such power that along with me I shall take all of them." That is a Vaiṣṇava. He can do so.

Therefore we have to become the dog of a Vaiṣṇava. *Chāḍiyā vaiṣṇava-sevā nistāra pāyeche kebā.* Without serving a Vaiṣṇava, nobody can be delivered. Why? Because a Vaiṣṇava is so merciful. He can demand from Kṛṣṇa, "Please, on my sake, please excuse him. I'll take him with me." So Kṛṣṇa grants him, "All right, you take him."

A Vaiṣṇava's only business is how to deliver fallen souls. Caitanya Mahāprabhu appeared as a Vaiṣṇava. He was born in a very nice *brāhmaṇa* family. He had a very beautiful body. Everyone liked Him. By His command He could in one night gather hundreds of thousands of people to make civil disobedience. He was so popular! He was only twenty or twenty-one years old. He had His beautiful wife, a very affectionate mother, and a very good position in the society. Still, He gave up everything.

Why? "If I do not deliver these fallen souls entrapped in *māyā,* then who will do it?" So for this purpose, Kṛṣṇa comes. For this purpose, Caitanya Mahāprabhu comes. And this is the same purpose of Prahlāda Mahārāja.

* * *

Prabhupāda expected his disciples to develop true compassion. Śrīla Bhaktisiddhānta Sarasvatī Ṭhākura spoke to the members of the Gaudiya Math before he departed from this world in a similar mood: "I wish that every selfless, tender-hearted person of Gaudiya Math will be prepared to shed two hundred gallons of blood for the nourishment of the spiritual corpus of every individual of this world."

A Special Gift Withdrawn

Most devotees left for Vṛndāvana after Gaura-Pūrṇimā. Prabhupāda would be going there in a few days and they would all meet him again. But Prabhupāda continued lecturing in Māyāpur, so I stayed on to hear him speak. I decided that as soon as Prabhupāda departed for Vṛndāvana, I would leave for Australia to prepare for my family's travel to the United States.

Before leaving Māyāpur, and in Calcutta as well, I continued to listen to Prabhupāda, but I felt my ability to hear attentively waning, as if I had been granted a special gift for a purpose that was now fulfilled.

Guaranteed Success

PRABHUPĀDA: There is regular propaganda, "Why should I go to the temple? God is everywhere." You can answer, "God is everywhere – except in the temple?" Their propaganda is, "God is everywhere. Why do you go to the temple?" But our answer is, "If God is everywhere, why He is not *also* in the temple? He must also be in the temple." But these rascals make propaganda, "Don't go to the temple."

There are so many rascals. But they came and they are gone. In India there is propaganda, "There is no God in the temple." But by this false propaganda the temples have not closed. Still in Vṛndāvana you'll find five thousand temples. You see the Jagannātha Purī temple. Many thousands of people go there. There is also Raṅganātha temple and so many other temples. So in India, this propaganda will not stay. These rascals will come and go. They make propaganda and go away. But the temples remain and so does the worship. Now the temples are increasing all over the world. Instead of stopping people from going to the temple, the temples are increasing.

For centuries, there was no temple in Europe and America. Now there are hundreds and thousands of temples. So it will increase. No one can stop Kṛṣṇa's glories. You cannot stop Kṛṣṇa's supremacy. That is not possible. *Mattaḥ parataraṁ nānyat kiñcid asti dhanañjaya.* That cannot be. Therefore it is sure and certain that if you work very sincerely for Kṛṣṇa to spread His message, the message of *Bhagavad-gītā,* there cannot be any check. It is not possible. *Ahaituky apratihatā. Apratihatā* means it cannot be checked by any material condition. You go on with your duty sincerely. There will be no power to check your progress.

* * *

While in Calcutta, Prabhupāda took his morning walk at the Victoria Memorial. I scooped up dirt from his footprints. Years before, on a similar walk in Calcutta, Prabhupāda had pointed to the Victoria Memorial and reminisced how he had climbed the construction scaffolding during his youth. A devotee noted the height of the memorial and remarked to Prabhupāda, "You must have been very brave." Prabhupāda replied, "I am still brave. Otherwise, how could I have come alone to your country?"

Prabhupāda was brave and, by his preaching words and preaching deeds, he inspired his disciples to bravely serve Kṛṣṇa. Based on Prabhupāda's bravery, devotees, filled with strength and encouragement, took great risks and spread Kṛṣṇa consciousness throughout the world.

After weeks in Śrīdhāma Māyāpur hearing Prabhupāda's potent preaching, I left Calcutta for Australia, inspired to do my part as his servant.

Melbourne, 1976

Traveling Plans via Air Kṛṣṇa

Prabhupāda's visit to Melbourne in April 1976, just after I had returned from seeing him in Māyāpur, found me busy making preparations to close my business. I was soon to leave Australia and become the president of ISKCON Laguna Beach. I arranged to buy inexpensive airplane tickets through the Australian Union of Students, but Kṛṣṇa had another plan. I caught a tram to downtown Melbourne to purchase the tickets at the Union's office. It was just after noon, but the storefront was locked. A "Closed" sign hung tilted on the door. "That's strange," I thought. "It's a regular business day and there are people inside flurrying around the office. Why is it closed?" I tapped on the glass door, but someone waved me away. I persisted, and finally a young woman pushed the door open a few inches and thrust her head out. "We're closed," she said.

"I already figured that out. When'll you be open again?"

"We won't," she said. "The government's giving us trouble, and at noon we closed for good." She closed the door again. "But one more ticket." I called as I tapped on the glass, thinking of the huge difference in price between three discounted tickets and three full-fare tickets. She shook her head no and returned to shuffling her papers. As a last "Just one more!" escaped my mouth, it occurred to me that Prabhupāda would be visiting Australia in a few weeks and then would fly on to Hawaii. I could travel to Hawaii with him and then onward to the mainland.

* * *

Up until this point, I hadn't even considered traveling with Prabhupāda. I was elated by this "minor miracle" of Kṛṣṇa's closing the ticket office. I immediately phoned the temple, found out Prabhupāda's onward flight bookings, and made parallel bookings for my family.

Godbrothers Will Fight

Tuṣṭa Kṛṣṇa Swami arrived from New Zealand to spend time with Prabhupāda. The local GBC at that time was Guru-kṛpa Swami. As Tuṣṭa Kṛṣṇa Swami was acting independently of ISKCON, Tuṣṭa Kṛṣṇa and Guru-kṛpa did not have a cordial relationship.

With both *sannyāsīs*, Tuṣṭa Kṛṣṇa and Guru-kṛpa, at his feet, Prabhupāda asked them a pointed question:

PRABHUPĀDA: What is the cause when two disciples of the same spiritual master cannot get along?

TUṢṬA KṚṢṆA: Envy, Prabhupāda.

[*Tuṣṭa Kṛṣṇa and Guru-kṛpa both look at each other*]

PRABHUPĀDA: Yes, but who is envious is hard to tell. But time will tell. One branch will blossom and the other will wither.

* * *

Prabhupāda's ominous statement reveals that an envious mentality, although often difficult to detect, will ultimately cut us off from devotional service and ruin our spiritual lives. Prabhupāda later wrote me about the squabbles and differences of opinion between godbrothers:

> Regarding the other matters, a difference between Godbrothers is natural. That difference of opinion will continue; what can be done.…So it is a natural thing for the brothers to fight, as long as they all stay obedient to the father. You do whatever you like, but do not forget chanting and following the rules and regulations. That will save you.

Fights among godbrothers should not be taken too seriously; they will always exist. Rather than taking sides, becoming envious of "the opposition," and committing offenses, we should stick to our spiritual business of performing our own service and strictly following the rules and regulations of spiritual life.

The Lord Helps Those Who Help Themselves

A devotee asked Prabhupāda for help, saying that he was not able to follow the four rules. Prabhupāda looked sternly at him. "If you do not follow the regulative principles, then no one can help you."

* * *

Prabhupāda's statement that we must follow the basic regulations before we are able to make advancement is not harsh. Nor is it meant to discourage those who are currently unable to strictly follow.

Sometimes when devotees stop following strictly, they become overtly critical. ISKCON and its leaders may need improvement, but it still seems more appropriate that before attempting to change or revolutionize ISKCON and thus save the world, one should first adhere to Prabhupāda's basic instruction of following the four rules and chanting sixteen rounds a day.

Tastes of Sweetness

I had so much to do before our departure for America that I was not able to participate in Prabhupāda's 1976 Melbourne visit other than to hear his evening *Bhagavad-gītā* classes.

Innocent or Guilty?

Guests, both known and unknown, filled the temple room. "A study of the *Bhagavad-gītā,*" he said, "could begin from either chapter one or chapter nine." Prabhupāda chose chapter nine. During the class, Prabhupāda said softly, "Don't ask a *sādhu* a question unless you are prepared to accept his answer."

He sat proudly after class on the purple velvet *vyāsāsana,* his back straight and his head high. He called for questions. A hand went up and a young man with long hair and glasses stood in the crowded temple room.

YOUNG MAN: "I'm asking this question...I'm concerned about the perverted caste system in India, right? I'm asking this question about a *brāhmaṇa.* If one of your *brāhmaṇa* initiated disciples falls from this platform, leaves the temple, and commits offenses, then returns demanding respect, should he be allowed to keep the sacred thread or should he be engaged in menial service, which never fails to cultivate humility?

PRABHUPĀDA: Well, that is to be judged by the spiritual master. You cannot judge.

YOUNG MAN: Well, I'm asking this because...

PRABHUPĀDA: You cannot judge who is following, who is not following. That is not your jurisdiction. Therefore he has accepted a spiritual master. It is his jurisdiction. He will do whatever necessary.

YOUNG MAN: Has there been a case...

PRABHUPĀDA: So that case you cannot judge. The case has to be judged by the spiritual master.

YOUNG MAN: Could you give me an example of a case that has been...

PRABHUPĀDA: Just like if somebody has done something wrong, he is taken to the court and the judge gives his decision, whether he is criminal or not. The man who has arrested him, he cannot give the decision. It has to be tried by the higher authority. Then the judgment will be. Anything more?

* * *

Prabhupāda had not been pleased when I left Hong Kong a few years earlier, but when I heard Prabhupāda's answer, I knew that although he wasn't pleased, he had judged me innocent.

In general, devotees should refrain from judging each other. That service should be left to the spiritual master.

Here are some other class highlights that struck me:

The Test of Love

PRABHUPĀDA: We are beings. We are individual persons. It is not very difficult to understand. Every one of us, individual. We think individually. We dress individually. We have got our egotism, individual. Everything... I don't agree with you; you don't agree with me. Voluntarily sometimes we agree. That means every one of us has individuality. This is called being "I am." Similarly, God is also a being like us, but He is the Supreme Being. That is the difference between God and me. I am also a being, you are also a being, but we are not the Supreme Being.

* * *

Tuṣṭa Kṛṣṇa Swami and other members of the "outside" group of devotees were present. My impression was that Prabhupāda was establishing that disagreements were natural due to our individuality, but we should nevertheless "suspend" this tendency and voluntarily unite around the desires of our spiritual master.

Freedom from Envy

PRABHUPĀDA: *Nirmatsara. Matsarata* means to become envious. So that is one of the qualification to understand God, not to become envious. But our enviousness is beginning from God. As soon as we present Kṛṣṇa as the Supreme Personality of Godhead, so many persons will protest, "Why is Kṛṣṇa the Supreme Personality of Godhead?" Why not? First of all, answer why not. If you think Kṛṣṇa is not the Supreme Personality of Godhead, then you present who is the Supreme Personality of Godhead. Either you do not know or you cannot present. If you do not know who is the Supreme Personality of Godhead, then take it from me: Kṛṣṇa. And if you know, then you present who is more efficient, more expert, more powerful, more rich than Kṛṣṇa. This is practically a challenge. So actually it has been challenged and it has been scrutinizingly examined and the verdict is *īśvaraḥ paramaḥ kṛṣṇaḥ sac-cid-ānanda-vigrahaḥ, anādir ādir govindaḥ*...

DEVOTEES: ...*sarva-kāraṇa-kāraṇam.*

PRABHUPĀDA: This has been decided. *Nṛpa nirṇitam.* It is already considered and decided.

* * *

Prabhupāda's mode of argument was strong and he would, at his discretion, apply the pressure of his arguments to individuals or groups during class.

Real Education in Real Knowledge

PRABHUPĀDA: There is no education actually. The modern education means simply craftsmanship. If you can prepare a nice motorcar, oh, what is that? It is craftsmanship – the blacksmith's work. It is not knowledge. Knowledge is different. Therefore it is called *jñānaṁ vijñāna-sahitam.* This is knowledge, "What I am? I am this body or something else? Why I am suffering? If there is any remedy? I do not wish to die, neither I am subjected to death." *Nityaḥ śāśvato 'yam...na hanyate han...* This is knowledge, that "If I am eternal, if I do not die after annihilation of this body, then why I am subjected to this body?" This is knowledge. And to manufacture a motorcar, that is not knowledge. That is craftsmanship. Knowledge is here, that "I am eternal. Why I am put into this condition of temporary body, not only one kind of body, but there are 8,400,000 different forms of body, and I have to accept one of them, *tathā dehāntara-prāptir,* according to my karma. This is my position. How to get out of it, to inquire about it?" That is knowledge.

* * *

To rectify the lack of transcendental knowledge in the world, Prabhupāda pushed devotees to educate themselves and others by studying, preaching, and distributing his books. Prabhupāda insisted that modern civilization lacked education in actual knowledge, and even the world's intelligentsia lacked it. Prabhupāda often pointed this out, as he did to Professor Kotovsky in Moscow:

PRABHUPĀDA: No, I'm not talking of religion, belief.

PROF. KOTOVSKY: Yes, yes.

PRABHUPĀDA: I'm talking of science and philosophy.

PROF. KOTOVSKY: Yes, yes... So science and philosophy.

PRABHUPĀDA: One religion may accept. That is not our purpose. We are talking on the point that if the owner of the body is permanent in spite of different change of the body, then what is the difficulty to understand that when this body will be changed, the owner of the body will have another body?

PROF. KOTOVSKY: But another approach is that there is no two phenomena, owner of the body and body.

PRABHUPĀDA: Yes.

PROF. KOTOVSKY: The body and its owner are the same.

PRABHUPĀDA: No.

PROF. KOTOVSKY: When body dies, the owner also dies.

PRABHUPĀDA: No.

PROF. KOTOVSKY: There is no separate...

PRABHUPĀDA: Why? Why there is no department of knowledge in university to study this fact scientifically? That is my proposition.

PROF. KOTOVSKY: Yes.

PRABHUPĀDA: So that means they are lacking. It may be as you say, or it may be as I say, but there must be a department of knowledge. Now recently, one cardiologist, a doctor, he has accepted that there is soul, in Montreal and Toronto. I had some correspondence with him. So he is strongly in belief that there is soul. So that is another point of view, but we accept knowledge from authority.

Finding the Root Solution

PRABHUPĀDA: We are manufacturing so many ways of happy life, this "ism," that "ism," this plan, that plan. So many plans. We are seeing so many suggestions, in the television. "This is the problem. This is the suggestion. This is problem." Full of new, new problems, new, new suggestions. But because we are lacking this *rāja-vidyā*, the king of knowledge, we are perplexed. But if you know that Kṛṣṇa is the root cause of everything and if you serve Kṛṣṇa, then every problem will be solved immediately.

* * *

Prabhupāda's determined conviction was that Kṛṣṇa consciousness could solve all problems. As a corollary to that, no problems can be solved outside of Kṛṣṇa consciousness.

Special Children, Special Parents

PRABHUPĀDA: We have got so many children among our *gṛhastha* devotees. How fine they are. They're getting Kṛṣṇa consciousness from the beginning of their life. That means in the past they advanced in Kṛṣṇa consciousness. Somehow or other they failed to complete. Now they have got again chance, again in the temple, dancing and chanting from the very beginning of life. So this is the opportunity....Suppose by karma, by material activities, fruitive activities, you become very rich man or very learned man and attain a very good office. But everything will be finished with your death. As soon as the body is finished, all your assets are finished. But if you become a devotee, your body may be finished but the soul is eternal. The soul will carry your assets of Kṛṣṇa consciousness, and nature will give you another chance of taking birth in a very rich family or in a Vaiṣṇava family.

* * *

Birth in a Kṛṣṇa conscious family is a great opportunity for a soul to advance in Kṛṣṇa consciousness and end his material existence. Prabhupāda therefore carefully explained the duty of a parent.

PRABHUPĀDA: This is real contraceptive method. If you think that "If a child is born, I shall educate him in such a way that this birth will be his last birth. Next he is going back to home, back to Godhead," then produce a child. Otherwise don't produce. This is spiritual contraceptive. This is real father and mother. Otherwise a dog is also becoming a father. That kind of father-becoming is not recommended in the Vedic civilization. Now, just become a real father to give the real benefit to the son. Then you become a father.

Bhagavad-gītā for Children

PRABHUPĀDA: The finger is the part and parcel of my body. So what is the duty? As soon as I say, "Finger, please come here," it comes. "Finger, come here. Do this, do that, pick up." This is a finger's business. A finger cannot remain independent. Or if the finger cannot give the service properly, then it is diseased. Similarly, our material condition means we are in diseased condition. We are not giving service to God, we are giving service to the dog. This is our diseased condition. So God is Himself explaining how you should live. That is *Bhagavad-gītā.*

* * *

Prabhupāda was such an expert preacher that he could explain difficult philosophy in such a way that everyone could understand.

The Foundation is Faith

PRABHUPĀDA: So if we accept that "Whatever Kṛṣṇa is saying, it is perfect," this is called *śraddhadhānāḥ,* faith. Without faith you cannot make any progress. In every action you must have faith. Just like if you go to a barber, you spread your neck and he is with a razor. He can immediately cut your throat. But because you have got faith – "No, this barber is honest. He'll not cut my throat. He'll cleanly shave..." So faith is required in every step. Without faith you cannot make one step. Simply you have to find out the person, "He is worthy of me keeping my faith." Here is Kṛṣṇa. He is worthy of you accepting His instruction. So take *Bhagavad-gītā* very seriously. Then your life is successful.

* * *

Śrīla Rūpa Gosvāmī stated, "*ādau śraddhāḥ,*" first there is faith. Faith in guru is faith in Kṛṣṇa. A faithful person thinks that his guru is accurately representing Kṛṣṇa and thus Kṛṣṇa will be pleased if he pleases his guru. No one progresses in Kṛṣṇa consciousness without faith.

Getting Correct Answers

YOUNG MAN: Śrīla Prabhupāda, how does one surrendering to

Kṛṣṇa discriminate between being tactful in his speech, on one hand, and, on the other hand, compromising?

PRABHUPĀDA: To surrender to Kṛṣṇa is the best tactful, and if you surrender, He will give you instruction. Then all tactfulness will be there.

teṣāṁ satata-yuktānāṁ
bhajatāṁ prīti-pūrvakam
dadāmi buddhi-yogaṁ taṁ
yena mām upayānti te

If you become a completely surrendered devotee of Kṛṣṇa – He is within your heart – He will give you the right instruction so that in every sphere of life you'll be perfect.

* * *

Kṛṣṇa as Supersoul is *caitya-guru,* the spiritual master in the heart. Because we lack the qualifications to consistently and accurately hear Him, we need an external manifestation of Him in the form of our spiritual master. Whenever practical, therefore, we confirm our realizations with our spiritual master, *śāstra,* and other trusted *sādhus* (devotees). Accepting the above, Prabhupāda nevertheless here explained the one principle that solves all "How do I know what to do?" problems: Be sincere enough to receive Kṛṣṇa's instructions from within.

Initiation Within the Heart

QUESTIONER: Śrīla Prabhupāda, does a disciple first accept his spiritual master within the heart when he takes initiation?

DEVOTEE: What is the question again?

QUESTIONER: When a disciple takes initiation, does he first take initiation in the heart?

PRABHUPĀDA: Initiation is the third stage. First stage is – just like you have come. This is called *śraddhā,* a little faith, not full faith. Then you have to increase this faith by association of devotees. That is required. And when the faith is increased, then the question of initiation. Initiation should not be immediately offered. That will be misused. Therefore when we initiate, we inquire from the head of the temple, "How long he is coming? What is his behavior?" If he certifies that "Yes, he is doing nice," then we initiate. Our initiation is not so cheap, "You come and be initiated." No, we do not do that. We must test you first of all. Then we initiate.

MADHUDVIṢA: His question was that can you take initiation by accepting the spiritual master in your heart without actually taking...

PRABHUPĀDA: This is bogus proposition. It has no meaning. [*Laughter.*] It has no meaning. If you think within yourself, "I am eating," will you be satisfied? You starve and simply think, "I have eaten everything." [*Laughter.*] Is that very practical proposal? You must eat. We don't say all these bogus propositions. All right. Thank you very much.

* * *

The actual intention of the question was not accurately rephrased by Madhudviṣa. (Prabhupāda himself told me in New Vrindaban in 1969 that he accepted his own spiritual master at their first meeting but did not take initiation until years later.) Yet Prabhupāda's answer to Madhudviṣa's question is extremely significant and relevant. Madhudviṣa asked whether a devotee could forego the initiation ceremony if he had already mentally accepted his spiritual master. Prabhupāda's reply is clear and uncompromising: "This is bogus proposition....We don't say all these bogus propositions."

Someone may mentally accept a guru, or may even accept him with his whole heart, but if he avoids actually taking initiation, his acceptance is insufficient. Prabhupāda's example about eating mentally is brilliant. If initiation can also be complete by our "mentally accepting a guru," the guru is not given the choice to accept or not to accept the disciple. Prabhupāda always ascribed importance to the initiation ceremony in which both guru and disciple formally accepted the mutual responsibilities of their relationship, and he insisted that a fire sacrifice be performed even after initiations were given through the mail.

Hear! Hear! Hear!

MAN: What if you hear in your heart, but don't act in your life?

PRABHUPĀDA: Hm?

PUṢṬA KṚṢṆA: What if you hear, but don't act accordingly in your practical life?

MAN: You feel it in your heart...

PRABHUPĀDA: No, hear means you do it in practical life. Otherwise what is the hearing? Then just like one stone, he has got ear. Hearing means it will react. That is hearing. The more you hear, the more it will react. Then you practically will do it. Everything comes by hearing. Hearing is so important. Just like even in your ordinary education you go to the school, college, and hear from your professor. Then you become perfect and take your degree. Similarly, the science of God, you simply hear about it. *Śravaṇaṁ kīrtanam.* Then gradually it will purify. Hearing means purifying the dirty things within the heart. That is hearing. *Ceto-darpaṇa-mārjanam. Śṛṇvatāṁ sva-kathāḥ kṛṣṇaḥ, puṇya-śravaṇa-kīrtanaḥ*. Because it is spiritual, hearing has got a potency to purify you. This is not ordinary hearing. This is spiritual hearing, so it has got a potency. *Śṛṇvatāṁ sva-kathāḥ kṛṣṇaḥ, puṇya-śravaṇa-kīrtanaḥ*.

Anyone who takes part in this process of hearing and chanting, he becomes pious, purified. Just like if you touch fire in some way or other, it will act.

* * *

Śrī Caitanya Mahāprabhu and Prabhupāda both followed Śrīla Vyāsadeva's conclusion about the potency of hearing, especially *Śrīmad-Bhāgavatam:*

nivṛtta-tarṣair upagīyamānād
bhavauṣadhāc chrotra-mano-'bhirāmāt
ka uttamaśloka-guṇānuvādāt
pumān virajyeta vinā paśughnāt

Glorification of the Supreme Personality of Godhead is performed in the *paramparā* system; that is, it is conveyed from spiritual master to disciple. Such glorification is relished by those no longer interested in the false, temporary glorification of this cosmic manifestation. Descriptions of the Lord are the right medicine for the conditioned soul undergoing repeated birth and death. Therefore, who will cease hearing such glorification of the Lord except a butcher or one who is killing his own self?

– *Śrīmad-Bhāgavatam* 10.1.4

Winning a Heart, Saving a Soul

GIRL: Śrīla Prabhupāda, would you please explain why Kṛṣṇa consciousness hadn't come to the West until now? Why didn't it come earlier?

PRABHUPĀDA: Because you were not born. After your birth we have come here to take you back to home, back to Godhead. Now take the opportunity; come with us. We were waiting for your birth.

* * *

Prabhupāda's answer endeared everyone, including the questioner, to his lotus feet.

Auckland, New Zealand, 1976

Steadiness in Service

My family and I joined Prabhupāda and his entourage, who were flying first to Auckland before continuing on to Latoka, Fiji, and then to Honolulu.

Alone with Prabhupāda in the Melbourne airport, Prabhupāda turned to me and asked, "Why are you leaving? Why have you decided to move?" I was quite surprised. I had been living outside the temple and was not able to serve in ISKCON full time. Now Prabhupāda seemed to be questioning, at the eleventh hour, my attempt to take up more direct service. "But I asked you in Māyāpur, Prabhupāda. They wanted me to become temple president in Laguna Beach, and I asked you in Māyāpur. You gave me permission to accept the position."

Prabhupāda's response paralleled the mood in which he had previously spoken. "Permission may be there, but why did you even want to leave?"

* * *

What pleased Prabhupāda? My analysis is that the essential ingredient in pleasing Prabhupāda was steadiness. When I could not remain in Hong Kong, I nevertheless was able to satisfy him by steadily – week by week – rendering service by sending donations. Prabhupāda's basic desire for his disciples was that they served steadily. Ultimately, steady service elevates one. Steady service will be more pleasing to our spiritual master than glowing but fleeting service, which shines brightly like a shooting star and then quickly becomes extinguished and disappears.

What one devotee needs to continue serving may be different from another. Later on this same tour, Prabhupāda wrote a purport (*Bhāg.* 8.2.30) underscoring this point: one should situate himself in a position wherein he can most steadily continue his devotional service and cultivate Kṛṣṇa consciousness.

> In the fighting between the elephant and the crocodile, the difference was that although the elephant was extremely powerful, he was in a foreign place, in the water. During one thousand years of fighting, he could not get any food, and under the circumstances his bodily strength diminished, and because his bodily strength diminished, his mind also became weak and his senses less powerful. The crocodile, however, being an animal of the water, had no difficulties. He was getting food and was therefore getting mental strength and sensual encouragement. Thus while the elephant became reduced in strength, the crocodile became more and more powerful. Now, from this we may take the lesson that in our fight with *māyā* we should not be in a position in which our strength, enthusiasm, and senses will be unable to fight vigorously. Our Kṛṣṇa consciousness movement has actually declared war against the illusory energy, in which all the living entities are rotting in a false understanding of civilization. The soldiers in this Kṛṣṇa consciousness movement must always possess physical strength, enthusiasm, and sensual power. To keep themselves fit, they must therefore place themselves in a normal condition of life. What constitutes a normal condition will not be the same for everyone, and therefore there are divisions of *varṇāśrama* – *brāhmaṇa, kṣatriya, vaiśya, śūdra, brahmacarya, gṛhastha, vānaprastha* and *sannyāsa.* Especially in this age, Kali-yuga, it is advised that no one take *sannyāsa.*

aśvamedhaṁ gavālambhaṁ
sannyāsaṁ pala-paitṛkam
devareṇa sutotpattiṁ
kalau pañca vivarjayet

– *Brahma-vaivarta Purāṇa*

From this we can understand that in this age the *sannyāsa-āśrama* is forbidden because people are not strong. Śrī Caitanya Mahāprabhu showed us an example in taking *sannyāsa* at the age of twenty-four years, but even Sārvabhauma Bhaṭṭācārya advised Śrī Caitanya Mahāprabhu to be extremely careful because He had taken *sannyāsa* at an early age. For preaching we give young boys *sannyāsa,* but actually it is being experienced that they are not fit for *sannyāsa.* There is no harm, however, if one thinks that he is unfit for *sannyāsa;* if he is very much agitated sexually, he should go to the *āśrama* where sex is allowed, namely the *gṛhastha-āśrama.* That one has been found to be very weak in one place does not mean that he should stop fighting the crocodile of *māyā.* One should take shelter of the lotus feet of Kṛṣṇa, as we shall see Gajendra do, and at the same time one can be a *gṛhastha* if he is satisfied with sexual indulgence. There is no need to give up the fight. Śrī Caitanya Mahāprabhu therefore recommended, *sthāne sthitāḥ śruti-gatāṁ tanu-vāṅ-manobhiḥ.* One may stay in whichever *āśrama* is suitable for him; it is not essential that one take *sannyāsa.* If one is sexually agitated, he can enter the *gṛhastha-āśrama.* But one must continue fighting. For one who is not in a transcendental position, to take *sannyāsa* artificially is not a very great credit. If *sannyāsa* is not suitable, one may enter the *gṛhastha-āśrama* and fight *māyā* with great strength. But one should not give up the fighting and go away.

"Just to Encourage My Disciples..."

Landing in New Zealand, Prabhupāda was greeted by a roaring *kīrtana* and a press conference.

INTERVIEWER: Well, what do you hope to achieve by your short visit here to New Zealand, where you don't have a very big following at all?

PRABHUPĀDA: Just to encourage my disciples. They're also trying their best to spread this Kṛṣṇa consciousness movement, so if I occasionally visit, they become encouraged. That's why.

* * *

Prabhupāda once mentioned that he had actually authored the many articles in his BTG magazine although his different disciples had signed them. Similarly, Prabhupāda was preaching throughout the world through his students. To ensure that the preaching would continue, he traveled constantly, despite his old age, and inspired his disciples to preach, act purely, and strictly follow the process.

The Potency of the Holy Names

INTERVIEWER: Well, I'm sure many New Zealanders would like to know the very reason why your followers chant the Hare Kṛṣṇa chant in the street? What is the reason behind this?

PRABHUPĀDA: Reason is that Hare Kṛṣṇa... Kṛṣṇa is the name of God, Kṛṣṇa. Kṛṣṇa is absolute, God is absolute. God's name and God, there is no difference. That is absolute idea. So if you chant Kṛṣṇa's name, that means you associate with Kṛṣṇa directly, God. And by associating with God, you become purified. You are now thinking "I am this body," as the dog is also thinking. We now think "I belong to America," "I belong to Australia," "I belong to New Zealand," "I... India." These wrong conceptions will go away by chanting. Then we'll understand that "I am not this or that; I am spirit soul, part and parcel of God." Then real knowledge begins, and if we act accordingly, our life becomes successful. So this movement is not simply meant for you or me – it is meant for every intelligent human being.

* * *

By their chanting in public, the devotees both purified themselves and allowed others to benefit from hearing Kṛṣṇa's names.

Sanātana Gosvāmī Shaves His Head

After the press conference, the devotees whisked Prabhupāda to their Gribblehurst Road temple. The temple was filled to capacity when Prabhupāda arrived. He greeted Śrī Śrī Rādhā-Giridhārī, the Deities he had installed in 1972.

Many chanters in the temple had long hair, and Prabhupāda's arrival address made his desires clear. He told the story of Sanātana Gosvāmī's meeting in Vārāṇasī with Śrī Caitanya Mahāprabhu. During that meeting, Mahāprabhu told Sanātana to shave off his long hair, beard, and mustache and look like a gentleman instead of a *daraveśa,* a hippie.

* * *

Prabhupāda knew about the tension between the two New Zealand groups – the regular temple devotees and the followers of Tuṣṭa Kṛṣṇa Swami. The temple devotees maintained Prabhupāda's standard of shaved heads while most of those living outside did not adhere to this practice. In his lecture, Prabhupāda expressed his standard: disciples must keep their heads shaved.

Paraṁ nijayate srī-kṛṣṇa-saṅkīrtanam

Later, Prabhupāda met with the temple leaders. Puṣṭa Kṛṣṇa Swami told Prabhupāda why the reporter had inquired about the devotees' public chanting.

PUṢṬA KṚṢṆA SWAMI: They're feeling threatened by our *kīrtana* parties.

PRABHUPĀDA: Who?

PUṢṬA KṚṢṆA SWAMI: He said that some of the town councils are trying to pass laws against our chanting in the streets.

DEVOTEE: Some of our men are going to meet with the council the day after tomorrow. The businessmen have complained. Some of the businessmen have complained.

PRABHUPĀDA: Not all of them. You take some signatures from other businessmen.

* * *

Prabhupāda was always extremely practical.

"Chanting Hare Kṛṣṇa is Bad" is Good

PRABHUPĀDA: So there is agitation against chanting. That is also good. Yes, "Hare Kṛṣṇa is bad." [*Laughs.*] So we want that. Let them chant Hare Kṛṣṇa somehow or other. [*Devotees laugh.*] "We don't want to be bothered by Hare Kṛṣṇa." That means chanting Hare Kṛṣṇa.

DEVOTEE: Because we have our *kīrtana* party now, we go on *kīrtana,* eighty men. We go two nights a week with eighty men. Huge *kīrtana* with five *mṛdaṅgas* and guitars, and we get huge crowds from the whole street.

PRABHUPĀDA: That will make you triumphant. Go on *kīrtana.* That is very nice. *Kīrtana* and book distribution. This is also *kīrtana.* Yes. So do it enthusiastically. Keep yourself pure. Nobody will be able to do any harm to you. Kṛṣṇa will give you protection.

Because they are sinful and in ignorance, they are suffering. Everyone, once they are educated, they will become peaceful, no disturbance. Then you can very happily chant Hare Kṛṣṇa and your life becomes successful. This is our program. But now, due to sinful activities they are suffering. And they will suffer and continue to suffer. So we want to stop that suffering. These rascals, they do not understand. They think, "Hare Kṛṣṇa movement is disturbing." A rascal civilization. So let us try our best. What can be done?

* * *

Prabhupāda had full faith in the transcendental effects of hearing and chanting the *mahā-mantra* and distributing transcendental knowledge through his books. He also had full faith that Kṛṣṇa would protect His devotees who were preaching earnestly, and he was determined to help the suffering people despite their ignorant resistance to Kṛṣṇa's mercy.

A Word of Caution for Preachers

Prabhupāda, aware of the issues between the two groups, spoke a word of caution to the temple leaders.

PRABHUPĀDA: Don't spoil the movement by manufacturing ideas. Don't do that. Go on in the standard way, keep yourself pure; then the movement is sure to be successful. But if you want to spoil it [by changing things] whimsically, then what can be done? It will be spoiled. If you manufacture whims and disagree and fight amongst yourselves, then it will be another edition of these so-called movements. It will lose the spiritual strength. Always remember this.

Now, actually, outsiders are surprised. "What power this Hare Kṛṣṇa mantra has got that it is changing people so quickly?" It has to be admitted. Unless it has got power, how it is changing? So we have to keep that power. Don't make it an ordinary musical vibration. It is a different thing, spiritual. Although it seems like musical vibration, it is completely spiritual. Mantra*uṣadhi-vaśaḥ*. By mantra, even the snakes can be charmed. So mantra is not ordinary sound vibration. So we have to keep the mantra in potency, potent, by offenseless chanting, by remaining pure. If you pollute the mantra, then it will lose its effect.

* * *

Prabhupāda again reminded the devotees that the *mahā-mantra*, when chanted purely, had great power in and of itself, regardless of how it was presented. The devotees, therefore, should not alter the process by which the mantra is received by polluting it with our own material concepts.

Displeasure and Disease

The next morning at the temple, just before Prabhupāda left for the airport, he oversaw a fire sacrifice and performed an initiation ceremony. I did not attend, as the temple was crowded with local devotees. When he saw me at the airport, Prabhupāda asked where I had been. His frown expressed his displeasure.

* * *

By attending the initiation ceremony, I would have been able to hear Prabhupāda speak. I didn't have an appropriate reason for missing this valuable opportunity. Prabhupāda immediately recognized this as a flaw, and indicated his disapproval by his frown.

By the Mercy of a Vaiṣṇava

Jita Girīśa, a devotee who was in New Zealand when Prabhupāda visited there in 1976, wrote a humble account of Prabhupāda's New Zealand visit from beginning to end. The chaos, the anxieties, the aspirations of a sincere disciple experiencing Prabhupāda's visit to a small temple are portrayed. I have included it here in its entirety to fill out details of Prabhupāda's 1976 visit.

> It's a chilly evening near the end of April; six of us from ISKCON's Gribblehurst Road temple are in a van speeding to the airport.
>
> As we arrive, Yamala Arjuna gasps, "Oh, Prabhu, look at this. There's at least fifty of them." A crowd of North Shore devotees are gathered in the arrival lounge, some in *dhotīs,* some with long hair, many appearing in public as devotees for the first time in a year. Yaśomatīnandana Prabhu, our temple president, starts an

uproarious *kīrtana*. I feel out of place – am I on the right team? Prabhupāda suddenly appears, smiling broadly. Guru-kṛpa Swami is wearing an outrageous white suit and a beret. They move quickly to the car, which slowly heads off to the temple.

"Hey, that's offensive – they're all overtaking Prabhupāda!" Yaśo snaps, as one by one, all the devotees' cars overtake Prabhupāda's and speed off to the temple. "We'd better go too, Yaśo. Nobody back at the temple will know what to do." At the temple there's a small crew of young devotees still cleaning and cooking, They haven't slept for three days. The place is a chaotic mess and they are in complete anxiety – Prabhupāda's coming! Our car pulls in to the temple ahead of Śrīla Prabhupāda and everyone runs in to make sure everything's in order. I stay on the nature strip waiting to see Prabhupāda. The North Shore devotees arrive and join me on the footpath. They start playing guitars and singing a melancholy slow tune "*nama oṁ viṣṇu-pādāya...*"

"Are you guys mad? Prabhupāda's here!" I think to myself. As Prabhupāda steps out of the car, I bound up and down like a puppy greeting its master at the end of the day. "*Jaya* Prabhupāda! *Jaya* Prabhupāda!" Śrīla Prabhupāda turns his head toward me and smiles right at me – he likes the enthusiasm.

We all start crowding around the entrance hall at the bottom of the stairs, and Prabhupāda slowly ascends as the *kīrtana* explodes with unrestrained, youthful exuberance.

Śrīla Prabhupāda sits calmly on a small *āsana* behind a desk. He has an air of complete ease. This is striking – he's taking *prasāda* silently in such a crowded room as though this were a completely normal way to eat – in front of seventy people staring at his every movement. He is regal and doesn't show even a trace of discomfort.

We watch as Prabhupāda pulls small pieces of *purī* off, deftly wraps them around some *sabjī*, and pops them gracefully into his mouth without touching his lips with his fingers. Finally, he leans his head back, opens his mouth wide, and expertly, with perfect poise, tips a stream of water from a silver cup. Swanlike perfect movements. This is not a practiced stage routine. "You are very lucky to live in such a nice country. You have enough of everything – enough land, enough grass, enough cows – everything is freely available. There is no difficulty. Use everything in Kṛṣṇa's service. Live nicely and peacefully and go back home, back to Godhead. Every living being is gradually evolving in consciousness. Even some rocks are growing – there is life there. Gradually evolving through different species to the human platform. The perfection of this evolution of consciousness is to meet Kṛṣṇa in Vṛndāvana. So, nothing is lacking here in New Zealand. Everything is here. I just have one request. You please don't concoct anything."

Prabhupāda finishes speaking. "We brought some sweets and ghee from the cows on our farm, Prabhupāda." Śrīla Prabhupāda opens the big jar of off-white *rasagullās* and tastes one. "Give one to everyone," he tells Hari Śauri. I get half a *rasagullā*. "So, you had one?" Prabhupāda asks Hari Śauri. He shakes his head. Softly and lovingly Prabhupāda says, "So, you take one."

It's early the next morning and we've entered the Domain Park from the Grafton Road entrance and huddled in behind Prabhupāda like a group of ducklings. I'm right up close behind him as he walks past a small pond. "Hare Kṛṣṇa, Hare Kṛṣṇa." I chant in a neophyte way, as though the mantra were a drug to make me high. Prabhupāda notices this and chuckles. We walk up to two small ponds. One has a Viking statue, a warrior on horseback blowing a trumpet.

"Prabhupāda," Yaśo queries, "were the Vikings *kṣatriyas?*"

"No," Prabhupāda answers. "*Kṣatriyas* fought on religious principles. They were noble warriors, religious, not murderers."

"Then what about the modern soldiers? Do they go to the heavenly planets when they die on the battlefield?"

"No, simply demons fighting demons for economic reasons. How can they go to heaven? They go to hell, both sides."

Prabhupāda walks onto a large green lawn behind the ponds. His mood is so serious it scares me. If he speaks to me I'll freeze. He stands, pointing his cane. "What is the name of this tree?" This is not a botanical knowledge test, it is a guru-disciple exchange. Will you speculate; will you be foolish and try to impress? If anyone does, he can be almost certain to be chastised: "You think? You do not know!"

Prabhupāda stands like the commander-in-chief of an army about to launch a major offensive. We move on. The same scene is repeated. Yaśomatīnandana and Tuṣṭa Kṛṣṇa Swami, the leaders of the two camps, contest for Prabhupāda's recognition and approval, but not many trees are named. The one thought that is reverberating in my head is, "I don't deserve to be here. I'm nobody. Prabhupāda is so grave and great."

His head tilted gently back as he aristocratically surveys the surroundings, Śrīla Prabhupāda and his group walk quietly toward the grand old museum building. "This is a nice building," Prabhupāda remarks.

"Yes, Śrīla Prabhupāda. We're going to get it for a temple," Yaśomatīnandana blurts. Silence follows. "In here, in this glasshouse, there are some lotus flowers," someone says. "Yes, I saw them last time," Prabhupāda replies. ("That last time was three or four years ago, Jita," says Yaśo.) Prabhupāda is not interested to see them again. He remembers. Our walk ends.

Next there will be an initiation. Kālasamvara, Parivādī, Sarvākṣa, Rudracandrī, Annapūrṇā, Advaita, and Gauravāṇī will be initiated.

We're all sitting in the temple room. Guru-kṛpa Swami is in a bad mood – everything's disorganized. "If you fall asleep one more time, you're not getting initiated," he snarls at Sarvākṣa. I start to put bananas and grains on paper plates for the initiates. "Not you! It should be a *brāhmaṇa,*" he tells me. Soon I'm back in the kitchen. Down the passageway comes Prabhupāda's melodious, even chant. "*Jayatāṁ suratau paṅgor...*" Then "*karṣan veṇu-svanair gopīr gopīnāthaḥ śriye...*"

The chanting stops. I can't miss this – we've all been waiting so long to see these devotees get their beads. I put down the pot, slink down the passage, and peer in the door just as Advaita and Gauravāṇī get their beads – what ecstatic names. Gauravāṇī, one who preaches the message of Caitanya Mahāprabhu. "Jita Girīśa! We need more pots!"

Some time passes before Tuṣṭa Kṛṣṇa Swami's strained face pokes in the kitchen window. "Prabhupāda's sitting, waiting on the *vyāsāsana,* and there's no *guru-pūjā* tray. Get it together, you guys. Stop spacing out!" Somehow I frantically manifest an *ārati* tray from the piles of homogeneously mixed kitchenware and Deity paraphernalia and race into the temple room. Two rows of silent devotees line the sides of the *vyāsāsana* where Prabhupāda sits waiting. "Hand out the flowers," comes an order. The flowers are all on a heavy marble slab at Prabhupāda's feet and there's no basket. Prabhupāda looks expectantly. I pick up the slab and carry it around feeling very silly. The *kīrtana* is starting; Prabhupāda nods his head and smiles, appreciating the sincere loving service of the devotees. Then majestically he gathers a handful of flowers in his right hand and sends a cascade streaming into the crowd of devotees, who start dancing as though magically infused with life. It is the loving gesture of an exalted father blessing his tiny, inexperienced children.

I'm in the kitchen with Dayāsāra most of the day, cooking for an afternoon feast. As it's being served out, we're called to Prabhupāda's room. "What is the noise downstairs?" Prabhupāda asks. "Oh, that's the feast, Prabhupāda," Dayāsāra replies. "Feast? What feast is that?" Prabhupāda is surprised. "Go and get Śrīla Prabhupāda a plate of *prasāda* right now!" barks Tuṣṭa Kṛṣṇa Swami. "How could we be so stupid to forget Prabhupāda?" laments Dayāsāra.

Later we hear Prabhupāda's angry voice shouting, "What rascal has done this?" A devotee accidentally locked Prabhupāda in the bathroom. We watch him creep up to the door, unbolt it quickly, and run off.

*

The evening *Gītā* class is on. Prabhupāda is wearing his glasses, looking old and scholarly as he sits on a *vyāsāsana* smothered in fruits, cellophane-wrapped presents, boxes of dried fruits, and all kinds of gifts. The guests overflow into the hallway and out the front door. "This is my last chance to be with my guru," I think, as I stand right at the side of the *vyāsāsana*. "I'm not going anywhere. I've been in the kitchen for two days, but now I'm not leaving for anything."

Prabhupāda asks for water and I immediately struggle through the crowd to get it. I bring it back, but I'm too timid to hand it to Prabhupāda, so I put it on the *vyāsāsana.*

Ahhh! Someone's punching me in the back. "Get back in the kitchen and cook, Jita!" More punches, but I stay. Damn the consequences. Question time comes. One arrogant hippie stands with folded hands. "If God exists, then why can't I see Him?" His question is demanding and rude.

"Yes," Prabhupāda's voice booms out angry, "you have turned your back on God. Kṛṣṇa is there, but you have your back to Him. How do you expect to see Him?" Prabhupāda's reply is so forceful and angry that the man sits down quietly. In the literal sense, his back had been turned to Rādhā-Giridhārī; in a deeper sense, his back had been turned to Śrīla Prabhupāda and his chance of becoming qualified to see Kṛṣṇa.

I'm washing pots at about 11p.m. in the kitchen when I'm jolted by a loud thud. Dayāsāra is stretched out asleep on the floor.

My job the next morning is to make *pañcagavya.* Or is it *pañcāmṛta?* Yaśo stayed up watching a Prabhupāda interview on TV, so he's not around. Prabhupāda is installing Gaura-Nitāi and big Jagannātha deities this morning, but as usual, nobody's in charge and nobody knows what to do. I take the *tilaka* and grind it. Next I get the cow urine and stool, put them in a huge bucket, throw in the sugar syrup, the ghee, and then the *tilaka.* I am stirring when Guru-kṛpa comes into the kitchen to see how things are shaping up. He's agitated. Nothing is arranged properly. "What's this?" he says, disgusted. "This is useless. Do it properly." And he walks out. I've spent over an hour grinding all the *tilaka* down and blistered my hands. Will I be able to do it again in time? Prabhupāda had showed great reluctance to install the Deities, agreeing at the last moment. Now will he change his mind again if the arrangements aren't *pakkā*?

At last my duties are finished and I run in to see Prabhupāda offering the ghee lamp, crowded by devotees and half-hidden in a cloud of smoke from the fire sacrifice. He stands stiff, straight, as a servant entrusted with a confidential service. He is indescribably sober, unspeakably grave. He is serving the infinite Supreme Godhead and it is an inconceivably enormous, loving duty.

I go back to the kitchen after Prabhupāda goes upstairs to pack. His breakfast remnants are there! I grab the tray and make for the garden – after all, one can steal *mahā-mahā*! Kālasamvara spots me and begins to scold me. He's joined by Sarvākṣa, who scolds me too, and then Parivādī, who is obviously also outraged. I start walking, but the whole temple's running after me. I don't remember getting any remnants.

Prabhupāda is about to leave. I have been thinking I am a competent, older devotee, but I'm a fool who has been mostly ignored by his spiritual master – how can I get his recognition and mercy?

At that moment Hari Śauri pops in. "Can you make sure Prabhupāda's eating bowls are clean, Jita?" I wash them as if they were fragile, priceless treasures, then race out to the driveway. Two rows of devotees flank the driveway leading to the car parked on the street. How will I be recognized? "Prabhupāda, please acknowledge me as your disciple" is my only thought, and it's driving me mad. My life is useless. One of the ladies hands me a garland. Here's a chance! But when I look at it I see it has no flowers on the neck area – just bare string. On yesterday's walk, Prabhupāda had removed a similar garland saying, " This is very troublesome." I hide the garland behind my back.

Prabhupāda seems to float down the steps, walking slowly with his cane. His skin is golden, smooth, and his forehead is smothered with orange *candana* paste. He is the epitome of loving, gentle dignity. He stops in front of me, bends his head down. "Put the garland on Prabhupāda," someone prompts. As I put the garland around his neck, Prabhupāda folds his palms together. I am amazed at what has happened. I cannot comprehend Prabhupāda's unbelievable humility and kindness. I am so worthless and unworthy.

We leap into the van and speed to the airport. All I can think of is how wretched I am. Prabhupāda's kindness has cut a gaping gash through my false conception of being "together." I will never be the same again. *"Gurudev! kṛpā-bindu diyā . . ."*

Showers of carnations bounce from Prabhupāda's lotus head, thoughtlessly thrown by enthusiastic devotees, but Prabhupāda doesn't complain as he walks, slow and stately, to the waiting lounge. He sits on a bench with crowds of disciples seated around his feet. He is serene and blissful, radiating an amazing heart-melting Vṛndāvana *śakti* like a transcendental force field. A few *"bhāgyavān jīvas"* pass into this zone as pedestrian traffic, by divine arrangement. Their hearts of steel are pierced by this *śakti,* their faces smashed like dry, clay masks revealing smiles that have been covered by a million births. We sit in awe, enveloped by this transcendental bubble as Prabhupāda smiles so lovingly.

Hare Rāma Dāsa begins strumming slowly and sings, "*Nama oṁ viṣṇu-pādāya*..." in a lingering, emotional eulogy. Prabhupāda is listening very carefully. Behind him, Guru-kṛpa Swami rings his *karatālas* vigorously, attempting to liven the *kīrtana* up, but Prabhupāda stops him – he likes it. He sits appreciating his disciple's mood in a way only Prabhupāda can. He removes his garland, smiles like a father, and hands it to Hare Rāma. Any misconceptions about the North Shore devotees being unbona fide disappear from my mind as I witness Prabhupāda's loving dealings. I stand, palms together, desperately trying to show that now I am sincere. Prabhupāda's glance is like a razor that cuts through to the soul and it seems to say, "You have not even started. Give your life to Kṛṣṇa. Give everything." Then, soon after, he goes up the stairs, boards his plane to Fiji, and is gone.

Prabhupāda, thank you for your unspoken instructions. Please, somehow – whatever it may take – let me be with you again, even for a second.

A Gift while Flying with Prabhupāda

An "outside" devotee, Ṛṣabha Dāsī, cooked some *barfī* for Prabhupāda and asked me to offer it to him during his flight. After we were safely airborne, I left my economy seat and carried the sweets in their metal container covered in plastic to the first-class section, where Prabhupāda sat with his servant. I offered him the sweets on behalf of Ṛṣabha Dāsī and he smiled and accepted them.

* * *

Hari Śauri later returned the plate to me. Half the sweets were eaten. We honored and distributed Prabhupāda's remnants and kept the plate with its plastic cover as *mahā-prasāda*. Ṛṣabha Dāsī had spontaneously made good use of an opportunity to cook for Prabhupāda, and Prabhupāda had accepted her gesture. I also had the good fortune of being the instrument of her serving mood; I benefited by handing Prabhupāda the *barfī* and by eating and distributing his remnants. And I got to keep the plate from which Prabhupāda had eaten.

Knowing Prabhupāda

Going through Fiji immigration, my daughter, Vrindaban Leela, who was one and a half years old, saw Prabhupāda. She excitedly stretched out her hand and pointed a finger in recognition. "Pra-boo-pad!" Prabhupāda looked at the small child and laughed with mild surprise, "She knows me!"

"Everyone knows you, Prabhupāda," I added.

Prabhupāda was pleased with her, and before she ran shyly back to her mother, for some moments he affectionately patted her on the head and stroked her face.

* * *

Vrindaban Leela had seen Prabhupāda's picture and heard his name since birth. Her first words were "Pra-boo-pad," and when she got a little older, she would say "Pra-boo-pad" when his picture was placed before her. Now she connected Prabhupāda with his picture and excitedly expressed her discovery with her outstretched finger.

Fiji, 1976

Upendra, along with a wealthy Fiji-Indian supporter and devotee, Deoji Punja, met Prabhupāda at the Lautoka airport and drove him and his entourage to his house. As soon as we arrived, Prabhupāda pointed to me and said, "Lead *kīrtana.*" I sang and my daughter danced. Prabhupāda said to me, "She was a great yogi in her past life." On hearing this comment from Prabhupāda, Jagattāriṇī looked at him and laughed. Prabhupāda replied, "Yes, it is so. It is *śāstra.* Without carrying Kṛṣṇa consciousness from the previous life, how can she be dancing in *kīrtana* at such an early age?"

* * *

My voice was not great. I felt Prabhupāda was encouraging me and including me in his entourage by asking me to lead *kīrtana.*

He told me that my daughter was previously a great yogi and to show that he was not just flattering me, he said that it was stated in *śāstra: śucīnāṁ śrīmatāṁ gehe yoga-bhraṣṭo 'bhijāyate.*

Why Not Cook Like They Cook?

Deoji Punja's wife, as well as the other ladies in their family, prepared tasty, Gujarati-style *prasāda*. Prabhupāda appreciated their delicious cooking, and after honoring it one day, commented, "Why the devotees in our movement cannot learn to cook like this?"

* * *

The Indian culture is sweet and indirect. In this case, Prabhupāda's complimenting the cooking expertise of his hosts took the form of a gentle criticism of ISKCON's cooks.

Listen to Him

Kevin, a devotee living outside the New Zealand temple, had been inspired by Prabhupāda's "shave-up" lecture in Auckland and had shaved up. He then decided to join Prabhupāda's entourage and accompany him to Fiji. When Kevin approached Prabhupāda in Fiji and told him he wanted to surrender, Prabhupāda pointed to Guru-kṛpa Swami and said, "Then surrender to him."

* * *

Prabhupāda had thousands of disciples. He could not privately instruct or guide them all. He had to rely on his senior disciples and *sannyāsīs* to help him guide the younger devotees, as a father may rely on older sons to care for younger ones. The senior disciples, therefore, carried a burden of love on behalf of their spiritual father to properly represent Prabhupāda's interests, mood, and affection.

Paths to Perfection

Guru-kṛpa Swami sat at Prabhupāda's feet and asked Prabhupāda a pointed question. "Prabhupāda, what about some devotees who are not interested in book distribution? These devotees don't really seem to be carrying the mood of their spiritual master. They are not into preaching, but instead get into other projects, like farms."

Prabhupāda replied firmly, "Do you think that the spiritual master is a dumb stone who cannot instruct different disciples in different ways?"

* * *

Prabhupāda's vision for worldwide preaching was broad. Therefore he instructed different disciples to develop different aspects of that vision, with their perfection being to surrender to the specific order they had been given. As Kṛṣṇa states in the *Bhagavad-gītā:*

śreyān sva-dharmo viguṇaḥ
para-dharmāt sv-anuṣṭhitāt
sva-dharme nidhanaṁ śreyaḥ
para-dharmo bhayāvahaḥ

> It is far better to perform one's own prescribed duties, even though faultily, than another's duties perfectly. Destruction in the course of performing one's own duty is better than engaging in another's duties, for to follow another's path is dangerous.
> – *Bhagavad-gītā* 3.35

Householders and Eating and Sleeping

Prabhupāda took his morning walk near the ocean. As we walked along the sidewalk, I saw neither waves nor palm trees, only the one-story factories that dotted the side of the road. Prabhupāda spoke about renunciation:

GURU-KṚPA: Sanātana Gosvāmī also depended on Kṛṣṇa to provide him food?

PRABHUPĀDA: Yes, but for the renounced order of life, the order is you must beg, *bhikṣā*. Not much. If I can subsist by taking one *capātī*, I'll simply ask for one *capātī*, not for two *capātīs*. That is *śāstra*. If you can live without any *capātī*, that is very good. But you can ask as much as you require. Not to eat sumptuously and sleep twenty-four hours, no.

BHŪRIJANA: And what about householders?

PRABHUPĀDA: Oh, householders? Householder can eat the whole world and sleep.

* * *

We all laughed at Prabhupāda's sarcastic remark. Prabhupāda was pointing out that we are neither householders nor *sannyāsīs;* we are souls with eternal relationships with Kṛṣṇa. Excessive material entanglement, regardless of our *āśrama* status, simply inhibits developing our love for Kṛṣṇa.

Prabhupāda continued to explain the purpose and limits to the concessions granted to householders: "Because he is householder, he has got the concession. Householders are unable [to refrain from sex indulgence]; that is their incapability. "Because I am householder, I have got the facility to have sex as many times and eat as much…" That is not householder. That is *gṛhamedhī*. There are two words: *gṛhamedhī* and *gṛhastha*. *Gṛhastha* is different from *gṛhamedhī*. *Gṛhastha-āśrama*. Although he's householder, it is *āśrama*, only for advancing in Kṛṣṇa consciousness. That is *gṛhastha*. But a *gṛhamedhī* cannot do that."

Opaque Projections

One evening, Prabhupāda wanted to show his hosts a letter he had received. He could have read the letter aloud, but instead he asked his servant to find an opaque projector to project the letter on the wall. When his servant said no projector was available, Prabhupāda expressed his desire that his entourage carry one with them from then on.

* * *

Prabhupāda didn't hesitate to use technology in Kṛṣṇa's service. Technology's ingredients, and the creative intelligence behind technology, "spring from but a spark" of Kṛṣṇa's splendor. Prabhupāda had no interest in dry renunciation. He saw everything Kṛṣṇa's and meant to be used in His service.

Freedom From Anxiety

After speaking to the devotees and guests present, Prabhupāda leaned back, relaxed, with his hand gracefully moving across and resting on his head, "In the beginning," Prabhupāda said, "I had nothing and there was no anxiety. Now Kṛṣṇa has given so much and still there is no anxiety." Prabhupāda then smiled in his unique way, illuminated the room as the sun illuminates the darkened earth at sunrise.

* * *

Prabhupāda struggled on so many fronts in his service of establishing the Kṛṣṇa consciousness movement throughout the world, yet his overall mood was full dependence on Kṛṣṇa. Therefore despite his struggling with managing a worldwide movement as well as his errant and unsteady disciples, he could describe himself as free from all anxiety.

A Child's Offering

Our morning programs in Fiji were simple. We gathered with Prabhupāda and offered guru-*pūjā*. We would then chant Hare Kṛṣṇa and hear his class. One morning, as Prabhupāda sat cross-legged on the plush, mauve couch, my daughter – with Jagattāriṇī's prodding to "show Prabhupāda your doll" – placed at Prabhupāda's feet her crudely carved, two-inch wooden doll. Prabhupāda accepted her offering, and smiling, picked up the doll. He held it in his fingers for a few moments and examined it, waiting for a possible interaction with her. Prabhupāda then looked at Vrindaban Leela before handing the doll back to me.

* * *

Prabhupāda had previously shown my daughter affection, but she was shy and unresponsive. Another time he offered her a sweet, but she turned and buried her face in her mother's *saree*. When Jagattāriṇī coaxed her to take the sweet from Prabhupāda, Vrindaban Leela began to cry. Prabhupāda motioned her not to disturb the child.

Prabhupāda remained affectionate, even from a distance. This morning at *guru-pūjā*, Prabhupāda received the doll as a loving exchange and handed Vrindaban Leela a burgundy flower. Whether dealing with a small child or an adult, Prabhupāda patiently awaited his chance to bestow his affection and mercy.

Chant Hare Kṛṣṇa

After a few days, several Indian families joined our morning program. One day, Guru-kṛpa Swami danced and led the singing of "*Jīv Jāgo*" and other *bhajanas* for Prabhupāda's pleasure. Prabhupāda stopped him in the middle of a song and told him to chant Hare Kṛṣṇa so the guests could also sing. Prabhupāda directed us to be conscious and considerate of others so that we would fan, not douse, their spark of enthusiasm to hear and chant.

An Artful Operation: Instructions for Householders

My wife and I approached Prabhupāda for guidance. I was eager to serve him and ISKCON more directly; my wife was hesitant. In the ensuing conversation, however, Prabhupāda encouraged both of us, especially my wife, to act dutifully as householders in Kṛṣṇa consciousness.

PRABHUPĀDA: Live separately. You're a family man – live separately, earn your livelihood. Where is the problem?

BHŪRIJANA: That's not what I want. I want to preach.

PRABHUPĀDA: Eh? You cannot preach. Those who are preaching, they are *sannyāsīs*. You cannot preach with the *sannyāsīs* and your wife and child. That's not possible. A preacher must be free man. You have got responsibility. You're married. You must maintain your wife and children. You cannot get out of this simple responsibility.…Your child is small. You have to take care. You have to take care of your wife. She has surrendered. On my word she went to marry you. She's so nice girl. That is unique in the Western countries. She never saw you previously. Simply I told her, "Go and marry that boy." So she went. So nice. You must take responsibility for your wife and children. There is no need of preaching.

BHŪRIJANA: Yes.

PRABHUPĀDA: Preaching is meant for the *sannyāsīs*. One who has no encumbrance. But a *gṛhastha* also can – as you were doing in Ḥong Kong. You were doing nice, husband and wife, but you changed your mind. But if you change your mind, there will always be problems. So you fix up your mind. This is my advice.

* * *

This conversation took place after Prabhupāda had taken his massage but before his *prasāda*. He corrected both Jagattāriṇī and I, and we felt relieved that Prabhupāda had diagnosed the problem. He then had us leave so he could eat. Directly after taking his *prasadām*, he called us back to his room.

* * *

PRABHUPĀDA: So what is the solution?

BHŪRIJANA: Well, I would like to serve someone who is serving you.

PRABHUPĀDA: And you?

JAGATTĀRIṆĪ: I guess the same, but I'm still very confused about it.

PRABHUPĀDA: What is the confusion? Many devotees are already doing. You can also... So now, what will be your program?

BHŪRIJANA: We're going to Hawaii on the same flight as you. And then I'll go to Los Angeles. Then I was supposed to assume the duties in Laguna Beach.

PRABHUPĀDA: Our temple.

BHŪRIJANA: Yes.

PRABHUPĀDA: That is good. How about you?

JAGATTĀRIṆĪ: There's still things I don't understand. I hear so many people being critical.

PRABHUPĀDA: Why do you worry so much about others? You are supposed to be a faithful wife to your husband. That's all. So why you are concerned about them?

JAGATTĀRIṆĪ: Because devotees are in conflict with those I respect.

PRABHUPĀDA: Respect you may have. That is good. We may respect even the ant. One who has no respect is another thing. But as a faithful wife, your duty is to follow your husband. That is your duty....Otherwise you will be hampered in your advancement in Kṛṣṇa consciousness. It is my duty to say that. There is no problem. You are husband and wife and you have to follow the instructions of your spiritual master wherever you live. Either you live in the temple or outside. A *gṛhastha* is supposed to live outside because one has to take care of wife and children. But if you remain within our temple, you will become temple president, that's nice. So manage nicely and keep yourself pure. What is wrong there? Then everything's all right. We have got arrangement for *gṛhasthas*. We don't make any distinctions. Simply one has to be in full Kṛṣṇa consciousness. Study the philosophy and try to distribute this philosophy. Where is the problem? I don't see the problem. [*Looking at Jagattāriṇī.*] Your duty is to keep peacefully with your husband, and his duty is to follow strictly the principles given to him by his spiritual master. You have got to live, so live cooperatively....A wife's duty is to remain faithful to her husband and if the husband is a pure devotee then both of them will be happy. What is the problem? [*Referring to an Indian couple.*] You see they are living happily, husband and wife.

The culture is so nice amongst Indians that in any condition the husband and wife live very peacefully.

JAGATTĀRIṆĪ: I've not been brought up in that culture.

PRABHUPĀDA: Ah, but if something is good you should accept.

JAGATTĀRIṆĪ: Yes.

PRABHUPĀDA: I know in your Western countries the ideas are different, but we have to pick up the best. In Vedic culture, the wife should remain faithful to husband. If the husband is bad, then that is another thing. Your husband is not bad; he's a devotee. So what is wrong there? Don't disturb your mind. Follow what I have laid down and chant Hare Kṛṣṇa. Follow the regulative principles and read the books.... You see this girl? [*Prabhupāda again refers to the Indian couple in whose house we are staying.*] She is maintaining a temple in the closet. This is Vedic way. It does not require any big hall. Even Kṛṣṇa is agreeable to keep Himself in a closet. I was doing in my childhood also.

JAGATTĀRIṆĪ: Like this I feel comfortable.

PRABHUPĀDA: Anywhere you can worship. You can keep in a box. It doesn't mean that you must have a very big temple. No. That is according to means. If you have got money then build temple, just like we have got in Bombay, Vṛndāvana. If money comes, then – otherwise, keep in box. Kṛṣṇa is agreeable. Kṛṣṇa does not say first of all build a big temple, then I will accept your service. He's agreeable. *Patraṁ puṣpaṁ phalam.* Simply devotion. The real thing is *bhakti.* Either you keep Him in a box or big temple, but if you have got means to build big temple, then don't keep Him in a box. That is cheating. Kṛṣṇa can understand that too. If you have got no means, He's agreeable. Keep Him in a box. So devotion to Kṛṣṇa cannot be checked in any circumstances. You can keep yourself anywhere very peacefully. Worship the Deity, small scale, big scale. Where is the problem?

JAGATTĀRIṆĪ: In a temple, it seems necessary to perform all worship in a complicated fashion and I can't do that.

PRABHUPĀDA: If you cannot manage big temple, make small temple. But keep it nice. These big temples can be also managed, and so can this temple [small one]. So whatever is feasible for you. Best thing is to stop taking instruction from anyone else. You take instruction from your husband, and if your husband does not give proper instruction, I will give. You can write. I will give.

JAGATTĀRIṆĪ: Yes.

PRABHUPĀDA: You can take instructions and if you think that he is not competent, then you can ask me. And do not take other instruction. That is not good for a woman.

JAGATTĀRIṆĪ: Yes.

PRABHUPĀDA: Woman should not divert her attention to anyone else except her husband. That will keep her pure. That is the Vedic culture. A woman's beauty is how much she's devoted to her husband. That is beauty, not personal beauty. One who is ugly, his beauty is his knowledge. Similarly, woman's beauty is how much she's devoted to her husband. One bird is black just like a crow, but her voice is so sweet. The more a woman is devoted to her husband, she's beautiful. That is Vedic culture.

Just like Sītā. Rāmacandra's stepmother served her husband Mahārāja Daśaratha so nicely that Daśaratha Mahārāja wanted to give her some benediction. She said, "I'll take in time." So when her stepson Rāma was announced to be king, she wanted that her son should be king. So she requested Mahārāja Daśaratha, "You wanted to give me one benediction." "Yes, you can take." "So my son should be king and Rāma should be banished, sent to the forest for fourteen years."

Mahārāja Daśaratha immediately fainted. But still, because he promised, he told Rāma, "This is the position. So, you have to go to the forest, my dear son." Rāma replied, "Oh yes, father," and He went. This is ideal. But he did not ask his daughter-in-law Sītā to go. She was also king's daughter. She was princess. So she could say, "All right, my husband is going to forest. I can go stay with my father's house." But instead she said, "No. Rāma, I shall go!" Rāmacandra said, "No! No, you were asked to stay here," but Sītā replied, "No, that I cannot do. My duty is that where my husband goes, I go." So she went with her husband and so many chaotic conditions were created simply for her pleasure. And she was kidnapped. Rāma was able to create millions of Sītās, but for one Sītā He fought Rāvaṇa and gave him a lesson in such a way that his whole family was destroyed. Then Sītā was rescued. This is the duty. These *śāstras* have to be learned for duty. Father's duty, son's duty, everything ideal. All ideal.

So first of all, you select, husband and wife, where you shall live very peacefully and live there and follow your husband peacefully. Worship the Deity, individually or collectively, whatever is possible. But don't be disturbed and create problems. That will spoil your life.

JAGATTĀRIṆĪ: It seems hard to change one's mentality when one is not already very submissive.

PRABHUPĀDA: That's up to you. That requires determination. This I was explaining. Anyone who is seeing woman, he's attracted. But if he is so determined, "No, I'll have no more sex life," then he is safe. Not that because I am thinking of woman I must have. No. I must know, "I am *sannyāsī*. I've taken vow before my guru. How can I? No."

Mind may be disturbed. Mind's business is to become disturbed. Accept and reject. But I should not be under my mind. That is called *gosvāmī*, not servant of the mind. Mind should be servant, that is all. Otherwise it will be very difficult – *māyā* is very strong. So I must be determined.

* * *

Later, Prabhupāda explained to other disciples, "[Arjuna] very intelligently appointed Kṛṣṇa as his spiritual master. Because everyone is in perplexity about the problem of life. So this very thing happened to Arjuna, and he wanted to go to his spiritual master for a solution. And the supreme spiritual master was present before him; therefore he submitted: *śiṣyas te 'haṁ śādhi māṁ tvāṁ prapannam. Kārpaṇya-doṣopahata-svabhāvaḥ...yac chreyaḥ syān niścitaṁ brūhi tan me.* The spiritual master's duty is how to benefit the disciple, *śreyaḥ.*"

Two Public Programs

Just after Prabhupāda spoke to Jagattāriṇī and I, he held two public programs. At one, he laid the cornerstone for Lautoka's Kṛṣṇa-Kāliya temple, and at the other he lectured in Hindi to a full house of locals at a Suva movie theater. Although Prabhupāda had allotted two weeks for his Fiji visit, he decided to travel earlier than expected to ISKCON's temple in Honolulu, Hawaii.

At the cornerstone-laying ceremony, the devotees held *kīrtana* with *shenāī* through the town to the future site of the Kṛṣṇa-Kāliya temple. Prabhupāda placed the sacred items in the cornerstone hole. He inspired Deoji Punja to take up the responsibility of temple construction. Although Deoji Punja failed to shave his head before the initiation ceremony as Prabhupāda had asked, Prabhupāda nevertheless initiated him and his wife as Vasudeva Dāsa and Bhagavatī Dāsī.

During the Suva movie theater engagement, Prabhupāda sat on a stage and lectured to a packed house of what appeared to be the working class of the Fiji-Indian community. The master of ceremonies, who ran the local Hindu school, brought out several classes of students. The children came on stage and nervously chanted several chapters of the *Bhagavad-gītā*. Prabhupāda watched patiently, fingering his *japa* beads and softly chanting Hare Kṛṣṇa.

After these engagements, Prabhupāda left for Honolulu. Although he had good facility for his translating work, the preaching opportunities in Fiji were minimal. Prabhupāda seemed to have no desire to relax, or even to spend his days in full-time writing. We, however, were satisfied seeing Prabhupāda every day with only a few devotees present and honoring his *mahā-mahā-prasāda* remnants.

Light in Darkness

The flight from Fiji to Hawaii was a night flight. The plane was almost empty. I stretched out along three seats when the cabin lights dimmed. I slept well for several hours, but suddenly awoke and sat up. Prabhupāda was directly before my seat and was walking through the sparse yellow light toward the front of the plane. He steadied himself on the armrests as he went. He looked pure and inwardly serene, deep and effulgent like a traveler from a higher dimension. I spontaneously asked, "Prabhupāda, can I help with anything?" His head nodded gently back and forth, and he smiled softly, "No, no need," and continued on.

* * *

This short vignette impresses a sweet picture on my consciousness. Prabhupāda, golden in the dim yellow light, walking slowly forward in the airplane cabin – I pray that Kṛṣṇa allows this moment to always remain with me.

Honolulu, Hawaii, 1976

Beneath a Banyan Tree

The ISKCON temple in Honolulu was donated by Ambarīṣa Dāsa, Alfred Ford. In an exclusive section of the city, this stately house-turned-temple included a sprawling banyan tree in the large back-yard. If it had been India, that tree would have sheltered either holy men, a temple, or a tea stall. Prabhupāda had previously spoken to the devotees about constructing a new temple building under the tree, but when he heard that we could not provide our own construction labor and that hiring laborers would cost eight dollars an hour per man, he gave up the idea.

* * *

Prabhupāda was extremely careful with Kṛṣṇa's money.

An End and a Beginning

The frequent and personal exchanges I had with Prabhupāda in Fiji were not possible in the busy Honolulu temple. As soon as we arrived, association with Prabhupāda was limited to hearing his morning classes about Ajāmila from the Sixth Canto of *Śrīmad-Bhāgavatam.* In those classes, Prabhupāda specifically addressed the situation in Hawaii.

The Enjoying Spirit

The Hawaii devotees were divided into the same two factions as the New Zealand devotees. In addition, Hawaii is permeated by an enjoying spirit. These tiny islands, advertised as the land of fun, sun, and surf, teem with tourists every year who bake on the white beaches and enjoy the night life. This spirit is so strong that ISKCON Hawaii's history was littered with mishaps of missing money, drugs, and sex.

Prabhupāda lectured here, in a capital of *māyā's* kingdom, that "Kṛṣṇa consciousness and sense gratification go ill together."

PRABHUPĀDA: This is the material world. So long as one will be engaged in sense enjoyment in different varieties, he will have to remain within this material world. Kṛṣṇa is so kind. We want to enjoy this material world; therefore He has given us full chance: "Yes, you enjoy."

But it should be stopped. Yes. Really it has to be stopped. If you want real life of eternal enjoyment, then you have to stop. If you don't stop, then you remain here. *Bhūtvā bhūtvā pralīyate.* You have to take birth according to your desire, either as Brahmā or as ant, as a cat, as a dog, as demigod, and according to your capacity, Kṛṣṇa will give you: "All right." *Ye yathā māṁ prapadyante tāṁs tathaiva bhajāmy aham.* If you want from Kṛṣṇa sense enjoyment, He will give you all facilities.

But Kṛṣṇa does not want. Kṛṣṇa says *sarva-dharmān parityajya mām ekaṁ śaraṇaṁ vraja*. That is His mission, that "You will never be happy in this process of sense enjoyment."

* * *

Prabhupāda once commented that enjoying in the material world was not possible, but if it were possible anywhere, it would be in Hawaii. Prabhupāda's Honolulu lectures noted the inconsistency of a devotee's simultaneous attempt to enjoy in the realm of matter and his or her blossoming spiritually.

Surfing is a regular part of Hawaii's "sun and fun" culture, and the temple devotees would religiously visit the Honolulu beaches each Sunday. Prabhupāda often teased their enjoying spirit. Although this appeared to be an innocent pleasure, Prabhupāda acknowledged its dangers and took exception.

PRABHUPĀDA: This morning we were talking about the sufferers, what is called? The sea suffers?

DEVOTEES: Surfers.

PRABHUPĀDA: Surfer, yes. [*Devotees laugh.*] Surfer. I call "sufferer." "Sea sufferer." [*Laughter.*] We are creating a situation by which we shall become a fish. Yes. Contamination. Just like if you purposely contaminate some disease you must suffer from that disease. Why there are different varieties of life? What is the reason? The reason is that we are infecting. Nature's law is so perfect that you infect something, some disease, some contamination, then you must suffer. This is nature's law automatically going on.

So the person who is taking very much pleasure, dancing in the sea like fish, so he is contaminating so that in his next life he will become a fish. He'll be very free to dance with the ocean. [*Laughter.*] Now it will take again millions of years to come to the stage of human being. *Jalajā nava-lakṣāṇi sthāvarā lakṣa-viṁśati*. He has to pass through 900,000 different species of fish life. Then again come to the land. You become trees, plants, and so on. Two million different forms he will have to go through.

* * *

Prabhupāda parodied the similarity of the words "surfer" and "sufferer" to point out the danger of becoming contaminated by the desire to enjoy in the water. He did not refrain from compassionately directing the "surfer/sufferers" toward real happiness.

PRABHUPĀDA: Kṛṣṇa says in the *Bhagavad-gītā,* "All living entities are My parts and parcels." This means "as good as I am." But they are concocting, manufacturing ideas to become happy.

He has no information how to become happy. Actually there is struggle for existence, but they are trying to be happy by manufacturing different types of struggles for existence. The other day someone was saying that they have now discovered another way of happiness. Flying in the air? Yes. Now the sufferers, or what is called?

DEVOTEE: Surfers.

PRABHUPĀDA: Now they want to fly. Another discovery. This is going on. Actually they are manufacturing different ways of suffering. There is no happiness – simply manufacturing different ways of suffering. That is our material disease.

But here it is recommended that we come to the right conclusion on how we shall become happy before our next death. Then we can end this process of continuously dying and again taking birth and again disease and again old age. That is not very good.

But they are so fools and rascals, they do not know how life is going on. They cannot see how nature is working upon us. Everything is darkness. Therefore, Kṛṣṇa consciousness is the only hope for human society. The only hope. It is not story; it is fact. So those who have come to Kṛṣṇa consciousness, I request that you take it very seriously. Read the books and make progress and simply try to understand Kṛṣṇa. Then everything, all problems, will be solved.

* * *

Prabhupāda again played on the similarity between "sufferer" and "surfer" to make his point about the never-ending, never-fulfilled search for material pleasure. The problems of material life, and also the problems of spiritual life – even the factions among the devotees, inside versus outside – could be solved by *śāstric* knowledge and Kṛṣṇa conscious advancement. How do we know if we are advancing?

PRABHUPĀDA: If one is trained up as a devotee of Kṛṣṇa, then what happens? Very soon one becomes detached. *Vairāgya. Bhakti-yoga* means *vairāgya-vidyā,* how to become detached. That is the test.

"Whether I am making progress in the *bhakti-yoga*?" The test is within myself. I haven't got to take a certificate from others. How much I am becoming detached from this material world, that is the test.

If you are still attached to material pleasures, that means you are not making progress in *bhakti-yoga.* It is a test.

* * *

Prabhupāda knew well the tendency of the conditioned soul to shrug off others' criticisms. He therefore prescribed a self-test for discerning our advancement in Kṛṣṇa consciousness: we should honestly examine our own position to discern whether adjustments in our life are required to enhance our spiritual progress. Only we ourselves will lose should we think that detachment from matter isn't an ingredient of advanced Kṛṣṇa consciousness.

Pure Enough to Dance with Kṛṣṇa

PRABHUPĀDA: Therefore it is said that *suśīlāḥ sādhavo yatra.* In the first word, *suśīlāḥ* – *śīlāḥ* means character and *suśīlāḥ* means very nice character. A devotee cannot be bad in character. Because Kṛṣṇa is *paraṁ brahma paraṁ dhāma pavitram* – *pavitra* means pure – so impurity cannot approach Him. If one wants to enter fire one must be fire, and if one is not fire, then he will burn.

If you want happiness, then you have to dance with Kṛṣṇa. But you cannot dance with Kṛṣṇa if you are not pure. Kṛṣṇa is the supreme pure. If you want to take pleasure in the company of Kṛṣṇa and dance in His *rāsa* dance, then you have to become purified. That is *sarvopādhi-vinirmuktam,* freedom from all designation. So this verse is the substance of the Kṛṣṇa consciousness movement: that those who are conducting this movement, they must be *suśīlāḥ,* very well-behaved. So nobody can find out any fault. That is *suśīlāḥ,* well-behaved. The behavior should be so nice. That is the test of how you have become Kṛṣṇa conscious. That is the test. Spotless. Just study Caitanya Mahāprabhu's behavior and His character. He is ideal. Throughout His whole life you'll not find a spot.

* * *

To make a diamond from coal requires pressure. Prabhupāda was encouraging all sincere devotees to apply pressure on themselves and advance.

The Essence of Material Life

PRABHUPĀDA: Every child should be trained up as *brahmacārī.* Then, when he is completely trained up, if he likes he can enter married life, which is a concession for sex life. But it is not required. You'll find in Vedic culture, therefore, many *naiṣṭika brahmacārīs* who had never any connection with woman.

And also *upakurvāṇa brahmacārīs. Upakurvāṇa brahmacārī* means he is married but not for enjoying. He is married to beget nice children under the order of his spiritual master. He is also *brahmacārī.* If a *gṛhastha* abides by the order of a guru he is also *brahmacārī.*

So here it is said: "*jitendriya.*" "*Suśila mita-bhuk dakṣaḥ śraddhadhāno jitendriyaḥ.*" The senses should not be used extravagantly. The modern civilization is such that if you can use your senses more and more, then you are civilized. Then you are enjoyer. Vedic civilization is different. The whole scheme is controlling the senses, especially sex, because if we become too much addicted to sex life, then our life is spoiled.

* * *

Unrestricted sex spoils one's life. Let Freud turn over in his grave and let the modern trendsetters stand in indignant protest. Both *śāstra* and experience prove Prabhupāda correct: our contemporary, hyped-up civilization has brought neither personal nor collective peace and happiness.

We are victims of this modern culture. Can we possibly avoid the chains of sex life? Prabhupāda's no-compromise answer was as clear in Honolulu as it was in Vṛndāvana: "Yes. By *tapasya*," or remaining fixed in one's vows.

The Tapasya of Avoiding Sex Life

Prabhupāda: Performing *tapasya* is difficult, but the recommendation is *tapasā brahmacaryeṇa*. So from *brahmacarya*, *tapasya* begins – celibacy, no sex life. If one becomes agitated by seeing a beautiful girl, or for a woman, a beautiful boy, that is natural. Young boy, young girl, they are naturally attracted. It is not surprising. But *tapasā* means that "I have taken vow, no illicit sex. Even if I am attracted, I shall not do this."

This is *tapasā*. Not "Because I am now attracted, now I shall enjoy." That is not *tapasya*. *Tapasya* means that even if one is attracted, he should not act. That is *tapasya*. It is not very difficult, but one has to practice determination. "I have taken a vow before the Deity at the time of initiation, before the fire, before the spiritual master, before the Vaiṣṇava, that 'I'll not have illicit sex.' That is promised. How can I break it?" This is *tapasya*. "I have taken vow before the Deity, before fire, before my spiritual master, before the Vaiṣṇavas, 'no illicit sex, no meat-eating, no drinking or intoxication, no gambling.' I have promised. If I am gentleman, how can I break my promise?"

* * *

And what realization fixes us, despite the disturbance of material desires, in this *tapasya* of Kṛṣṇa consciousness? Prabhupāda's answer: practice – based on knowledge.

Dhīra and Adhīra

PRABHUPADA: To be agitated in mind is not unnatural. But by practice, then you'll not be agitated anymore. That is called *dhīra.* You have to become *dhīra. Dhīra* and *adhīra. Dhīra* is sober. Even there is cause of agitation, still he remains firm. And *adhīra* means as soon as there is cause of agitation, he becomes a victim. That is called *adhīra.*

In lower animal life I have enjoyed the senses in so many ways. So sense enjoyment is not very difficult. Even the hogs and pigs have got facility for sense enjoyment. They do not care even who is who. Even she is mother or she is sister or she is daughter, they will enjoy sex. That is hog life. There is no discrimination. And the monkeys, they are enjoying sex life. So everyone enjoys sex life. "So why should I, who have got this valuable, human form of life, act as hogs and dogs?" Thinking like this is called *tapasya.*

* * *

Actual knowledge and full sincerity of purpose impels us to perform *tapasya,* the voluntary acceptance of hardship for advancement in Kṛṣṇa consciousness.

Becoming Safe from Māyā

PRABHUPĀDA: So our main problem is sex life, because sex life is the basic principle of material life. Either you are human being, a demigod, a bird, a beast, a fly, a fish, a tree, a plant – in every species the basic principle is sex.

You have got books. You study and follow the practices. Be a little sober. You'll become able and Kṛṣṇa will help. As soon as you are very eager, then Kṛṣṇa will help. Therefore the Deity worship is there. Along with Deity worship, we should always pray, "Kṛṣṇa, kindly save me from the pitfalls of *māyā.*" He'll do it. But if you want to cheat Kṛṣṇa and cheat guru, then you'll be cheated. That's all. The guru will not be cheated. Neither will Kṛṣṇa be cheated. You'll be cheated.

That's all. If you want to be cheated, then do whatever you like and prolong your term of repetition of birth and death. And if you want to stop it, then here: *tapasā brahmacaryeṇa śamena ca damena ca.*

* * *

Prabhupāda again brought the question back to the individual devotee: do you want *māyā* or Kṛṣṇa? He made it clear that those who want to advance in Kṛṣṇa consciousness must strictly follow the rules and regulations, especially the prohibition against illicit sex. Prabhupāda's words, as usual, were to the point. He was consistently straightforward as he explained the Absolute Truth and the processes of attaining it.

In this way, Prabhupāda directed his followers, the devotees, and warned them of pitfalls on the spiritual path. Prabhupāda's classes at this time also stressed the need to forego our independent plans and surrender to guru and Kṛṣṇa.

Surrender to Guru and Kṛṣṇa

PRABHUPĀDA: How to get this perfect knowledge? *Tad viddhi.* First of all you try to learn. How to learn? *Praṇipātena.* By full surrender. Our process of Vedic knowledge is how to surrender, not that I hear and I reject it. That is not the way. That is another rascaldom.

First of all find out the person where you can surrender. Not that we take a guru as a fashion. No. Do not do. Don't keep an order-supplying guru like somebody keeping a dog that the master will order him, "Do this," and he does. No. It is not fashion. You must approach a guru to whom you can surrender. Otherwise don't take a guru. And the guru also should not accept such a rascal as a disciple. First of all things is surrender. *Tad viddhi praṇipātena.* The first necessity is you surrender.

Just like a diseased person goes to the physician and the physician gives him medicine. He takes the medicine and is cured. But he is again afflicted with the disease, and he again goes to the physician. Why does this happen? Because one does not follow the rules and regulations given by the physician.

Going to a physician means you have to accept some "do not" and some "do." That is called regulative principle. Without regulative principles you cannot correct yourself. But if simply we say, "Follow the rules and regulations," it will not stay unless you become a devotee. That is the test of Kṛṣṇa consciousness. Because Kṛṣṇa consciousness is so powerful, as soon as you become a devotee, gradually or immediately, all the good qualities come as in your original position.

So it is recommended that we follow rules and regulations. Unless we do so, there is no possibility of curing our material disease. The whole problem is that we are materially diseased. So if we want to be cured from this disease, we have to follow rules and regulations. Just like a patient, if he wants to be cured from the disease, he has to follow the rules prescribed by the physician.

"Why shall I surrender?" That is our mentality. If somebody says, "You surrender, I shall give you good instruction," our answer is, "Oh, why shall I surrender to you?" That is material life. But this Kṛṣṇa consciousness movement begins when you are ready to surrender. That is beginning. *Tad viddhi praṇipātena. Praṇipāt* means surrender. *Prakṛṣta-rūpena nipāta.* "Yes, I surrender to you." That is the beginning. *Bahūnāṁ janmanām ante jñānavān māṁ prapadyate.* To learn the surrender, it will take many, many births. *Bahūnāṁ janmanām ante.*

But those who are intelligent surrender immediately, thinking, "Kṛṣṇa says, 'Surrender,' and why not? Kṛṣṇa is the Supreme Lord. Let me surrender." Then his life is successful immediately.

Within a second his life is successful. But we are not prepared to surrender. That is our material disease.

So if we do not surrender to Kṛṣṇa and take His instruction as our life, that is our choice. But if you like, you can make your life successful within a moment simply by surrendering to Kṛṣṇa.

* * *

Prabhupāda exposed the tendency to superficially accept a spiritual master but not follow his instructions. Without following his instructions, Prabhupāda explained, how could we be cured of our coverings of material contamination?

Meeting for Unity

Prabhupāda met with one of his disciples, who was also a follower of Siddha-svarūpānanda Goswami. Prabhupāda first emphasized the foolish condition of materialistic society.

PRABHUPĀDA: Everywhere, living entities, they are taking birth. That's all. And they are dying also. And between birth and death there is disease and old age. During birth one cannot understand because there is unconscious stage. So even the fetus is killed, it cannot understand because of his fully unconscious stage. But there is life undoubtedly; otherwise how the fetus all of a sudden gets life?

But these *mūḍhas* cannot see it. In matter there is no life; it will never show any symptom of life. But if there is life, at some time it will come to consciousness. Just like a fainted man is lying like a dead man, but he is not dead. There is life. So because there is life, he may lie down in that unconscious state for two, three hours, but he'll later again come to consciousness. It is common sense.

And if a log, wood log, is lying flat, will it come to life? But because these *mūḍhas,* they are taking that "Fetus has no life. Kill it, finish it, and eat it." It is going on...There are so many things, so many nice instructions. There are many other attempts for awakening the human society to the right platform, but their basic principle is wrong. They cannot do it. It is not possible....So this movement should be pushed very vigorously.

* * *

How much compassion Prabhupāda must have felt for the fallen and miserable condition of the contemporary society, where abominable activities are fully accepted and people are becoming so degraded that they're even eating human fetuses.

Can society be redirected? Prabhupāda hoped his society, ISKCON, would propagate actual knowledge and thereby continue his empowered attempt to educate and help the world.

PRABHUPĀDA: So far, we have become successful. There will always be enemies as soon as there is something good. That is the way of the material world. Even Kṛṣṇa had enemies, what to speak of us. So many enemies, but He was powerful; He killed them all. Nobody could kill Him, but there were attempts to kill Him right from the very beginning of His birth. He had so many enemies.

Kaṁsa knew his sister is now newly married, but as soon as there was some foretelling, "Ah, you are taking care of your sister so nicely. The eighth child of this sister will kill you." He became angry. "Why wait for the eighth child? Kill my sister."

Long, long before the birth of Kṛṣṇa, the mother was to be killed. This is the position of this material world. He did not consider, "She is my sister. She is just newly married. Where is pregnancy? Where is child? And that is the eighth child, and what will happen after that?" No consideration. Immediately, "Kill her!" This is the position.

So we are instructing: no intoxication. So those who are flourishing by selling cigarettes and wine and liquor, they do not like: "Immediately kill him." Oh, yes, they are thinking, "If this movement becomes very strong, then our business will be lost. Kill him." So naturally there will be enemies.

We have forbidden: no illicit sex, no intoxication, no meat-eating, and no gambling. The whole Western world is living on these four pillars. Just see our position. And in the same way, everyone is thinking, "If this movement goes on, then how all these nightclubs will go on? How all breweries will go on? How all slaughterhouses will go on? How the cigarette factories will go on?"

So you cannot expect that we will have many friends. That is not possible, because the world is full of Kaṁsas, demons. So we have to struggle. In the face of so many obstacles we have come to this standard that there is a Hare Kṛṣṇa movement. It is very dangerous to the modern way of life. They're feeling the pulse, and everywhere we are meeting obstacles. In Singapore.

PUṢṬA KṚṢṆA SWAMI: We went to the airport.

PRABHUPĀDA: Yes.

PUṢṬA KṚṢṆA: And practically they didn't even want to let us stay in the airport. We had to stay there only for four hours to catch the next flight.

PRABHUPĀDA: This is our position. So don't be disappointed because that means it is successful. Kṛṣṇa and Kṛṣṇa's movement are not different. Identical. So as Kṛṣṇa was attempted to be killed many, many years before He appeared... An eighth child, even if the mother produces a child yearly, still it will be eight years before His birth. Yet the mother was attempted to be killed. So there may be attempt like that. And Lord Jesus Christ was killed. So they may kill me also.

DISCIPLE: I don't think that is possible.

PRABHUPĀDA: No, I mean to say, I am not so important man. But this is the way of the law. If we become weak by factioning, then that is not good. We must be strong. Don't expect that this movement will be accepted.

* * *

Because the prohibitions Prabhupāda preached challenge the pillars of modern society, such preaching is a threat to those whose lives, pleasures, and profitable enterprises are based on these sinful practices of Kali-yuga. In ISKCON's early days, Prabhupāda was pleased to hear that Alan Watts, a Western-born eclectic, anti-authoritarian, impersonalist popularizer of Eastern religion, who was famous in the '60s and '70s, wrote a negative, angry response when asked to read and review Prabhupāda's original *Bhagavad-gītā* manuscript. Prabhupāda's reply: "Our preaching is proved successful when the demons are disturbed."

Prabhupāda's conclusion was that we should remain united: strength grows in unity and weaknesses are minimized.

PRABHUPĀDA: Our cause is common, how to push on. That soberness must be there. I can give you points, instructions, but you will have to put it into shape. Otherwise, how it will go on?

PUṢṬA KṚṢṆA SWAMI: We can understand that Your Divine Grace does not want factions.

PRABHUPĀDA: That will better the movement.

Prabhupāda then spoke about something he had recently translated from the end of the Seventh Canto of *Śrīmad-Bhāgavatam*, making the point that a guru is nondifferent from Kṛṣṇa because he represents Kṛṣṇa in distributing "Kṛṣṇa-knowledge." Similarly, he points out, the Kṛṣṇa consciousness movement is also Kṛṣṇa, for it too performs the same function of giving Kṛṣṇa-knowledge.

Prabhupāda continued to explain that a guru may be considered ordinary by ordinary people, but he is nevertheless extraordinary because he functions purely in Kṛṣṇa's service. Prabhupāda then cautioned that two dangers can dilute his mission's potency: thinking "I'll enjoy," and the attempt to appease people, thinking "I'll be unacceptable" if I don't offer compromises. His conclusion was that the devotees should cooperate to spread the Kṛṣṇa consciousness movement.

* * *

Thus Prabhupāda clearly expresses his desire that the devotees "combinedly" and "vigorously" preach. The urgency of the preaching mission necessitates the strength fostered by unity. Despite the acceptance of that necessity, problems cooperating nevertheless occur.

GURU-KṚPA: Sometimes, Śrīla Prabhupāda, it just seems there is a difference in the way Kṛṣṇa consciousness is being…

PRABHUPĀDA: Why different?

GURU-KṚPA: Well, there's only one way…

PRABHUPĀDA: So now why there should be different? The formula is there. Why there should be difference?

GURU-KṚPA: Then there is someone who's not doing it properly according to the…

PRABHUPĀDA: That should be settled up. Suppose you are not doing properly. I can say, "This is this," and show you how to do it another way.

PUṢṬA KṚṢṆA: We should work together.

PRABHUPĀDA: That I want.

HARI ŚAURI: There's no problem, but the thing is they simply don't want to cooperate with the ISKCON movement.

PRABHUPĀDA: But why?

HARI ŚAURI: That no one knows. They simply just don't want to mix.

PRABHUPĀDA: That we can settle up by sitting together. Why there should be difference?

* * *

The devotees will now bring specific issues of contention to Prabhupāda's attention. Tension between the individual's present over methods of spreading Kṛṣṇa consciousness becomes apparent, yet Prabhupāda nevertheless remains hopeful that they can reach a positive resolution by "sitting together" in his presence.

HARI ŚAURI: Just like in New Zealand. Originally they split from ISKCON, and now gradually you are bringing them back to the same standard again, like now you're encouraging them to build a temple and install Deities. That means they have to come up to the required brahminical standard again. So why was there any need to go away in the first place? But still they won't cooperate. Now they'll have to do it their own way. This is... that's their problem.

DISCIPLE: There are a lot of devotees here who follow the principles but who don't shave up. And they still wear *karmī* clothes pretty much. But they're clean. They're devotees. And in this way they're attracting many of the local people, because they're able to relate to them.

PRABHUPĀDA: So that...

DISCIPLE: They're not lowering your standard.

PRABHUPĀDA: No, naturally, but when they are initiated they must shave. They must keep to the standard. If one becomes initiated and he still keeps the hippie form, that does not look nice. Do you think that is all right? No, that is not good. So long they are coming as outsider, joining *kīrtana,* they may have their own dress. It doesn't matter. But when they are to be initiated, they must follow the rules and regulations given by the spiritual master.

DISCIPLE: So...

PRABHUPĀDA: Otherwise they should not be initiated. It is simple thing. Let them go on chanting, taking *prasāda.* But when they are to be initiated, they must follow. If you don't want to disturb them, let them come, chant, dance, take *prasāda.* We have no objection. But don't recommend them for initiation unless he agrees to the rules and regulations given by the spiritual master. Where is the wrong? Where is the difficulty? You can talk with him like that.

Prabhupāda speaks further and the conversation continues:

DISCIPLE: I think it is pretty clear, Śrīla Prabhupāda. But just for clarification, they're working. They have a very nice store, and they're distributing foodstuffs to all the other stores on the island. And they're working a lot within the society with the *karmīs,* I guess. So their thinking is that "If we shave our heads and wear robes, like that, then they'll look at us...

PRABHUPĀDA: Who is prohibiting to chant? You can chant, you can dance, you can take *prasāda*.

* * *

Prabhupāda insists that those chanting Hare Kṛṣṇa who desired to take initiation come to the standard of surrender to his order, his rules, and his regulations. Those not up to that standard may chant Hare Kṛṣṇa and remain independent, as friends. He had seen that many "outside" devotees, both in New Zealand and Hawaii, had long hair: "If one becomes initiated and he still keeps the hippie form, that does not look nice. Do you think that is all right? No, that is not good." Despite Prabhupāda's stressing these points, no great contention seems yet to have arisen.

PUṢṬA KṚṢṆA: Can they actually say that "His Divine Grace A.C.Bhaktivedanta Swami Prabhupāda is my spiritual master" if they haven't accepted all of the instructions?

PRABHUPĀDA: Eh?

HARI-ŚAURI: One of the differences that first sprang up between the two groups was that one group was going out when you were saying, "Go out and distribute books profusely," so they were going and distributing. And they had various means of doing it. Some were not so good, but still the books were going out. Then the group that split away, they were saying, "Ah, you're disturbing the public by these methods of book distribution. We don't want..." This is what happened in Australia, the one temple in Brisbane. They became very much against the *saṅkīrtana* methods and as a result they gave up the *saṅkīrtana* program altogether and went to live on farms like this. They left the temple and the temple was finished. So like this, they were saying, "We're still following Prabhupāda's instructions, but we..." But they were saying that the devotees who were distributing the books, they were not following instructions. Like that.

PRABHUPĀDA: His Divine Grace has said that "You distribute book," and why do you say that?

Hari-śauri: Well, their idea was that because sometimes the public is becoming disturbed by the book distribution, therefore it's not being done correctly. So it should be stopped.

Prabhupāda: Public may be disturbed, but we are following our own course of action. It is not obligatory. We are requesting you, "Take this book." That is not obligatory. "If you like, you can take. If you don't like, don't take."

Disciple: I think that…

Hari-śauri: So what their idea was that we shall build some public relations, like you said with this store. They prefer to try to spread Kṛṣṇa consciousness by public relations, by giving a good impression, and then people will come.

Prabhupāda: Then you are dictated by the public, not by the dictation of your spiritual master. Spiritual master has ordered you to distribute books. You shall do that. That is called obedience. Now the public may take or not take, that is public's option. But my duty is – because spiritual master has said – I must try my best.

Spiritual master has not said that "You must sell so many books daily, otherwise I will reject you." He has not said that. So everyone may try his best. That's all. The public may take or not take. It doesn't matter. And if you want to please the public, the public says that "You dance naked, I will be very happy with you." So I'll have to do that? Then what is the use of taking a spiritual master? Public, they have got their whims how to become pleased. So we are to follow all these things? We have to follow our instruction of the spiritual master. Why to manufacture, "The public will be pleased like this?" Public may or may not give you, what you can do?

Hari-śauṛi: Our success is in the spiritual master's pleasure, not the public's pleasure.

Prabhupāda: Yes, that is *bhakti*. Otherwise, why Kṛṣṇa says, *sarva-dharmān parityajya mām ekaṁ śaraṇaṁ vraja?* "You haven't got to please so many religious instructions. You simply please Me."

Disciple: I don't think the devotees who factioned out were against book distribution. I think that a little bit was that some of the devotees were using very, very forceful tactics and trying to give people books and take their money, and people were becoming very offended...

PRABHUPĀDA: That is not good.

DISCIPLE: That is not what you want.

HARI-ŚAURI: That's all right, but don't give up the book distribution.

DISCIPLE: Yes.

HARI-ŚAURI: This is what happened. The temples fell down, the devotees went away. The ones who were distributing the books went on and distributed more books, became more expert, so that the public was not so much disturbed, and still they're distributing books. But these people who factioned off are not distributing books even now, two or three years later. So it was simply actually a question of faultfinding more than earnest desire to please the spiritual master.

PRABHUPĀDA: Yes. [*Pause.*] Discuss.

DEVOTEES: All glories to Śrīla Prabhupāda.

* * *

For better and/or worse, the passage of time seems to have decided many of these contention-filled issues. From the viewpoint of today's Kṛṣṇa consciousness movement, which is largly congregational, one may find oneself wondering if Prabhupāda's words are as relevant now as they were in 1976, when almost every ISKCON devotee lived in an ISKCON temple. The answer of course is yes, for fulfilling Prabhupāda's desires will always be at the heart of his movement. Yet one's presentation to Prabhupāda could determine Prabhupāda's reply. Prabhupāda's reaction to Hari Śauri's description of being "against the *saṅkīrtana methods,* and as a result they gave up the *saṅkīrtana program* altogether" brought Prabhupāda to comment that we are not dictated by the public but by the attempt to please our spiritual master. But Prabhupāda responded to the presentation of forceful, inappropriate book distribution and money collection tactics that offended people with "That is not good." All points seemed acceptable to both Prabhupāda and the assembled devotees. Amid the clash of history, opinions, and personalities, the conversation ended with Prabhupāda's request to "Discuss." Prabhupāda had expressed his desires and reached his own conclusions. He left the matter somewhat open and asked his disciples to combinedly settle their differences with the goal of satisfying their spiritual master.

A Beloved Lost Son Visits Home

Govinda Dāsī and Gaurasundara had opened the first temple in Honolulu in 1969. After a few years of struggle, the temple began to flourish. By the end of 1973, however, ISKCON Hawaii fell apart. Gaurasundara abandoned his wife and sold the temple. Prabhupāda questioned what had happened to the money from the sale of the building, but Gaurasundara remained aloof from both Prabhupāda and the movement. Although remaining always affectionate, Prabhupāda heavily criticized Gaurasundara.

In 1976, Gaurasundara visited Prabhupāda for the first time in more than two years. I was not in the room during Gaurasundara's *darśana* with Prabhupāda, but when Gaurasundara came out of Prabhupāda's room, his heavy brow seemed even heavier. I asked him what Prabhupāda had said. He answered, "Don't try to become guru prematurely. You should serve your guru."

* * *

Prabhupāda had long ago analyzed Gaurasundara's problem. I remember him mentioning it to me in 1974 when we were together in Hong Kong. Prabhupāda now had the opportunity to give the same analysis directly to Gaurasundara: a premature, possibly lethal, desire to become guru.

An actual guru always remains the servant of his own guru and the predecessor *ācāryas*. Attempting to become a guru without one's own guru's order is a materialistic ambition. Accepting followers and circumventing one's own guru is offensive. Prabhupāda implored Gaurasundara to rectify this serious fault in his Kṛṣṇa consciousness and humbly return to the shelter of his spiritual master. One year later, when Gaurasundara visited Prabhupāda in Vṛndāvana, Prabhupāda conversed with Gaurasundara with great affection, like a lost son who had returned home:

PRABHUPĀDA: Why not stay here for some time? So what are your activities now?

GAURASUNDARA: In Hawaii we have Rādhā-Kṛṣṇa deities and bathing, Deity worship, and reading your books.

PRABHUPĀDA: Very good.

GAURASUNDARA: Feast program.

PRABHUPĀDA: May Kṛṣṇa help you. How many inmates are there?

GAURASUNDARA: Right now there's about one dozen people on the farm, and on Sundays maybe forty, fifty people coming for feast.

PRABHUPĀDA: Very good. You are my old disciple. So I'll be very pleased if you keep the principles. It doesn't matter wherever you live and spread Kṛṣṇa consciousness wherever you feel happy, and do not forget the real business.... Because you are maintaining the temple as private. So make nice clothes, decorations. Deity is small Kṛṣṇa or big Kṛṣṇa, the same thing. When Kṛṣṇa was child on the lap of His mother, the same Kṛṣṇa killed Pūtanā. And when He was killing other demons in His young age, the same. Avyaya. He does not change. Acyuta. These are the names of Kṛṣṇa, so it does not make any difference. So you have got small Deity. Very nicely...So you can bathe Them nicely, decorate Them nicely, give Them... And big Deity will be difficult to handle. Better keep this Deity and increase the devotion. More time devoted for taking class, for cleansing... About *Śrīmad-Bhāgavatam* consider. That is main business.

arcāyām eva haraye
pūjāṁ yaḥ śraddhayehate
na tad-bhakteṣu cānyeṣu
sa bhaktaḥ prākṛtaḥ smṛtaḥ

If you simply worship the Deity in gorgeous way and do not preach, see to the interest of devotees and other common men, then you'll remain in the *prākṛta* state, material stage. You should go further, see the interest of ordinary people, how they are understanding Kṛṣṇa consciousness.

Tad-bhakteṣu. To give worship to the guru and honor them. Simply to worship Deity is material platform. *Gṛhasthas,* we want, this preaching.

In Hawaii where you are living, that is quite comfortable?

GAURASUNDARA: It's in the country.

PRABHUPĀDA: Seaside?

GAURASUNDARA: A few miles up on the side of the mountain. About one thousand feet elevation.

PRABHUPĀDA: All the inmates, they are following rules and regulations?

GAURASUNDARA: Oh, yes, yes.

PRABHUPĀDA: That's nice. No intoxication?

GAURASUNDARA: No, no intoxication.

PRABHUPĀDA: [*Chuckles.*] Be intoxicated with Kṛṣṇa.

Medicine for Uniting the Factions

The devotees in the outside faction lived separately from the temple, preferring to practice their *sādhana* at home. The other faction, the temple devotees, stressed temple life and group living.

Prabhupāda, of course, did not say that devotional service could only be performed while living in the temple, but he did insist that all devotees strictly follow the rules and regulations given by their spiritual master.

Prabhupāda encouraged temple life because the temple routine makes it easy to both follow *sādhana* and associate with devotees. Living in a temple strengthens a devotee's spiritual practices. Yet, a temple has to be managed. There has to be efficient organization, maintenance of the building, and managerial headaches. Should (or can) an individual devotee avoid this and live alone if he has the spiritual strength to do so? And if not, why not? Prabhupāda's morning *Bhāgavatam* lectures helped devotees understand what they would have to do to unite the factions in ISKCON Hawaii.

By listening closely to Prabhupāda's message, I understood that although he was specifically addressing the Hawaiian situation, his words would create a spiritual revolution anywhere they were heard and applied.

Compassion: the Mood of Vaiṣṇavas

PRABHUPĀDA: That is Vaiṣṇava. Parīkṣit Mahārāja is Vaiṣṇava. He is very unhappy that so many living entities are rotting in a hellish condition of life. So he is asking, *adhuneha mahā-bhāga yathaiva narakān naraḥ, nānogra-yātanān neyāt tan me vyākhyātum arhasi* "I am very sorry that so many living entities are suffering. Is there any way to give them relief?"

That is Vaiṣṇava. One who is not a Vaiṣṇava sees another person is suffering and he doesn't care: "Let him suffer." Society has come to that state. I heard from one of my disciples that here, or in New York, if somebody is killed on the road, nobody will care. Is it a fact?

DEVOTEE: Yes.

PRABHUPĀDA: So we have come to that stage of civilization. But Parīkṣit Mahārāja is feeling compassion simply by hearing from Śukadeva Gosvāmī that "A person, if he commits sinful activities, he suffers." He is not even seeing, yet he feels compassion: "How such a person can be delivered?"

This is the inquiry, that "They are suffering from some sinful activities. How they can be saved?" This is Vaiṣṇava. Vaiṣṇava means *para-duḥkha-duḥkhī*. A Vaiṣṇava is unhappy by seeing others' unhappiness. Personally he has no unhappiness. Like Nityānanda Prabhu. *Hā hā prabhu nityānanda, premānanda sukhī, kṛpābalokana koro āmi boro duḥkhī. Nitya* means eternally and *ānanda* means happy. So Nityānanda has no unhappiness.

He is happy personally, but because He knows that "These drunkards, woman-hunters, prostitute-hunters will suffer very, very severely, so why not deliver them?" This is Nityānanda Prabhu. This is a Vaiṣṇava. In your country there is Lord Jesus

Christ. When he was being crucified, still he was saying, "My Lord, excuse them. They do not know what they are doing." This is Vaiṣṇava.

They are not unhappy themselves and they can tolerate any unhappy position. They come to deliver so many fallen souls. Here Parīkṣit Mahārāja, out of compassion, inquired from Śukadeva Gosvāmī, "These persons are rotting in hell. Is there any means to deliver them?"

* * *

In this lecture, Prabhupāda gave us an insight into his own mood – the mood of a compassionate Vaiṣṇava. His description of Nityānanda Prabhu's kindness to those addicted to intoxication and prostitution points to a need for a monsoon of mercy to inundate those living during Kali-yuga.

Prabhupāda hoped that we would become compassionate Vaiṣṇavas, but if that was not possible, then we should become the servants of a compassionate Vaiṣṇava. He did not want the devotees to remain aloof from the outside world; he wanted them to mend their differences and cooperate to actively and expertly preach Kṛṣṇa's glories in *māyā's* kingdom.

The Expertise of a Devotee

PRABHUPĀDA: Whatever business is entrusted to him, a devotee does very nicely. That is called *dakṣa,* expertise. Just like Raghunātha Dāsa Gosvāmī. He had no interest in material things. Although his father's estate was very big, he was not interested. But when put in a political situation, he tackled it very nicely. This is *dakṣa.*

Not that because he has become Kṛṣṇa conscious and a Vaiṣṇava, he is unable to do anything of this material world. No. One who is Kṛṣṇa conscious, he is conscious of everything and he knows how to deal with everything. That is called *dakṣa.* Not that "Because I have become Kṛṣṇa conscious I can have no knowledge in other things." No. You must have. If not complete knowledge, a devotee knows something of everything. That is intelligence. To know something of everything and to know everything of something. That is wanted. You know everything of devotional service, but a devotee should not be callous in material dealings. He should know something of everything. That is called *dakṣa*.

* * *

Impersonalists see the world as illusion; therefore, they attempt to renounce all worldly interactions. A devotee's vision, however, is different. A devotee sees the world as Kṛṣṇa's. Therefore he renounces not his own activities (which are performed in Kṛṣṇa's service), but the attachment to enjoying the fruit of those activities. Devotees preach on behalf of Kṛṣṇa, and they are often called on to deal with the world in Kṛṣṇa's service. Our success, as Prabhupāda pointed out, will be to both accomplish our mission and maintain our devotion. Accomplishing one and not the other is insufficient.

Even within the surf and sunshine of heavenly Hawaii Prabhupāda yearned for his disciples to graft to their hearts his desire that Kṛṣṇa consciousness be spread throughout the world. Without his "big" desire becoming ours, our own petty desires would triumph.

Surrender to the Desire for Service

PRABHUPĀDA: It is not possible to give up desires. That is not possible. To give up desires means I am dead body, a stone. If I have got life, if I am not a stone, there must be desires.

If we make a desire, it must be fulfilled. Kṛṣṇa will give you facilities. Desire is so strong.

We must change the platform to no material desires by simply desiring how to serve Kṛṣṇa. *Nārāyaṇa-parāyaṇāḥ* means those who are always ready to abide by the orders of Nārāyaṇa.

Those who have taken the path of Nārāyaṇa, devotional service, as their life and soul, are called *nārāyaṇa-parāyaṇāḥ*. So what is the qualification of *nārāyaṇa-parāyaṇāḥ?* It does not require any qualification to become *nārāyaṇa-parāyaṇāḥ* other than voluntarily agreeing that my life is now dedicated for Nārāyaṇa. If you simply take it as vow that "From this day my life is dedicated to Nārāyaṇa, Kṛṣṇa,"...As soon as we take this vow that "From this day my life is dedicated to Kṛṣṇa. I surrender," from that day you become free. Simply this determination that "From this day I belong to Nārāyaṇa, or Kṛṣṇa. Whatever He wants..."

* * *

Desire continues as long as life remains within the body. Accepting Kṛṣṇa's desire as our desire is spiritual life. Prabhupāda was confident that all factionalism would disappear if the devotees would simply adopt his desire, which was Kṛṣṇa's desire, as their own.

Come to the Side of Kṛṣṇa

PRABHUPĀDA: That is the teachings of *Bhagavad-gītā*. Just to teach us, Arjuna thought as if he was for his family. In the war field, when there was to be fighting, he came to the family side and he said, "My dear Kṛṣṇa, how can I fight with my family? They are my brothers. They are my nephews. They are my grandfathers. They are my teachers. Fight means to fight with enemies. What kind of war it is that I have to fight with my family?"

Because he belonged to the Kuru's family, he took the side of the family. But after hearing *Bhagavad-gītā,* after understanding Kṛṣṇa, when he came to the conclusion that "I must be on Kṛṣṇa's side, not the family side," then he became perfect. After speaking the *Bhagavad-gītā* Kṛṣṇa said, "Now what you will do? To the family side or My side?" Freedom is there. "Whatever you like, you can do. I have given My instruction." That freedom is there always. Kṛṣṇa or His representative, the spiritual master, he can give you good instruction, good advice. But to do it or not to do it is your option.

That is your option. You decide yourself. Kṛṣṇa said, *yathecchasi tathā kuru:* "I am not interfering with your independence. I am dealing as your spiritual master, and you accepted Me as your spiritual master." Arjuna had already accepted earlier by saying, *śiṣyas te 'haṁ:* "Kṛṣṇa, no more friendly talk. I accept You as my spiritual master." What kind of disciple? *Prapannam,* fully surrendered. "Now whatever You will say, I'll do." This is *śiṣya.*

I have several times explained, *śiṣya: śas-dhātu* – he who voluntarily accepts the ruling of a person. He is *śiṣya.* And otherwise, "You go on talking whatever nonsense you can. I'll do my own business." That is not *śiṣya. Śiṣya* means *śiṣyas te 'haṁ śādhi māṁ tvāṁ prapannam. Tad viddhi praṇipātena.* That is *śiṣya.* So Kṛṣṇa taught him *Bhagavad-gītā.* Then, still, He gave him the freedom, *yathecchasi tathā kuru:* "Now Arjuna, you decide what to do." It is not force.

Arjuna's reply was, "My illusion is now over. I am now remembering what I am." That remembering means, "I am not belonging to this family." *Tvat-prasādān…mayācyuta. Smṛtir labdhā.* In the material world we have lost our memory that "I am part and parcel of Kṛṣṇa and my duty is to serve Kṛṣṇa."

* * *

Sarvopādhi-vinirmuktaṁ tat-paratvena nirmalam is the *Nārada Pancarātra's* definition of pure devotional service. Prabhupāda's example was to serve Kṛṣṇa by serving his spiritual master's instructions and acting for his pleasure.

Further Surgery

I was not present during the conversation between Prabhupāda, his disciple who followed Siddha-svarūpa, and the other devotees, nor did I find out about it until years later. Still, it proved important for me because based on that conversation, Prabhupāda called me into his presence.

"Prabhupāda wants to see you," Hari Śauri told me one day. Knowing Kṛṣṇa had a plan, I raced to the balcony of the Honolulu temple where Prabhupāda waited, sitting in a chair. Puṣṭa Kṛṣṇa Swami and Hari Śauri sat at his feet. I offered my obeisances.

BHŪRIJANA: Would you like me to do anything? What would you like me to do? I know I don't want to be independent.

PRABHUPĀDA: Why you are inclined to follow Siddha-svarūpa? What is your special attraction?

BHŪRIJANA: While we were in Hong Kong, we couldn't always be corresponding with you. I needed some personal instruction.

PRABHUPĀDA: But what is the special attraction? Your wife said that their instruction is very clear. So what is the distinction between clear and ambiguous? What do you find ambiguous? What do you find clear? What is that?

BHŪRIJANA: I think the part I found clear, the more introspective points about humility, and changing one's desires...

PRABHUPĀDA: Humility means not to follow the instruction of guru?

BHŪRIJANA: No, that is not humility.

PRABHUPĀDA: I'm asking you what is the special attraction? What is clear and ambiguous?

BHŪRIJANA: The clearness may be a deeper understanding to want to be humble. A deeper understanding to want to...

PRABHUPĀDA: Humble, but if you do not follow your spiritual master's instruction, you follow others, then where is the humbleness? Your wife says that what Siddha-svarūpa says, it is very clear, and others are not so clear. Is it not? What is that clear? What is not clear?

BHŪRIJANA: He says chant Hare Kṛṣṇa.

PRABHUPĀDA: So who says that you don't chant?

BHŪRIJANA: Maybe the emphasis of others isn't so much on chanting. Everyone says *harer nāma harer nāma harer nāmaiva kevalam,* but everyone only chants their sixteen rounds a day, chants a half-hour *ārati* in the evening and a half-hour *ārati* in the morning.

PRABHUPĀDA: So what do you want more? What is your program? Twenty-four hours?

BHŪRIJANA: No, but I like more *kīrtana* than that.

* * *

Prabhupāda's probing forced me to consider my relationship with Siddha-svarūpa. He seemed intent on penetrating my consciousness with his questions. He asked what I found different, clearer, or especially attractive that would explain my inclination specifically to follow Siddha-svarūpa and to not follow the regular ISKCON program. He would not accept the difference as "more humility" because my leaving Hong Kong had not demonstrated to him a humble disciple's submission to his guru's order. My reply that the difference was more emphasis on chanting the holy names caused him to offer a sarcastic reply.

The specific memory I have of this conversation with Prabhupāda was that he was pushing me to reveal my mind. I clearly remember how difficult it was to clarify my thoughts and speak openly and honestly. Prabhupāda was such an awe-inspiring figure. His presence evoked the desire to please him. I feared expressing my possibly wrong or foolish thoughts to his scrutiny, and my tendency was to superficially agree. But Prabhupāda was determined to push through to a deeper, more trusting affection. He forced me to pull out and reveal whatever doubts and complaints I truly harbored. As the conversation continued, I found myself becoming more relaxed and open.

Although I thought that I had both increased my humility and my desire to chant Kṛṣṇa's names, Prabhupāda wished to point out what he had concluded as the actual difference between ISKCON and the followers of Siddha-svarūpa. It seems that he had already decided what the difference was and he wished me to accept it as well.

PRABHUPĀDA: So you don't like to sell books.

BHŪRIJANA: No, I think I like very much. I mean I think I would like to.

PRABHUPĀDA: So what is the difference?

BHŪRIJANA: Between selling books and *kīrtana*?

PRABHUPĀDA: No, no, between others and you. Where is the difference? Point out that this is the point on which we differ. What is that point?

BHŪRIJANA: Well, maybe the point about more *kīrtana* or less *kīrtana*.

PRABHUPĀDA: So if you chant more, they're objecting?

BHŪRIJANA: No.

PRABHUPĀDA: Then where is the difference? Has anyone objected if you chant more?

Bhūrijana: No.

PRABHUPĀDA: Then where is the objection? What is the point of difference?

BHŪRIJANA: I think there's no point of difference.

PRABHUPĀDA: Then why do you say we find these instructions more clear?

BHŪRIJANA: It's just the emphasis that was given to chanting. For myself, I know that in my heart I built up an enmity toward your disciples and thinking that by their distributing books, they were making people angry at Kṛṣṇa and...

PRABHUPĀDA: That is the real point. That is the real point.

* * *

I was in Japan and Hong Kong from 1970–1974 and then lived outside mainstream ISKCON from 1974–1976. During these foundational years of ISKCON, Prabhupāda had made known his desires about book distribution. Even as I sat at Prabhupāda's feet on the balcony outside his rooms in ISKCON Hawaii, I was unaware of the depth of Prabhupāda's desire that his disciples distribute his books. Yet by his pushing me to analyze the actual difference, it eventually popped out: the difference between how the inside and the outside factions were prosecuting Kṛṣṇa consciousness was the emphasis on book distribution, or deeper than that, the depth of surrender to Prabhupāda's order to distribute books.

BHŪRIJANA: That's what I felt. When I was in Hong Kong, people I would meet, they used to yell... they'd yell at me, "What have you done to Kṛṣṇa?" Some Indians used to say that. People we'd meet, they'd tell us they see the Hare Kṛṣṇa devotees and they hate Kṛṣṇa. I remember one specific time when I was speaking to one businessman who was helping us and...

PRABHUPĀDA: He said that, "We hate Kṛṣṇa?"

BHŪRIJANA: No, no. He said that "Your members of the Hare Kṛṣṇa, they're making people in Australia hate Kṛṣṇa. They make people inimical." Making people inimical to Kṛṣṇa.

PUṢṬA KṚṢṆA: They feel threatened simply that we're preaching something that will discourage their sinful way of life. Simply they feel threatened. Not they're hating. Their argument is that because of our strong emphasis on preaching and book distribution, they say therefore that the mass of people have a bad impression of Kṛṣṇa.

BHŪRIJANA: And also because...

PRABHUPĀDA: Because we are selling books.

BHŪRIJANA: Not so much the selling of books. Maybe because of the emphasis on how much money can be taken. Like if someone says on the street, "Please give me a donation," so they give him a donation. "No, you must give more," and more and more. So the people think that the devotees are only interested in getting money and they get a bad impression that ISKCON is a money-making movement.

PUṢṬA KṚṢṆA: We're selling one-half million large-sized books each year.

PRABHUPĀDA: That is envious. So if they sell books, so that is making Kṛṣṇa unpopular?

* * *

Prabhupāda is agreeing with Puṣṭa Kṛṣṇa's point that books are being distributed, and it is not only that money is being collected. At other times and in other circumstances, and while talking to a different individual, Prabhupāda acknowledged and spoke strongly against inappropriate tactics that could turn the public's sentiment against the Kṛṣṇa consciousness movement:

> Regarding the controversy about book distribution techniques, you are right. Our occupation must be honest. Everyone should adore our members as honest. If we do something which is deteriorating to the popular sentiments of the public in favor of our movement, that is not good. Somehow or other, we should not become unpopular in the public eye. These dishonest methods must be stopped. It is hampering our reputation all over the world. Money collected for feeding people in India should be collected under the name "ISKCON Food Relief." Not any other name. And every farthing of that money must be sent to India, or better yet, buy food grains there and ship them here and we will distribute. But every farthing collected for that purpose must be used for that purpose. I have already sent one letter to these points. (Śrīla Prabhupāda's letter to Rūpānuga Dāsa, January 9, 1975)

BHŪRIJANA: But one must learn to be a good book salesman, I think.

PRABHUPĀDA: But selling book about Kṛṣṇa, does it mean that the booksellers are creating unpopular opinion? Does it mean?

BHŪRIJANA: Automatically, no.

PRABHUPĀDA: When you say that they are making enemies because they are pushing this, what is wrong there? Actually, I can so far understand that you do not like to sell books, or you cannot sell books.

BHŪRIJANA: I've never really tried so much.

PRABHUPĀDA: Those who are selling books, you think of them that they're not very advanced.

BHŪRIJANA: I don't think that they can continue for a very long time if they are not advanced.

Prabhupāda: But actually they're doing, so why do you say they cannot continue long?

* * *

Prabhupāda points out that book distributors who are engaged year after year in fulfilling his desire are surrendered souls and therefore advanced devotees.

BHŪRIJANA: It used to make me angry when people would collect money and lie and say that they're collecting money for the welfare center here, or to feed the children here, or to bus the children there. They'd collect money, but it wasn't straightforward.

PUṢṬA KṚṢṆA: Prabhupāda has many times given the instruction to the devotees that they should try as much as possible to distribute the books on their own merit.

BHŪRIJANA: But they emphasize collecting, not distributing books.

PUṢṬA KṚṢṆA: No, but the point is that Prabhupāda's instruction is there.

BHŪRIJANA: But all the devotees want to hear is Prabhupāda also said, "By hook or by crook."

PUṢṬA KṚṢṆA: Sometimes it may be required to interest someone in a book that they may find out their interest. Just like people are interested in philanthropic activity.

PRABHUPĀDA: Just like our... What is his name?

HARI-ŚAURI: Tripurāri? [*Laughter.*]

PRABHUPĀDA: Some lady inquired, "Is there any instruction about the power shortage?" "Oh, yes." [*Laughs.*] So she purchased, and the next day she said, "There is nothing about power." So suppose Tripurāri has sold one book. The lady inquired, "Is there any basic instruction about power shortage?" And he said, "Yes." So you think it is wrong. That is your version.

BHŪRIJANA: I think a simple lie like that is not bad.

PRABHUPĀDA: But a devotee's view is that whatever may be her inquiry, if she purchases one book, she'll be benefited. This is the point. But you, as big moralist, you, [*laughs*] you think that he has cheated. He has not cheated. He has benefited her. Somehow or other he has given a book to her. Someday she'll read and she'll benefit. But you people, you think that why we should sell like that, "Yes, there is some solution of power shortage." Actually there is, but you think that he has lied. Just like sometimes the father's child is suffering from fever, so the father wants that the child may take the medicine and promises, "You take the medicine. I'll give you this cake." The purpose is not to give the cake actually. The purpose is the child may take the medicine. That is the purpose. But when the father promises, "If you take the medicine, I'll give you the cake." But cake is dangerous for the child who is suffering from fever, but still the father allures him. "If you take the medicine and I'll give you cake." So is the father wrong?

BHŪRIJANA: No.

PRABHUPĀDA: Similarly, if somehow or other one can sell one book to a person, it is good for him. Don't take how he is selling, but he's giving the book and that person is paying something. That is good.

But big moralist, they cannot understand. They'll see, "Why the father has spoken lie to his son. He's not a good father." They'll mistake. Father is always friend. Father cannot be enemy. But for the benefit of the rascal child, sometimes he has to say like that, that "If you take the medicine, I'll give you cake." Those who are mundane moralist, they cannot understand because they are on the mundane platform.

Another example is Yudhiṣṭhira Mahārāja. He was asked by Kṛṣṇa, "You speak a lie to Droṇācārya, 'Your son is dead.'" Yudhiṣṭhira Mahārāja refused. For this he had to see hell. He was more a moralist than Kṛṣṇa. For this moral activity he had to visit hell.

* * *

I had previously read a different version of why Yudhiṣṭhira had to see hell in an English translation of the *Mahābhārata*. That translation said that Yudhiṣṭhira had to see hell because he lied on Kṛṣṇa's order. Obviously, that did not concur with the Kṛṣṇa conscious conclusion. I had been meaning to ask Prabhupāda for the correct understanding, and Kṛṣṇa arranged for Prabhupāda to answer my question without my having to ask it.

PRABHUPĀDA: This philosophy cannot be understood by neophyte devotees. Our purpose is to push so much this sales of books, because through it our missionary activities will be very widely known. That we want. Somehow or other let him purchase a book. That is our mission.

There is no question of transgressing moral principles. Arjuna was arguing with Kṛṣṇa that killing my relatives is horrible, abominable. Better I beg and maintain myself than I kill my relatives and become a king. Did he not say? That is an ordinary man's argument. But as Yudhiṣṭhira Mahārāja refused to speak lie, Arjuna wanted to refuse to fight. But Arjuna, in spite of his conviction that it is sinful to kill my relatives, he still agreed to kill. Why?

BHŪRIJANA: That is the supreme morality, following Kṛṣṇa's desire.

PRABHUPĀDA: What Kṛṣṇa desires is above all this material. But it should not be manufactured. The thing is that our spiritual master wants to preach Kṛṣṇa consciousness and he has repeatedly stressed distribution of books. We shall distribute books by any means. That is good. And if you become moralist that "Oh, they're taking this means, that means for selling of book. I'm a big moralist. I'm bigger than him."

BHŪRIJANA: I don't think there is so much enmity because of the books themselves.

PRABHUPĀDA: No, I do not know what they are doing, but I have information that they're not selling books.

BHŪRIJANA: Some I think. I think some.

PRABHUPĀDA: But not...

BHŪRIJANA: Comparable amount.

Prabhupāda: Yes. Others who were transgressing the moral principle, they were selling more books. And those who are big moralists, they could not.

PUṢṬA KṚṢṆA: They're also distributing one pamphlet printed by Siddha-svarūpānanda. Then if they like, they can buy one of Prabhupāda's books. Prabhupāda's book comes second.

PRABHUPĀDA: Sometimes I've heard so many things.

BHŪRIJANA: But they give those away for free. I mean just in the sense that someone maybe doesn't want to purchase anything so they give him something for free about Kṛṣṇa.

PUṢṬA KṚṢṆA: First they do that.

BHŪRIJANA: Only because it's free as far as I know.

PRABHUPĀDA: If they can get knowledge for free, then why they should purchase? If you give them the opportunity that we take knowledge free, then why they will purchase?

* * *

At another time, Prabhupāda told me he didn't object to free book distribution. Here he did not agree that distributing a free introductory book was an effective way to get people to buy his books.

PRABHUPĀDA: They should follow what their spiritual master says: bookselling. There is no question of moral and immoral. They must sell. Just like in fighting. Where there is fight, the soldiers, to gain victory, there is no question of moral and immoral.

BHŪRIJANA: Śrīla Prabhupāda, but I think the thing I understand least is that if they are not doing what you want... I mean... I'm sitting before you now and you're telling me and I'm listening, and you are my spiritual master. I must accept.

* * *

I began to ask Prabhupāda why, since he was their spiritual master, he didn't simply and definitively order them to act as he desired. I couldn't get my question out, for as I spoke I understood that Prabhupāda, as Siddha-svarūpa's spiritual master, was instructing him in the best possible way, even if I could not understand it.

PRABHUPĀDA: We want that bookselling must be increased as much as possible. This we want. The same thing. Let the child take medicine. Never mind the father is speaking lies.... Because as soon as he takes the medicine, he'll be benefited. End justifies the means. End is that everyone should have a Kṛṣṇa literature. Doesn't matter what is the means. Because he has taken one Kṛṣṇa literature, that justifies everything. This is the principle.

BHŪRIJANA: How about just collecting without giving any literature? Just collecting. Three months ago I saw it in Australia, with a lying line too. Not telling the truth. And that wasn't very long ago.

HARI-ŚAURI: Sometimes the devotees are just distributing incense.

BHŪRIJANA: Nothing.

HARI-ŚAURI: They collect and distribute incense. Sometimes they don't distribute books.

PUṢṬA KṚṢṆA: Maybe they have to pay off a loan on the temple. All the devotees are well aware that Prabhupāda's books have first priority. Everyone knows it.

HARI-ŚAURI: Prabhupāda's point is that if you see fault with the method of implementing the spiritual master's instructions, you'll fail to follow the instructions.

PRABHUPĀDA: No, the point is not that they have not done any wrong. Don't think like that. But my point is that my instruction is to sell books.

* * *

This mood had been a stumbling block for me – that I had to neglect my common sense and intelligence and accept what I perceived as a faulty following of Prabhupāda's order as faultless. That type of acceptance was difficult, perhaps even impossible, for me.

But Prabhupāda's answer satisfied me completely. "No, no, the point is *not* that they have *not* done any wrong. Don't think like that." His hair-splitting answer allowed me to accept the correctness of what the devotees did do without being forced to accept as correct what I understood as inappropriate.

On hearing Prabhupāda's explanation, my mind became instantly illuminated and I understood.

BHŪRIJANA: I understand. In other words, if you think they're doing it wrong, you do it better. If you see others are doing it wrong, make sure you do it, but do it without the wrong thing. Don't stop doing it.

PRABHUPĀDA: Yes. Besides that, if you do not take to Deity worship, then you shall remain unclean. That's a fact.

* * *

Prabhupāda was satisfied that I had properly understood, and he immediately left the book distribution point to cite a second "fault" in the devotional stance adopted by the outside devotees: neglecting the temple means neglecting Deity worship, which is meant to keep us internally and externally pure.

By the end of this conversation, I felt a more honest and deepened relationship with Prabhupāda. I had lost my fear, and my affection, devotion, and surrender to Prabhupāda as father and wise master had increased. Prabhupāda's calling me into his association had removed both misconceptions and ignorance about his actual desire. He had corrected me, but in an exacting way: he removed that which he judged inappropriate yet left that which others had judged inappropriate. He made clear a principle and offered me a template to make further discriminations. He had exposed the error in my thinking without judging *all* my thoughts as incorrect.

Later, I saw one of Prabhupāda's *sannyāsī* disciples after he had just heard the tape of my conversation with Prabhupāda. His eyes were dreamy and star-filled, like the young in love. He obviously felt fully sanctioned and said, "Prabhupāda said the end justifies the means. We should distribute books by hook or by crook."

Prabhupāda had said it. Years later when I reminded that *sannyāsī* of his words he remarked, "And then I proceeded to wreak havoc." Prabhupāda had ordered his books distributed. The *sannyāsī* had tried, thinking that as long as the number of books he distributed increased, his actions were pleasing to Prabhupāda. He had, however, caused difficulties both within the temples and with the public. How mysterious is spiritual life – completely incomprehensible to a materialist. We must serve our spiritual master sincerely and abide by his order without hesitation, even if we are unable to do it perfectly. Nevertheless, mistakes, even those committed in all sincerity, may prove costly both to ourselves and to others.

Prabhupāda had rejected my claim of increased humility and thus advancement because it was not accompanied by the performance of my duty (remaining in Hong Kong). Yet the mixed results accruing from the immature performance of duty leads us to recognize that not only must we do our duty, but we must learn to do it in mature consciousness, for Kṛṣṇa's pleasure. This takes advancement in Kṛṣṇa consciousness. By following the standard *sādhana*, especially hearing and chanting about Kṛṣṇa without offense, our subtle and gross material tendencies naturally decrease and our desire to act simply for Kṛṣṇa's pleasure increases. Thus as we advance, the increased devotion to Kṛṣṇa with which we perform our duties further empowers those duties – especially our preaching – with spiritual potency, *bhakti*.

Although at this time I had neither the scriptural knowledge nor the maturity to grasp the depths of Prabhupāda's point, I eventually understood it more clearly. We must continue doing our duty, even though we may perform our duty acting from a self-centered, selfish platform. That is natural because we are fresh from material life (*Bhagavad-gītā* 2.31–37). As we advance, we become less self-centered and selfish (*Bhagavad-gītā* 3.10–16). Later, as our transcendental knowledge and goodness increases, we perform that same duty but with detachment (*Bhagavad-gītā* 2.39–53; 3.16–25; 9.27). Still later, while performing the same activity, we act beyond detachment, for Kṛṣṇa's pleasure on the platform of full surrender (*Bhagavad-gītā* 9.26; 18.65–66). This platform of activity is true *bhakti*, although the other platforms should neither be minimized nor criticized. Those preliminary stages are also *bhakti* in the sense that they lead to *bhakti*. Renunciation of duties without causing ourselves an adverse effect may take place only on the most advanced platform, the *uttama-bhāgavata* platform, at either *bhāva-bhakti* or *prema-bhakti* (*Bhagavad-gītā* 3.4–8).

Kṛṣṇa Himself cautions Arjuna to neither criticize nor disrupt the minds or the activities of those who are materially attached but who are nevertheless working dutifully (*Bhagavad-gītā* 3.26–31). It is by offering their work along with the fruits of that work that they will advance. These points had clearly flowed from the mouth of Śrī Kṛṣṇa as a river of nectar in the *Bhagavad-gītā*, and Prabhupāda had elaborated on them in his purports.

Due to my own lack of realization I had reacted improperly to the immature application of Prabhupāda's order – the book distribution and other activities of the devotees. Prabhupāda was displeased by my critical attitude and over the years, he had found me guilty of losing my perspective on three counts: neglecting to follow the standard ISKCON program, becoming critical of devotees who were performing their duty on the order of their spiritual master, and giving up my own duty.

In addition, Prabhupāda made clear his desire that the "outside" devotees remain in ISKCON with his other disciples. Personality clashes, overly self-assured opinions, hot tempers, and arguments will always be part of institutional life. Yet, despite that fact, through devotion to Prabhupāda – his society, his order, and his mission – we should somehow cooperate. As difficult as it may be, we should take advantage of each other's realizations and strengths. We should actively seek to understand and benefit from the validity of each other's points of view, even if those opinions oppose our own, and even if we are "more correct" than they. "Discuss," Prabhupāda had said. Remain united to invigorate and push on Prabhupāda's mission, which is the mission of Śrī Caitanya Mahāprabhu.

Answering Kṛṣṇa's Call

I mulled over Prabhupāda's words again and again as the days passed in Honolulu. I wanted to understand them fully. One day, after being in Honolulu for about ten days, I was called to the pay phone outside the temple complex. "Hurry! It's Jagadīśa calling from the mainland."

I ran to the phone and heard Jagadīśa's familiar voice. After we exchanged obeisances and hellos, Jagadīśa said he had something to tell me before I arrived in California. ISKCON Laguna Beach no longer needed a temple president. Revatīnandana needed to be encouraged and would now perform that service.

"Thanks," I shouted into the phone. "I'm in the middle of jumping from Australia to Laguna Beach and just before landing, you tell me I shouldn't have jumped. Glad you wanted to tell me before I arrived." Jagadīśa remained calm as I stormed on for a few moments. Then he suggested several alternatives. I could open a new temple in Santa Barbara, California, I could help him in his *gurukula* service in Dallas, or I could travel with him on his preaching rounds. When I hung up, I wondered what Kṛṣṇa had in store for Bhūrijana Dāsa.

My wondering started me wandering, and I met Bhaktījana, my eccentric devotee friend whom I had last seen in Māyāpur. I told him about my situation. Bhaktījana gave me the same advice he had offered in Māyāpur: "Why not go see Prabhupāda and ask him what you should do?"

So obvious! Why hadn't I thought of it? Go to Prabhupāda and ask him. I thanked Bhaktījana and ran toward Prabhupāda's rooms.

* * *

Prabhupāda had once told me, "I wish I could train all my disciples personally, but what can I do?" The great fortune of having such an exalted and powerful spiritual master did carry for most disciples the "price tag" of infrequent physical association. Of course, we understood even then that "*vāṇī* is more important than *vapu,*" and that we should simply serve Prabhupāda in his vast mission. We never begrudged our circumstances, which were overwhelmingly fortunate, yet since my conversation with Prabhupāda in Honolulu, I found myself always longing for more of his personal association.

An Order from Guru

I entered Prabhupāda's rooms and offered my obeisances. He sat alone at his low desk, the yellow glow of his desk lamp highlighting his already golden face.

I explained my dilemma to Prabhupāda and relayed the choices I had been offered. Prabhupāda, his face grave, listened and considered the options. I felt as if he was examining my file. "No new temples," was his first statement. Then, after thinking for a few moments more, he told me how to serve him.

"You and Jagadīśa organize *gurukulas*. Not just centrally in one place, but all around the world. We don't want these children to become technicians or factory workers. Make sure that they are properly taken care of."

"With love," I added, and Prabhupāda nodded his head in agreement.

Prabhupāda told me that our temples can also have nursery schools wherein one mother could supervise many children. "I have seen it," he added. "One can care for fifty. If a mother only wants to take care of her own children, then she should not live in the temple."

* * *

My first reaction to Prabhupāda's instruction that I work in education was negative, but within moments, I surrendered internally and soon became enthusiastic, relieved to have regained service under the shelter of Prabhupāda's order.

I offered my obeisances and left the room. Within a few days, I said goodbye to Prabhupāda, and flew with Jagattāriṇī and Vrindaban Leela to Los Angeles. I could not know when I left Hawaii that Prabhupāda would depart from this world in November of 1977 and that I would not have the fortune of seeing him again.

Epilogue

I met Jagadīśa in Los Angeles. After a few weeks there, my family and I moved to Dallas, and I assumed the duties of headmaster of the small school that remained after ISKCON's original *gurukula* had closed. I also had the opportunity for the first time since joining ISKCON to serve installed Deities.

I remember the shock of first entering Rādhā-Kālācandjī's altar. The atmosphere on the altar was exactly the same as being close to Prabhupāda. I then understood that Prabhupāda had captured Rādhā and Kṛṣṇa in his heart.

Prabhupāda wrote to Jagattāriṇī and I in Dallas. He said he was pleased that we had settled into a steady ISKCON service. That service in the Dallas *gurukula*, however, was an administrative post, not a teaching post. One day I received a phone call from Jagadīśa requesting me to visit ISKCON's farm in Port Royal, Pennsylvania, and possibly become the sole teacher/supervisor of that school. When I spoke to him on the phone, I intuitively knew that Port Royal would become my home.

Jagattāriṇī and I went to Gītā-nāgarī and gradually took up the responsibility of educating the ten devotee children who were in residence with their parents at the farm. As I knew nothing about teaching, these students became my teachers at "The School of Essential Experience." I had no books, no curriculum, no training, and no one with whom to consult. My students, on the other hand, were all experienced *gurukula* veterans, capable of pushing a novice teacher far beyond his limits. Yet we continued, based on Prabhupāda's order and a desire to please him.

While I was in Dallas, Prabhupāda traveled first to Los Angeles, then to New York, then to India. His final illness had begun. From Los Angeles and a few months later from Vṛndāvana, Prabhupāda wrote and encouraged me to be steadily engaged in teaching and to "Please take this movement very seriously."

Gradually his health deteriorated. When I traveled from Australia with Prabhupāda, I was able to give him the $1,000 I had hoped to give him the year before. Over the next year, I continued to send Prabhupāda donations in my regular letters to him. When I understood Prabhupāda was ill, I sent him half of all the money I had left, about $1,000. When Prabhupāda left Bombay for Vṛndāvana in May 1977, I understood that my only shelter would soon be leaving. I cried like a small child who knew he was soon to become an orphan, although I could not really understand what that meant.

Prabhupāda's health didn't improve, and I again sent him half the money I had. By this time (June 1977), Prabhupāḍa's secretaries were answering his mail on his behalf. I knew it was inevitable that Prabhupāda would leave, but I could not actually conceive of a life without Prabhupāda's strong and concerned shelter.

Prabhupāda's health continued to decline steadily. Fearing that my opportunities to offer him donations were running out, I sent Prabhupāda my final donation. I sent every penny I had.

Again I received a reply from Prabhupāda's secretary.

In November 1977, three days after observing Śrī Govardhana-pūjā, I was with Dhṛṣṭadyumna in Harrisburg, Pennsylvania. We heard that Prabhupāda had left this world.

We cried, we consoled the younger devotees, we lectured about the passing of our beloved Prabhupāda, but we could not fathom the significance of Prabhupāda's departure. We knew the philosophy. We had studied, practiced, and lectured on it for years.

We knew *vāṇī* was more important than *vapu* – that imbibing the spiritual master's instructions was much more important than associating with the spiritual master's physical form, from which we may be separated at any time. We knew this, but when Prabhupāda actually left, no philosophy gave us shelter. He was our shelter. He was the person *bhāgavata*, the giver of the book *bhāgavata*, and he had set like the sun from this world.

Who would pull us out of *māyā* when we stumbled? Who would give us another chance? To whom could we write and be overjoyed at being handed a yellowish aerogram, striped in orange and blue, with Tridandi Gosvami A.C.Bhaktivedanta Swami written on its back in that special, purple-red ink? On whose feet could we place our heads as he patted our *śikhās* with the affection of a loving father?

We cried intermittently for days and weeks and months. We clung to his instructions and our memories of him. We had no choice.

Oh, how we miss that personality, His Divine Grace A.C. Bhaktivedanta Swami Prabhupāda, our Guru Mahārāja, our lord and holy master, our dearest friend, our most concerned father. How we miss him. We were mere children when he left this world. Although his blessings continuously rain upon us as he promised, and although we do not feel he is actually gone, how we miss that personality. While he was in this world I asked him about the trivial, the foolish, and the mundane. What could a baby, with his small hands and limited consciousness, beg from Kṛṣṇa's dearest devotee?

It is now more than eighteen years since his departure. I have been his disciple for twenty-seven years. Still, I can only glimpse his greatness, which seems, regardless of how I grow, to always loom ahead like a great mountain peak. Feeling like an elderly orphan, I long for his association more and more. I pray for his eternal service.

Śrīla Prabhupāda *kī jaya!*